INUYASHA™

VOL. 26
VIZ Media Edition

Story and Art by
RUMIKO TAKAHASHI

English Adaptation by Gerard Jones

Translation/Mari Morimoto
Touch-Up Art & Lettering/Bill Schuch
Cover and Interior Graphic Design/Yuki Ameda
Editor/Urian Brown

Managing Editor/Annette Roman
Editorial Director/Elizabeth Kawasaki
Editor in Chief/Alvin Lu
Sr. Director of Acquisitions/Rika Inouye
Senior VP of Marketing/Liza Coppola
Exec. VP of Sales & Marketing/John Easum
Publisher/Hyoe Narita

Printed in the U.S.A.

Published by VIZ Media, LLC
P.O. Box 77010
San Francisco, CA 94107

10 9 8 7 6 5 4 3 2 1
First printing, July 2006

RATED T+ FOR OLDER TEEN

PARENTAL ADVISORY
INUYASHA is rated T+ for Older Teen. This book contains violence. It is recommended for ages 16 and up.

www.viz.com

store.viz.com

InuYasha

VOL. 26

VIZ Media Edition

STORY AND ART BY
RUMIKO TAKAHASHI

CONTENTS

Long ago, in the "Warring States" era of Japan's Muromachi period (*Sengoku-jidai*, approximately 1467-1568 CE), a legendary dog-like half-demon called "Inuyasha" attempted to steal the Shikon Jewel—or "Jewel of Four Souls"—from a village, but was stopped by the enchanted arrow of the village priestess, Kikyo. Inuyasha fell into a deep sleep, pinned to a tree by Kikyo's arrow, while the mortally wounded Kikyo took the Shikon Jewel with her into the fires of her funeral pyre. Years passed.

Fast-forward to the present day. Kagome, a Japanese high school girl, is pulled into a well one day by a mysterious centipede monster and finds herself transported into the past—only to come face to face with the trapped Inuyasha. She frees him, and Inuyasha easily defeats the centipede monster.

The residents of the village, now 50 years older, readily accept Kagome as the reincarnation of their deceased priestess Kikyo, a claim supported by the fact that the Shikon Jewel emerges from a cut on Kagome's body. Unfortunately, the jewel's rediscovery means that the village is soon under attack by a variety of demons in search of this treasure. Then, the jewel is accidentally shattered into many shards, each of which may have the fearsome power of the entire jewel.

Although Inuyasha says he hates Kagome because of her resemblance to Kikyo, the woman who "killed" him, he is forced to team up with her when Kaede, the village leader, binds him to Kagome with a powerful spell. Now the two grudging companions must fight to reclaim and reassemble the shattered shards of the Shikon Jewel before they fall into the wrong hands...

THIS VOLUME While battling the Band of Seven, Inuyasha and crew encounter a stange mountain with an energy so holy it repels all impure spirits. Meanwhile, blood is in the air as the Band of Seven slaughter a small army of humans to exact revenge for their original deaths! What is the secret of the mountain's power? And how

KAGOME
Modern-day Japanese schoolgirl who can travel back and forth between the past and present through an enchanted well.

INU-YASHA
Half-demon hybrid, son of a human mother and demon father. His necklace is enchanted, allowing Kagome to control him with a word.

MIROKU
Lecherous Buddhist priest cursed with a mystical "hellhole" in his hand that's slowly killing him.

NARAKU
Enigmatic demon-mastermind behind the miseries of nearly everyone in the story.

SANGO
"Demon Exterminator" or slayer from the village where the Shikon Jewel was first born.

KOGA
Leader of the Wolf Clan, Koga is himself a Wolf Demon and, because of several Shikon shards in his legs, possesses super speed. Enamored of Kagome, he quarrels with Inuyasha frequently.

BAND OF SEVEN
A group of undead killers brought back to life by Naraku through the powers of the Shikon Jewel Shards.

SCROLL ONE

THE SHIELD OF MOUNT HAKUREI

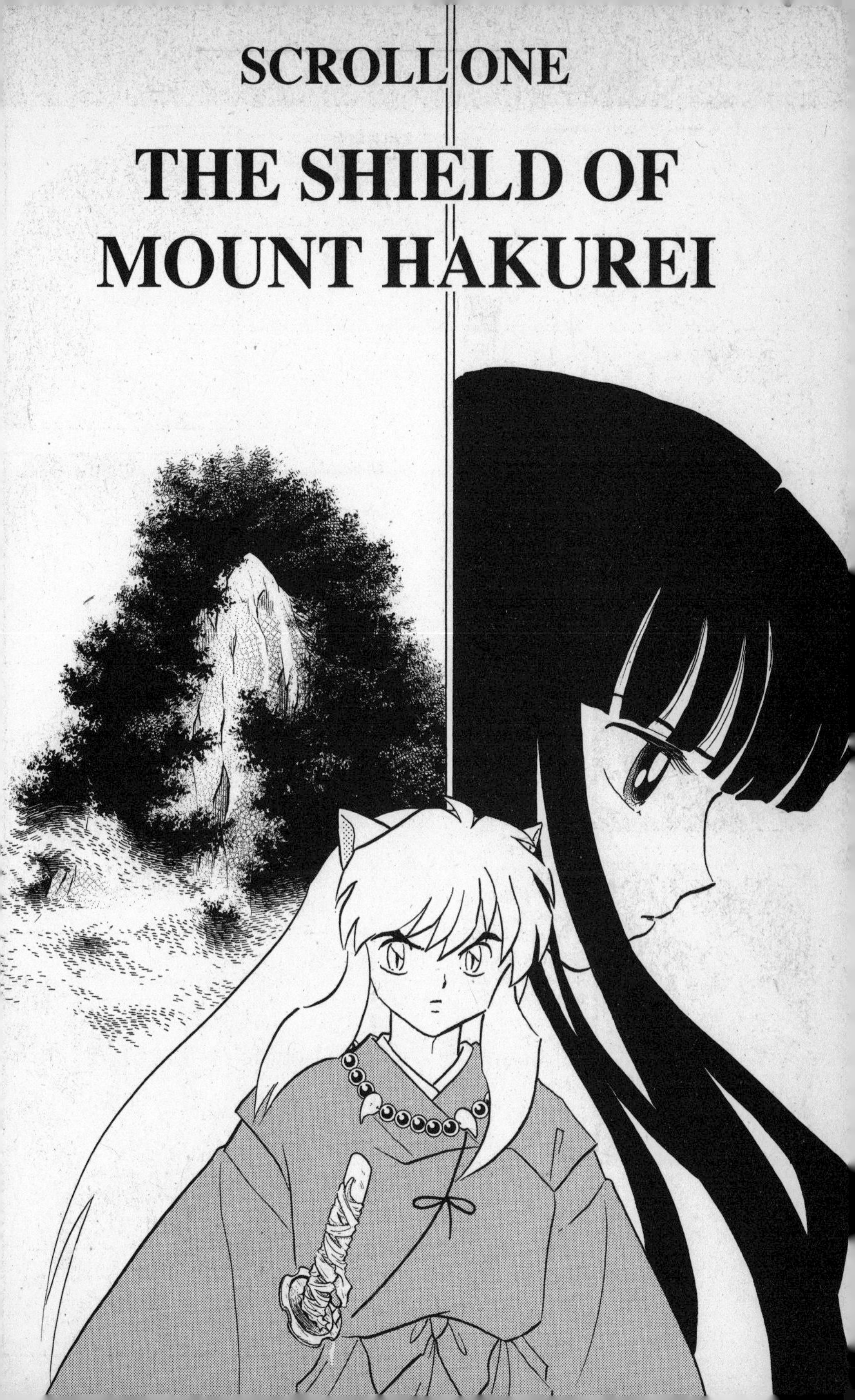

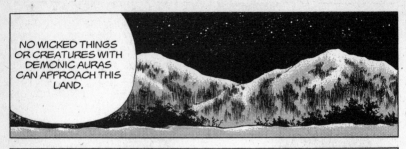

NO WICKED THINGS OR CREATURES WITH DEMONIC AURAS CAN APPROACH THIS LAND.

IT IS BECAUSE HAKUREI PURIFIES THE AIR ABOVE US.

HAKU-REI...?

I HAVE HEARD OF IT.

A SACRED MOUNTAIN THAT ABSOLVES SINNERS...

YES...

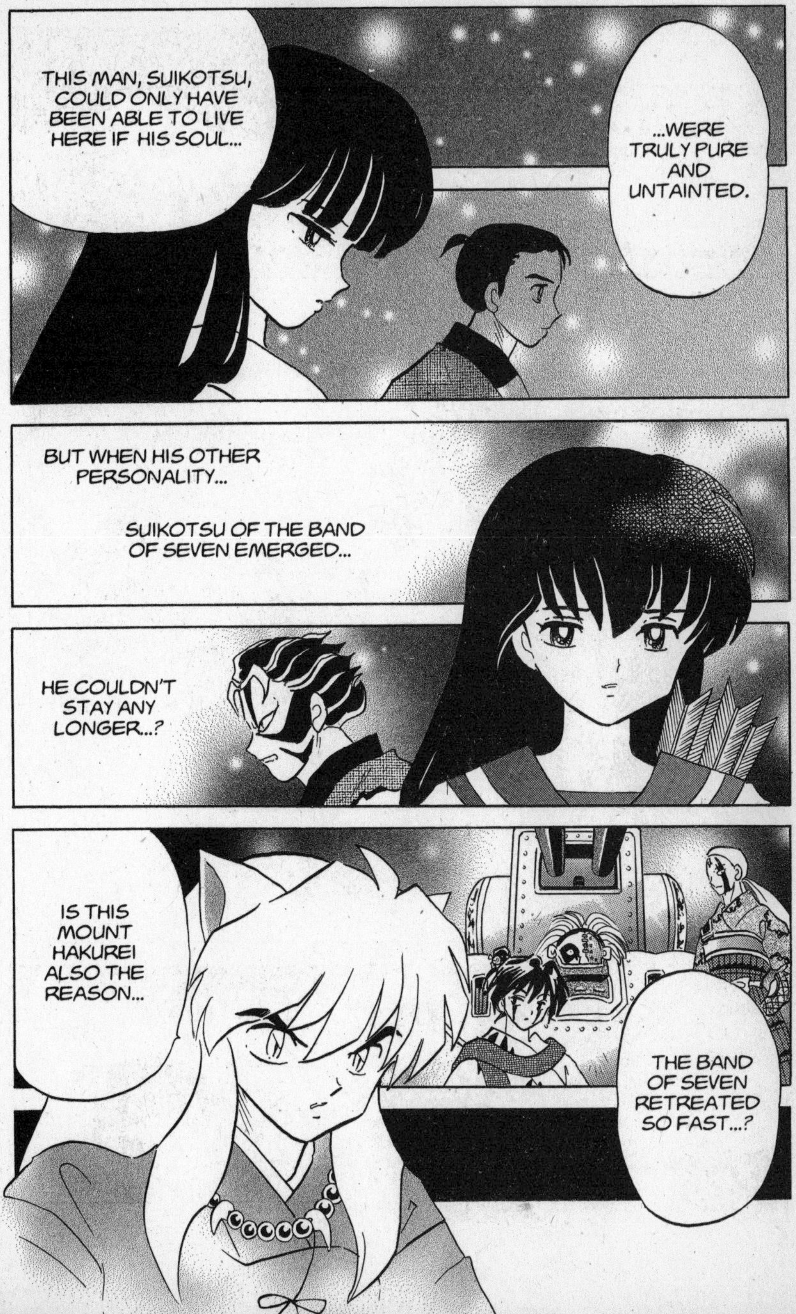
THIS MAN, SUIKOTSU, COULD ONLY HAVE BEEN ABLE TO LIVE HERE IF HIS SOUL...
...WERE TRULY PURE AND UNTAINTED.
BUT WHEN HIS OTHER PERSONALITY...
SUIKOTSU OF THE BAND OF SEVEN EMERGED...
HE COULDN'T STAY ANY LONGER...?
IS THIS MOUNT HAKUREI ALSO THE REASON...
THE BAND OF SEVEN RETREATED SO FAST...?

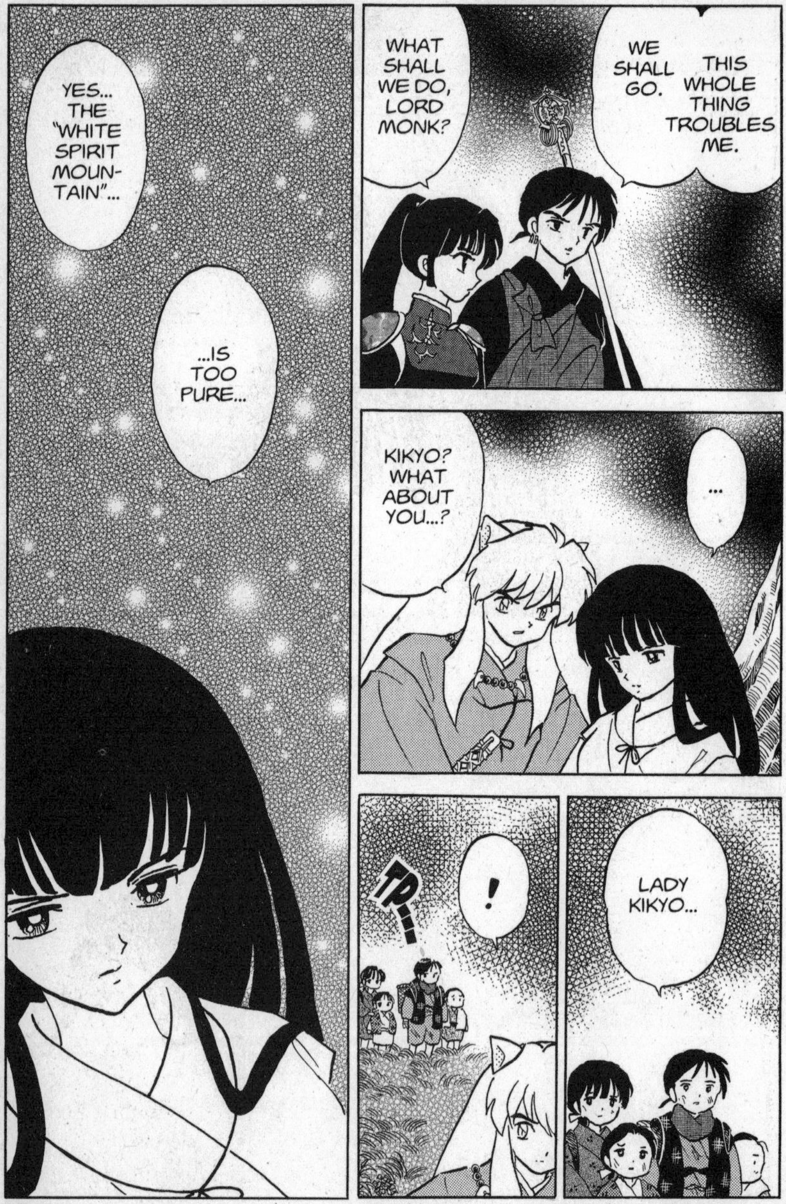
YES... THE "WHITE SPIRIT MOUN-TAIN"...
...IS TOO PURE...
WHAT SHALL WE DO, LORD MONK?
WE SHALL GO.
THIS WHOLE THING TROUBLES ME.
KIKYO? WHAT ABOUT YOU...?
...
TP
!
LADY KIKYO...

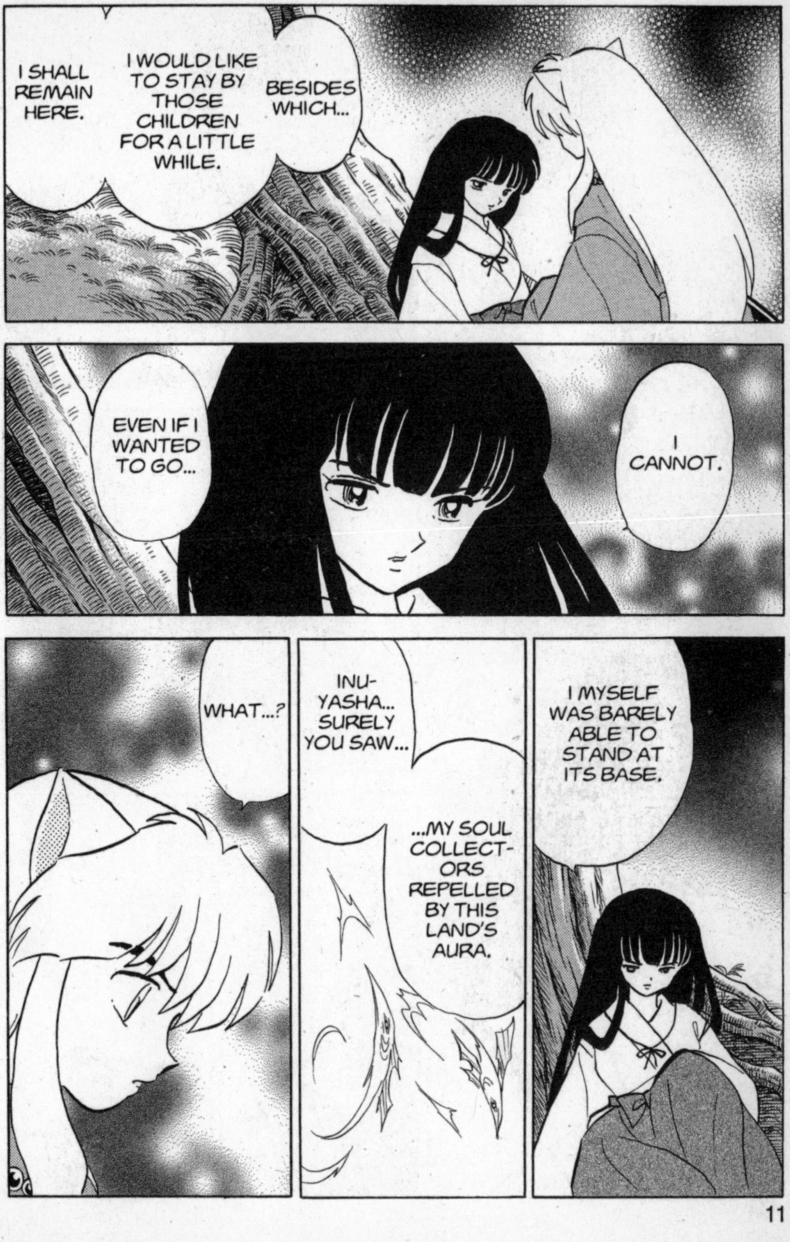
I SHALL REMAIN HERE.
I WOULD LIKE TO STAY BY THOSE CHILDREN FOR A LITTLE WHILE.
BESIDES WHICH...
EVEN IF I WANTED TO GO...
I CANNOT.
WHAT...?
INU-YASHA... SURELY YOU SAW...
...MY SOUL COLLECT-ORS REPELLED BY THIS LAND'S AURA.
I MYSELF WAS BARELY ABLE TO STAND AT ITS BASE.

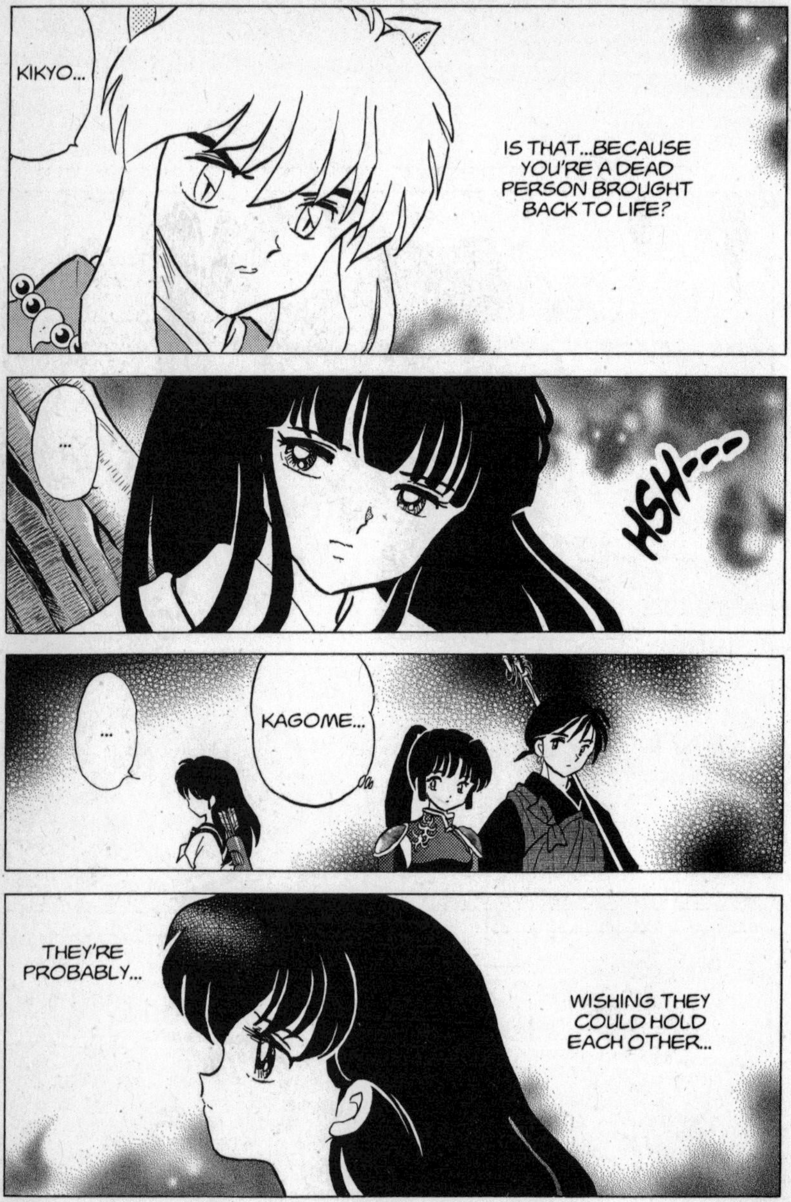
KIKYO...
IS THAT...BECAUSE YOU'RE A DEAD PERSON BROUGHT BACK TO LIFE?
...
HSH---
...
KAGOME...
THEY'RE PROBABLY...
WISHING THEY COULD HOLD EACH OTHER...

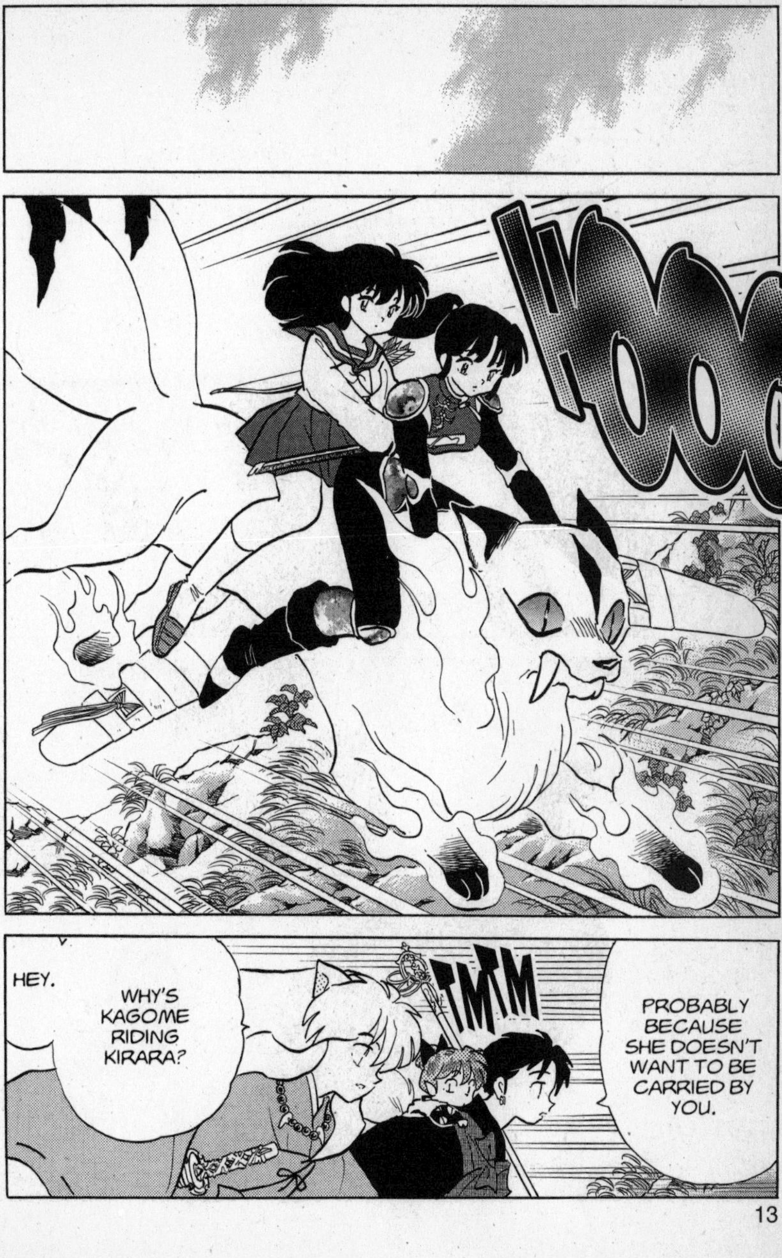
HOOO
HEY.
WHY'S KAGOME RIDING KIRARA?
TMTM
PROBABLY BECAUSE SHE DOESN'T WANT TO BE CARRIED BY YOU.

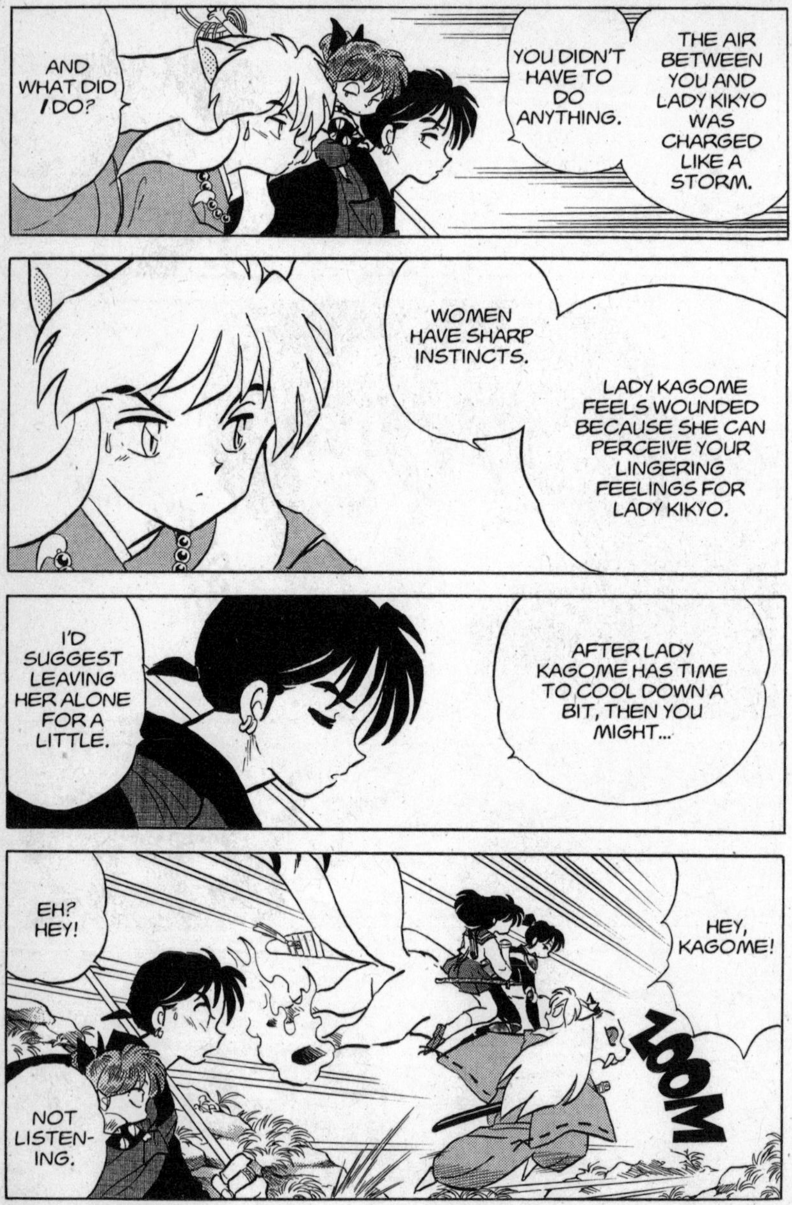
AND WHAT DID I DO?
YOU DIDN'T HAVE TO DO ANYTHING.
THE AIR BETWEEN YOU AND LADY KIKYO WAS CHARGED LIKE A STORM.
WOMEN HAVE SHARP INSTINCTS.
LADY KAGOME FEELS WOUNDED BECAUSE SHE CAN PERCEIVE YOUR LINGERING FEELINGS FOR LADY KIKYO.
I'D SUGGEST LEAVING HER ALONE FOR A LITTLE.
AFTER LADY KAGOME HAS TIME TO COOL DOWN A BIT, THEN YOU MIGHT...
EH? HEY!
HEY, KAGOME!
ZOOM
NOT LISTEN-ING.

WHAT'S YOUR PROBLEM?!
WHAT ARE YOU IGNORING ME FOR?!
DID YOU SAY SOME-THING?
BLINK
VSSSH
PEEK
IF THERE'S SOMETHING YOU WANT TO TELL ME, JUST SAY IT.
TELL *YOU?*

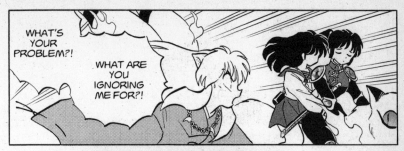

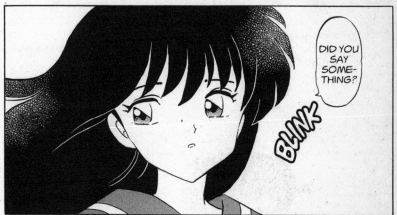

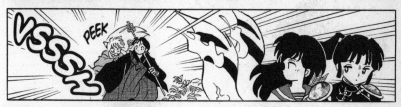

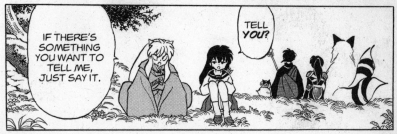

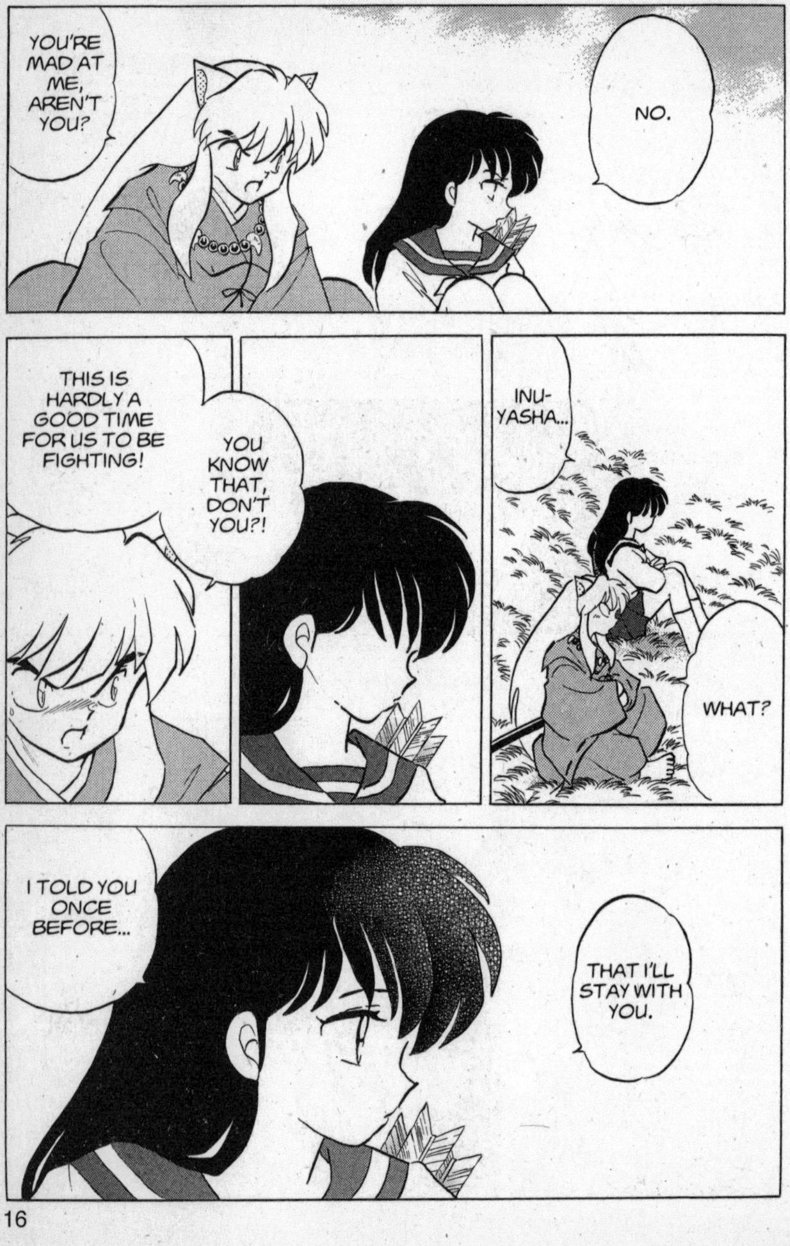
YOU'RE MAD AT ME, AREN'T YOU?
NO.
THIS IS HARDLY A GOOD TIME FOR US TO BE FIGHTING!
YOU KNOW THAT, DON'T YOU?!
INU-YASHA...
WHAT?
I TOLD YOU ONCE BEFORE...
THAT I'LL STAY WITH YOU.

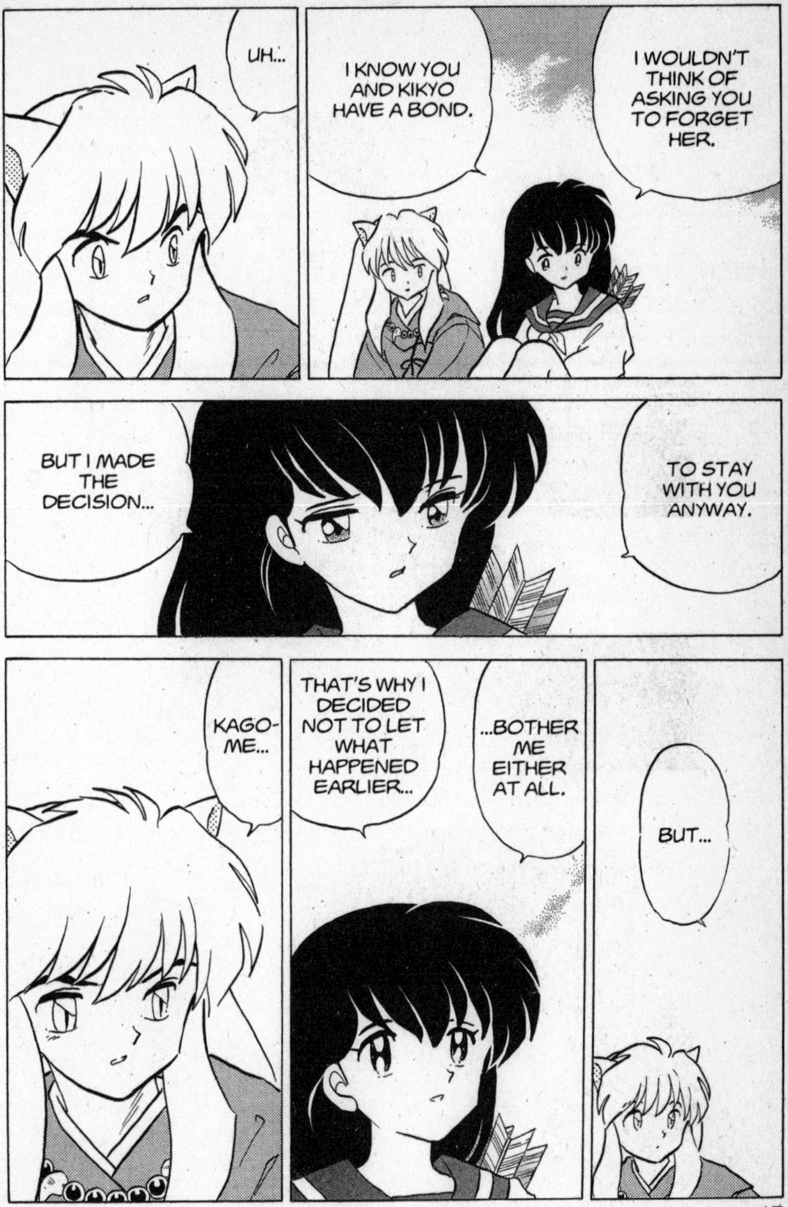
UH...
I KNOW YOU AND KIKYO HAVE A BOND.
I WOULDN'T THINK OF ASKING YOU TO FORGET HER.
BUT I MADE THE DECISION...
TO STAY WITH YOU ANYWAY.
KAGO-ME...
THAT'S WHY I DECIDED NOT TO LET WHAT HAPPENED EARLIER...
...BOTHER ME EITHER AT ALL.
BUT...

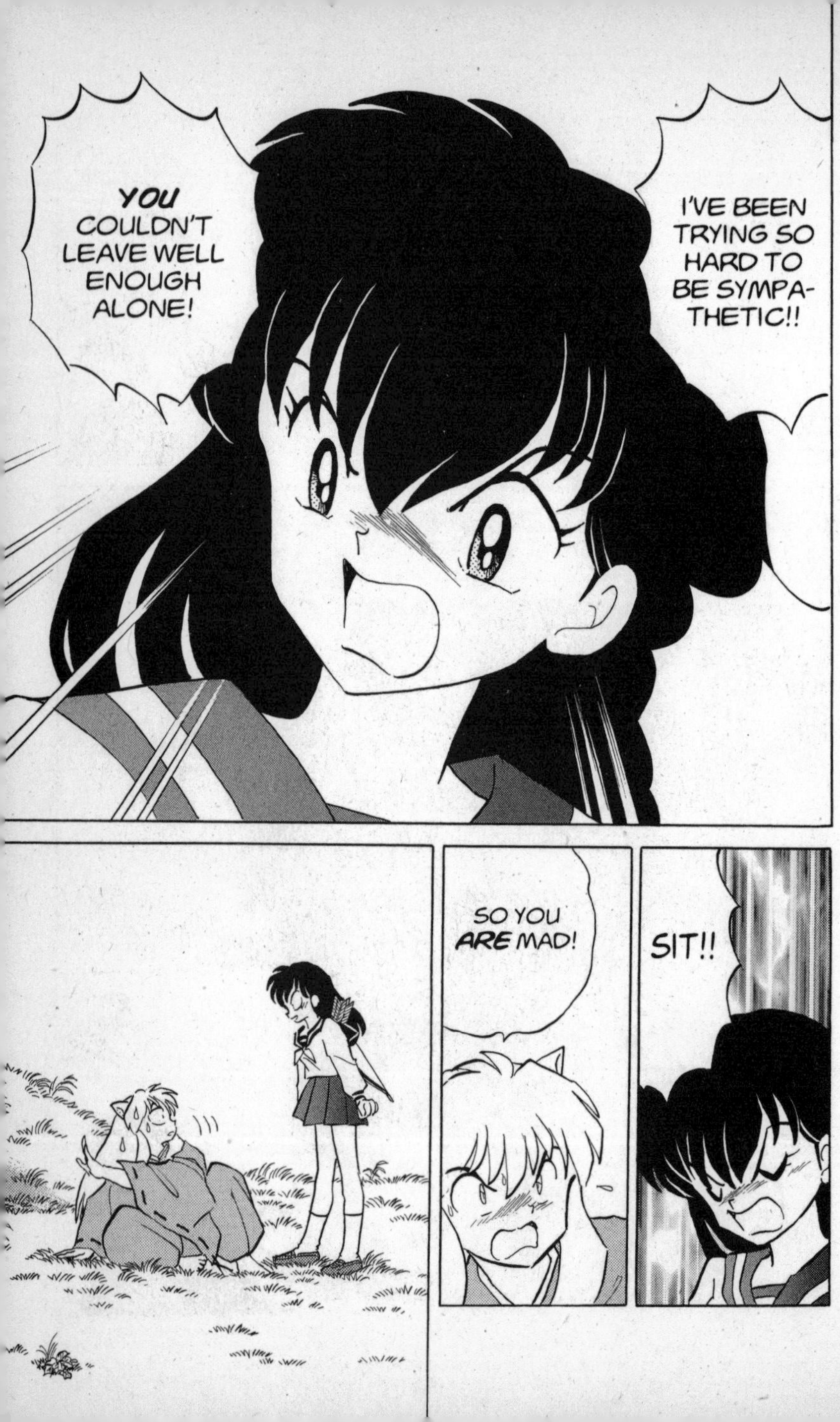
YOU COULDN'T LEAVE WELL ENOUGH ALONE!
I'VE BEEN TRYING SO HARD TO BE SYMPA-THETIC!!
SO YOU ARE MAD!
SIT!!

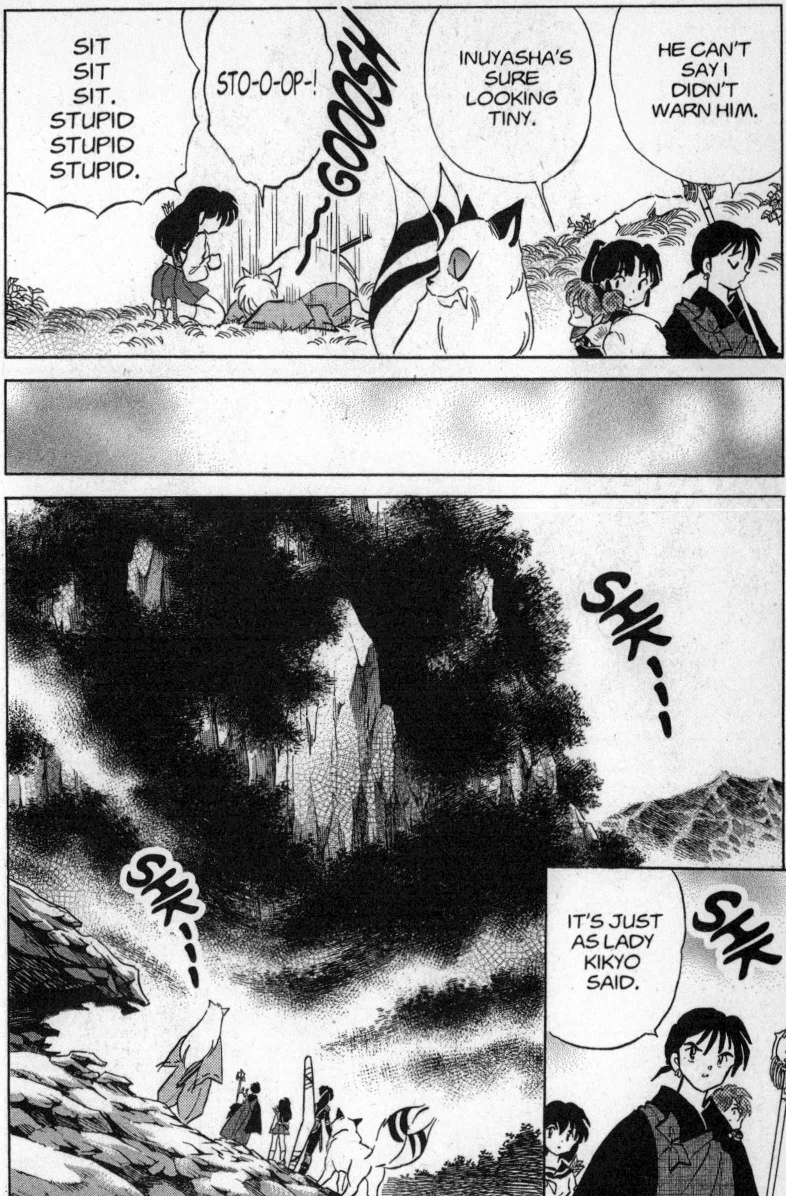
SIT SIT SIT. STUPID STUPID STUPID.
STO-O-OP-!
GOOOSH
INUYASHA'S SURE LOOKING TINY.
HE CAN'T SAY I DIDN'T WARN HIM.
SHK...
SHK...
IT'S JUST AS LADY KIKYO SAID.
SHK

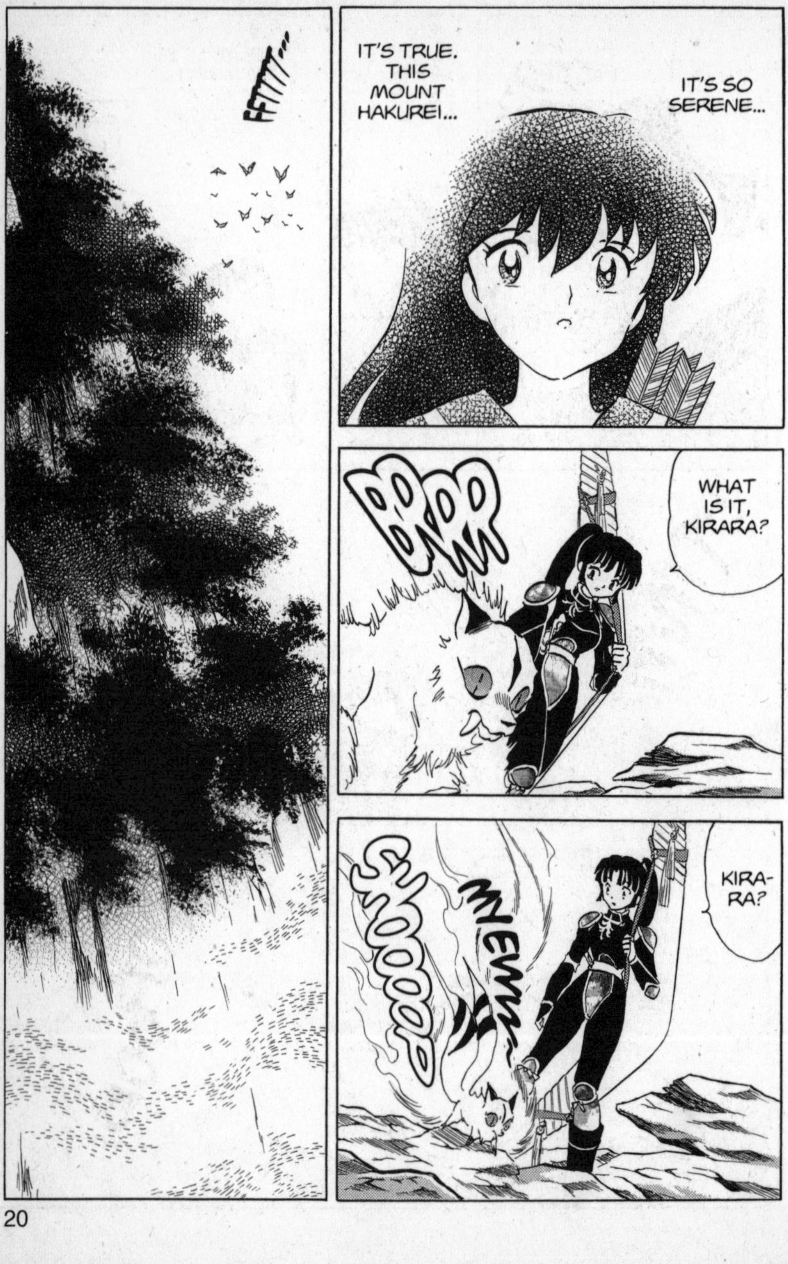
FFTTTT...
IT'S TRUE. THIS MOUNT HAKUREI...
IT'S SO SERENE...
BROWW
WHAT IS IT, KIRARA?
SHOOOOP
MYEWW
KIRA-RA?

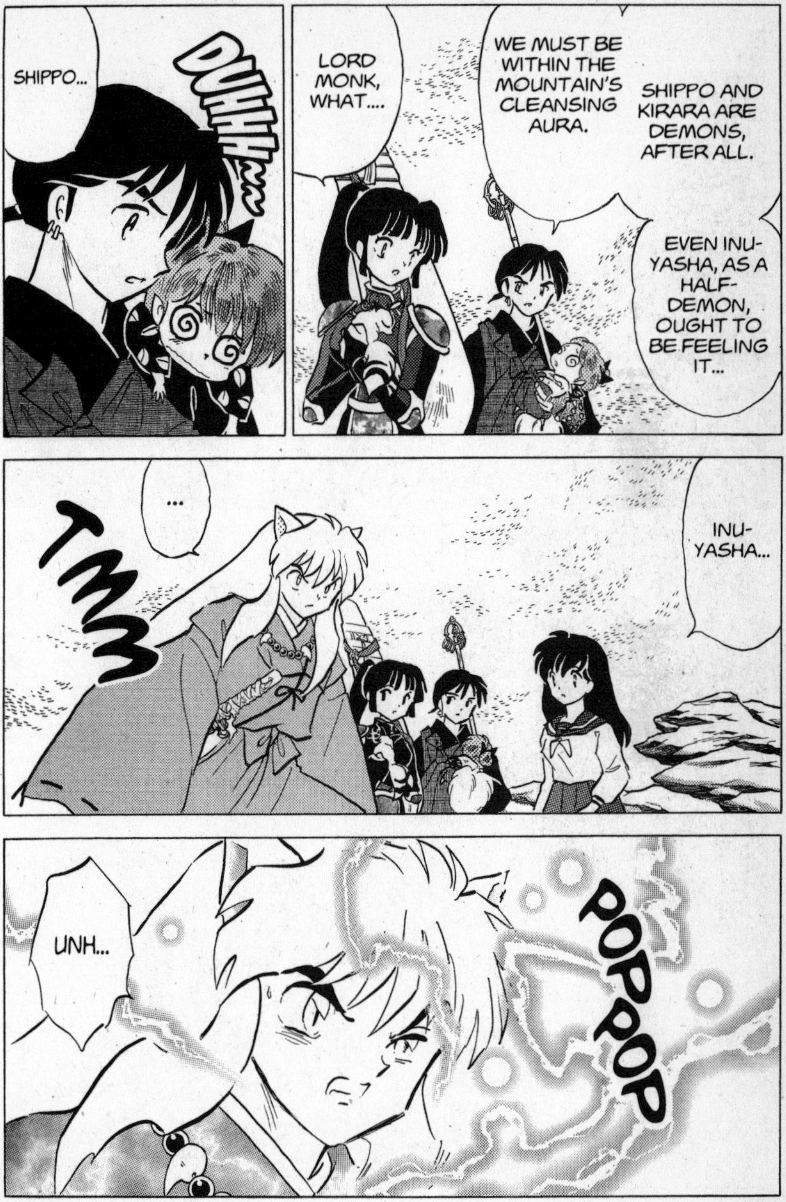
SHIPPO...
DUHHH
LORD MONK, WHAT....
WE MUST BE WITHIN THE MOUNTAIN'S CLEANSING AURA.
SHIPPO AND KIRARA ARE DEMONS, AFTER ALL.
EVEN INU-YASHA, AS A HALF-DEMON, OUGHT TO BE FEELING IT...
...
TMM
INU-YASHA...
UNH...
POP POP POP

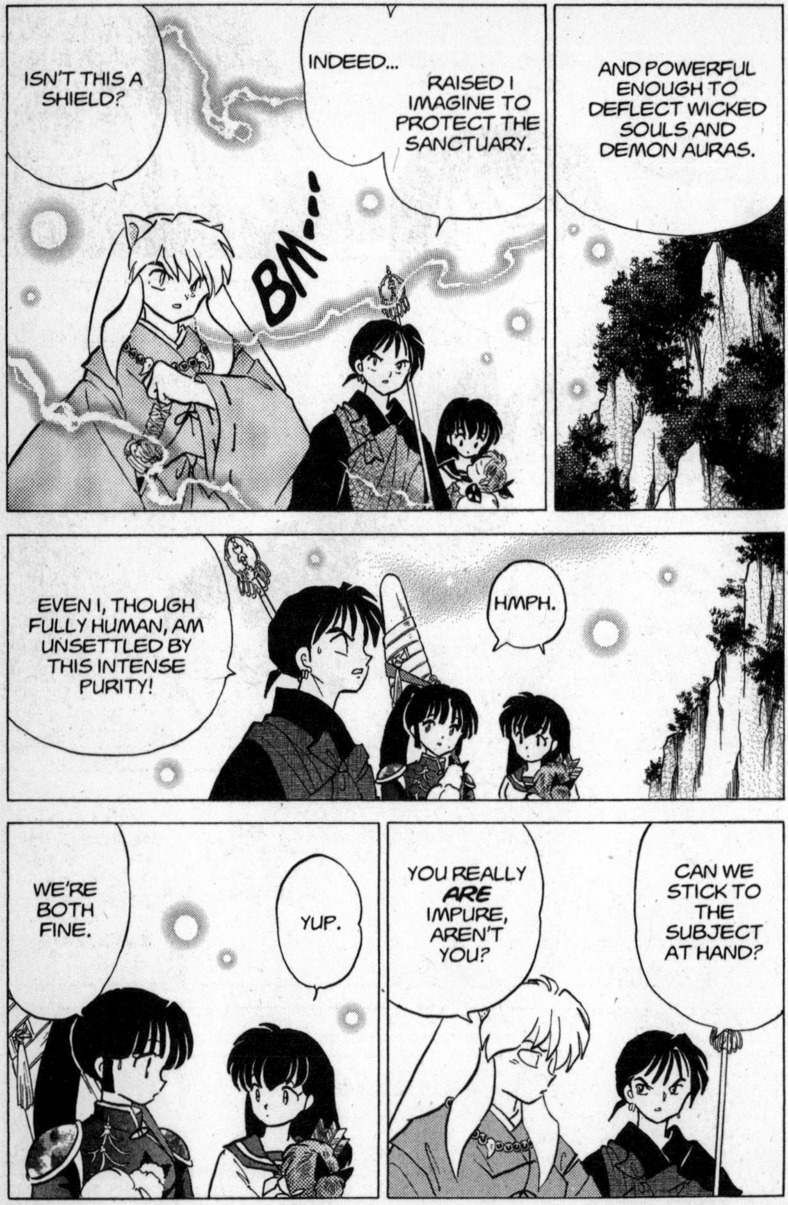
ISN'T THIS A SHIELD?
INDEED...
RAISED I IMAGINE TO PROTECT THE SANCTUARY.
BM
AND POWERFUL ENOUGH TO DEFLECT WICKED SOULS AND DEMON AURAS.
EVEN I, THOUGH FULLY HUMAN, AM UNSETTLED BY THIS INTENSE PURITY!
HMPH.
WE'RE BOTH FINE.
YUP.
YOU REALLY *ARE* IMPURE, AREN'T YOU?
CAN WE STICK TO THE SUBJECT AT HAND?

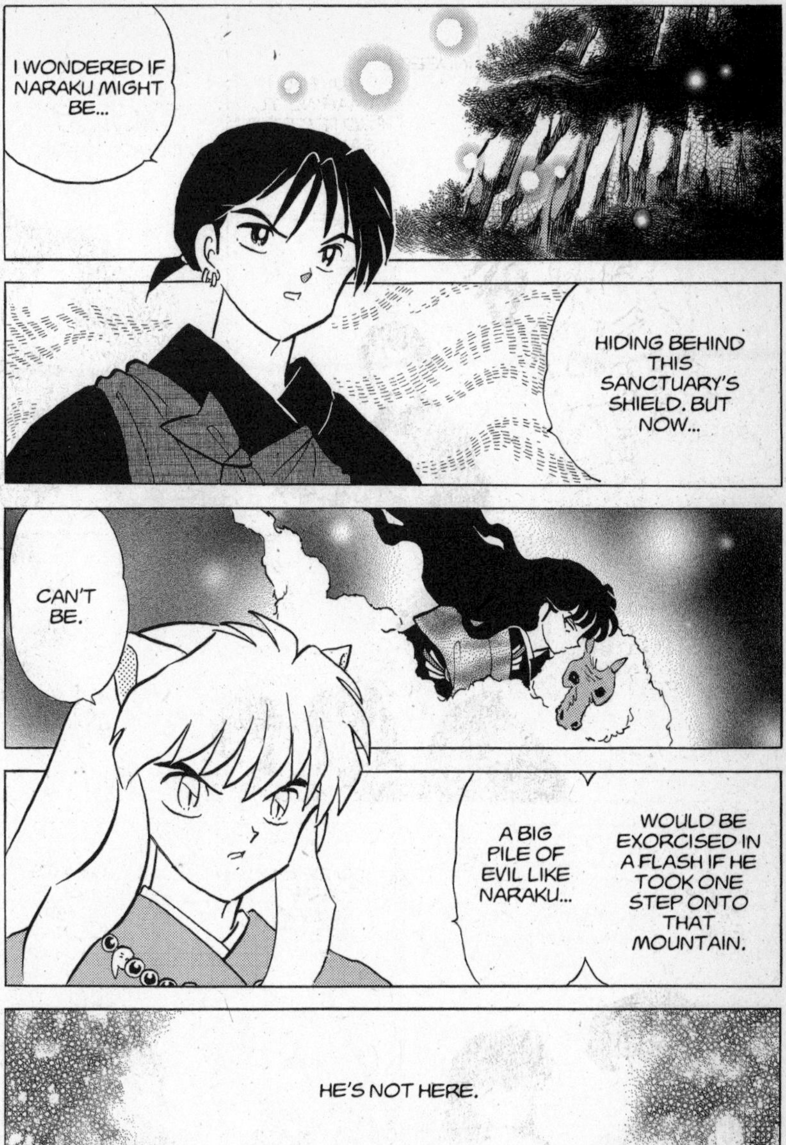
I WONDERED IF NARAKU MIGHT BE...
HIDING BEHIND THIS SANCTUARY'S SHIELD. BUT NOW...
CAN'T BE.
A BIG PILE OF EVIL LIKE NARAKU...
WOULD BE EXORCISED IN A FLASH IF HE TOOK ONE STEP ONTO THAT MOUNTAIN.
HE'S NOT HERE.

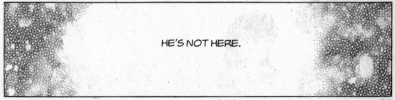

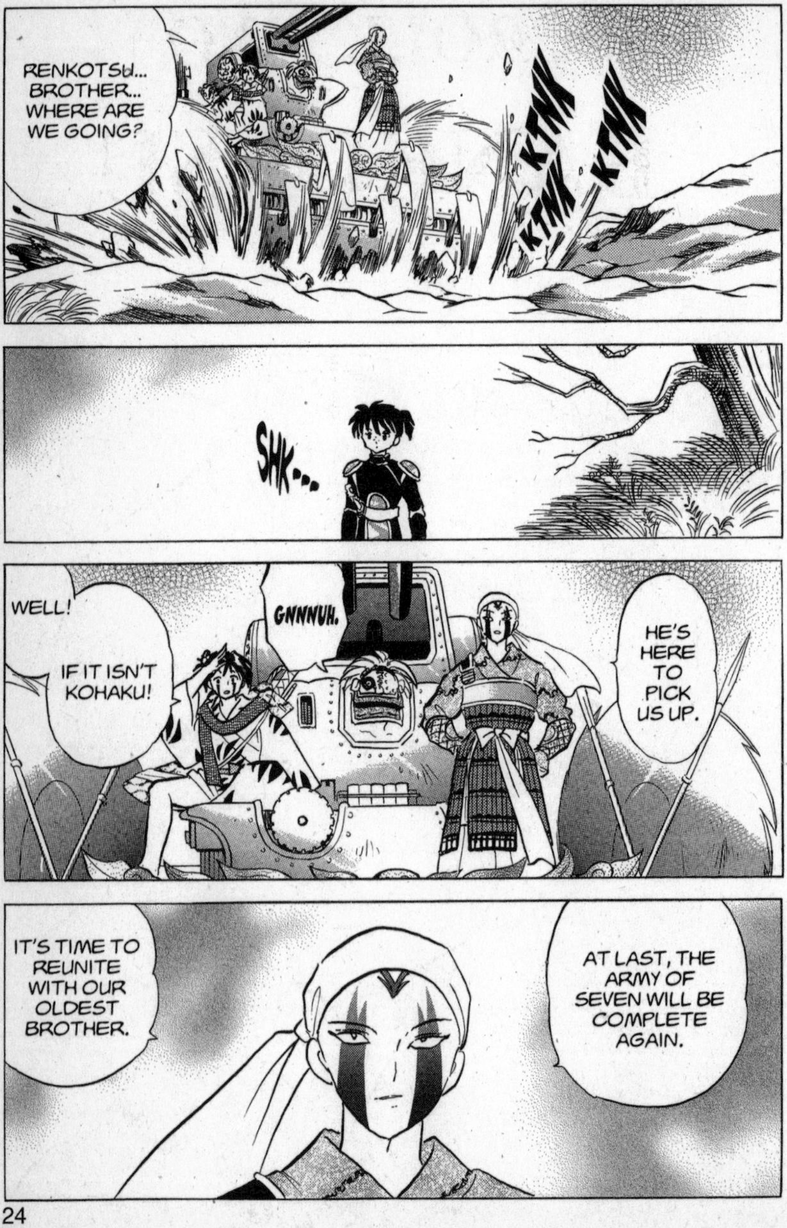
RENKOTSU... BROTHER... WHERE ARE WE GOING?
KTNK KTNK
KTNK KTNK
SHK...
WELL!
IF IT ISN'T KOHAKU!
GNNNUH.
HE'S HERE TO PICK US UP.
IT'S TIME TO REUNITE WITH OUR OLDEST BROTHER.
AT LAST, THE ARMY OF SEVEN WILL BE COMPLETE AGAIN.

SCROLL TWO
BANKOTSU

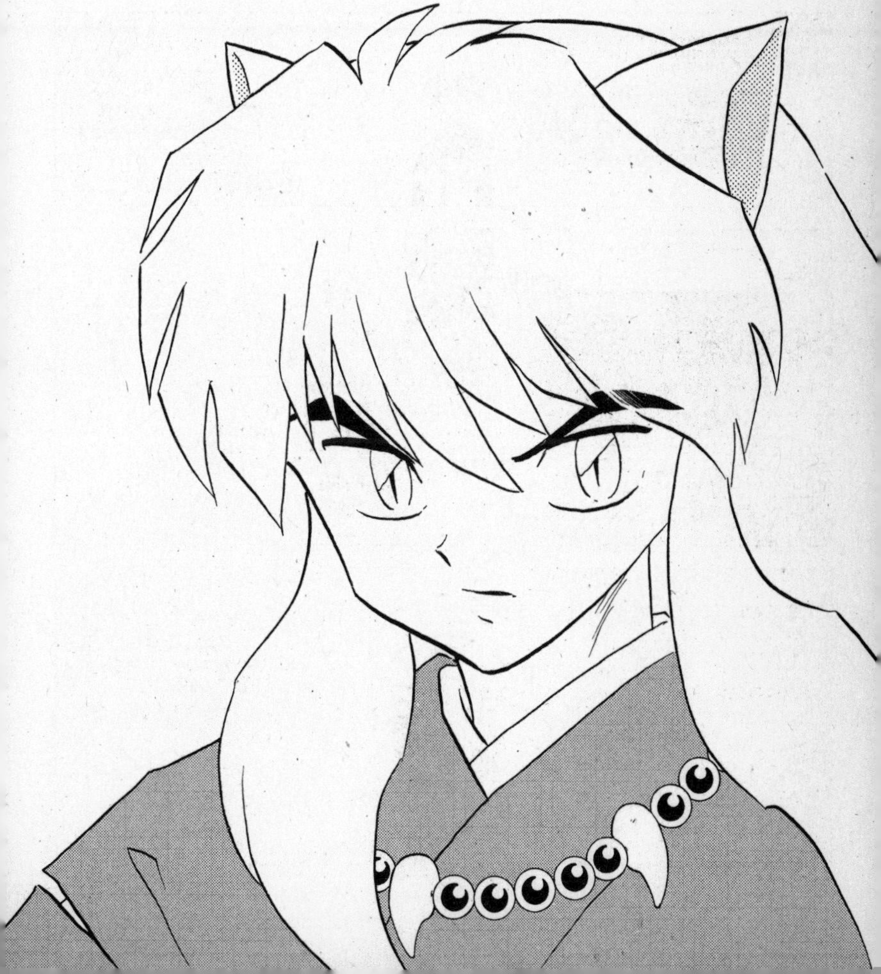

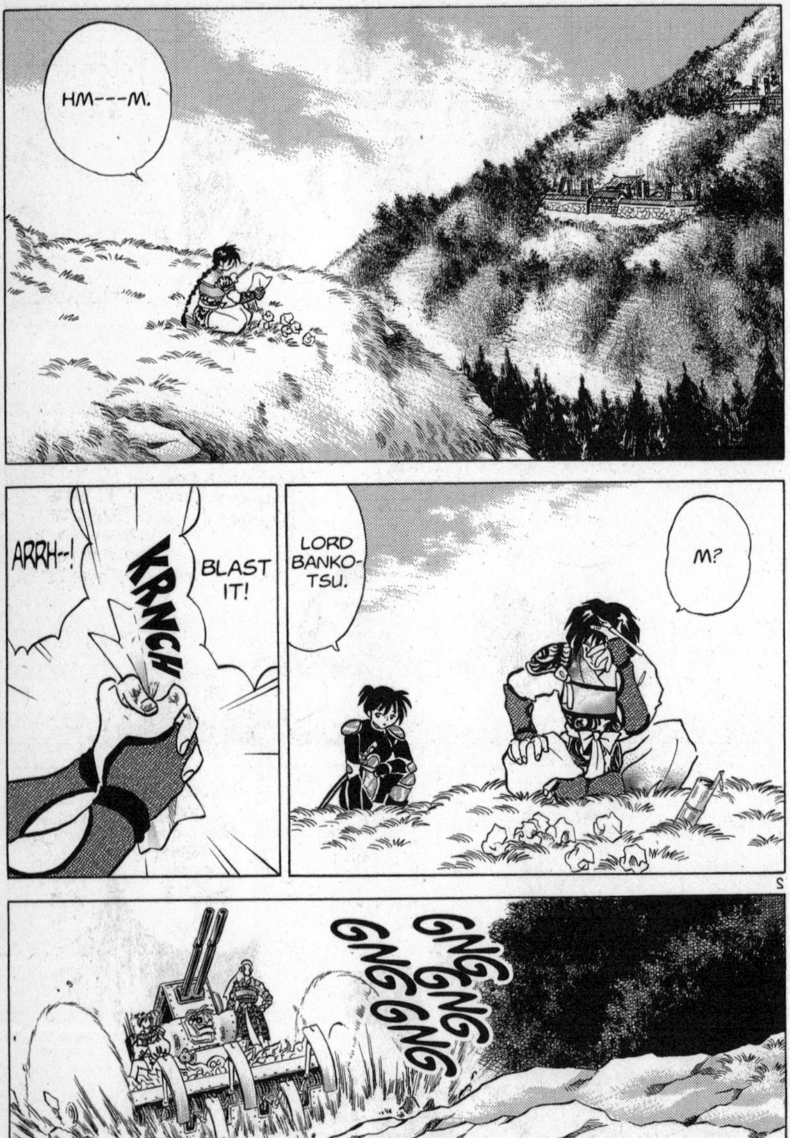
HM---M.
ARRH--!
KRNCH
BLAST IT!
LORD BANKO-TSU.
M?
GNG GNG GNG
GNG GNG GNG

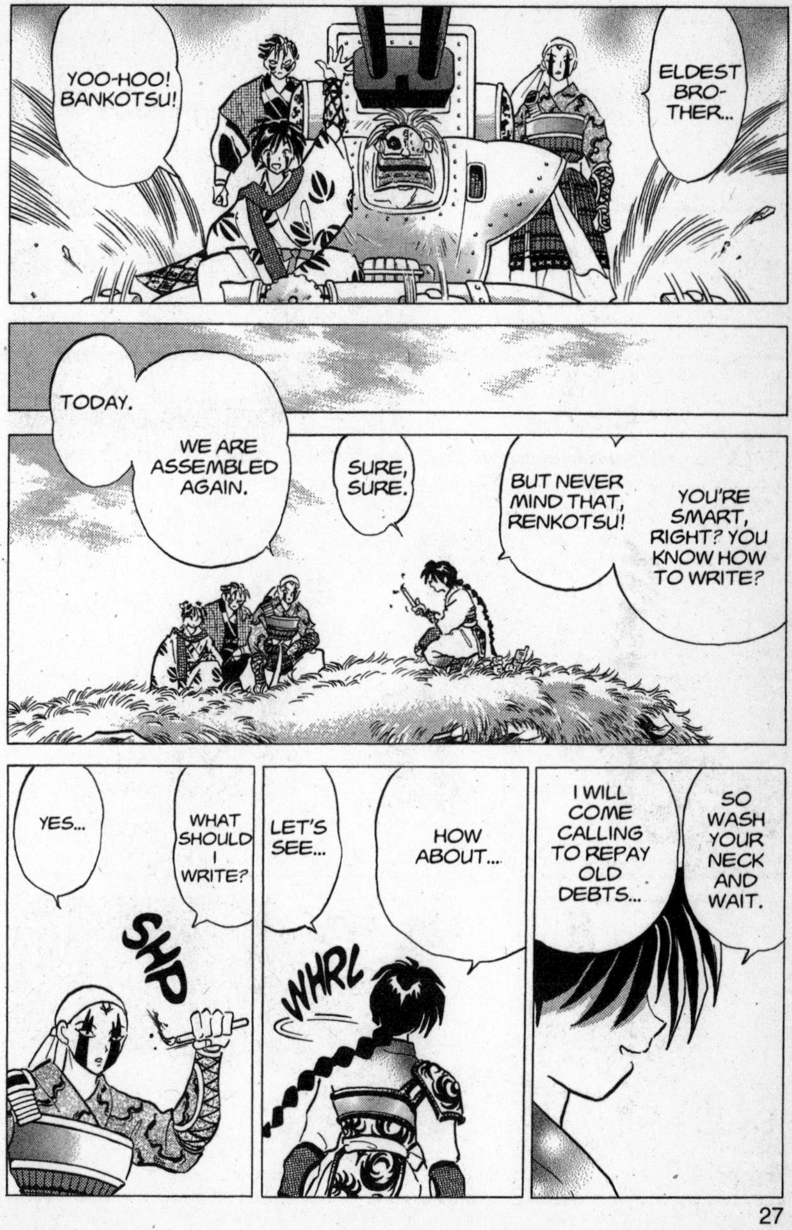
YOO-HOO! BANKOTSU!
ELDEST BRO-THER...
TODAY.
WE ARE ASSEMBLED AGAIN.
SURE, SURE.
BUT NEVER MIND THAT, RENKOTSU!
YOU'RE SMART, RIGHT? YOU KNOW HOW TO WRITE?
YES...
WHAT SHOULD I WRITE?
SHP
LET'S SEE...
HOW ABOUT....
WHRL
I WILL COME CALLING TO REPAY OLD DEBTS...
SO WASH YOUR NECK AND WAIT.

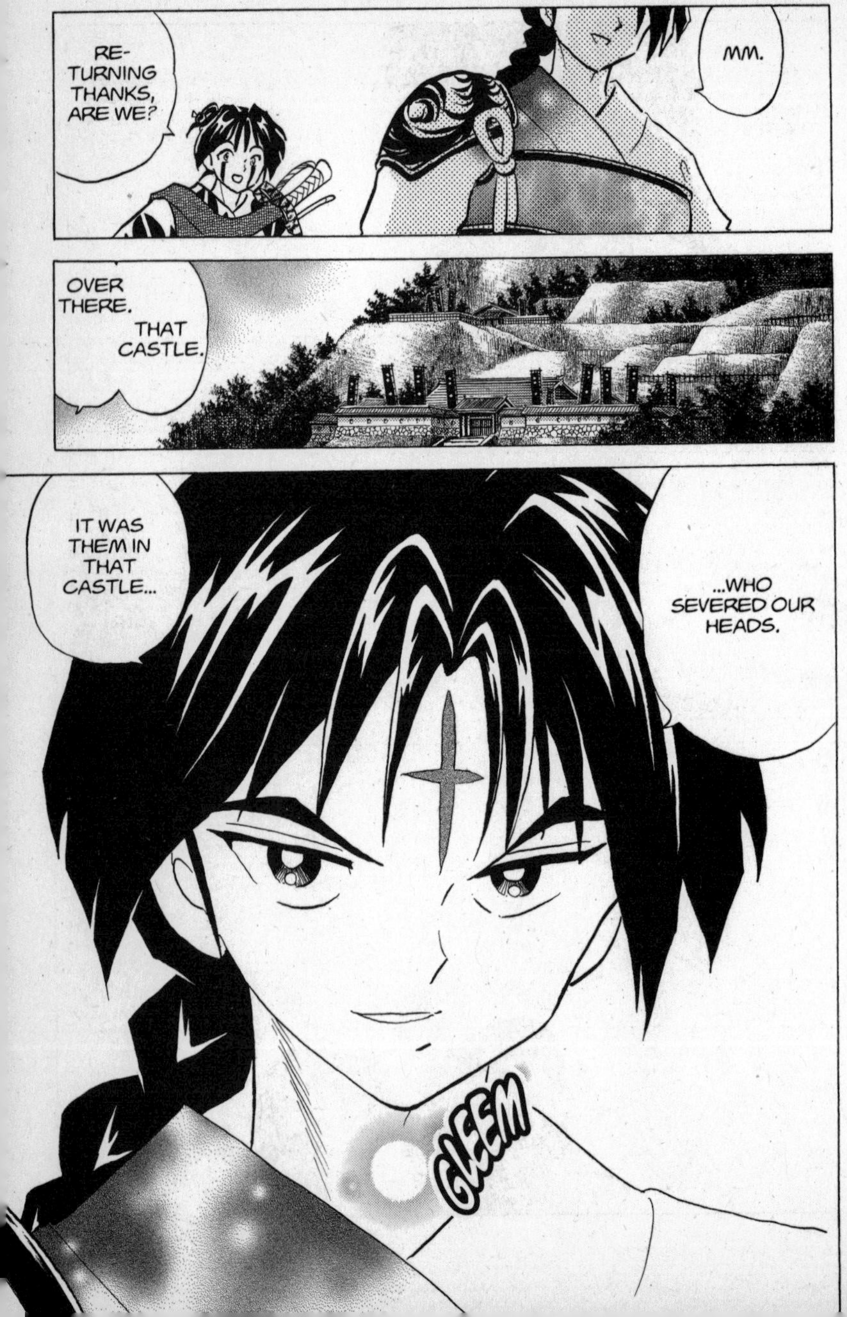
RE-TURNING THANKS, ARE WE?
MM.
OVER THERE.
THAT CASTLE.
IT WAS THEM IN THAT CASTLE...
...WHO SEVERED OUR HEADS.
GLEEM

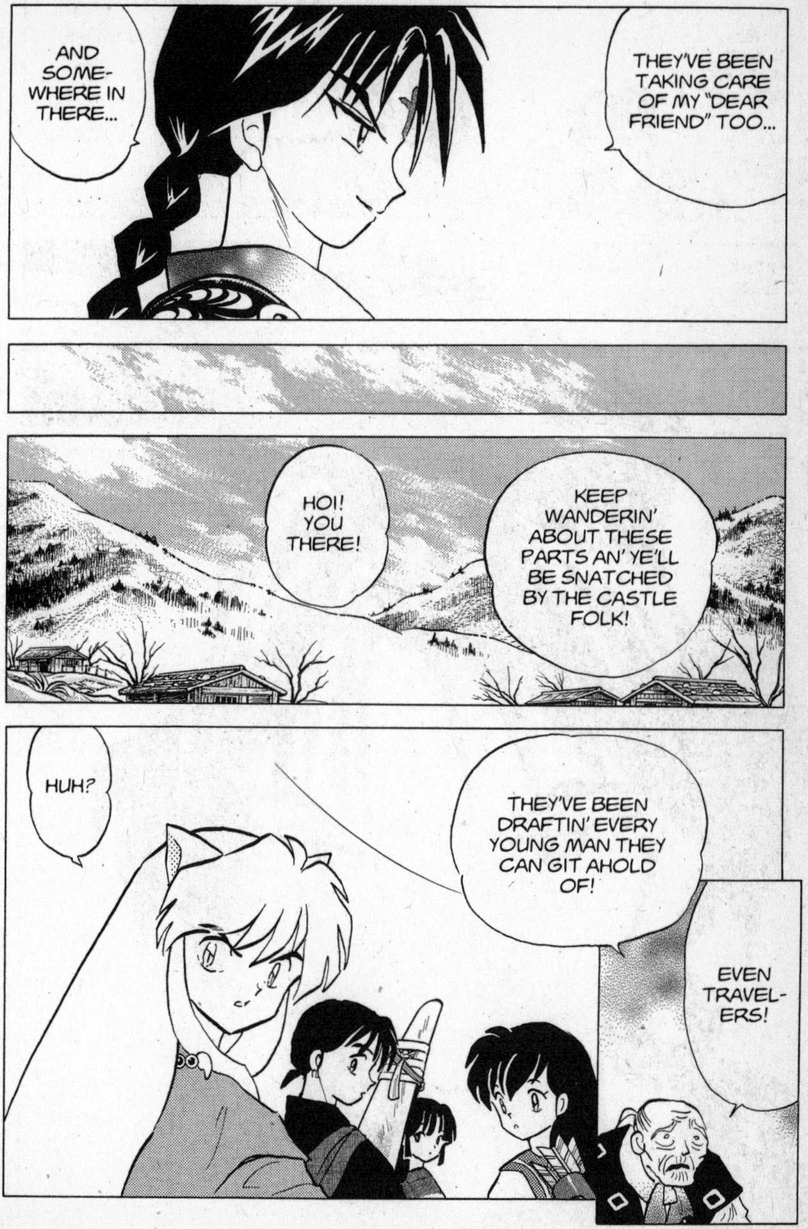
AND SOME-WHERE IN THERE...
THEY'VE BEEN TAKING CARE OF MY "DEAR FRIEND" TOO...
HOI! YOU THERE!
KEEP WANDERIN' ABOUT THESE PARTS AN' YE'LL BE SNATCHED BY THE CASTLE FOLK!
HUH?
THEY'VE BEEN DRAFTIN' EVERY YOUNG MAN THEY CAN GIT AHOLD OF!
EVEN TRAVEL-ERS!

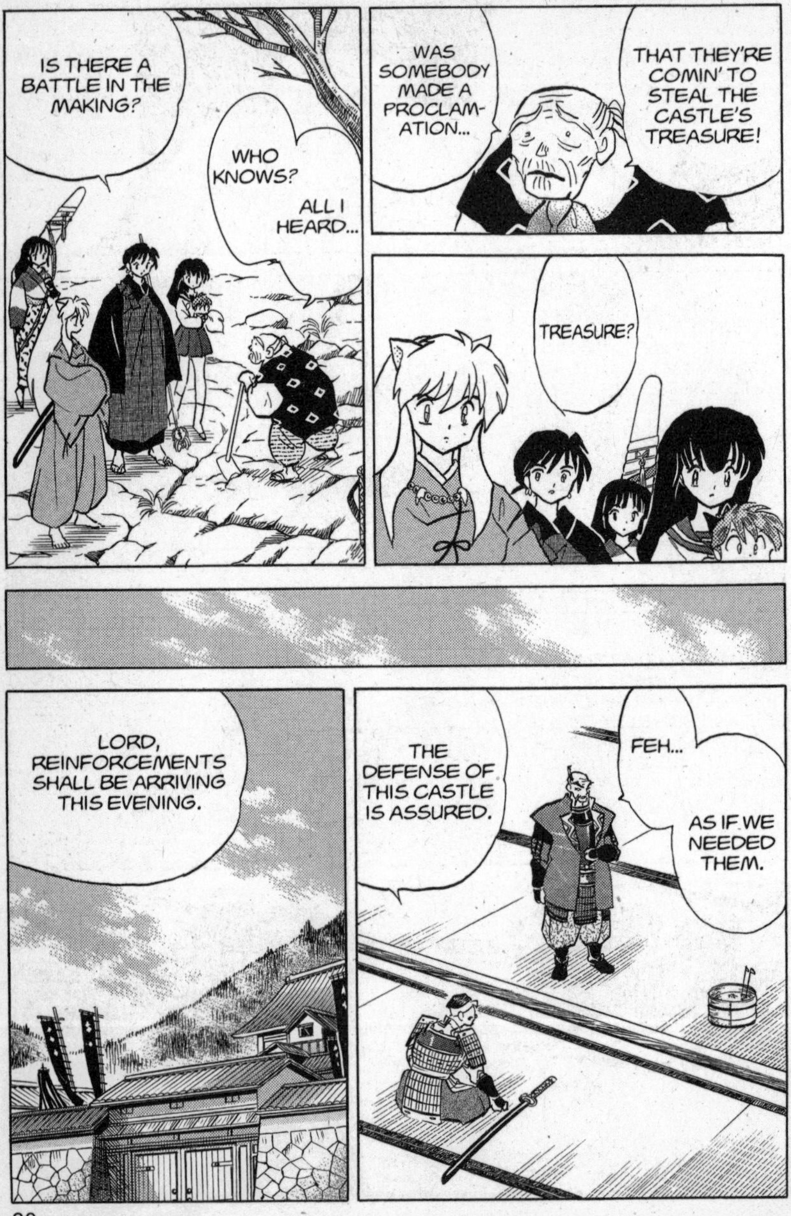
IS THERE A BATTLE IN THE MAKING?
WHO KNOWS?
ALL I HEARD...
WAS SOMEBODY MADE A PROCLAMATION...
THAT THEY'RE COMIN' TO STEAL THE CASTLE'S TREASURE!
TREASURE?
LORD, REINFORCEMENTS SHALL BE ARRIVING THIS EVENING.
THE DEFENSE OF THIS CASTLE IS ASSURED.
FEH...
AS IF WE NEEDED THEM.

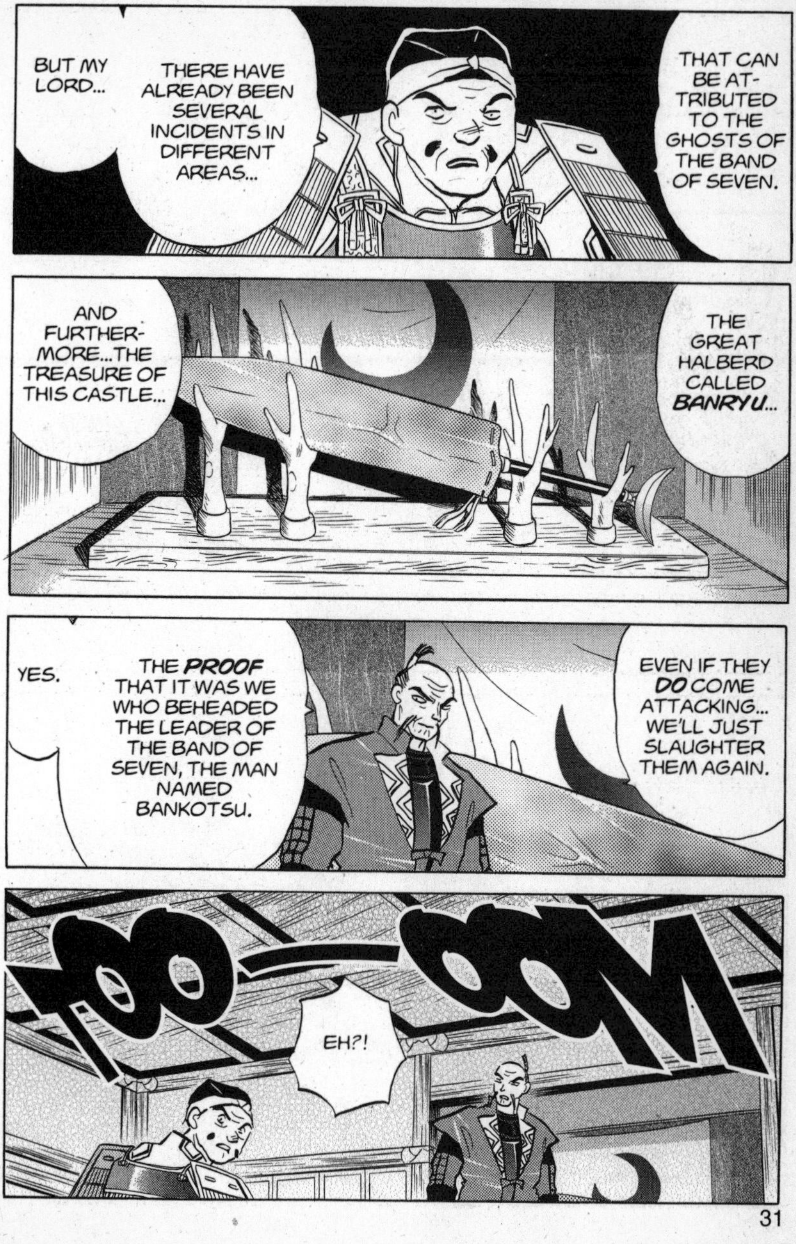
BUT MY LORD...
THERE HAVE ALREADY BEEN SEVERAL INCIDENTS IN DIFFERENT AREAS...
THAT CAN BE AT-TRIBUTED TO THE GHOSTS OF THE BAND OF SEVEN.
AND FURTHER-MORE...THE TREASURE OF THIS CASTLE...
THE GREAT HALBERD CALLED BANRYU...
YES.
THE PROOF THAT IT WAS WE WHO BEHEADED THE LEADER OF THE BAND OF SEVEN, THE MAN NAMED BANKOTSU.
EVEN IF THEY DO COME ATTACKING... WE'LL JUST SLAUGHTER THEM AGAIN.
OO—OOM
EH?!

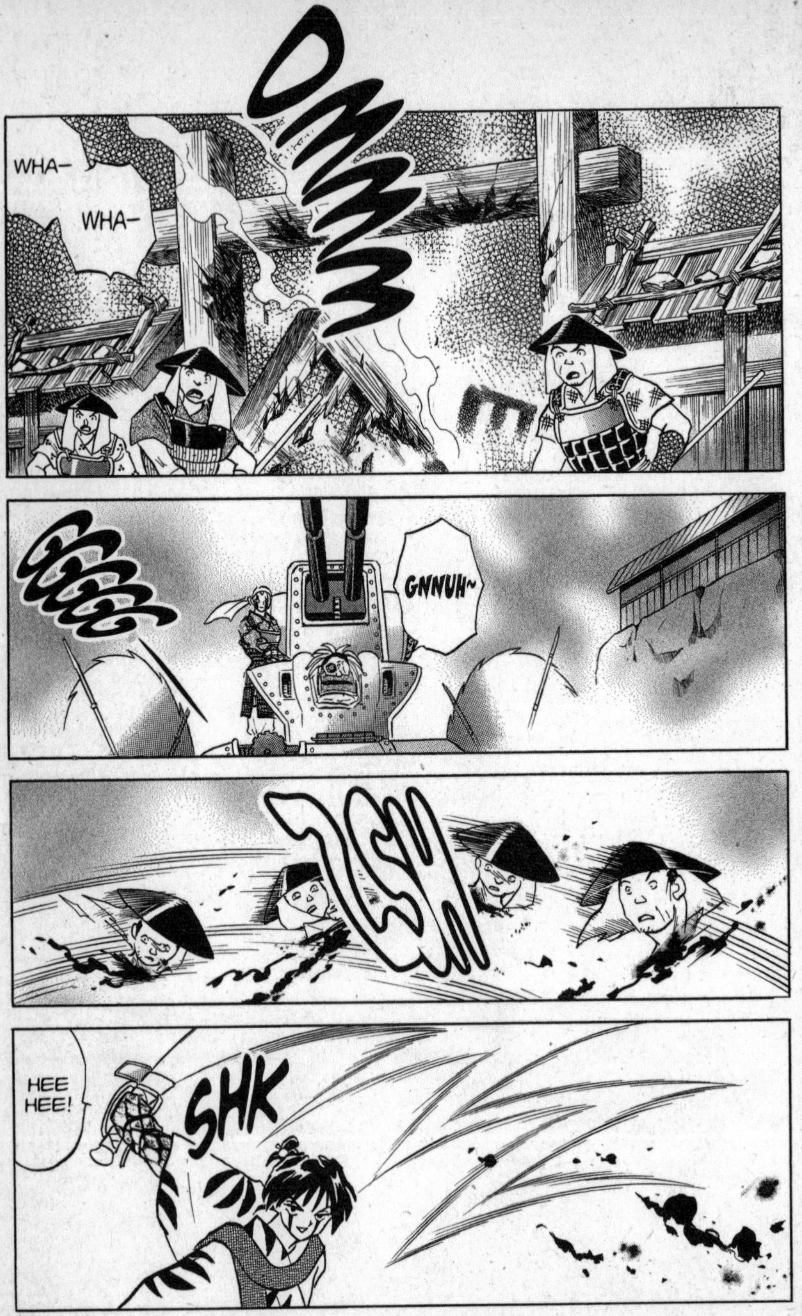
DMMMM
WHA-
WHA-
GNNUH~
HEE HEE!
SHK

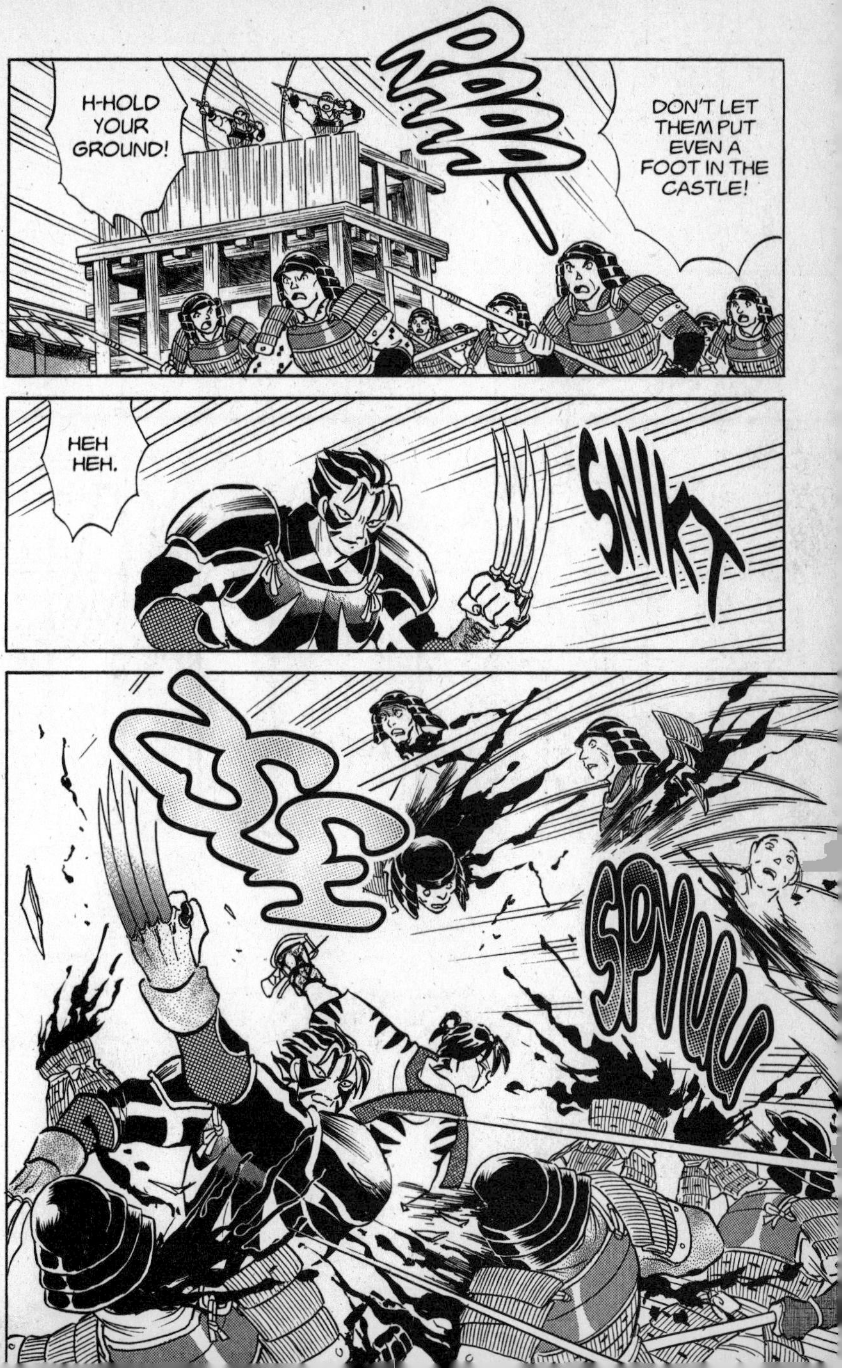
H-HOLD YOUR GROUND!
DON'T LET THEM PUT EVEN A FOOT IN THE CASTLE!
HEH HEH.
SNIKT

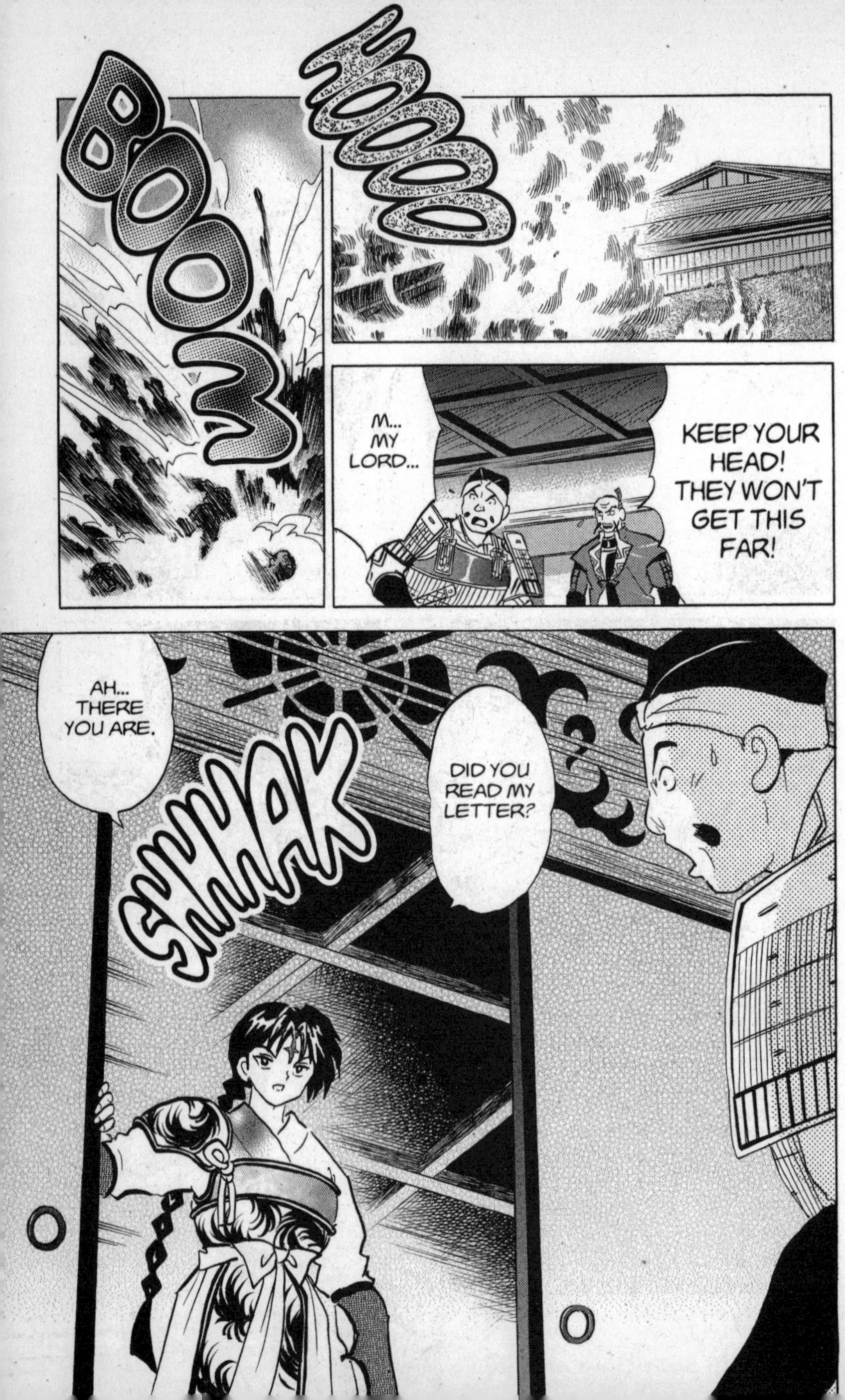
BOOOM
WHOOOO
M... MY LORD...
KEEP YOUR HEAD! THEY WON'T GET THIS FAR!
AH... THERE YOU ARE.
SHHAK
DID YOU READ MY LETTER?

Y...YOU...

WHERE IS THE GUARD?!

MM?

YOU MEAN THEM?

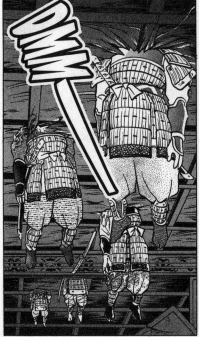

DMM

NOW.

W-WAIT!

KRACK

YOU WANT THE GREAT HALBERD, YES?

I'LL GIVE IT BACK TO YOU...!

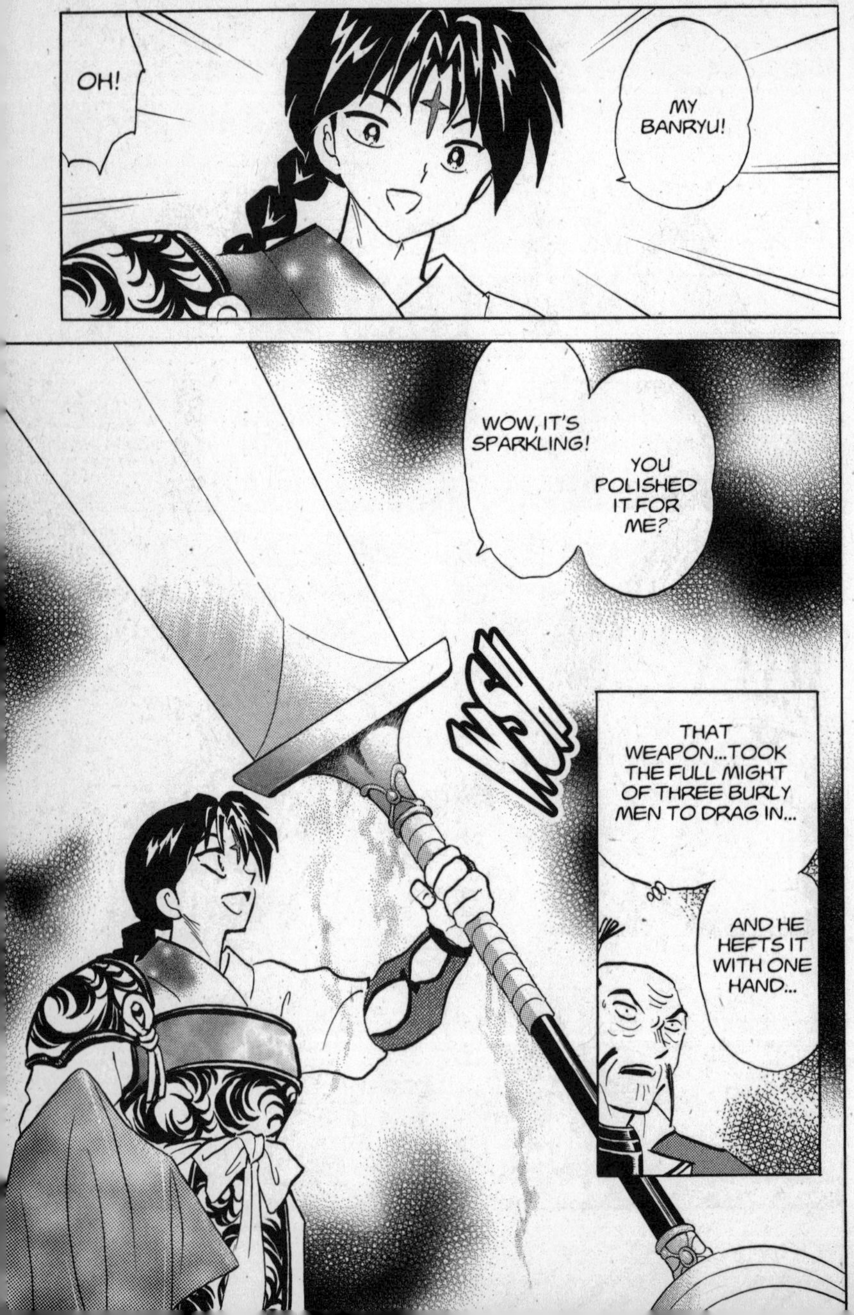
OH!
MY BANRYU!
WOW, IT'S SPARKLING!
YOU POLISHED IT FOR ME?
THAT WEAPON...TOOK THE FULL MIGHT OF THREE BURLY MEN TO DRAG IN...
AND HE HEFTS IT WITH ONE HAND...

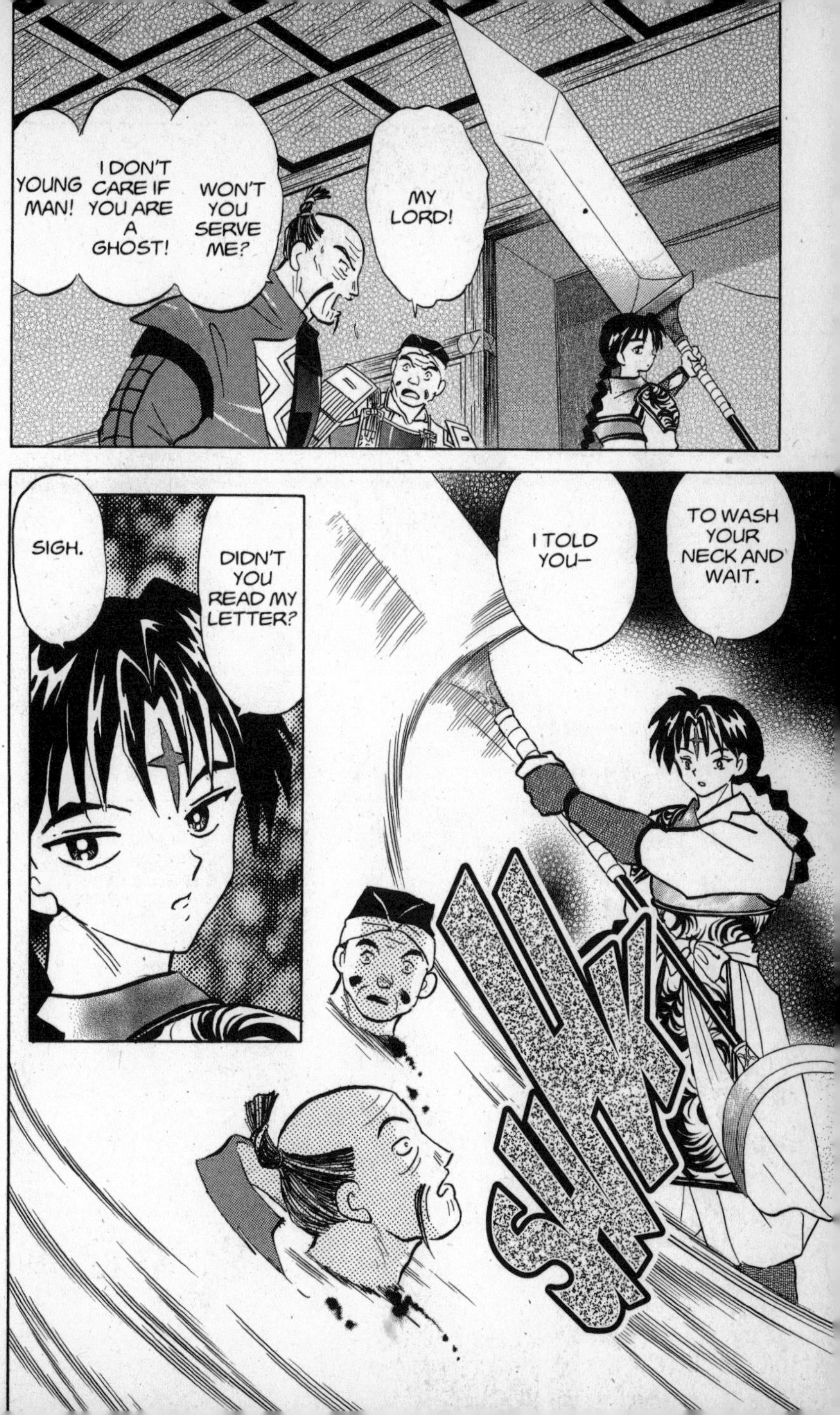
YOUNG MAN!
I DON'T CARE IF YOU ARE A GHOST!
WON'T YOU SERVE ME?
MY LORD!
SIGH.
DIDN'T YOU READ MY LETTER?
I TOLD YOU—
TO WASH YOUR NECK AND WAIT.

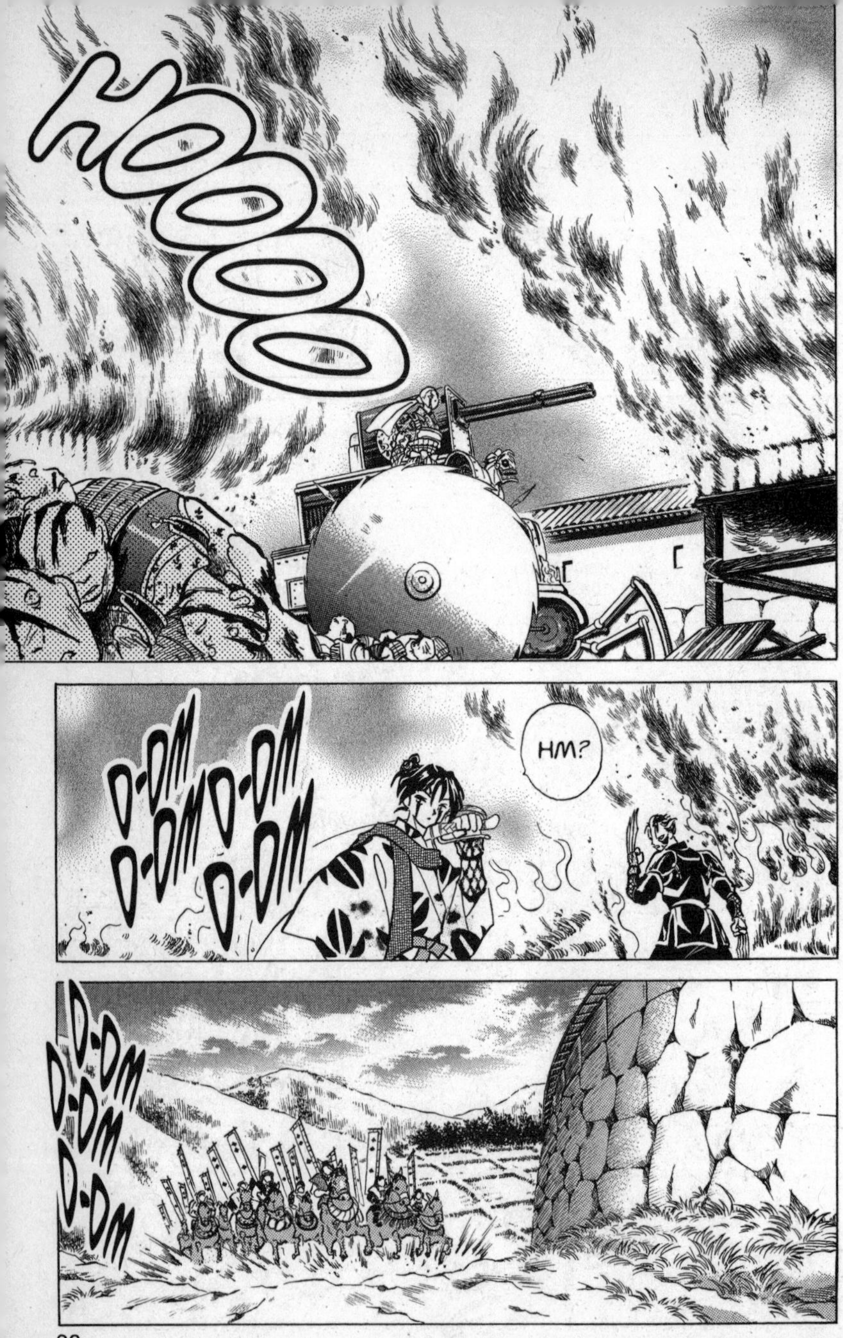
HOOOOO
D-DM D-DM D-DM
D-DM D-DM D-DM
HM?
D-DM D-DM D-DM

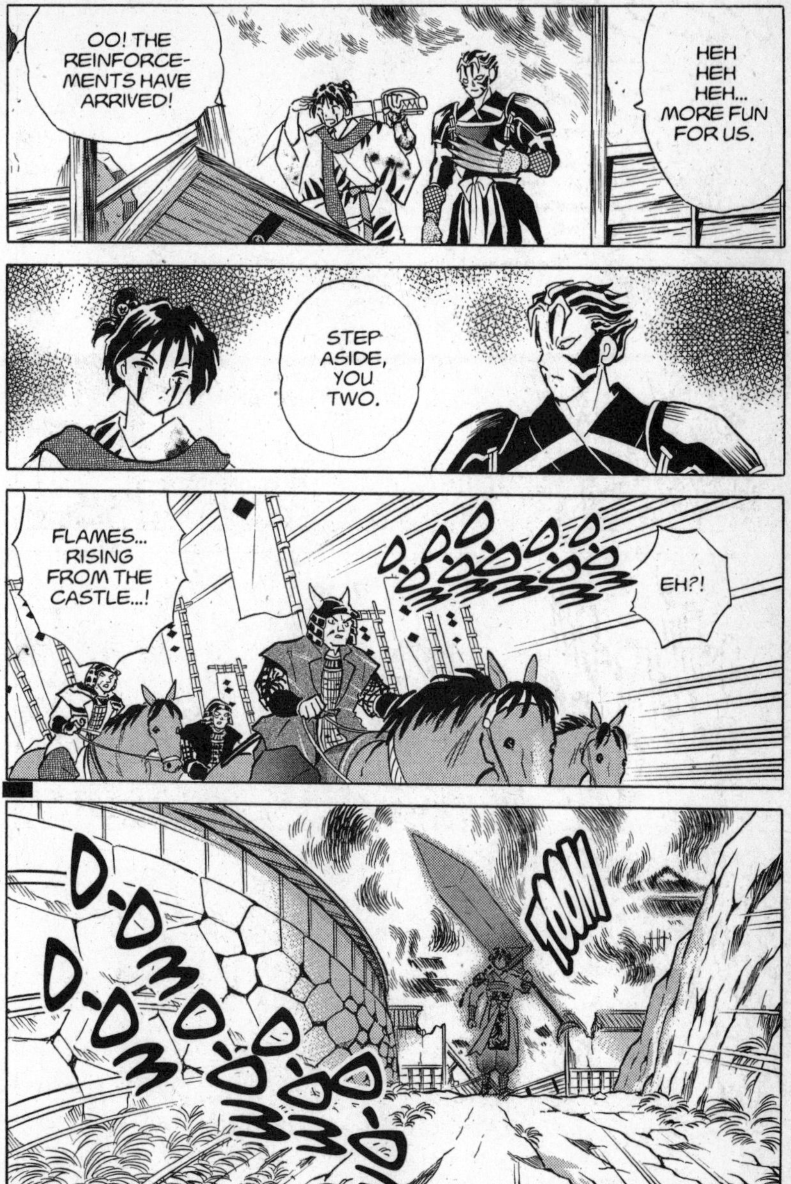
OO! THE REINFORCE-MENTS HAVE ARRIVED!
HEH HEH HEH... MORE FUN FOR US.
STEP ASIDE, YOU TWO.
FLAMES... RISING FROM THE CASTLE...!
EH?!
TOOM

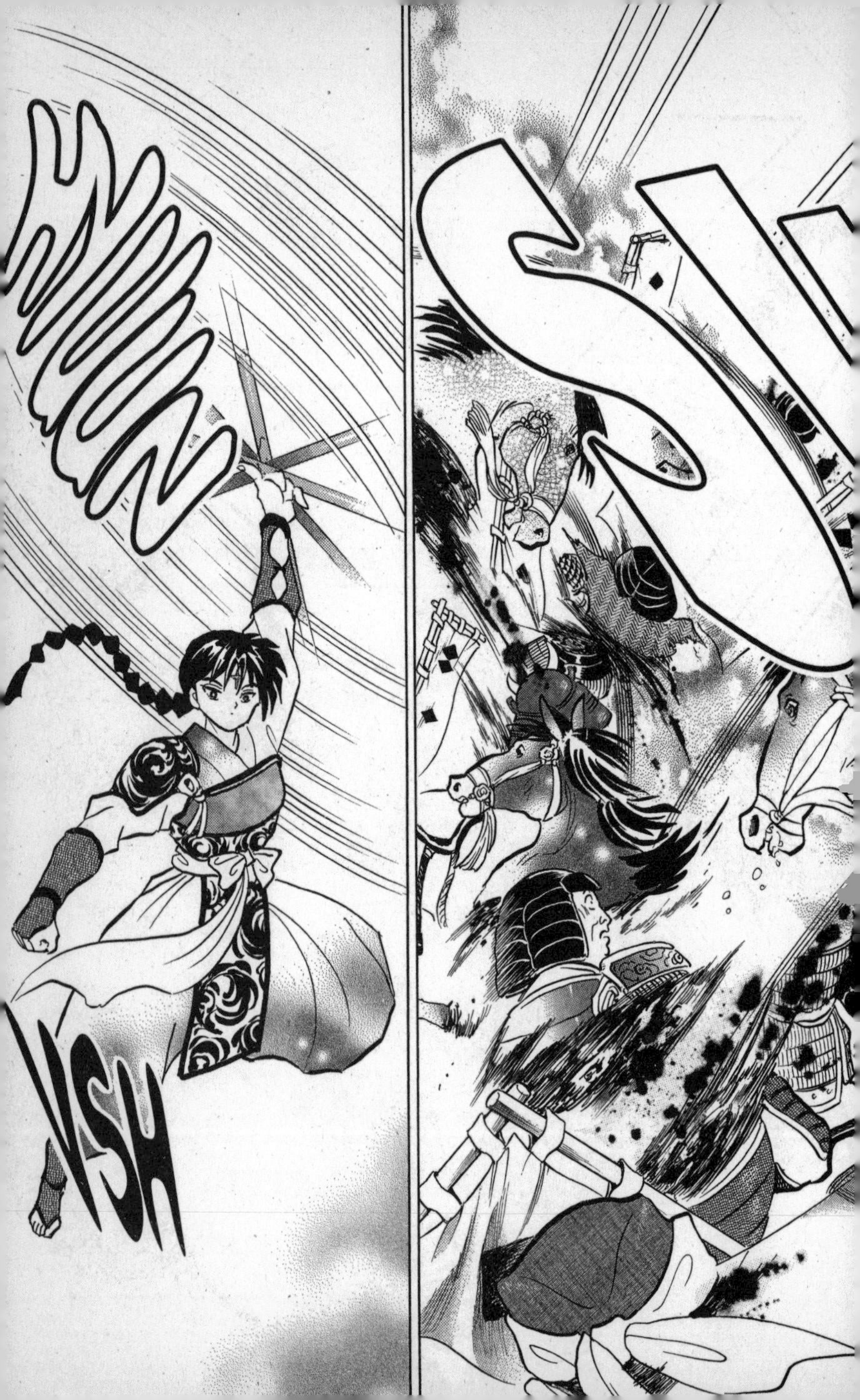

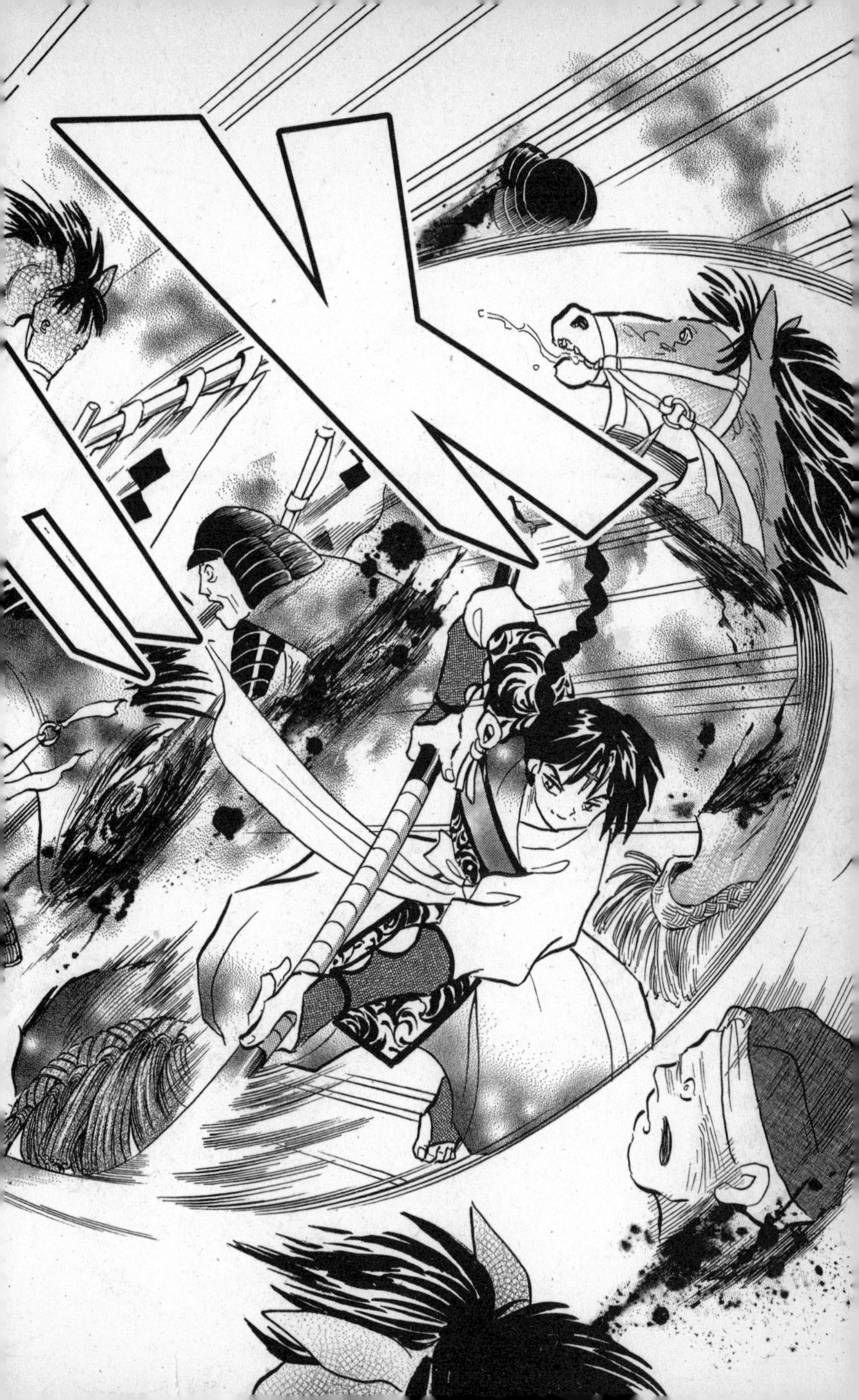

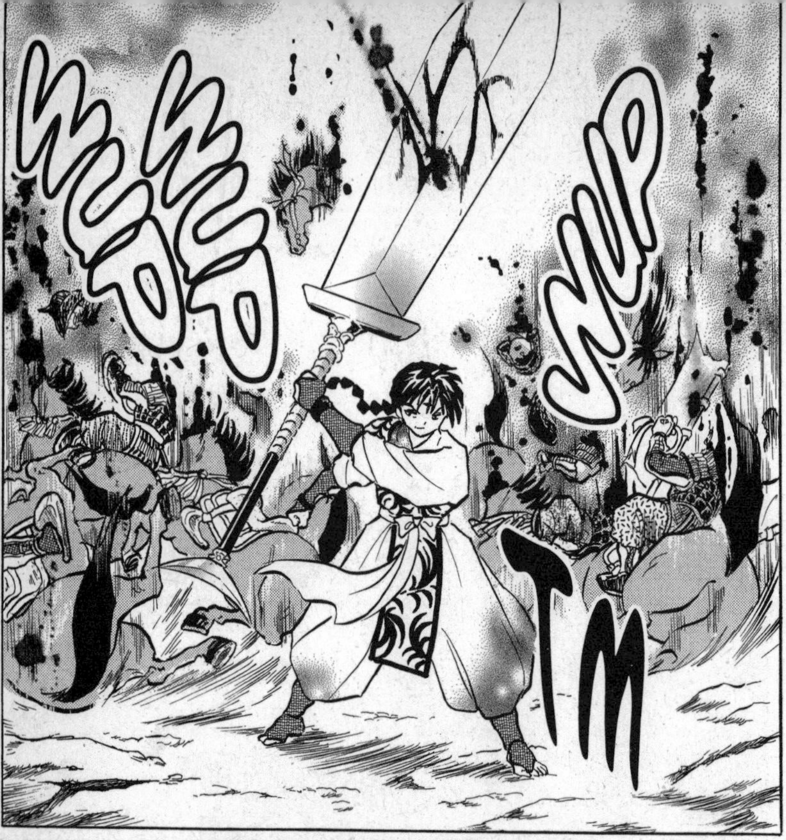
WUWUP
WUP
TM
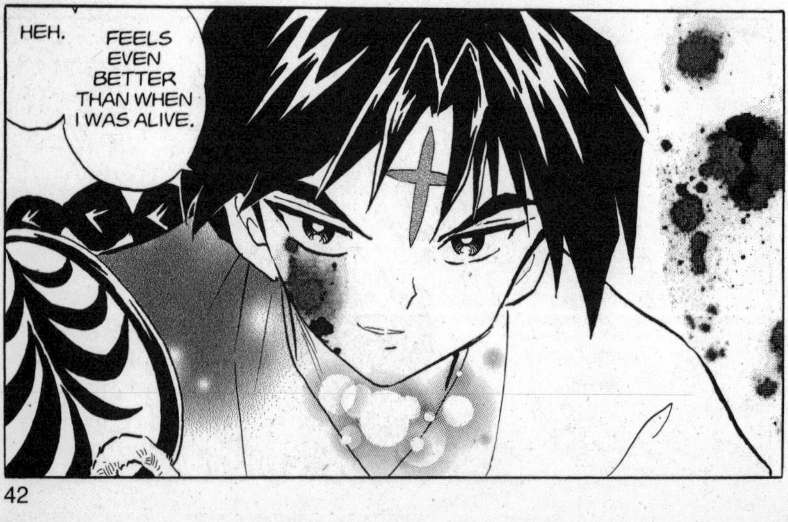
HEH.
FEELS EVEN BETTER THAN WHEN I WAS ALIVE.

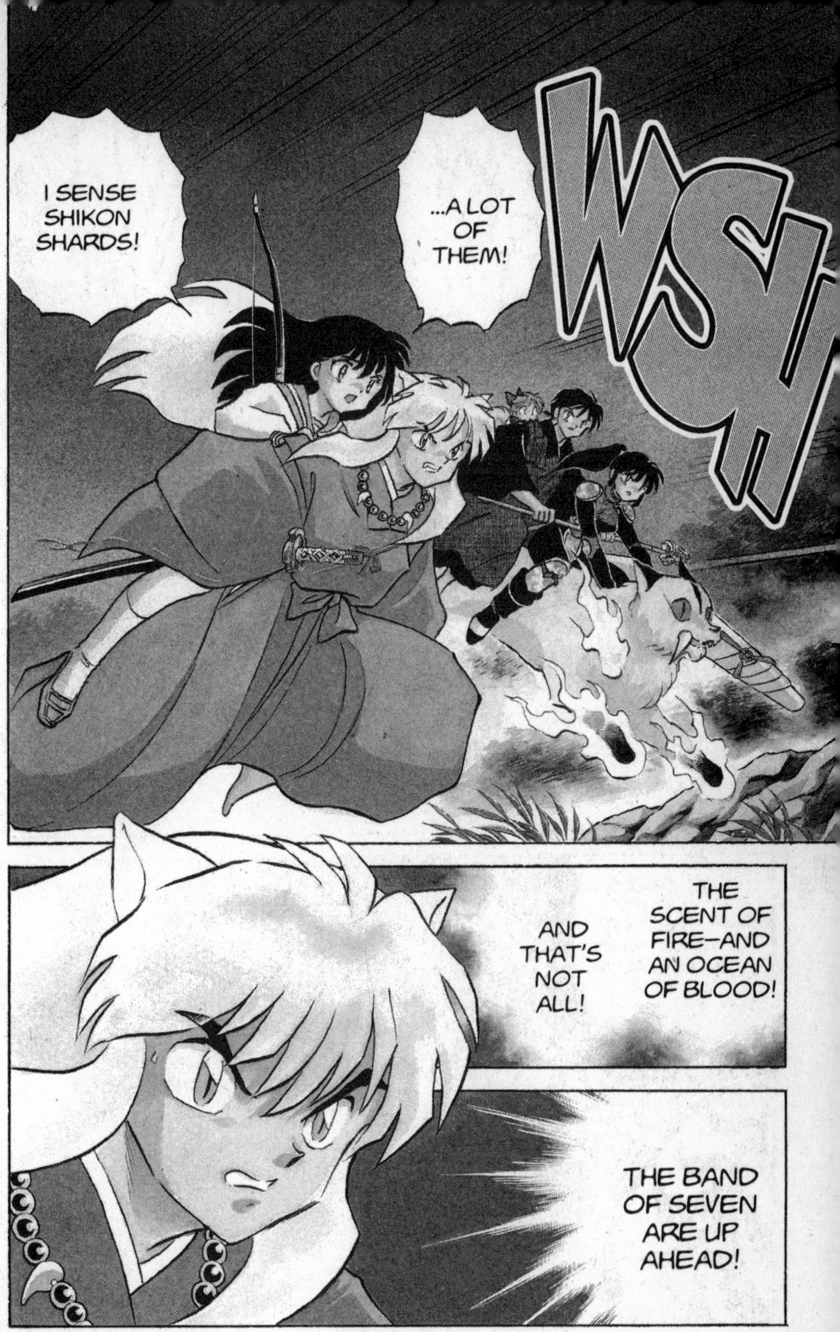
I SENSE SHIKON SHARDS!
...A LOT OF THEM!
WSH
AND THAT'S NOT ALL!
THE SCENT OF FIRE—AND AN OCEAN OF BLOOD!
THE BAND OF SEVEN ARE UP AHEAD!

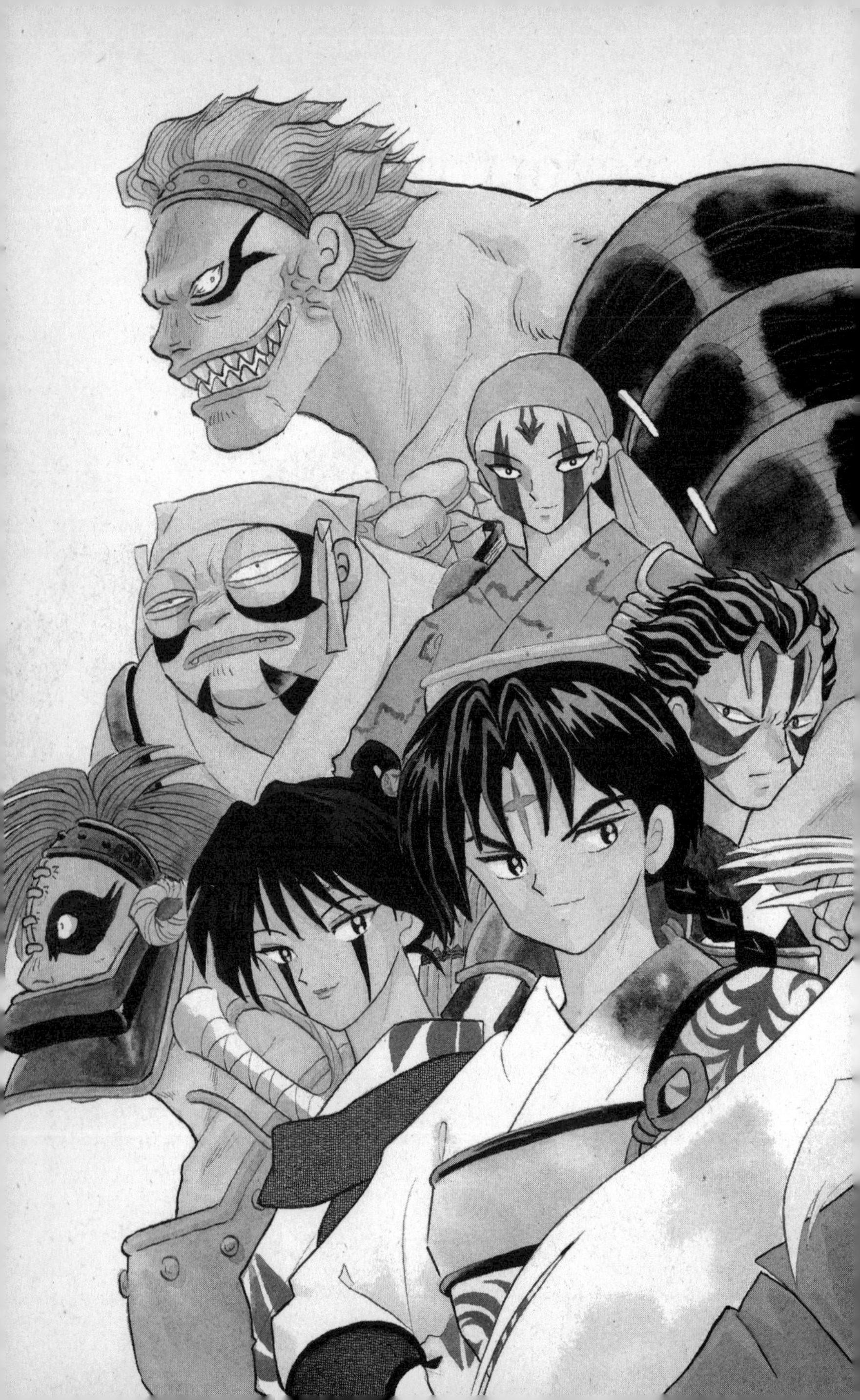

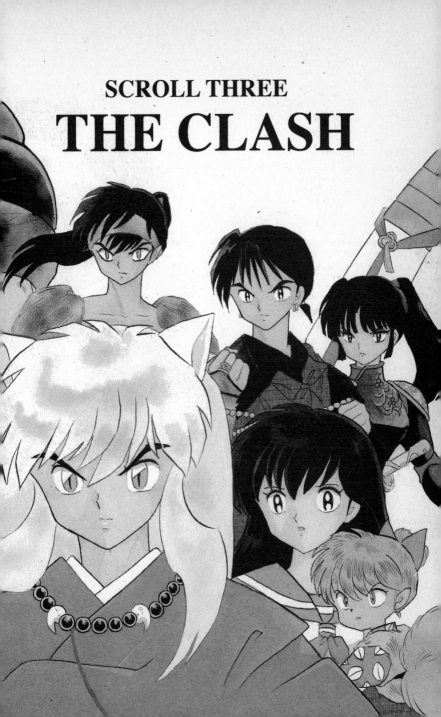

SCROLL THREE

THE CLASH

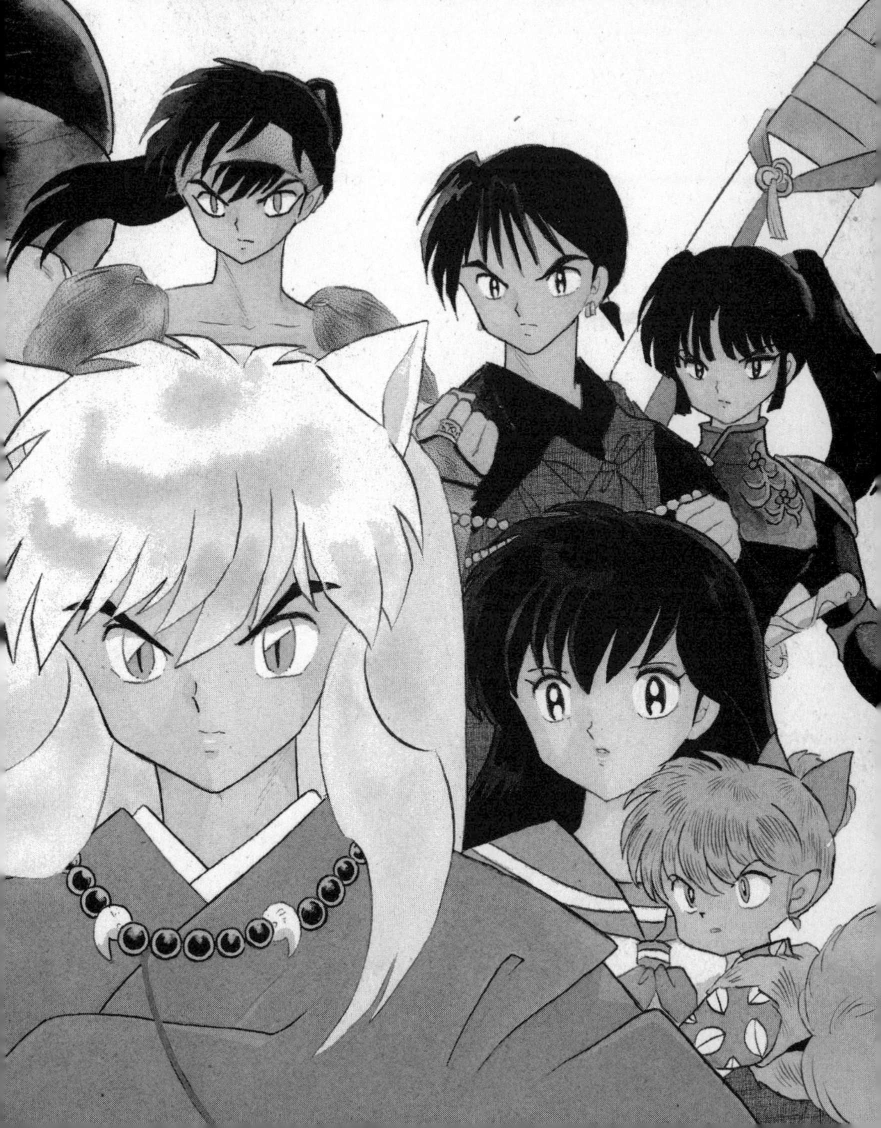

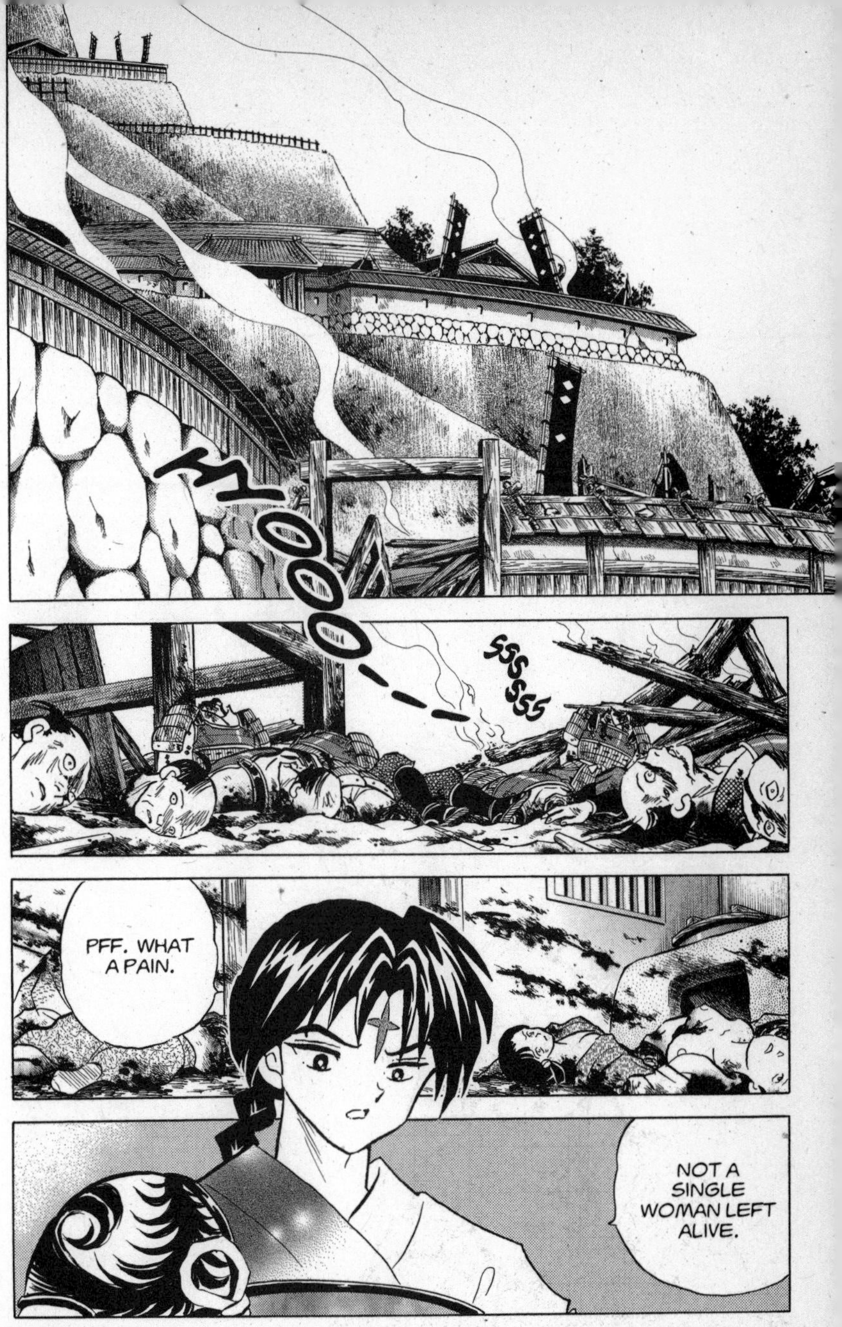
KYOOOO---
SSSSSS
PFF. WHAT A PAIN.
NOT A SINGLE WOMAN LEFT ALIVE.

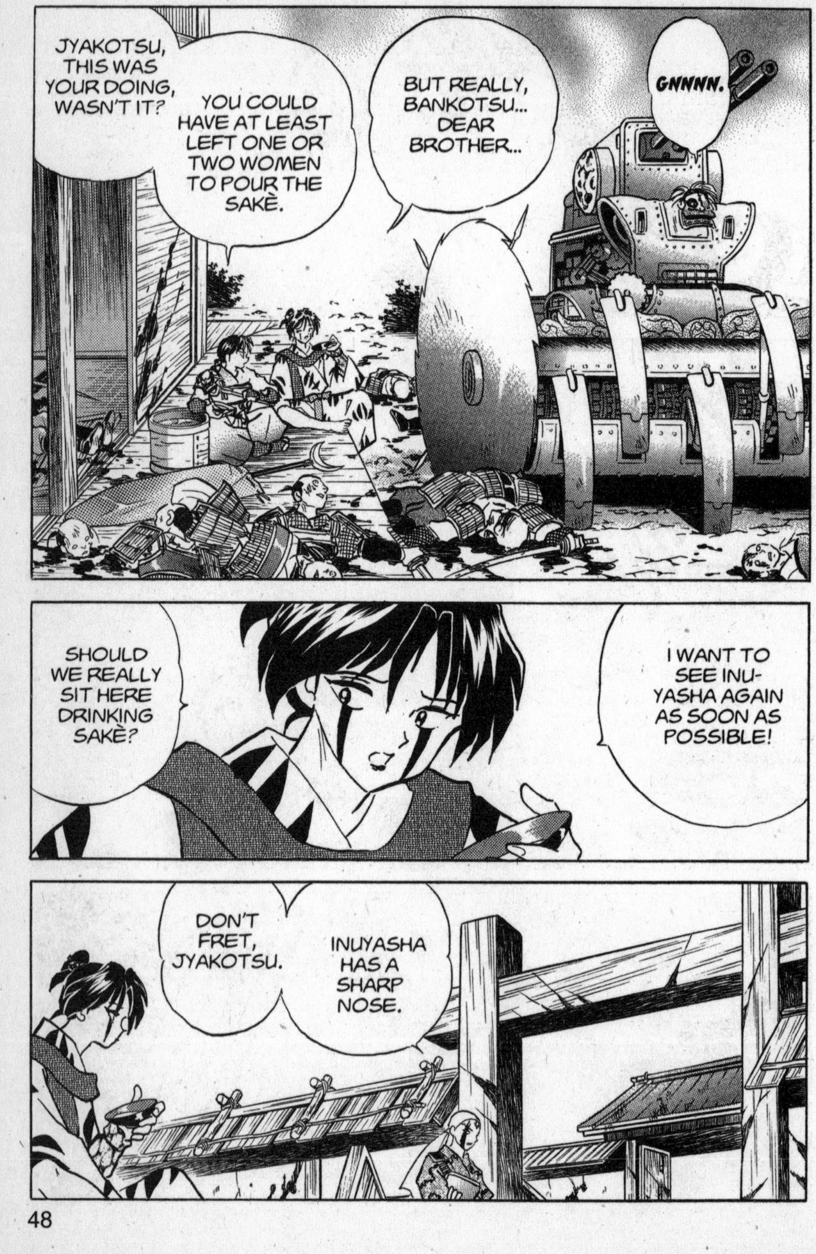
JYAKOTSU, THIS WAS YOUR DOING, WASN'T IT?
YOU COULD HAVE AT LEAST LEFT ONE OR TWO WOMEN TO POUR THE SAKÈ.
BUT REALLY, BANKOTSU... DEAR BROTHER...
GNNNN.
SHOULD WE REALLY SIT HERE DRINKING SAKÈ?
I WANT TO SEE INU-YASHA AGAIN AS SOON AS POSSIBLE!
DON'T FRET, JYAKOTSU.
INUYASHA HAS A SHARP NOSE.

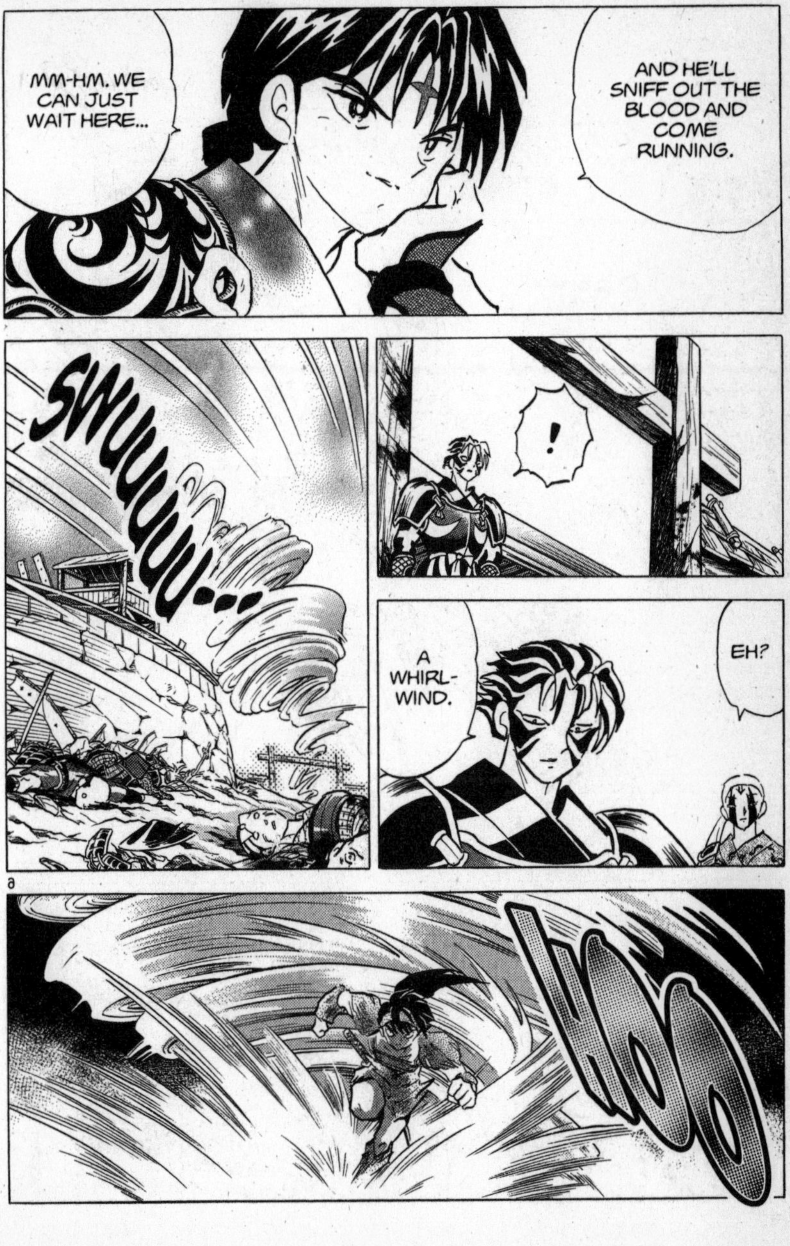
MM-HM. WE CAN JUST WAIT HERE...
AND HE'LL SNIFF OUT THE BLOOD AND COME RUNNING.
SWUUUUU...
!
A WHIRL-WIND.
EH?
HOOO

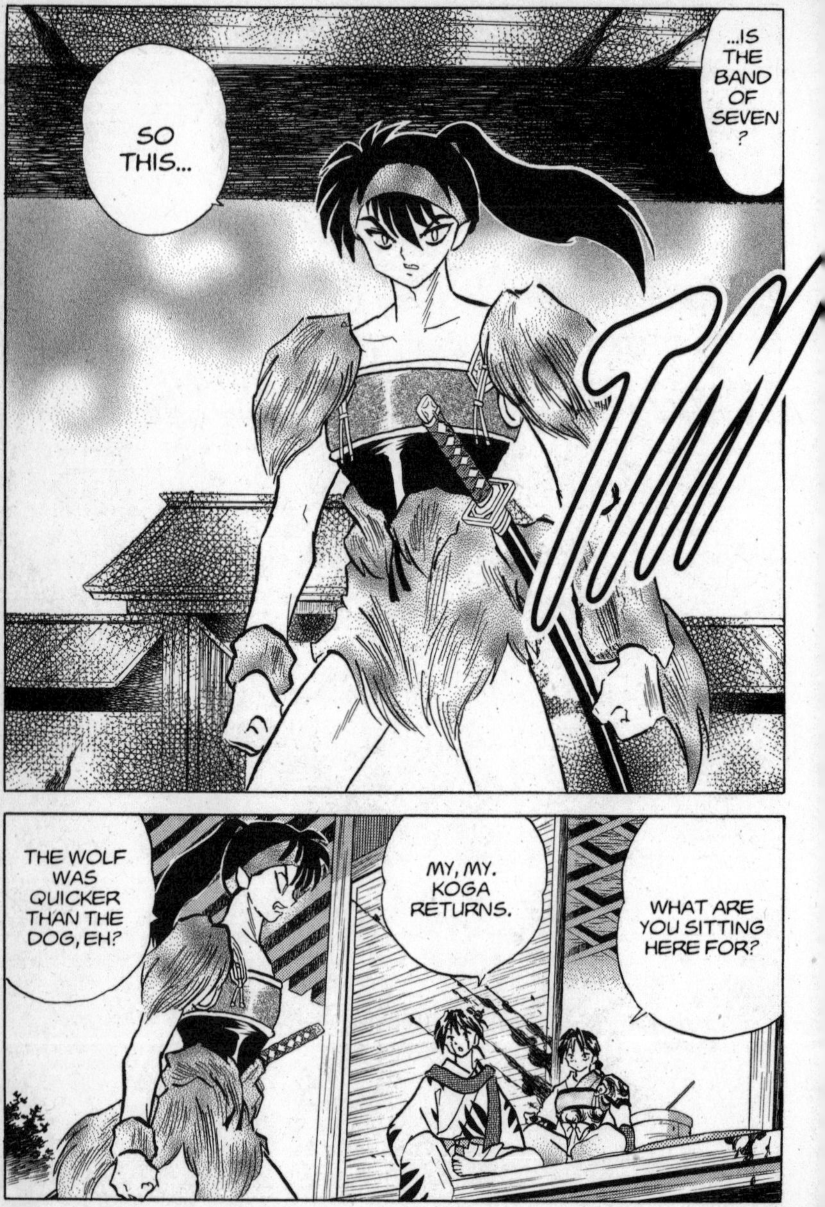
SO THIS...
...IS THE BAND OF SEVEN?
THE WOLF WAS QUICKER THAN THE DOG, EH?
MY, MY. KOGA RETURNS.
WHAT ARE YOU SITTING HERE FOR?

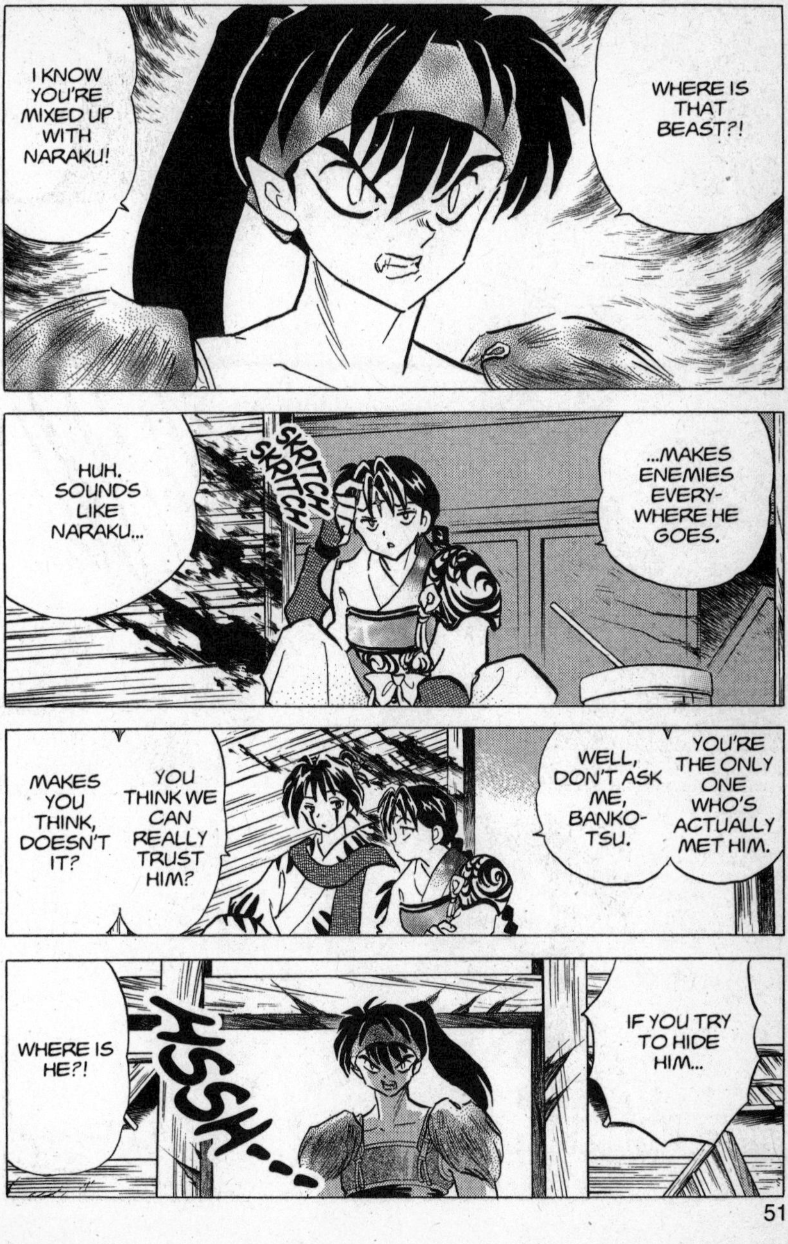
I KNOW YOU'RE MIXED UP WITH NARAKU!
WHERE IS THAT BEAST?!
HUH. SOUNDS LIKE NARAKU...
SKRITCH SKRITCH
...MAKES ENEMIES EVERY-WHERE HE GOES.
MAKES YOU THINK, DOESN'T IT?
YOU THINK WE CAN REALLY TRUST HIM?
WELL, DON'T ASK ME, BANKO-TSU.
YOU'RE THE ONLY ONE WHO'S ACTUALLY MET HIM.
WHERE IS HE?!
HSSH...
IF YOU TRY TO HIDE HIM...

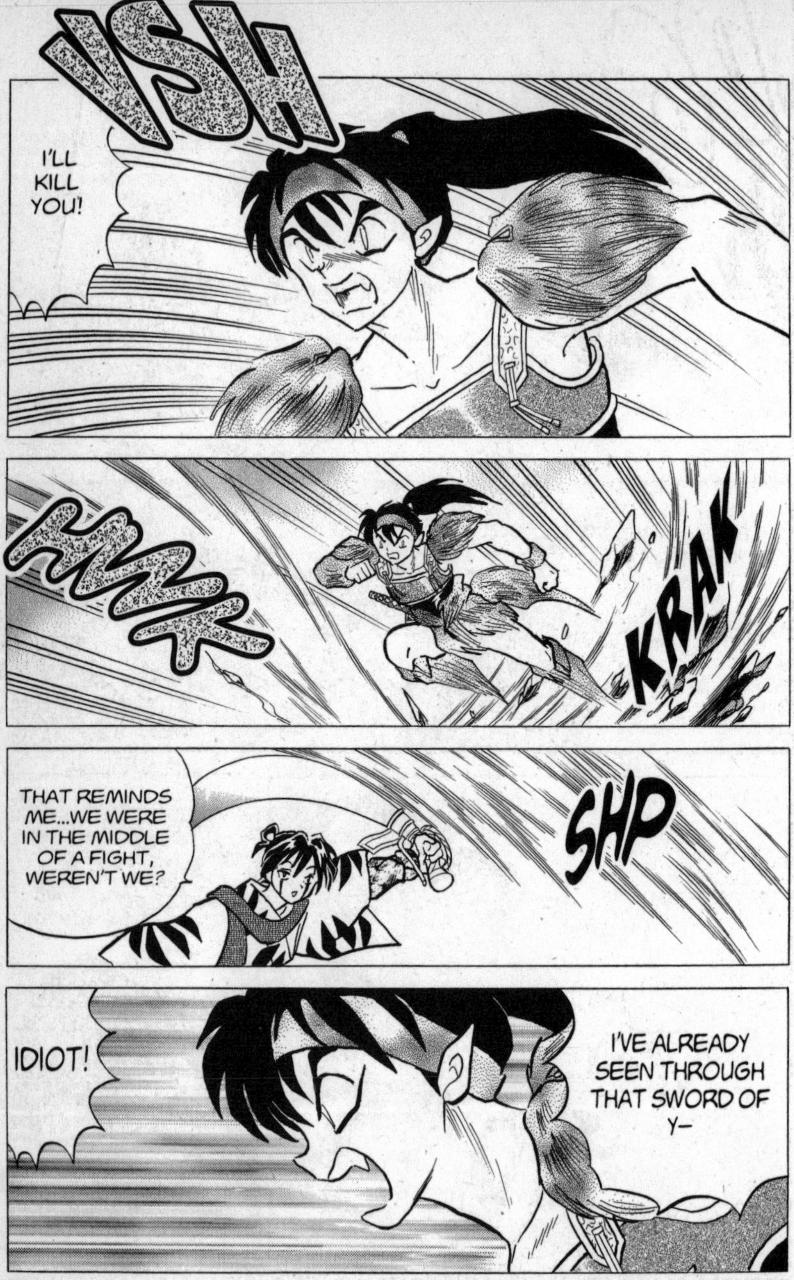
VSH
I'LL KILL YOU!
HWK
KRAK
THAT REMINDS ME...WE WERE IN THE MIDDLE OF A FIGHT, WEREN'T WE?
SHP
IDIOT!
I'VE ALREADY SEEN THROUGH THAT SWORD OF Y—

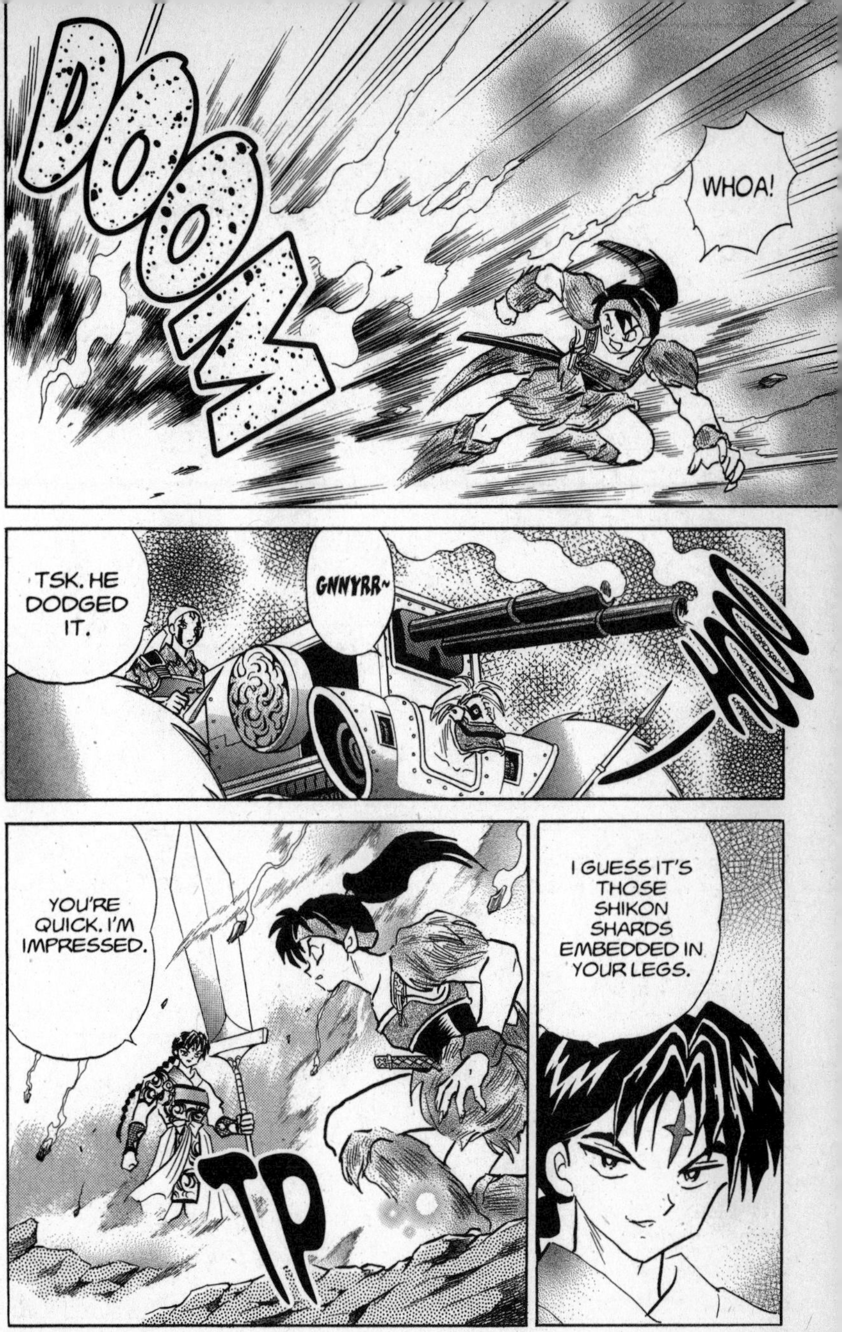
DOOOM
WHOA!
TSK. HE DODGED IT.
GNNYRR~
YOU'RE QUICK. I'M IMPRESSED.
TP
I GUESS IT'S THOSE SHIKON SHARDS EMBEDDED IN YOUR LEGS.

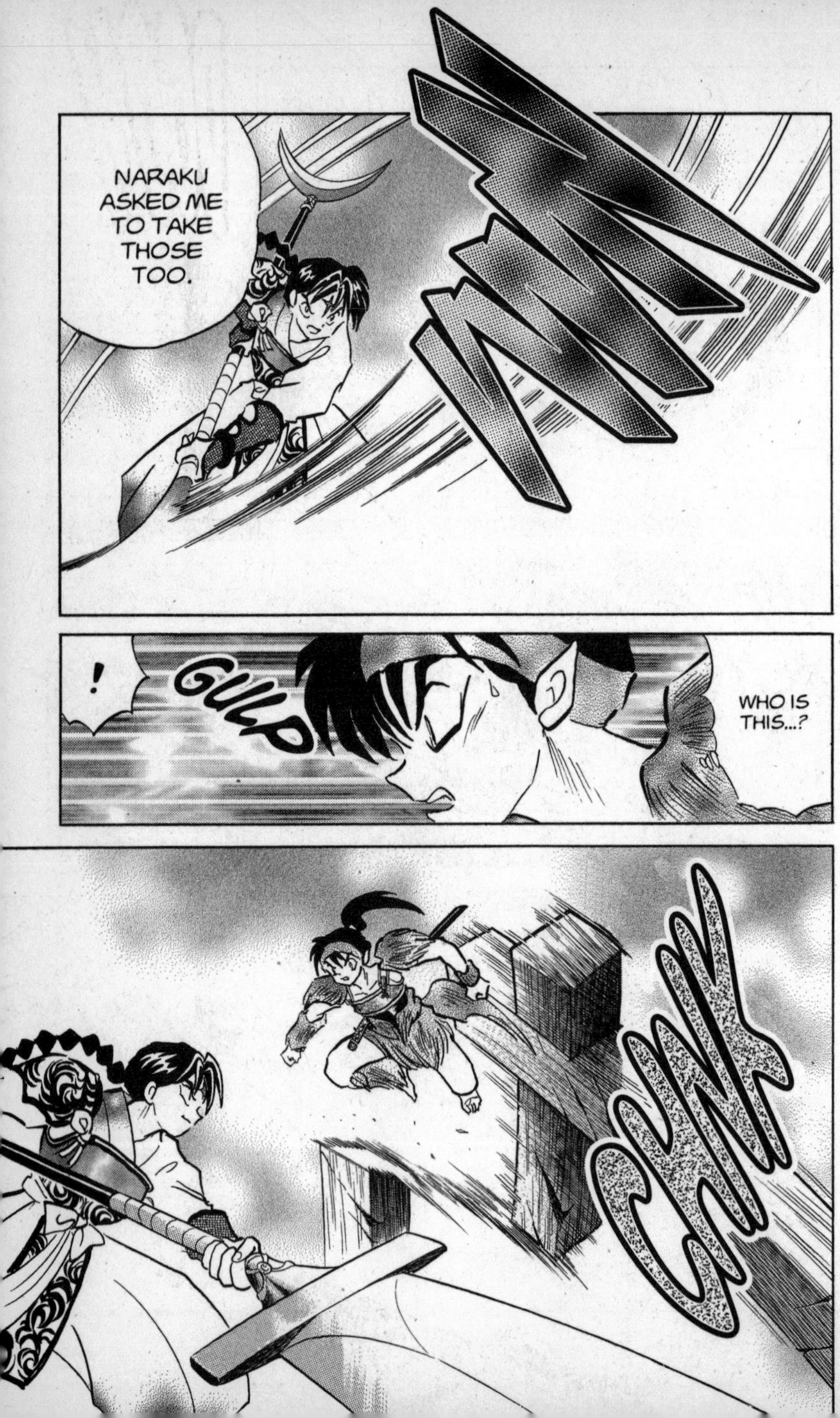
NARAKU ASKED ME TO TAKE THOSE TOO.
!
GULP
WHO IS THIS...?

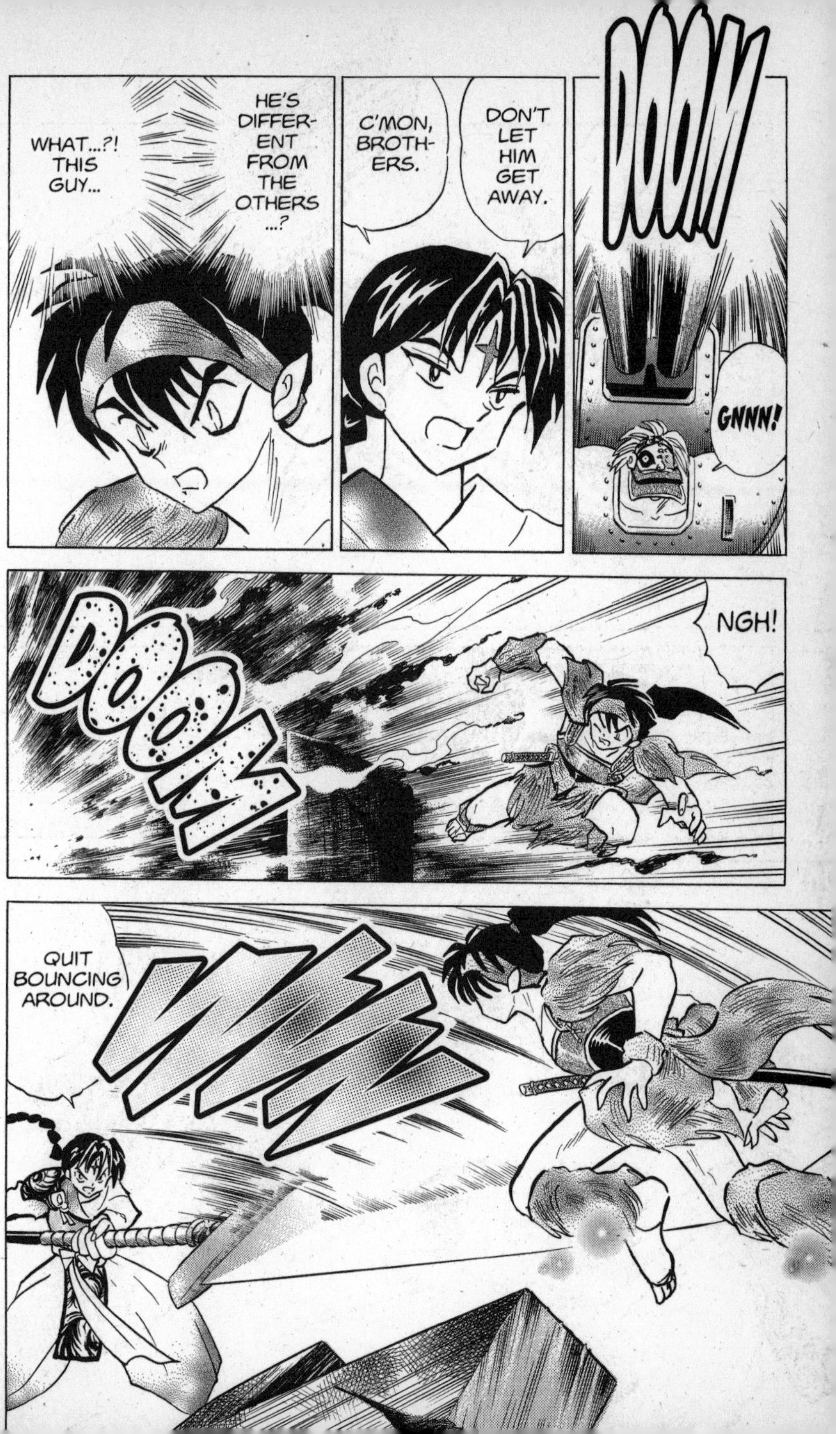

WHAT...?! THIS GUY...
HE'S DIFFERENT FROM THE OTHERS ...?
C'MON, BROTHERS.
DON'T LET HIM GET AWAY.
DOOM
GNNN!
DOOOM
NGH!
QUIT BOUNCING AROUND.

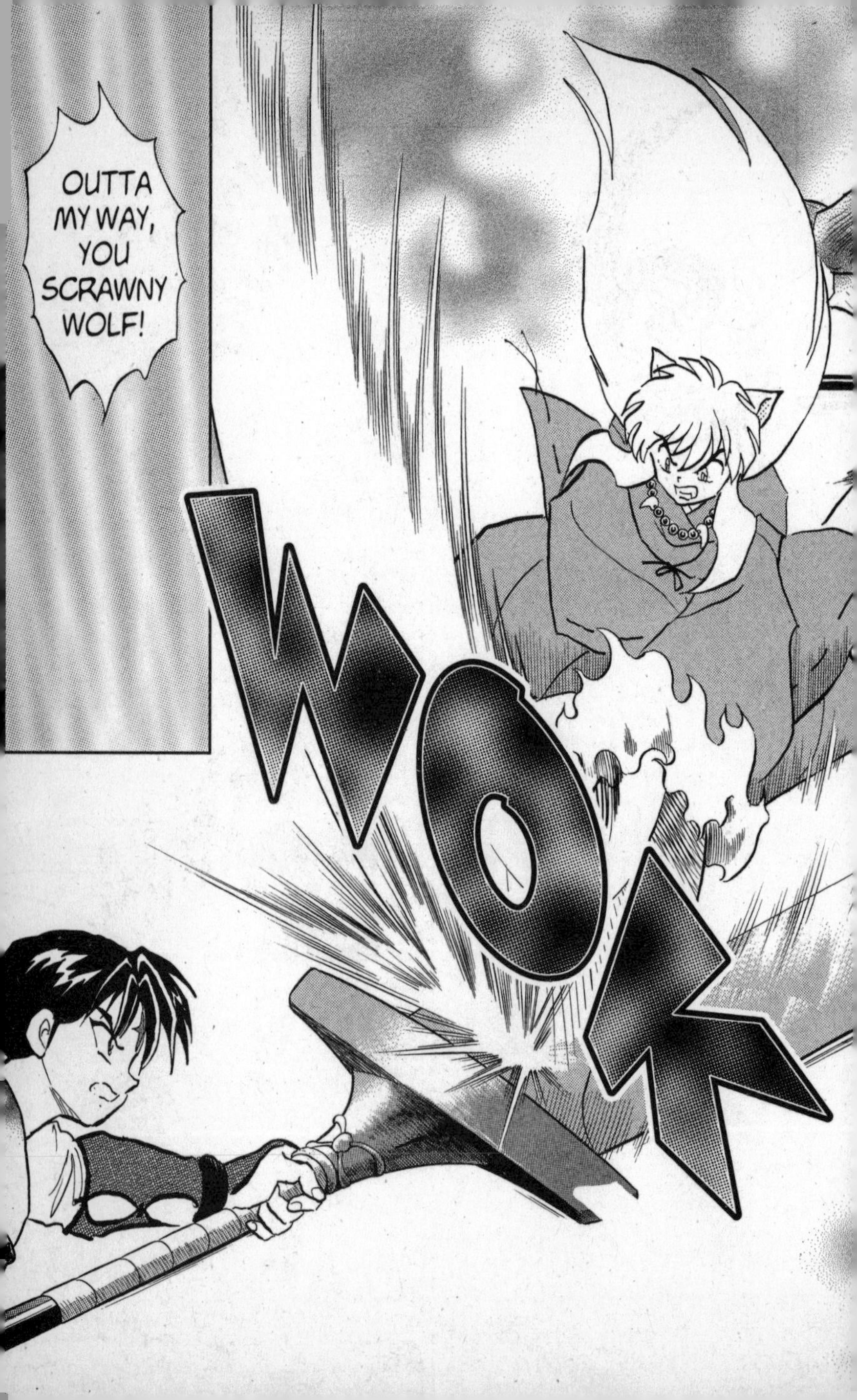
OUTTA MY WAY, YOU SCRAWNY WOLF!
WOK

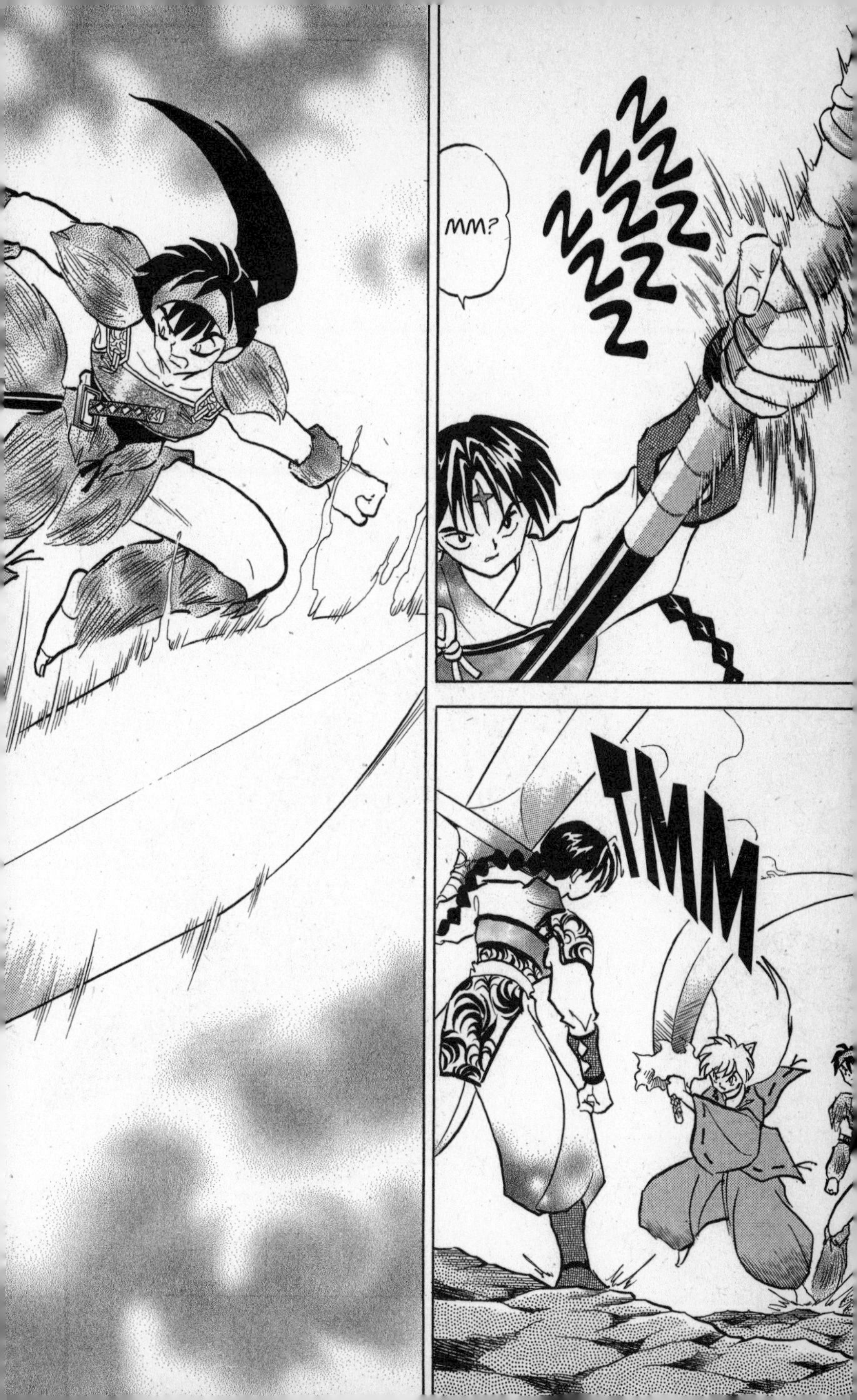
MM?
ZZZZZZZZZ
TMM

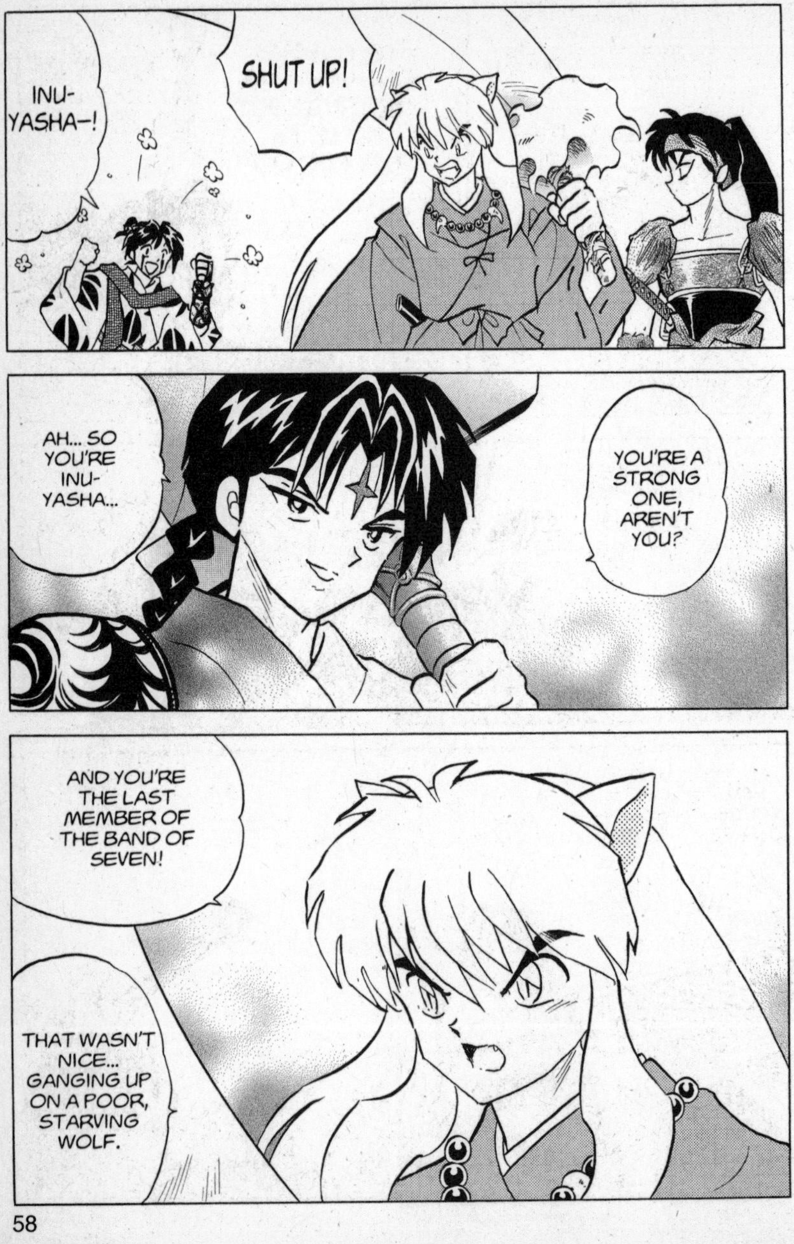
INU-YASHA-!
SHUT UP!
AH... SO YOU'RE INU-YASHA...
YOU'RE A STRONG ONE, AREN'T YOU?
AND YOU'RE THE LAST MEMBER OF THE BAND OF SEVEN!
THAT WASN'T NICE... GANGING UP ON A POOR, STARVING WOLF.

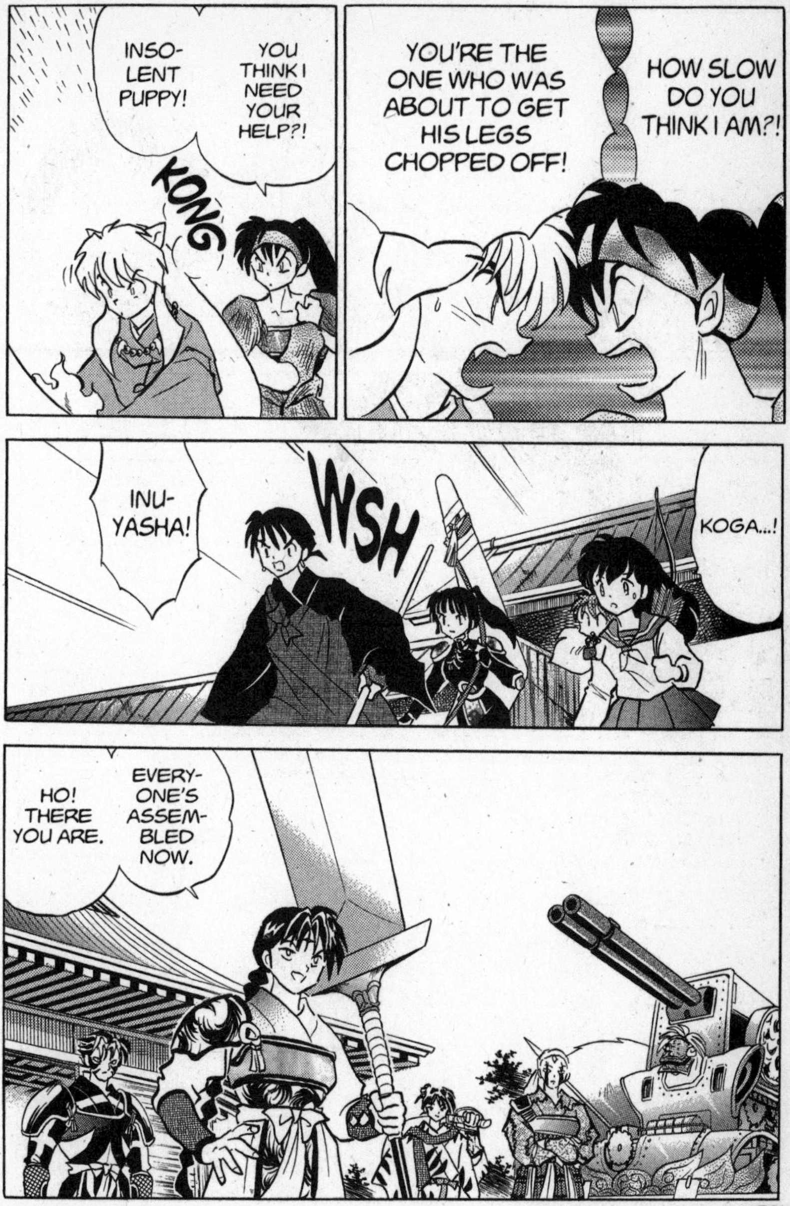
INSO-LENT PUPPY! YOU THINK I NEED YOUR HELP?!
KONG
YOU'RE THE ONE WHO WAS ABOUT TO GET HIS LEGS CHOPPED OFF!
HOW SLOW DO YOU THINK I AM?!
INU-YASHA!
WSH
KOGA...!
HO! THERE YOU ARE. EVERY-ONE'S ASSEM-BLED NOW.

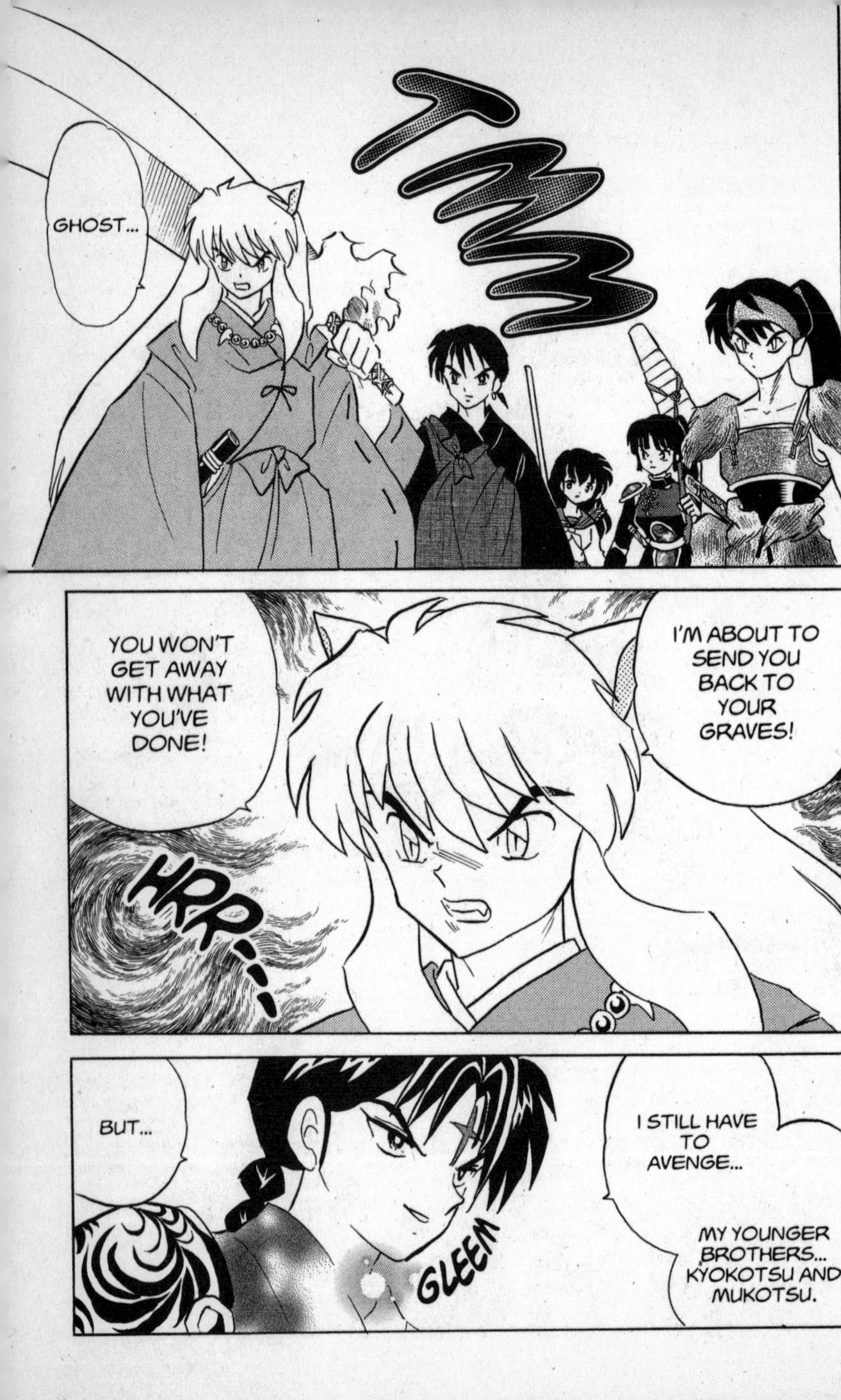
GHOST...
TMMM
YOU WON'T GET AWAY WITH WHAT YOU'VE DONE!
I'M ABOUT TO SEND YOU BACK TO YOUR GRAVES!
HRR...
BUT...
I STILL HAVE TO AVENGE...
MY YOUNGER BROTHERS... KYOKOTSU AND MUKOTSU.
GLEEM

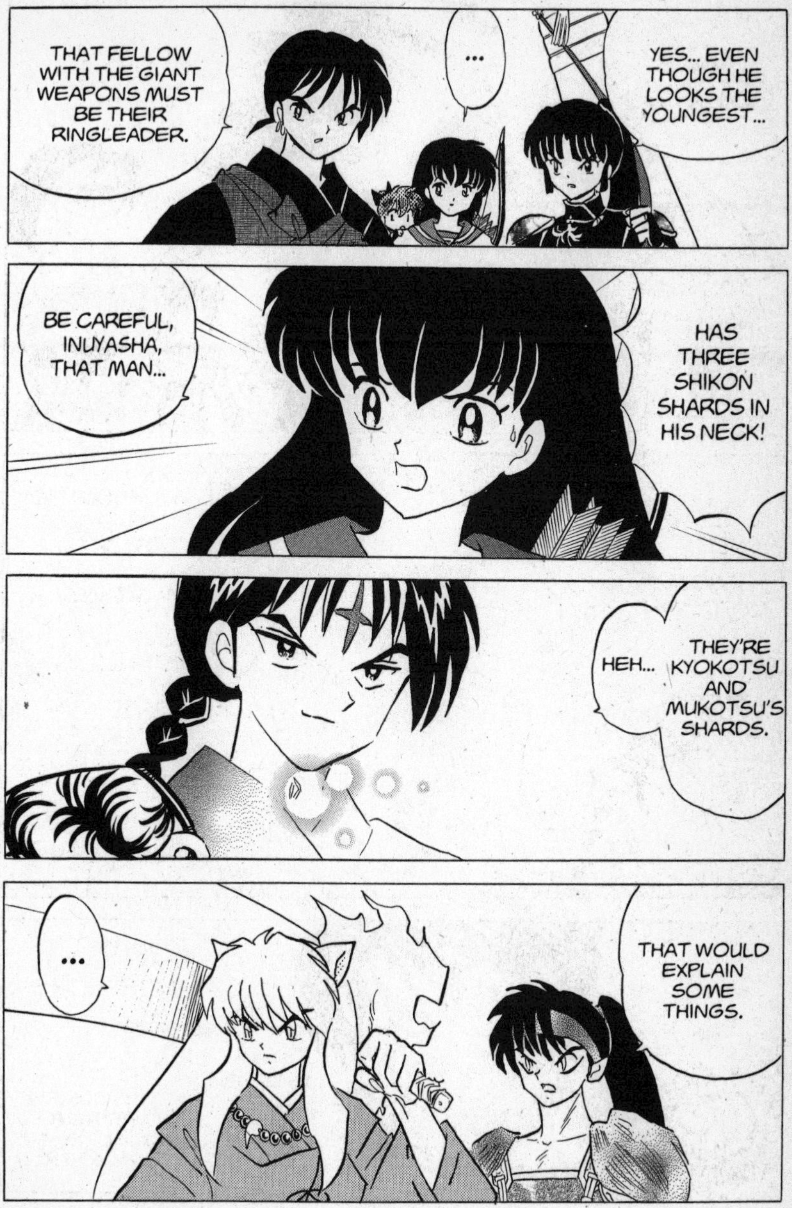
THAT FELLOW WITH THE GIANT WEAPONS MUST BE THEIR RINGLEADER.
...
YES... EVEN THOUGH HE LOOKS THE YOUNGEST...
BE CAREFUL, INUYASHA, THAT MAN...
HAS THREE SHIKON SHARDS IN HIS NECK!
HEH...
THEY'RE KYOKOTSU AND MUKOTSU'S SHARDS.
...
THAT WOULD EXPLAIN SOME THINGS.

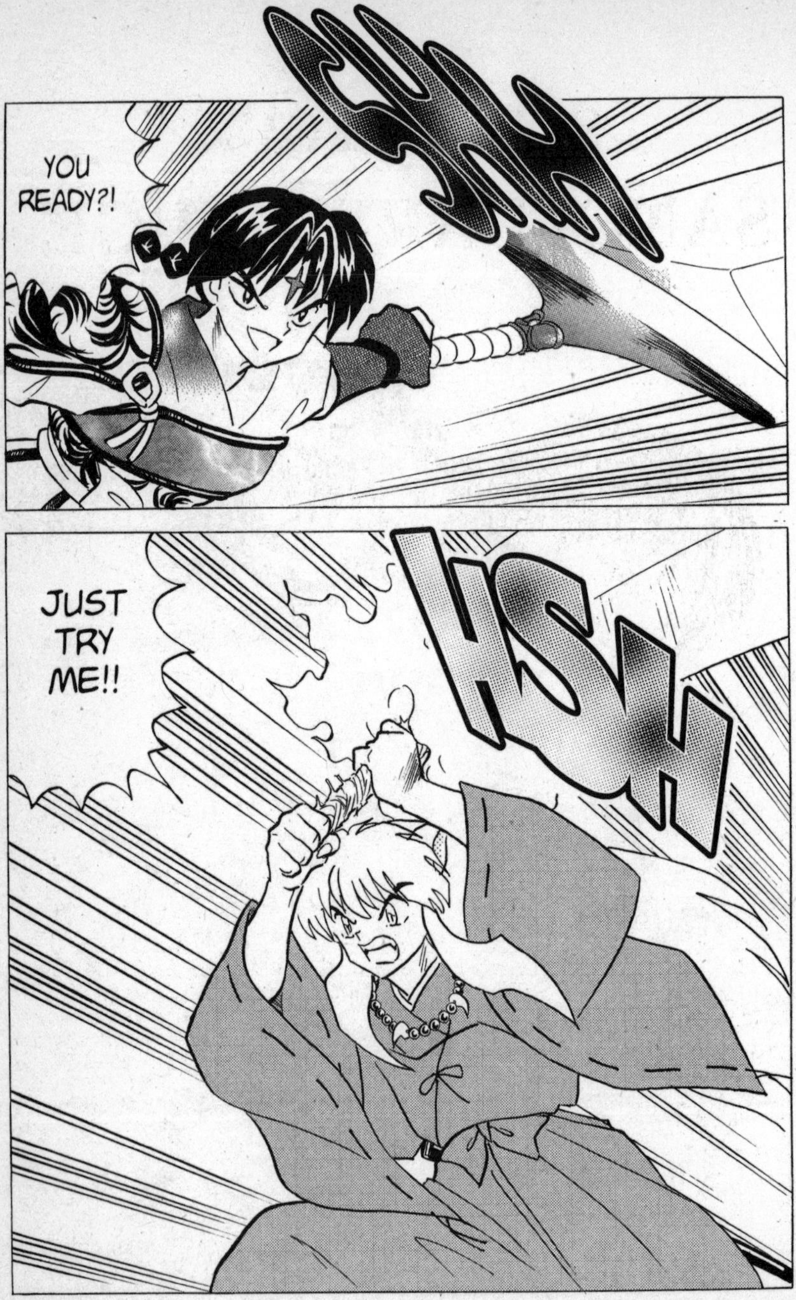
YOU READY?!
JUST TRY ME!!

SCROLL FOUR
SANCTUARY'S EDGE

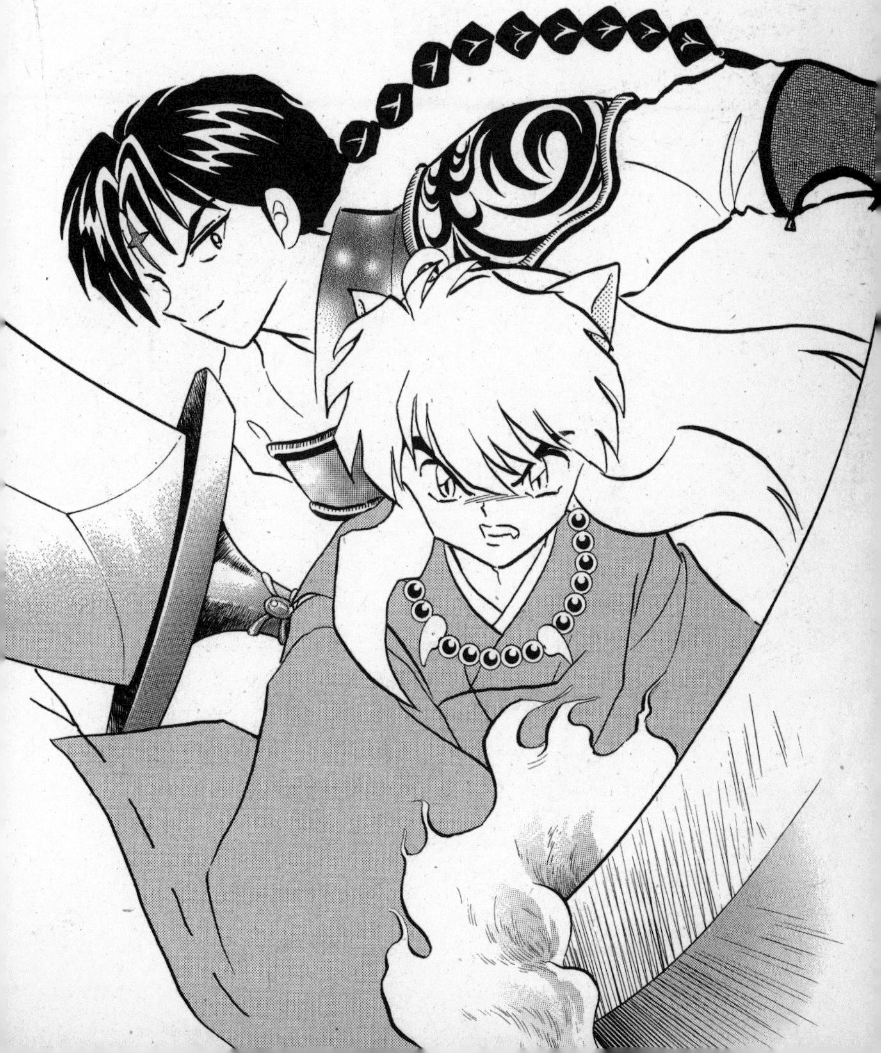

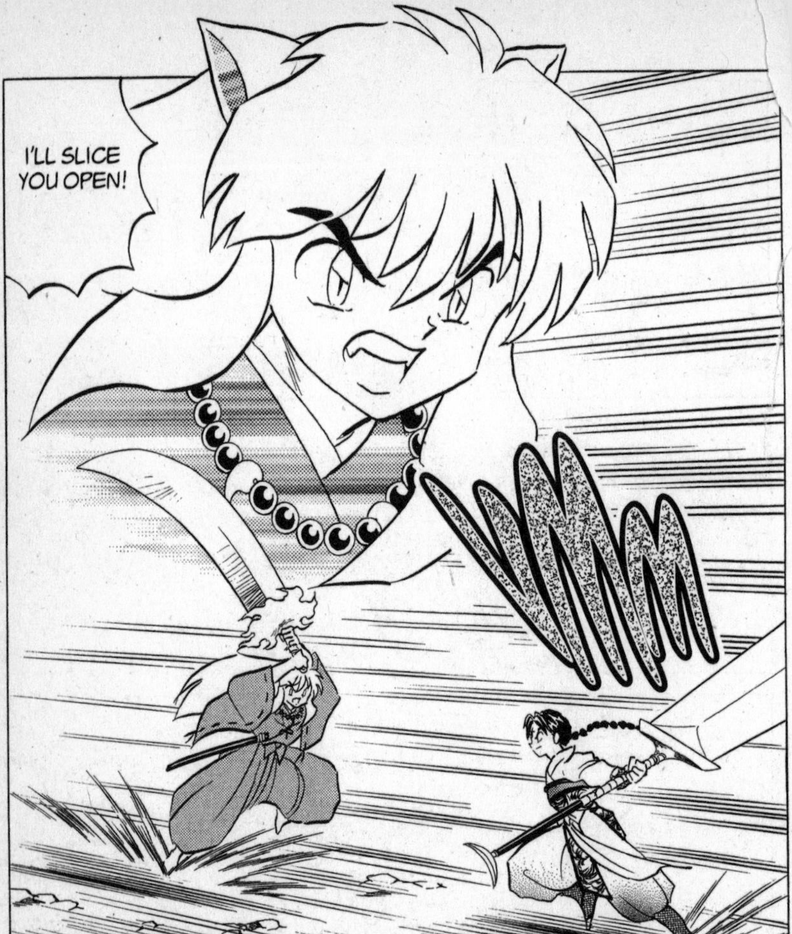
I'LL SLICE YOU OPEN!
VMMM

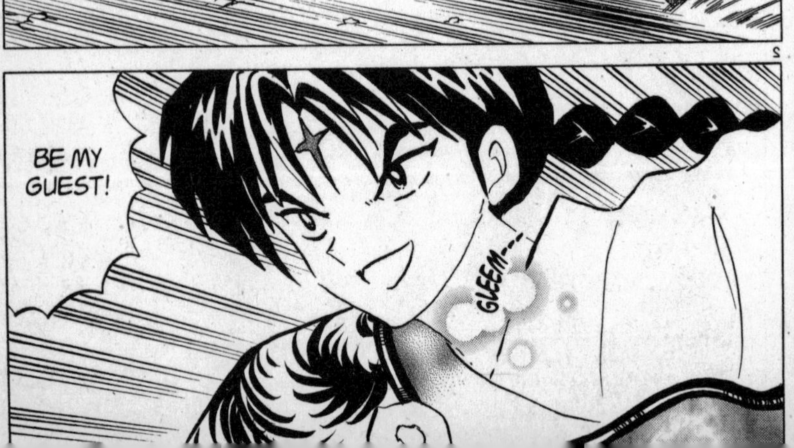
BE MY GUEST!
GLEEM...

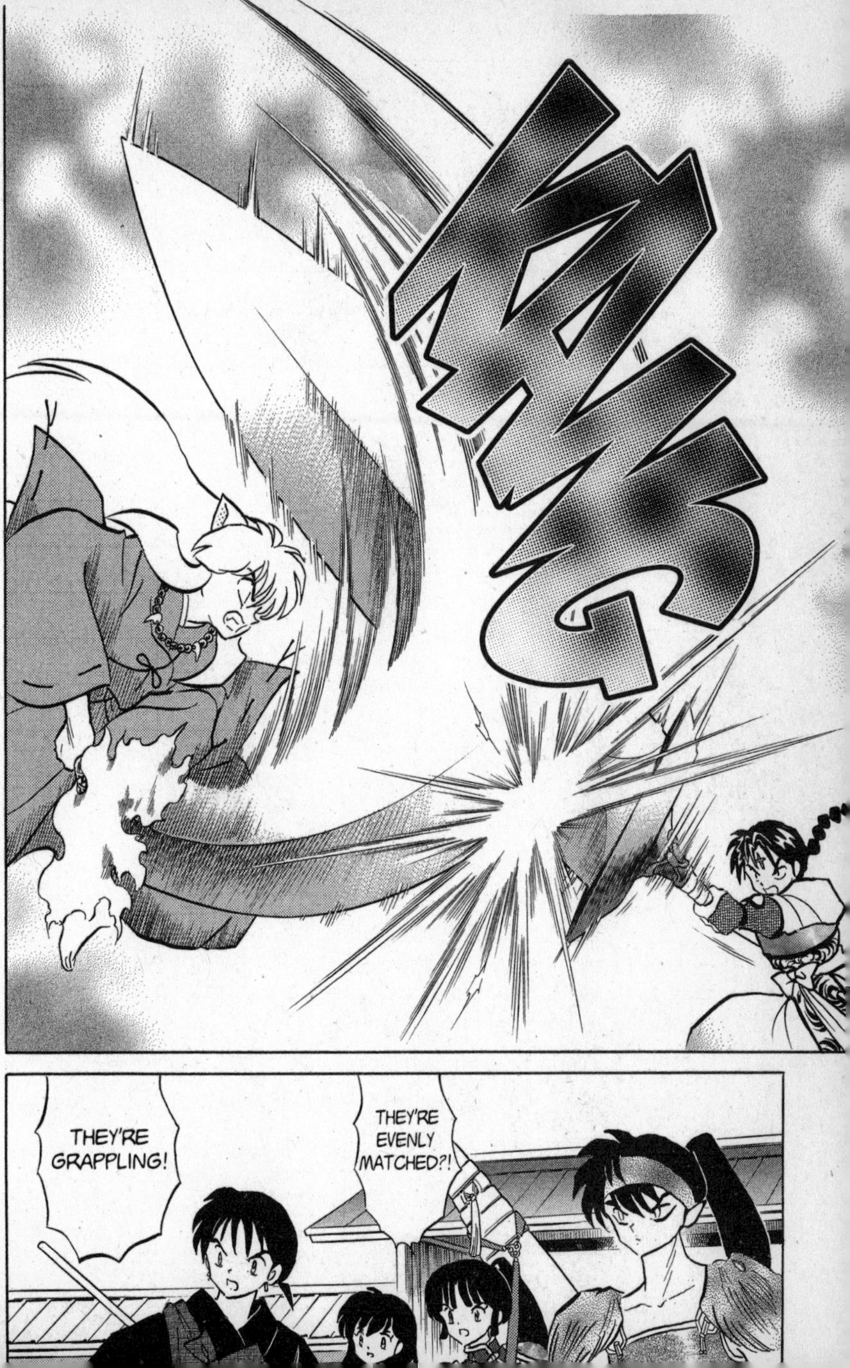
KANG
THEY'RE GRAPPLING!
THEY'RE EVENLY MATCHED?!

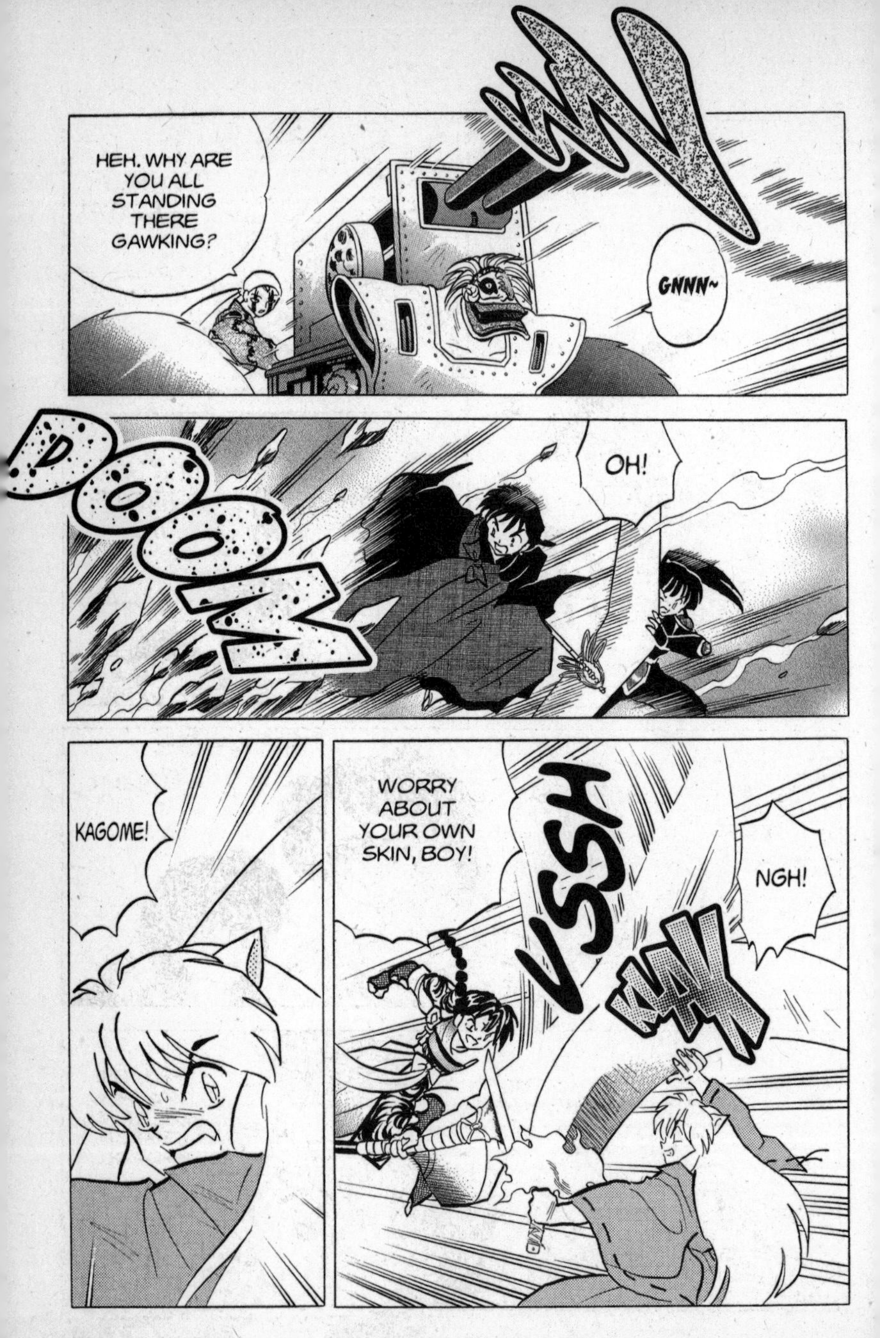
WMM
HEH. WHY ARE YOU ALL STANDING THERE GAWKING?
GNNN~
DOOOM
OH!
KAGOME!
WORRY ABOUT YOUR OWN SKIN, BOY!
VSSH
NGH!
KNAK

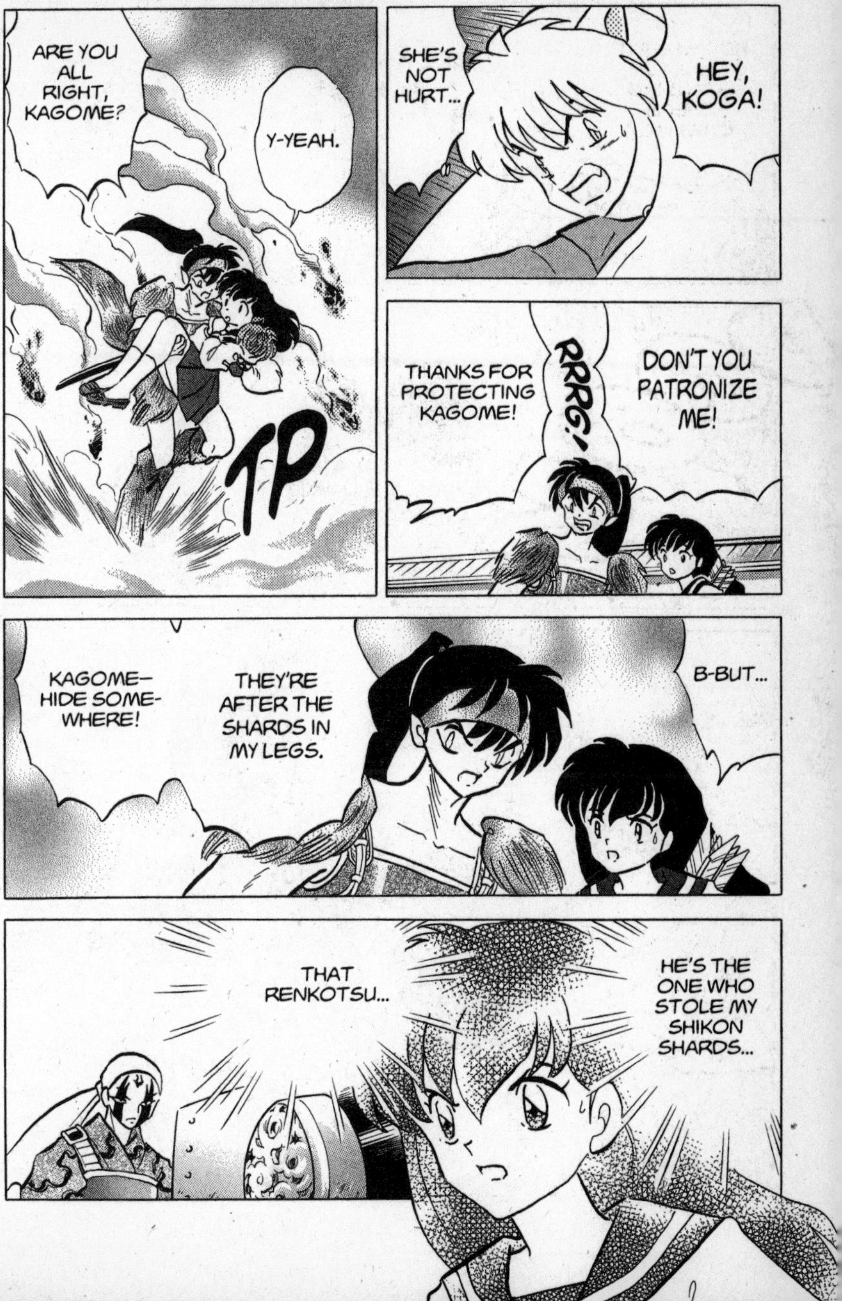
ARE YOU ALL RIGHT, KAGOME?
Y-YEAH.
TP
SHE'S NOT HURT...
HEY, KOGA!
THANKS FOR PROTECTING KAGOME!
RRRG!
DON'T YOU PATRONIZE ME!
KAGOME— HIDE SOME-WHERE!
THEY'RE AFTER THE SHARDS IN MY LEGS.
B-BUT...
THAT RENKOTSU...
HE'S THE ONE WHO STOLE MY SHIKON SHARDS...

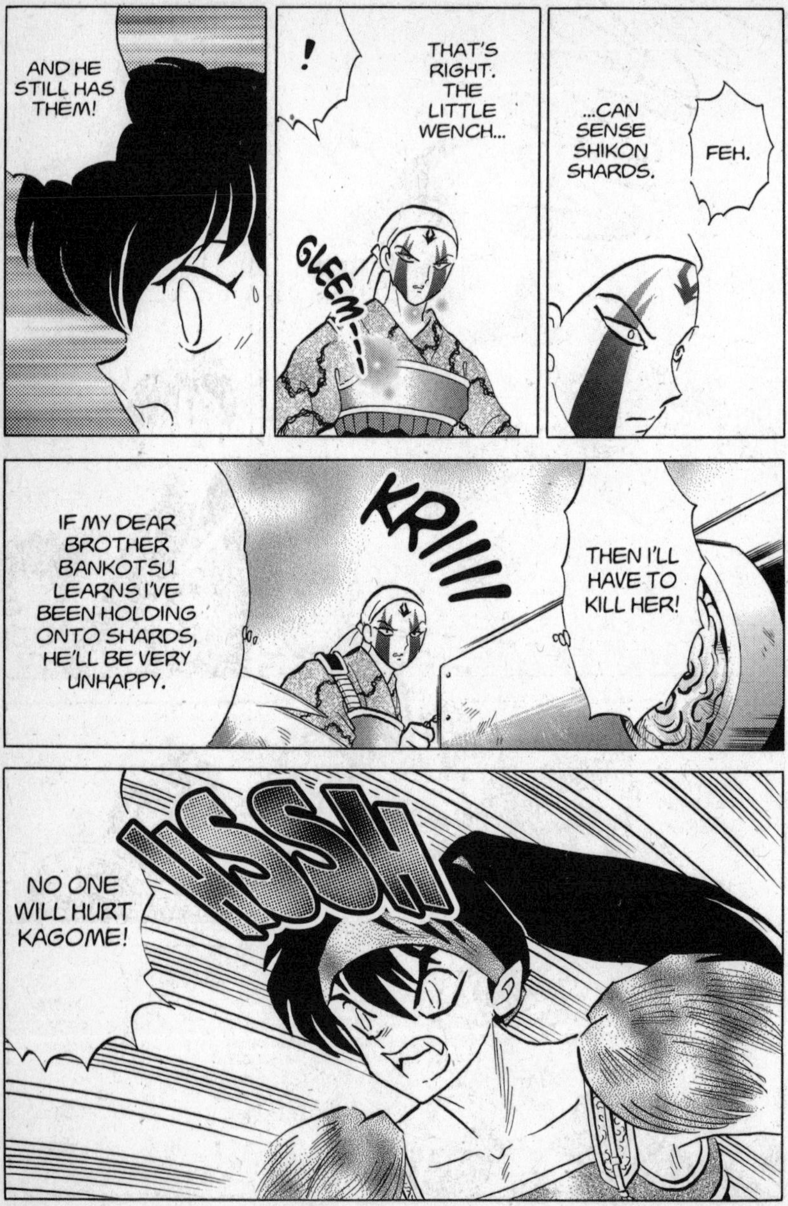
AND HE STILL HAS THEM!
!
THAT'S RIGHT. THE LITTLE WENCH...
GLEEM...
...CAN SENSE SHIKON SHARDS.
FEH.
IF MY DEAR BROTHER BANKOTSU LEARNS I'VE BEEN HOLDING ONTO SHARDS, HE'LL BE VERY UNHAPPY.
KRIIIII
THEN I'LL HAVE TO KILL HER!
NO ONE WILL HURT KAGOME!
ISSH

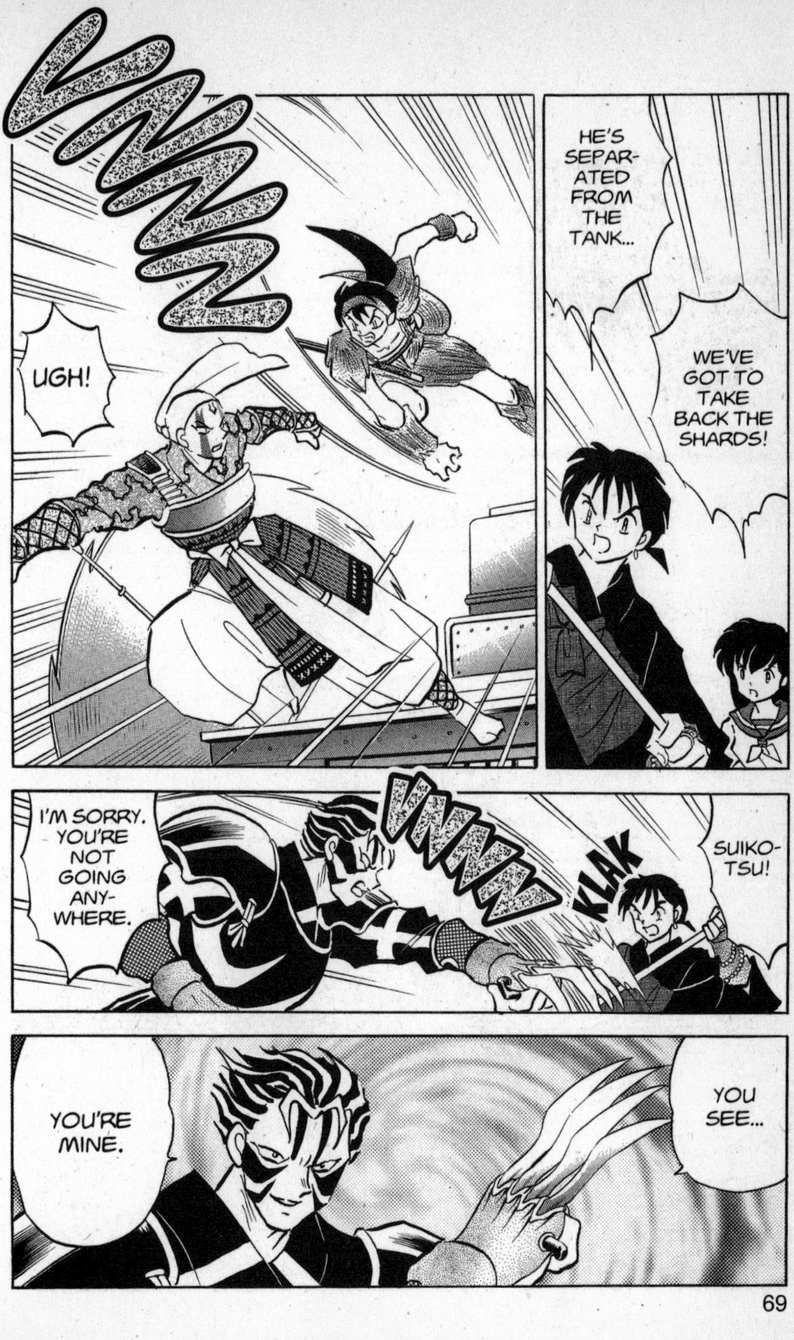
UGH!
HE'S SEPAR-ATED FROM THE TANK...
WE'VE GOT TO TAKE BACK THE SHARDS!
I'M SORRY. YOU'RE NOT GOING ANY-WHERE.
VNNNN
KLAK
SUIKO-TSU!
YOU'RE MINE.
YOU SEE...

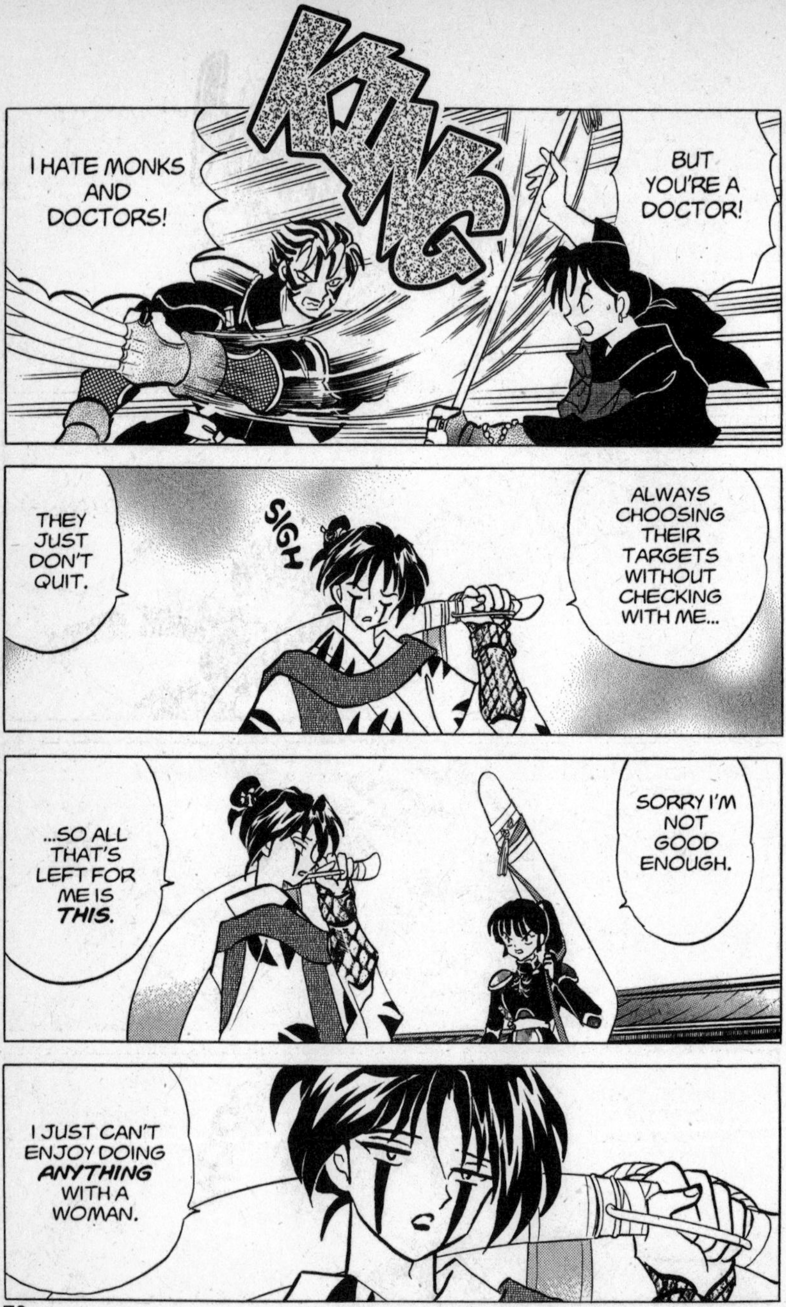
KANG
I HATE MONKS AND DOCTORS!
BUT YOU'RE A DOCTOR!
THEY JUST DON'T QUIT.
SIGH
ALWAYS CHOOSING THEIR TARGETS WITHOUT CHECKING WITH ME...
...SO ALL THAT'S LEFT FOR ME IS **THIS**.
SORRY I'M NOT GOOD ENOUGH.
I JUST CAN'T ENJOY DOING ***ANYTHING*** WITH A WOMAN.

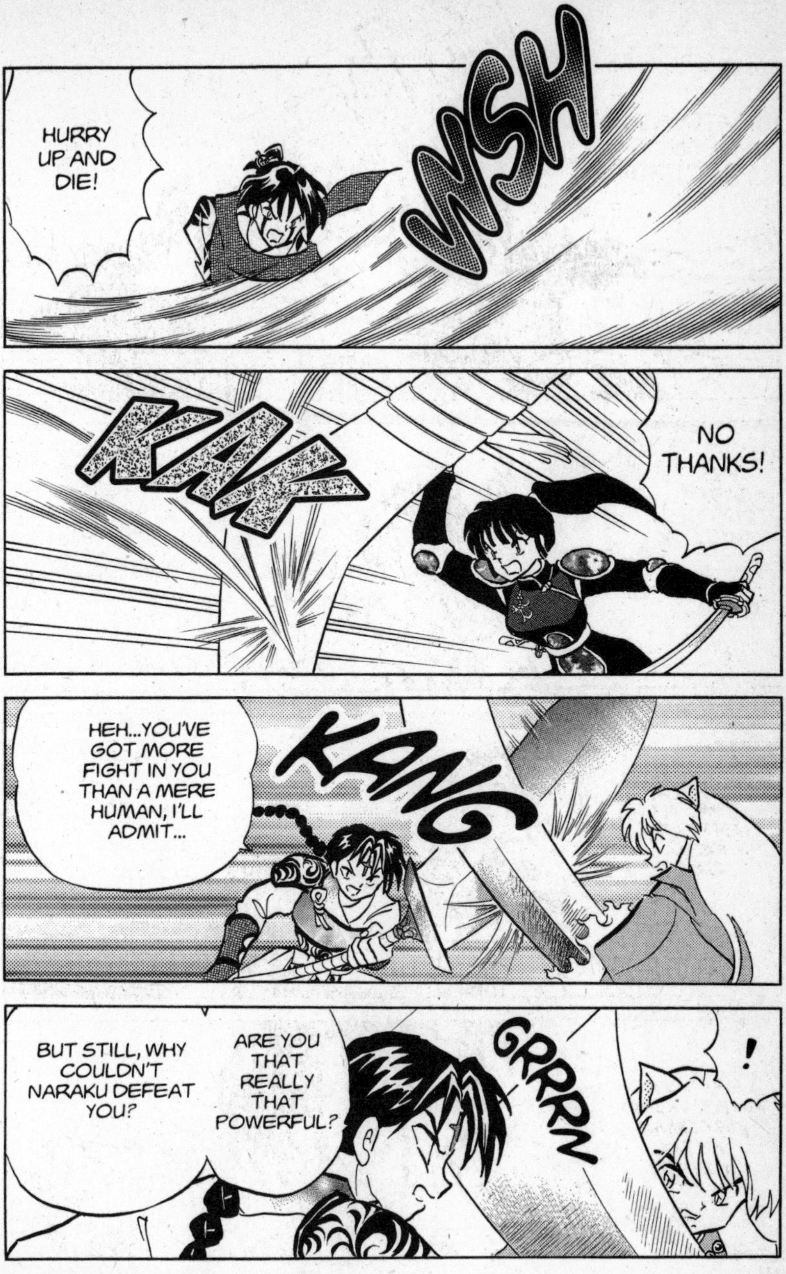
HURRY UP AND DIE!
WSH
KAK
NO THANKS!
HEH...YOU'VE GOT MORE FIGHT IN YOU THAN A MERE HUMAN, I'LL ADMIT...
KANG
BUT STILL, WHY COULDN'T NARAKU DEFEAT YOU?
ARE YOU THAT REALLY THAT POWERFUL?
GRRRN
!

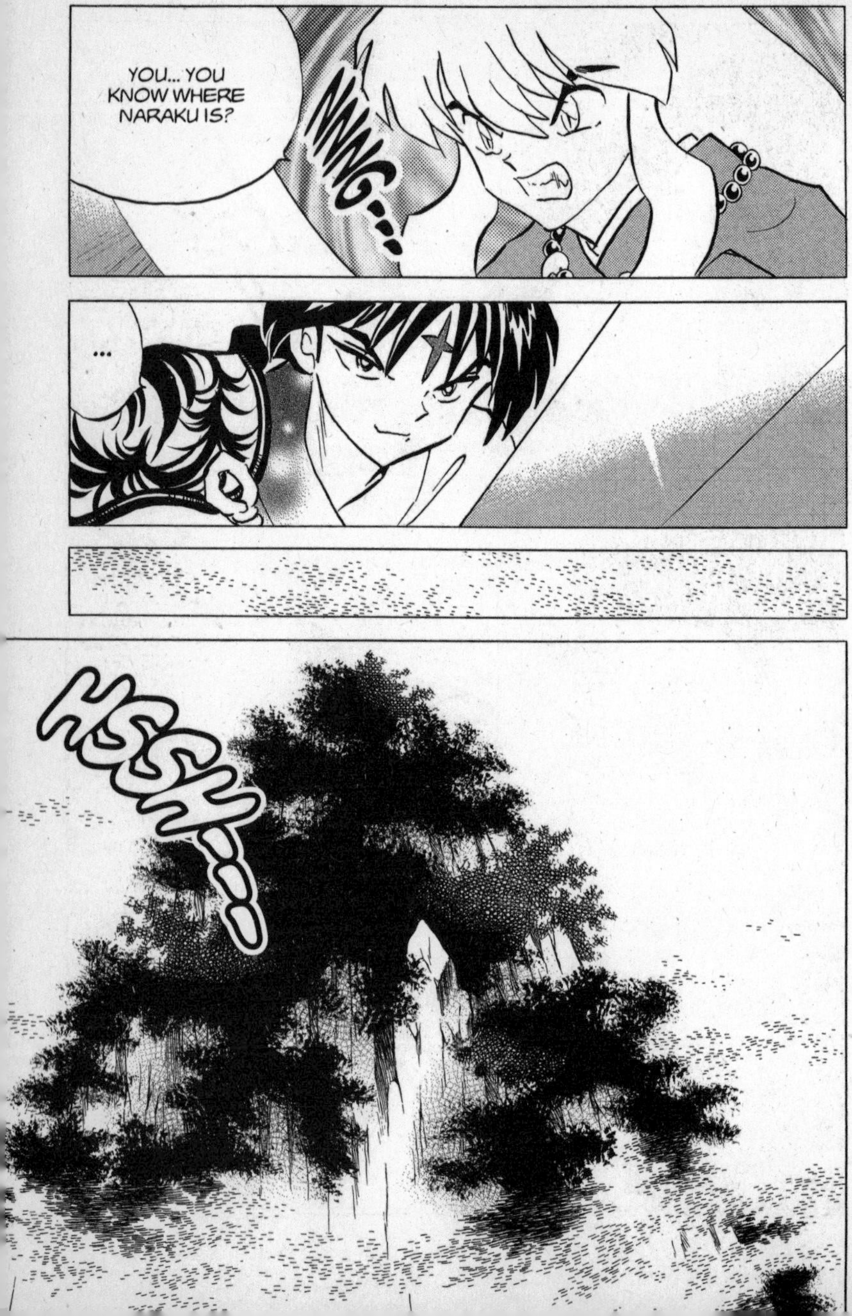
YOU... YOU KNOW WHERE NARAKU IS?
NNNG...
...
HSSH...

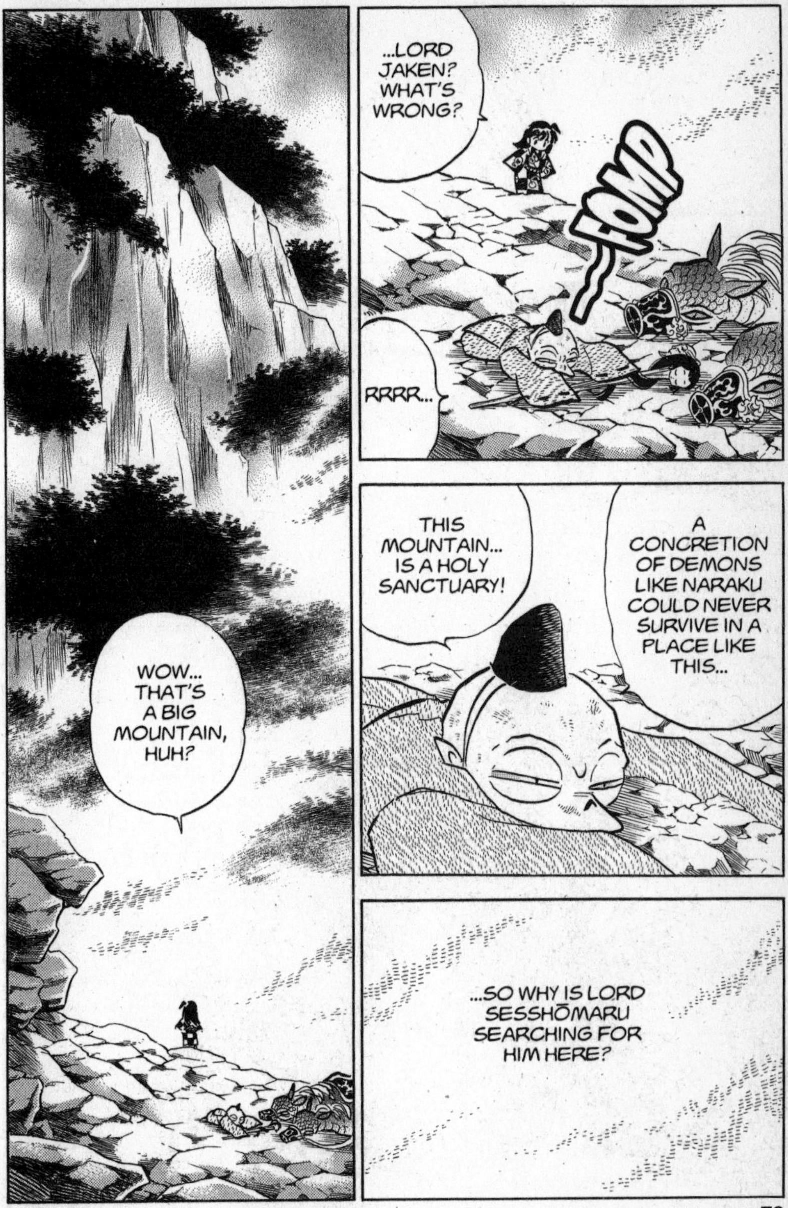
...LORD JAKEN? WHAT'S WRONG?
FOMP
RRRR...
THIS MOUNTAIN... IS A HOLY SANCTUARY!
A CONCRETION OF DEMONS LIKE NARAKU COULD NEVER SURVIVE IN A PLACE LIKE THIS...
...SO WHY IS LORD SESSHŌMARU SEARCHING FOR HIM HERE?
WOW... THAT'S A BIG MOUNTAIN, HUH?

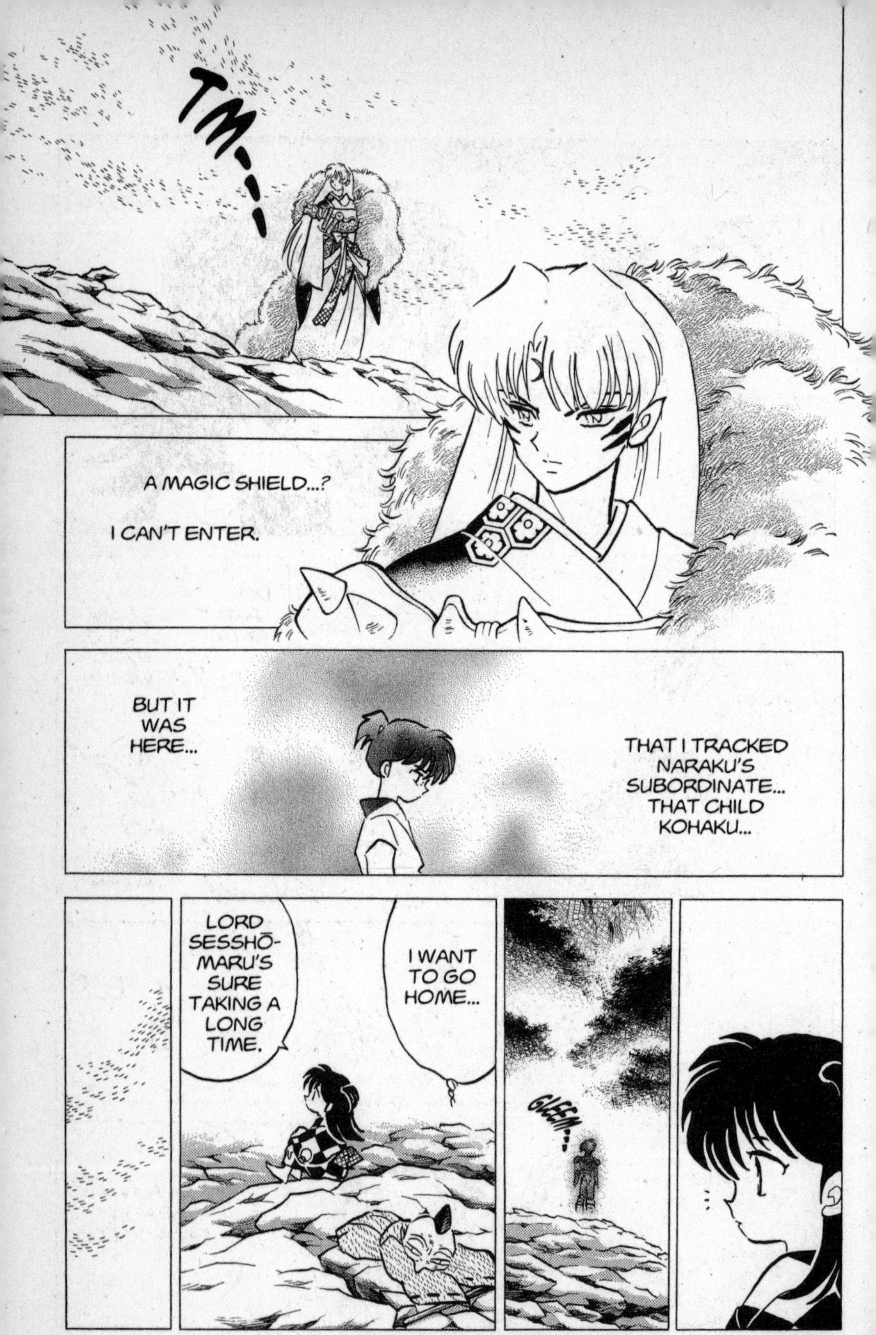
TM...
A MAGIC SHIELD...?
I CAN'T ENTER.
BUT IT WAS HERE...
THAT I TRACKED NARAKU'S SUBORDINATE... THAT CHILD KOHAKU...
LORD SESSHŌ-MARU'S SURE TAKING A LONG TIME.
I WANT TO GO HOME...
GLEEM...
...

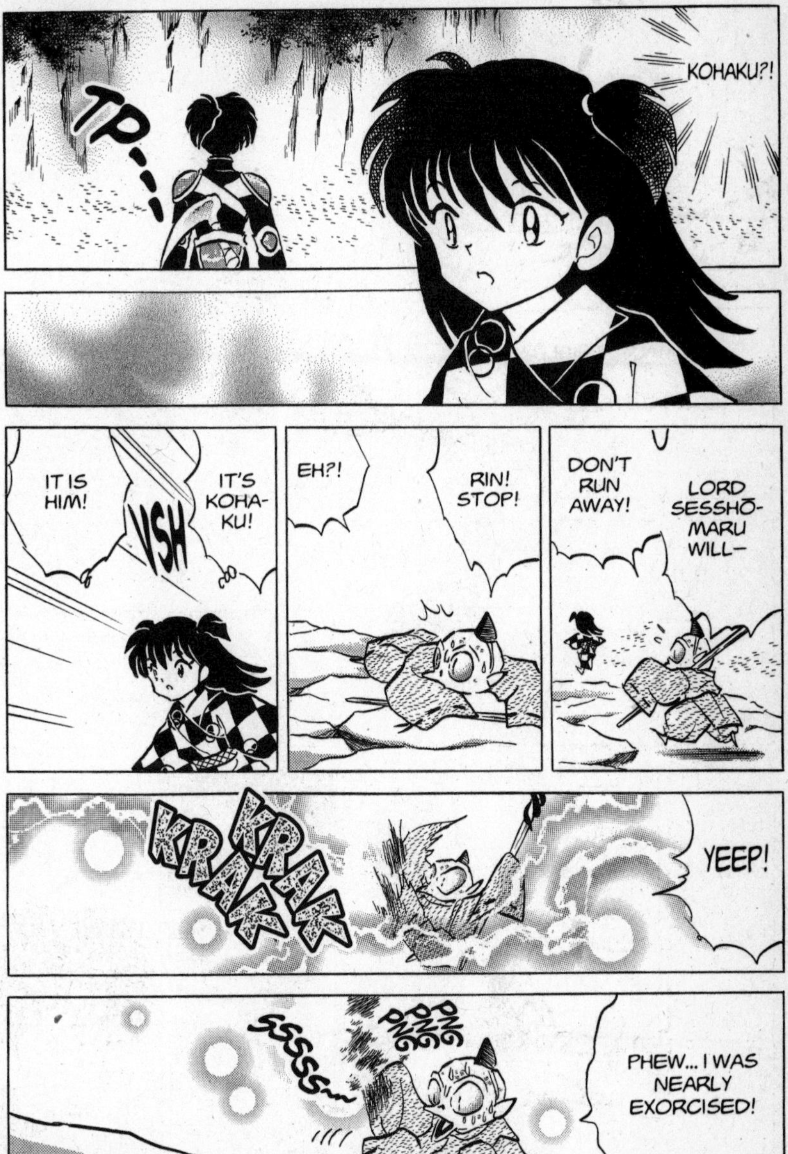
TP...
KOHAKU?!
IT IS HIM!
VSH
IT'S KOHA-KU!
EH?!
RIN! STOP!
DON'T RUN AWAY!
LORD SESSHŌ-MARU WILL–
KRAK KRAK
YEEP!
SSSSS
PNG PNG PNG
PHEW... I WAS NEARLY EXORCISED!

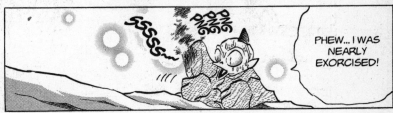

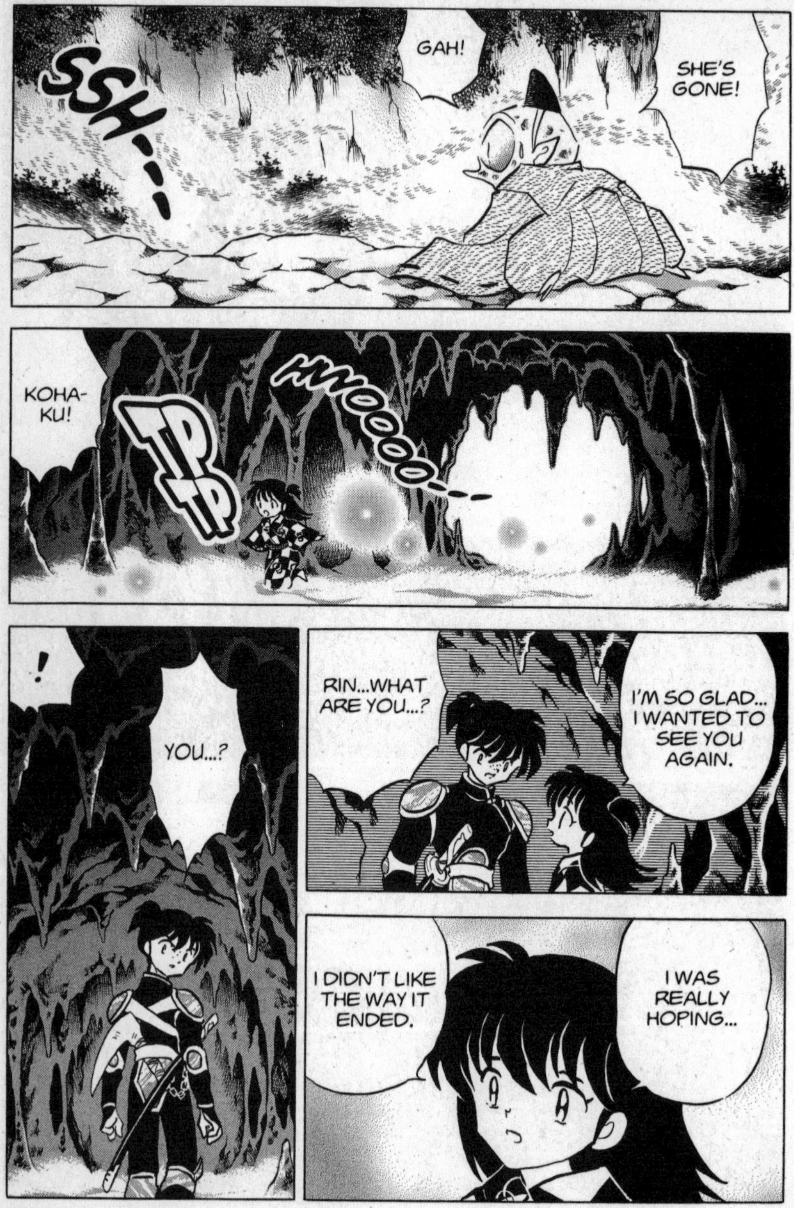
SSH...
GAH!
SHE'S GONE!
KOHA-KU!
TP TP
WOOOOO...
!
YOU...?
RIN...WHAT ARE YOU...?
I'M SO GLAD... I WANTED TO SEE YOU AGAIN.
I DIDN'T LIKE THE WAY IT ENDED.
I WAS REALLY HOPING...

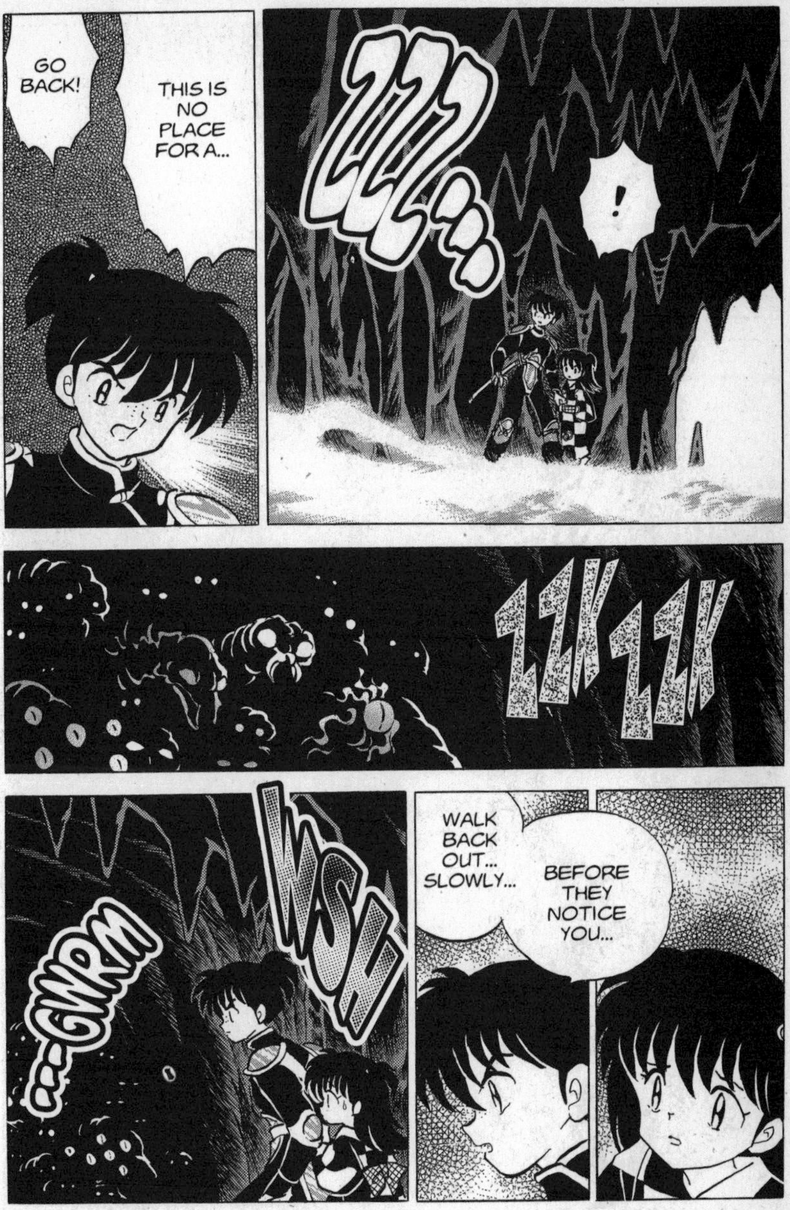
GO BACK!
THIS IS NO PLACE FOR A...
ZZZ...
!
ZZK ZZK
GWRM
WSH
WALK BACK OUT... SLOWLY...
BEFORE THEY NOTICE YOU...

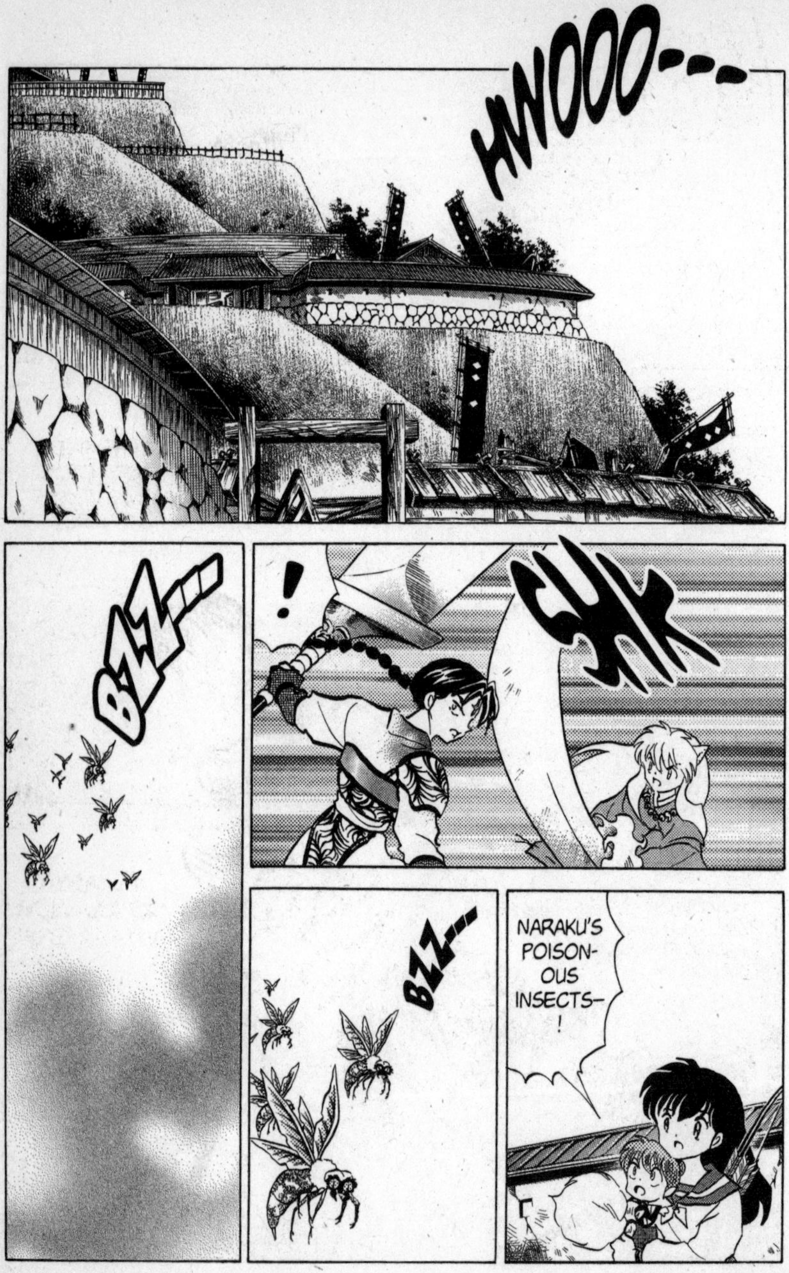
HWOOO---
BZZ---
!
CHK
BZZ---
NARAKU'S POISON-OUS INSECTS—!

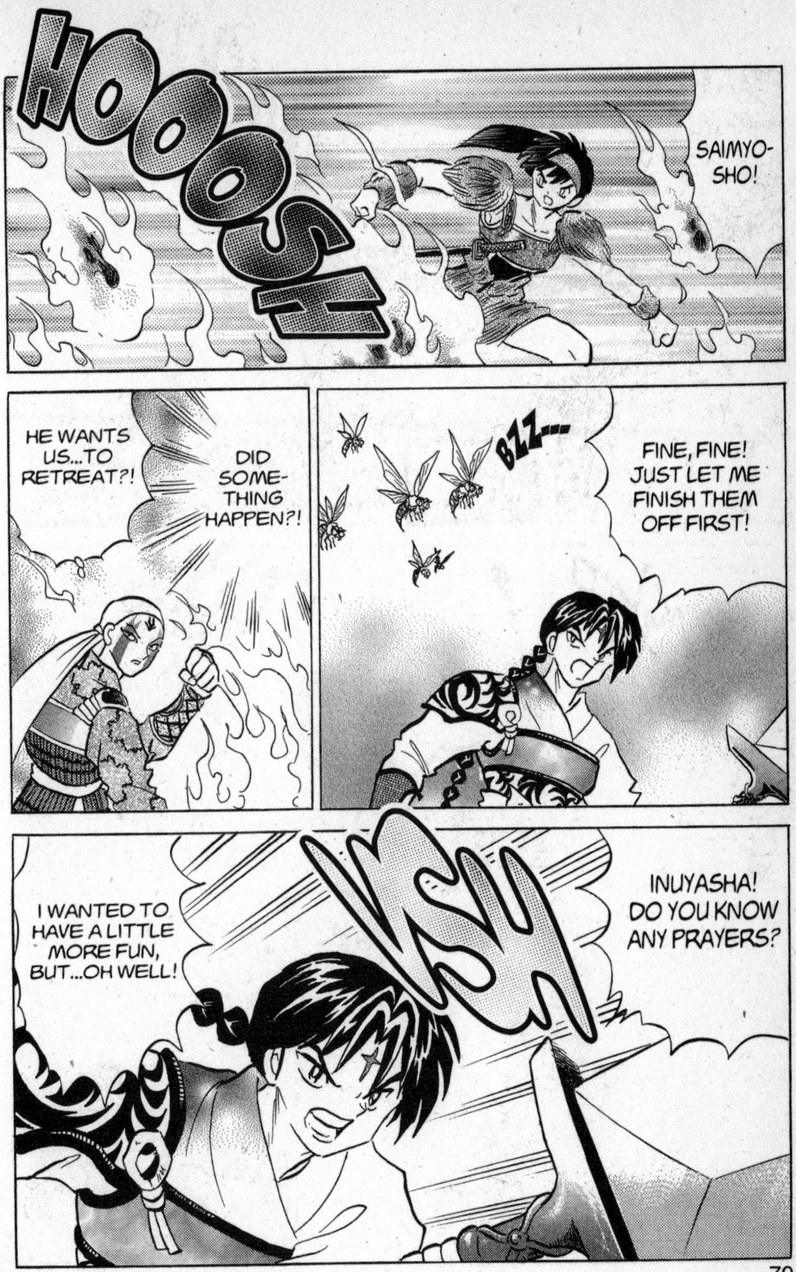
HOOOOSH
SAIMYO-SHO!
HE WANTS US...TO RETREAT?!
DID SOMETHING HAPPEN?!
BZZ...
FINE, FINE! JUST LET ME FINISH THEM OFF FIRST!
I WANTED TO HAVE A LITTLE MORE FUN, BUT...OH WELL!
WSH
INUYASHA! DO YOU KNOW ANY PRAYERS?

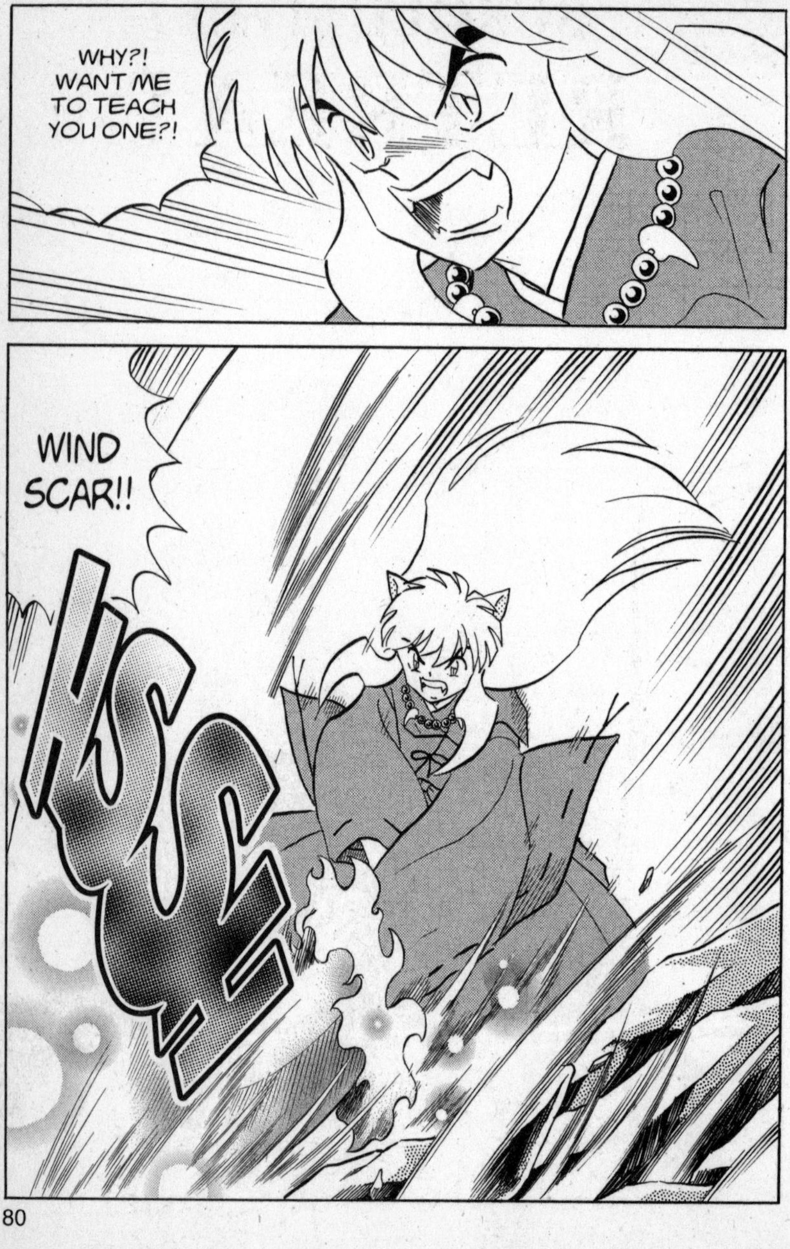
WHY?!
WANT ME
TO TEACH
YOU ONE?!
WIND
SCAR!!
HSSS

SCROLL FIVE
RETREAT

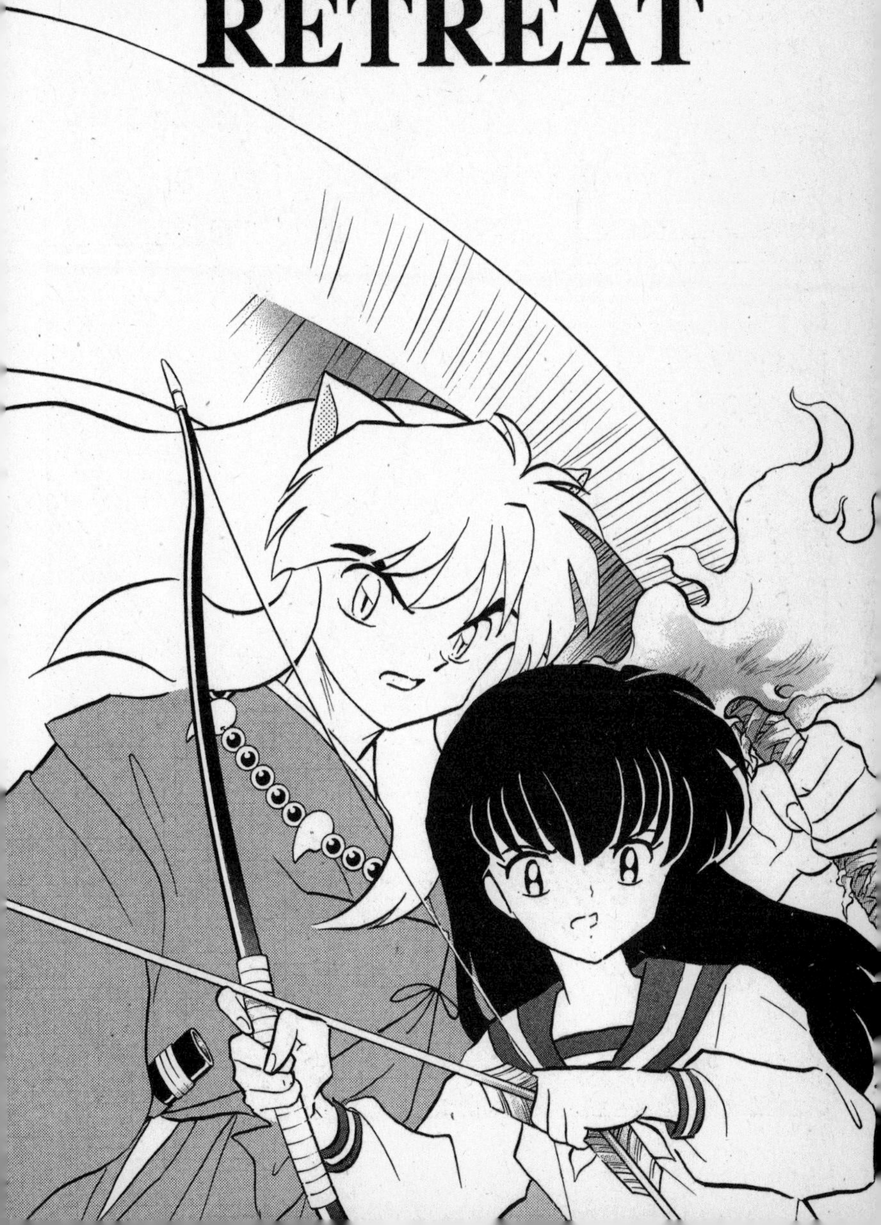

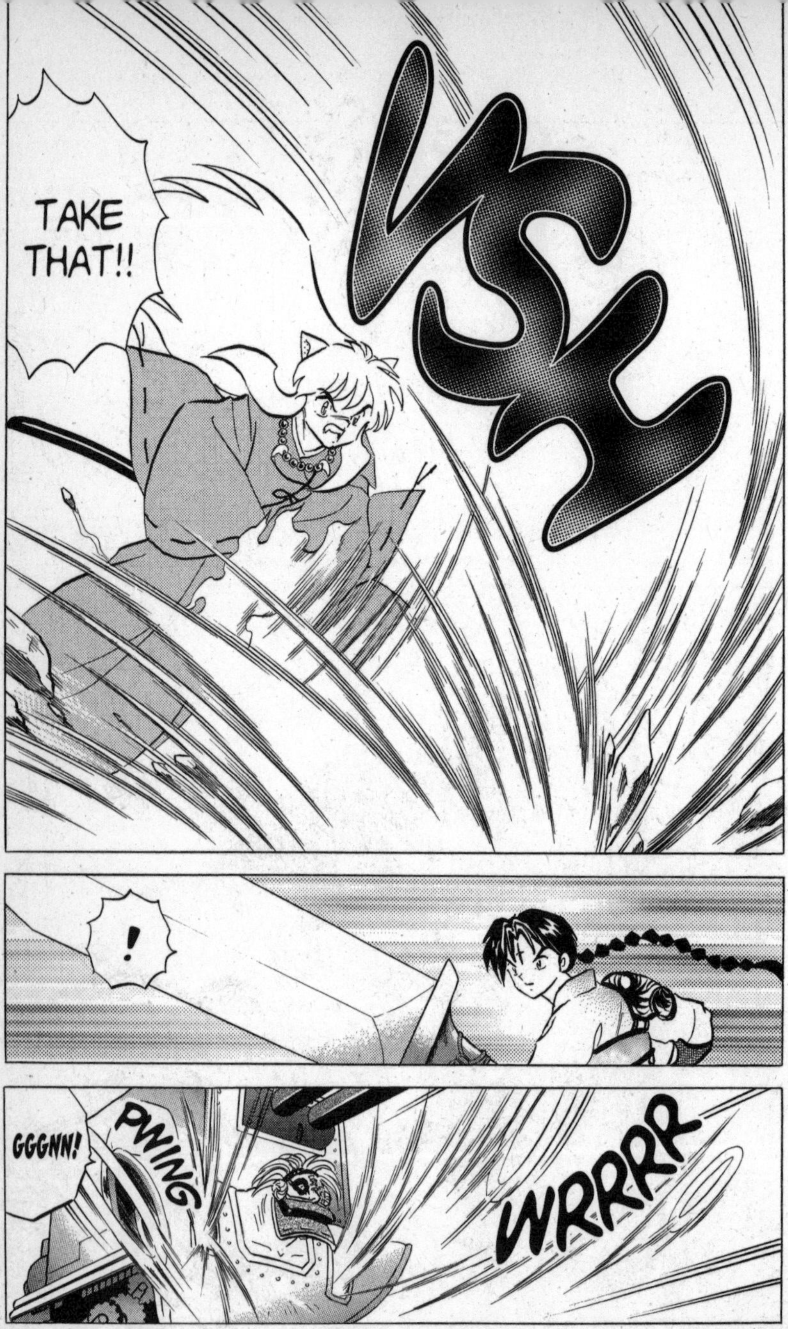
TAKE THAT!!
VSH
!
GGGNN!
PWING
WRRRR

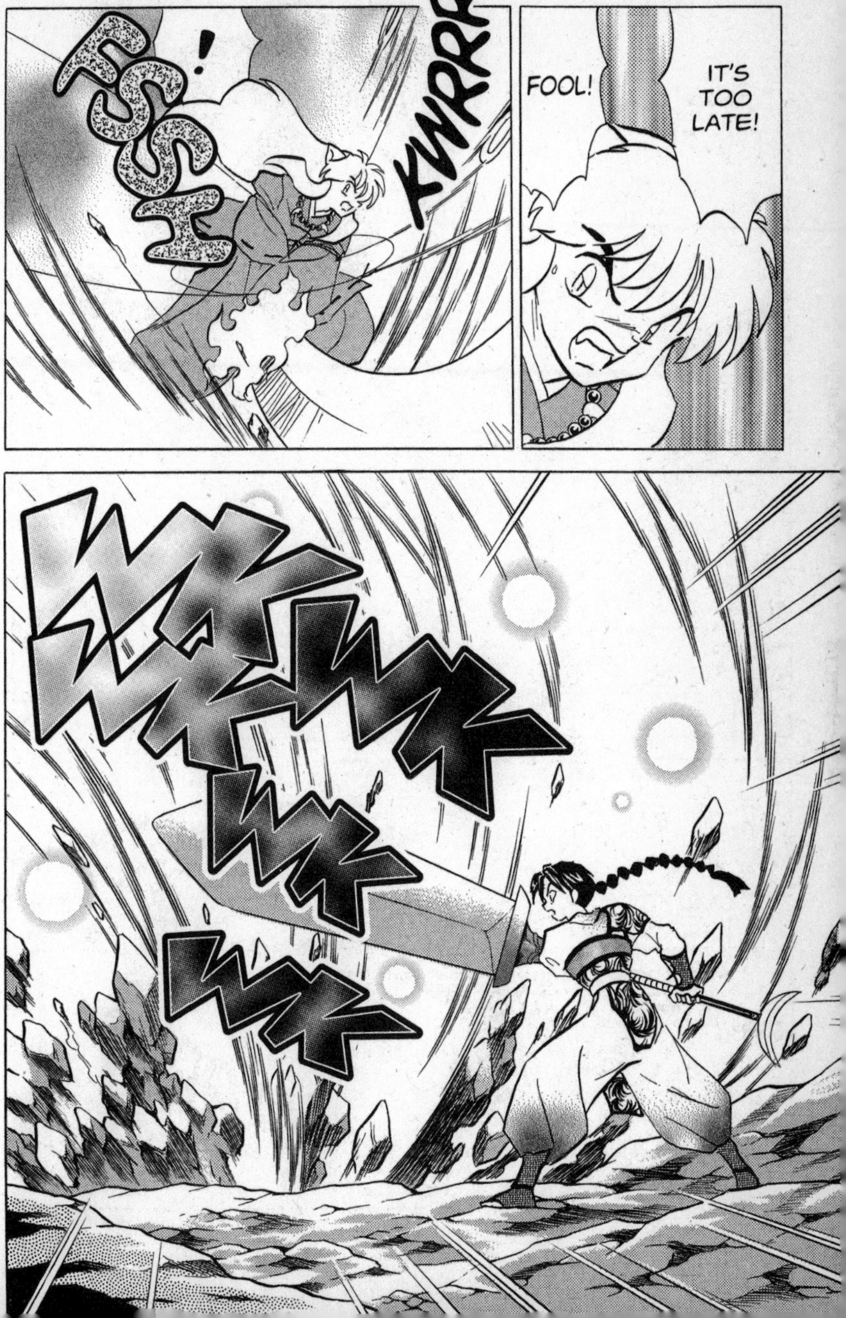
FSSH!
KWRRR
FOOL!
IT'S TOO LATE!

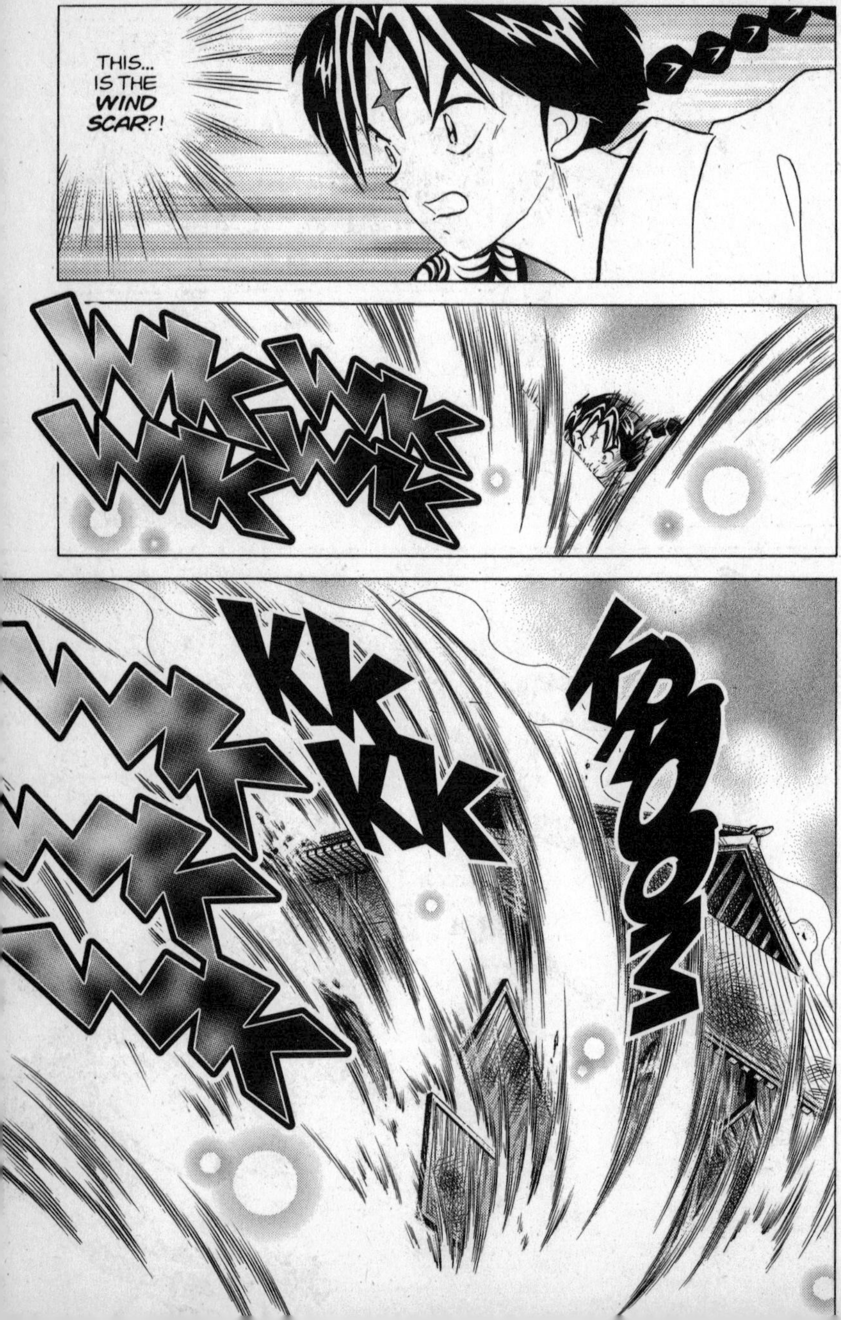
THIS... IS THE WIND SCAR?!
KRAKOOM

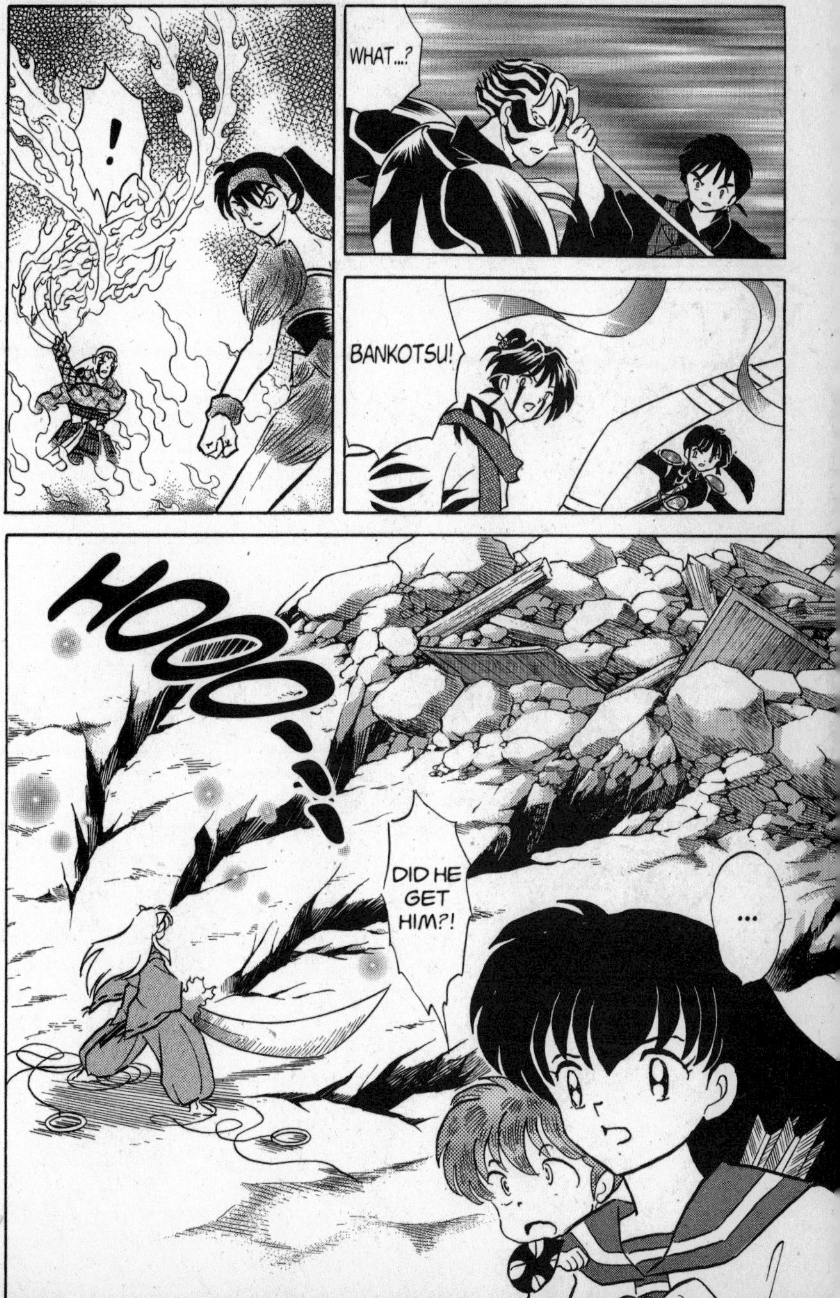
!
WHAT...?
BANKOTSU!
HOOO...!!
DID HE GET HIM?!
...

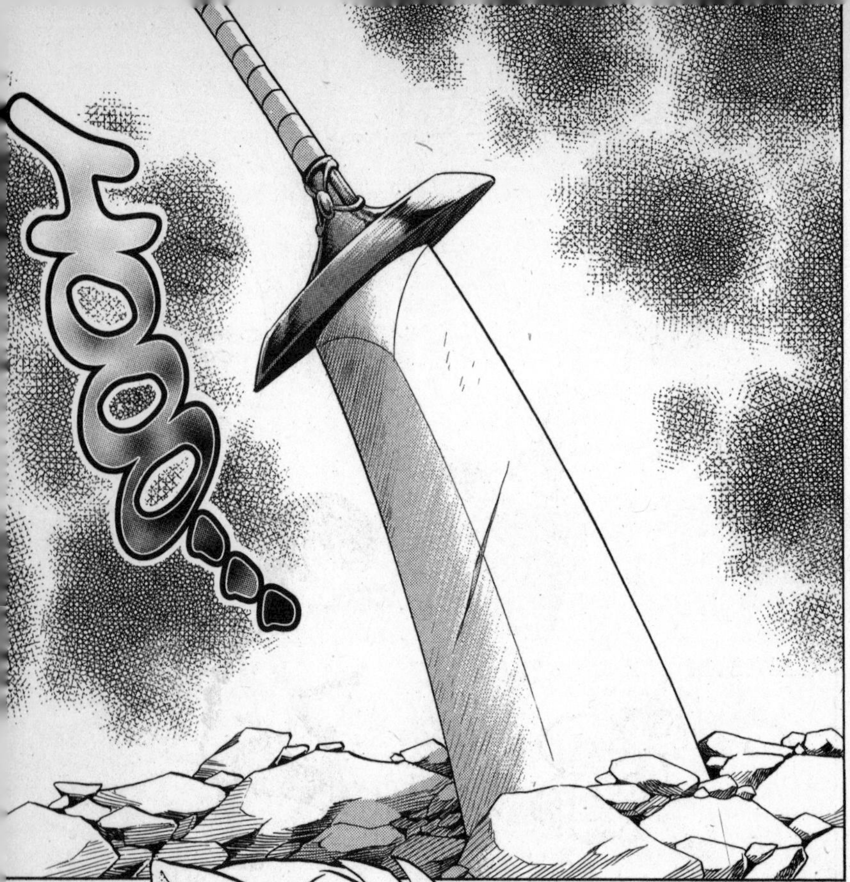
VOOOM...

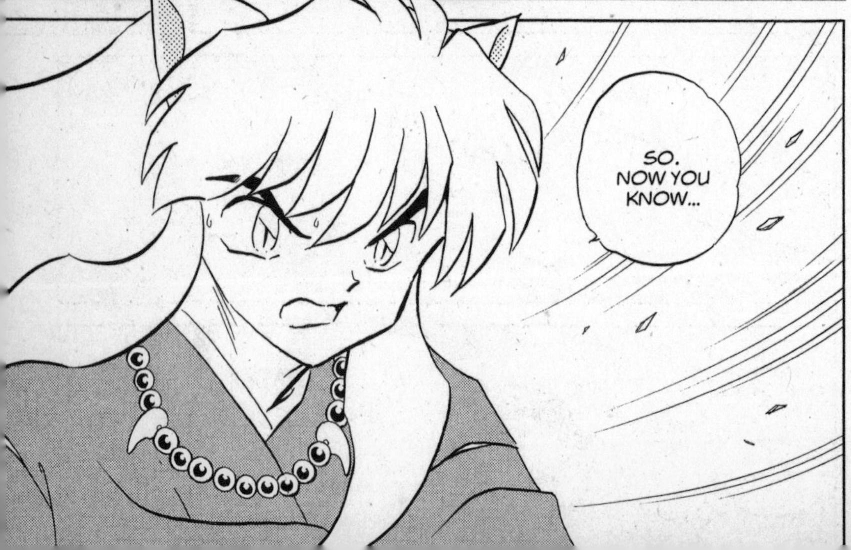
SO. NOW YOU KNOW...

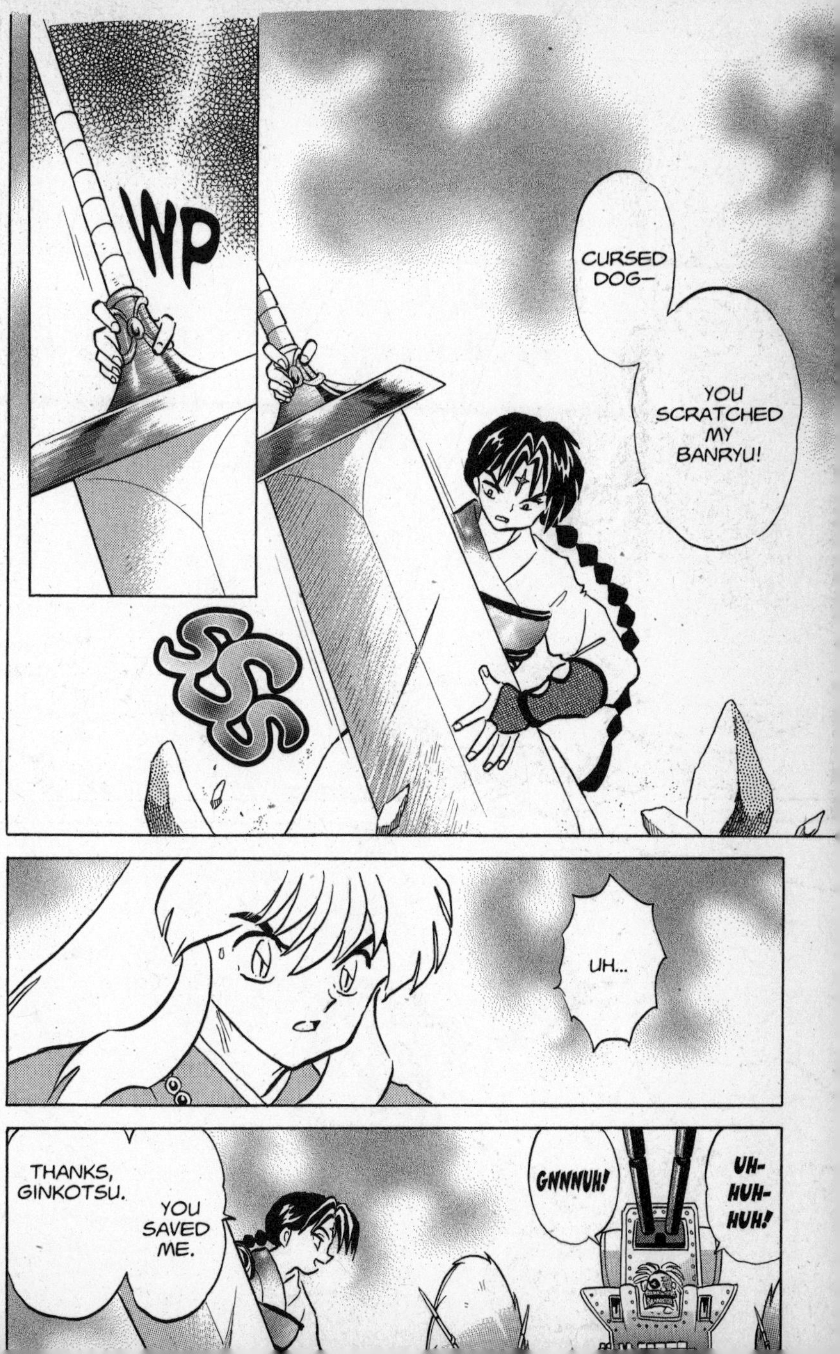
WP
CURSED DOG—
YOU SCRATCHED MY BANRYU!
SSS
UH...
THANKS, GINKOTSU.
YOU SAVED ME.
GNNNUH!
UH-HUH-HUH!

ALL RIGHT! FINE, FINE!

INU-YASHA— WE'LL MEET AGAIN!

WE'LL....?

YOU'VE GOT TO BE JOKING!

...

SSP

AWAY!!

AH!

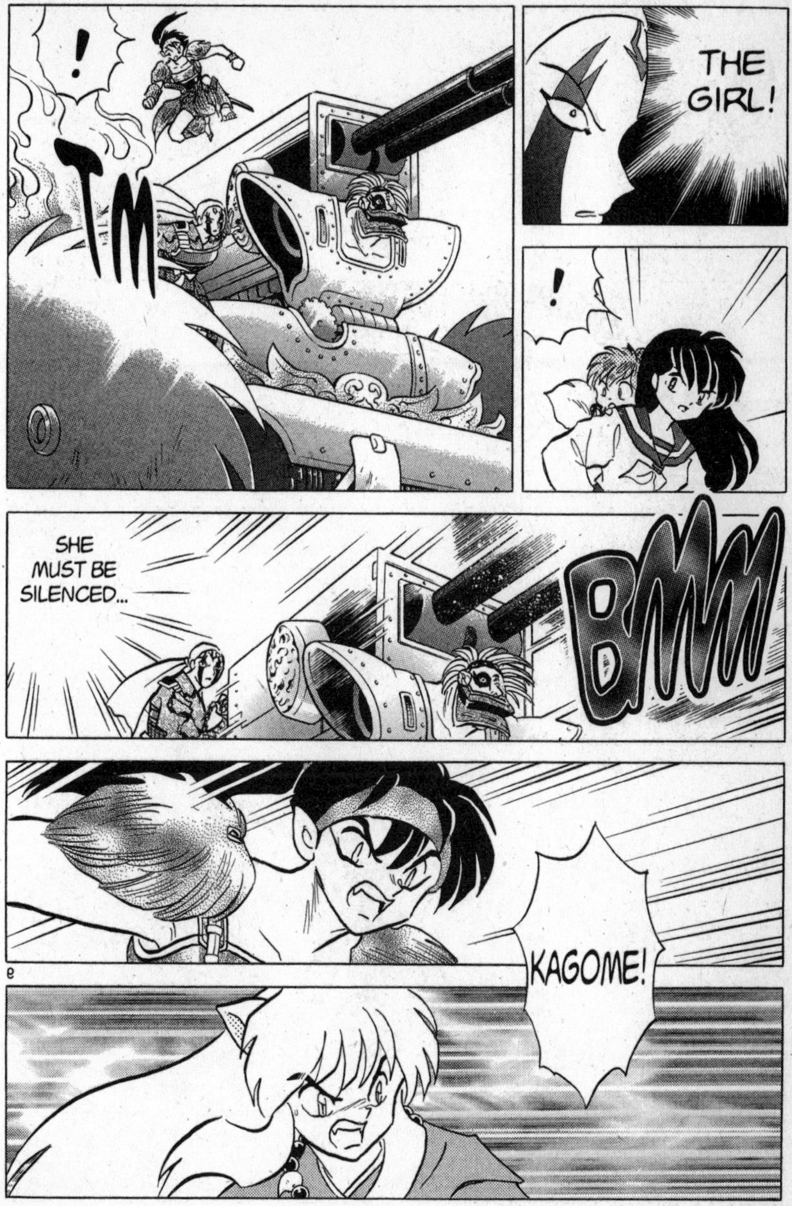
!
TM
THE GIRL!
!
SHE MUST BE SILENCED...
BMMM
KAGOME!
8

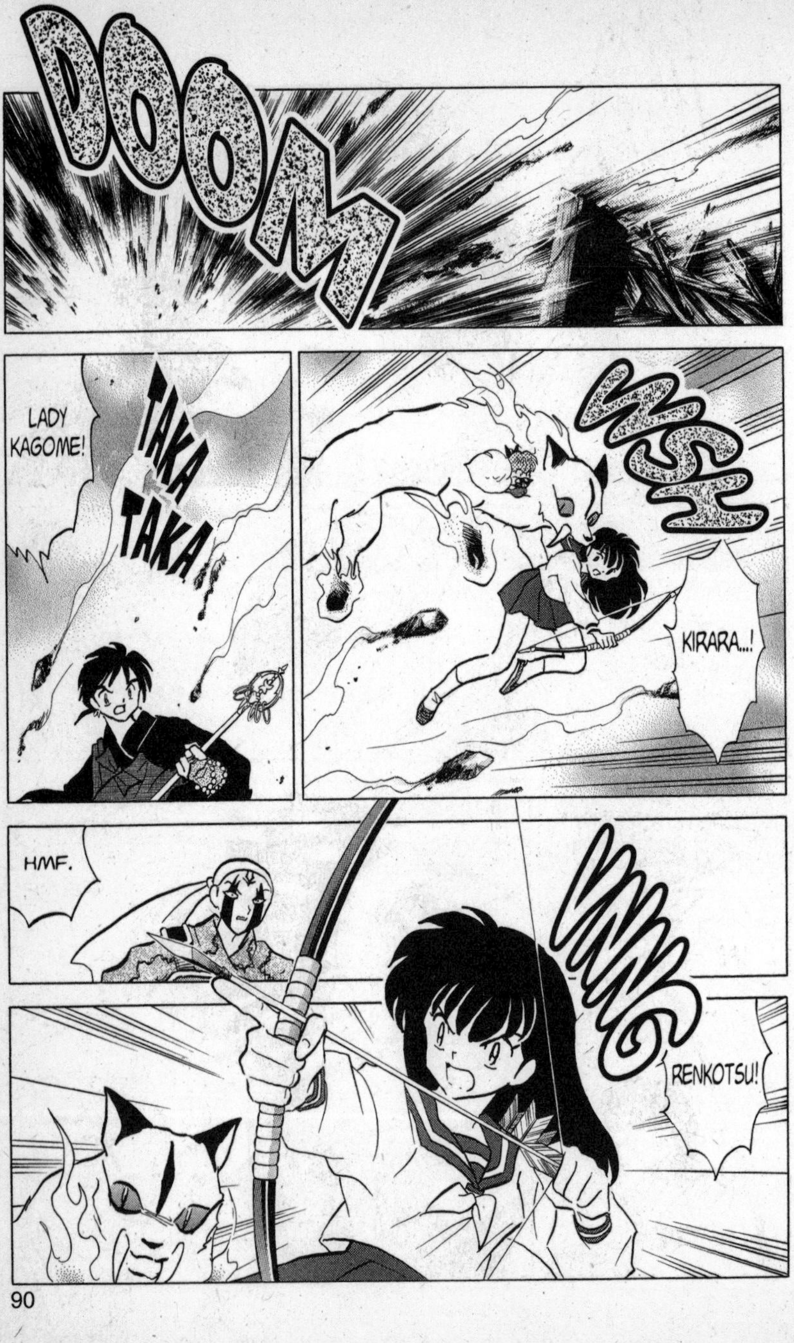
DOOM
LADY KAGOME!
TAKA TAKA
WSH
KIRARA...!
HMF.
VWNG
RENKOTSU!

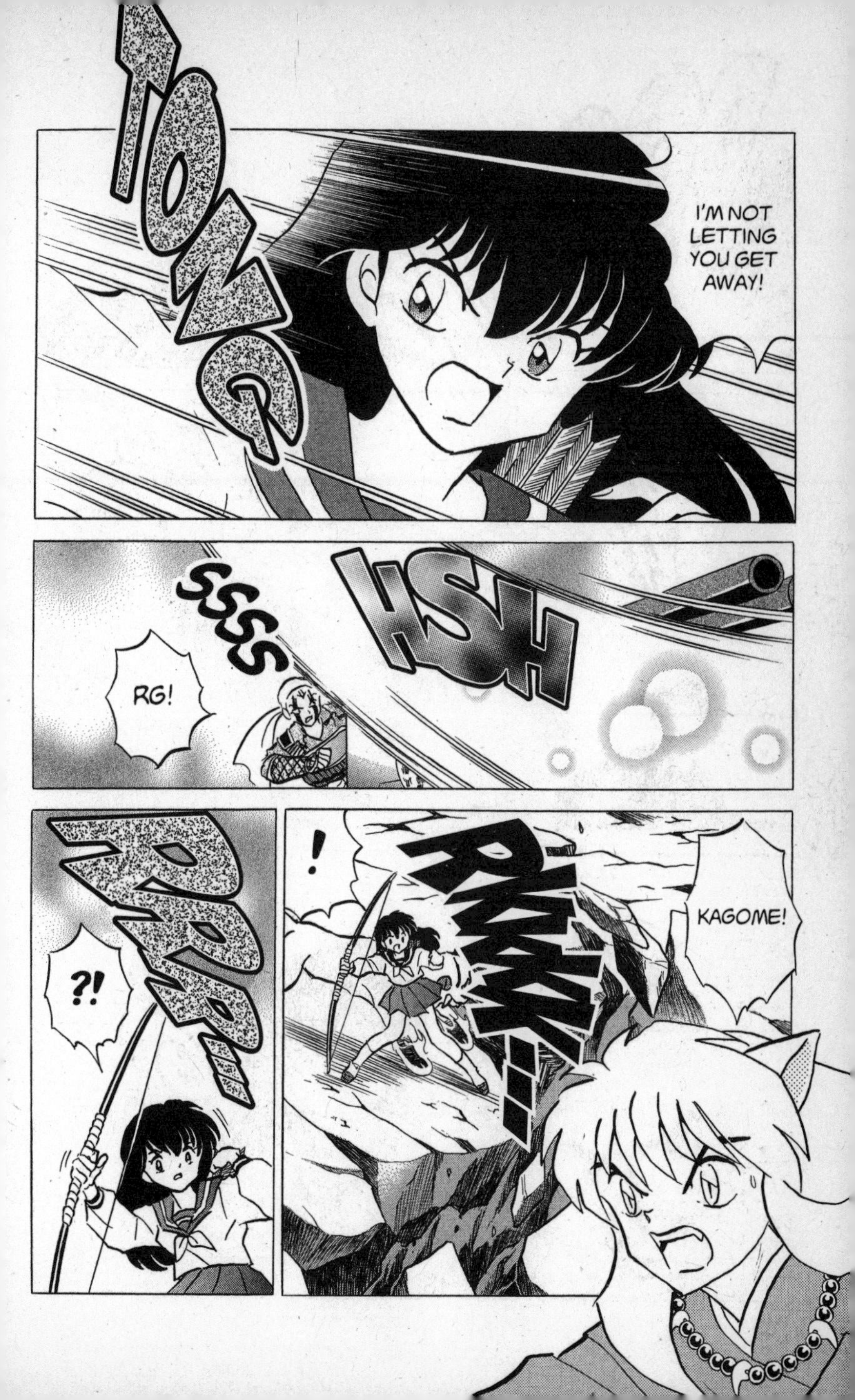
TONG
I'M NOT LETTING YOU GET AWAY!
SSSS
HSH
RG!
PRRR!!
?!
!
PWANG!!
KAGOME!

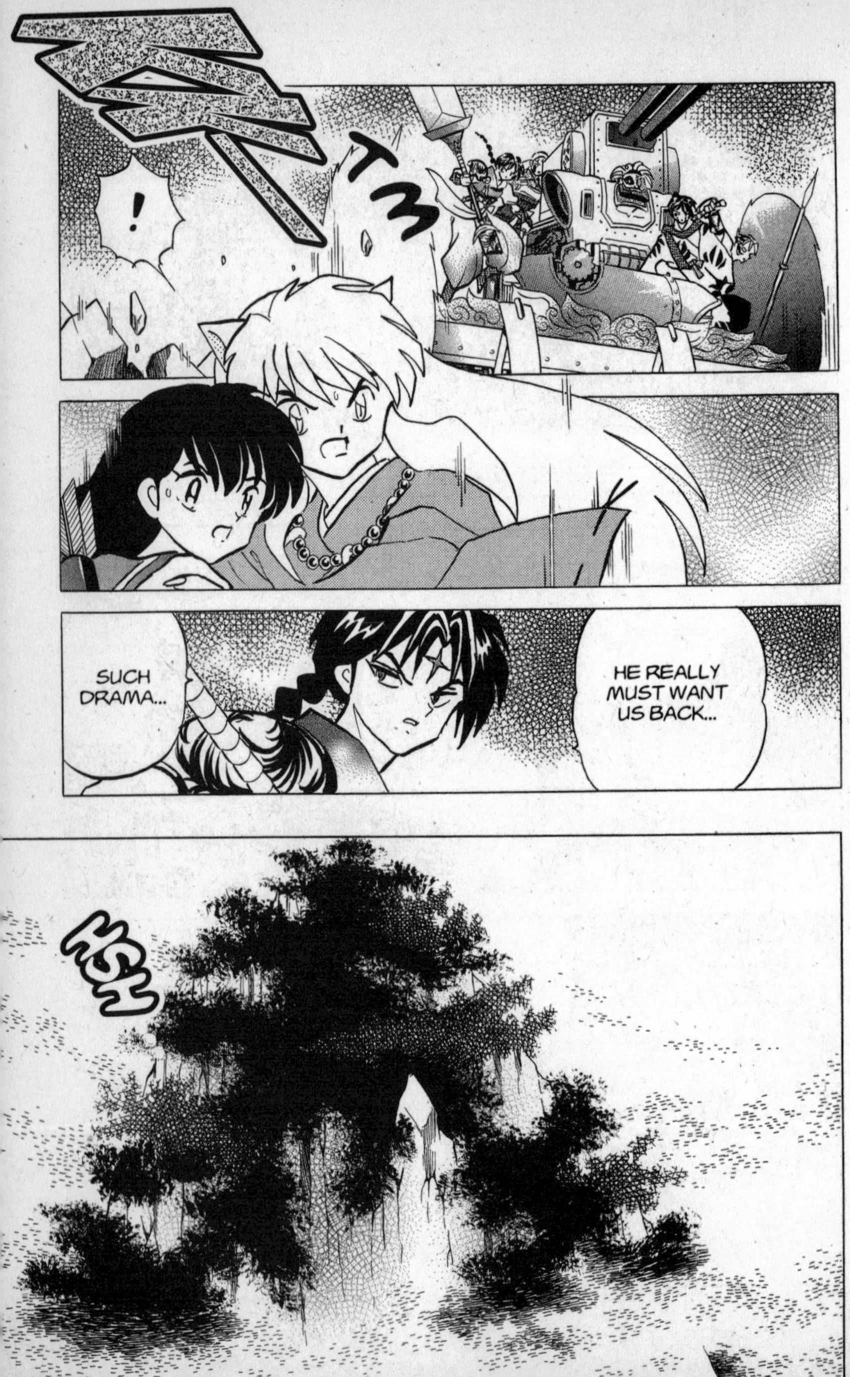
TM
SUCH DRAMA...
HE REALLY MUST WANT US BACK...
HSH

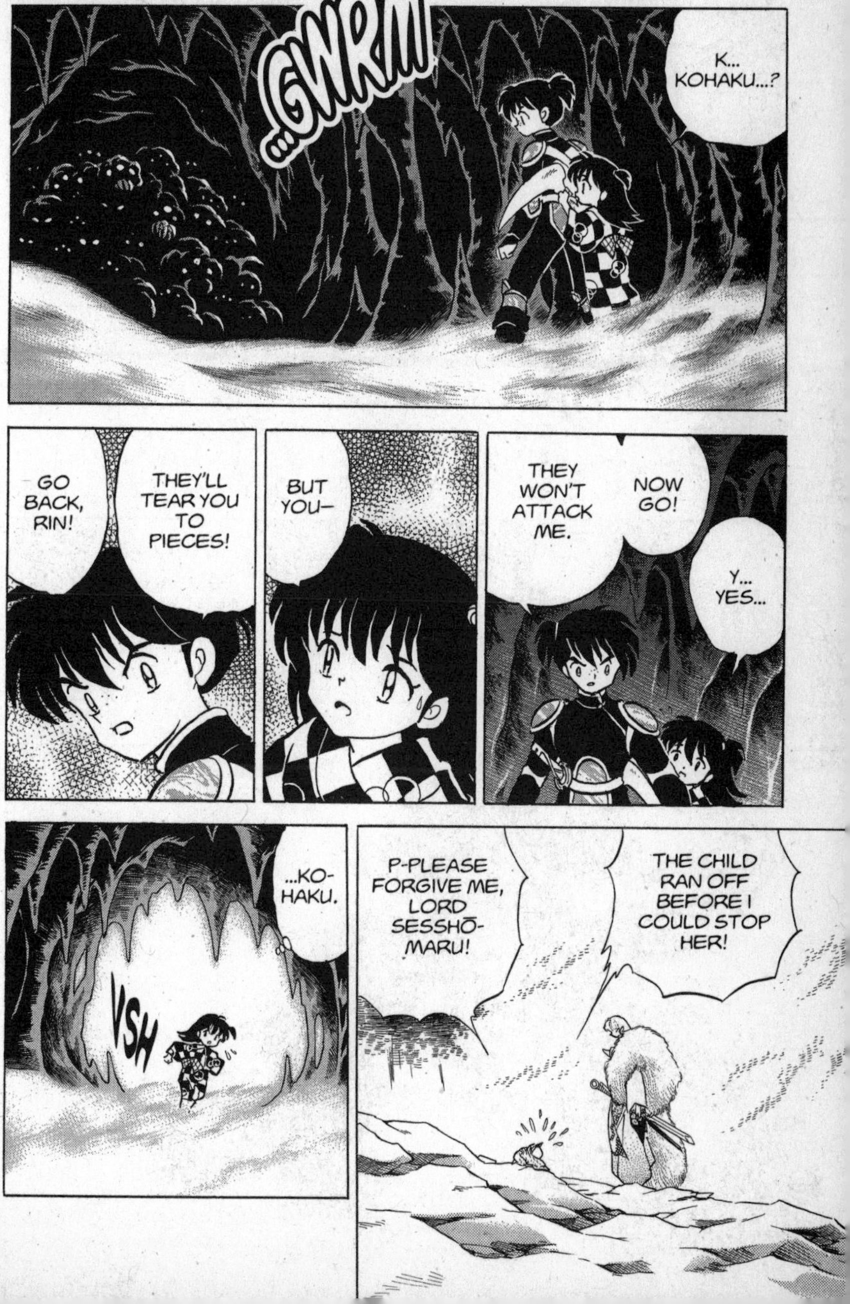
...GWRM
K... KOHAKU...?
GO BACK, RIN!
THEY'LL TEAR YOU TO PIECES!
BUT YOU—
THEY WON'T ATTACK ME.
NOW GO!
Y... YES...
...KO-HAKU.
VSH
P-PLEASE FORGIVE ME, LORD SESSHŌ-MARU!
THE CHILD RAN OFF BEFORE I COULD STOP HER!

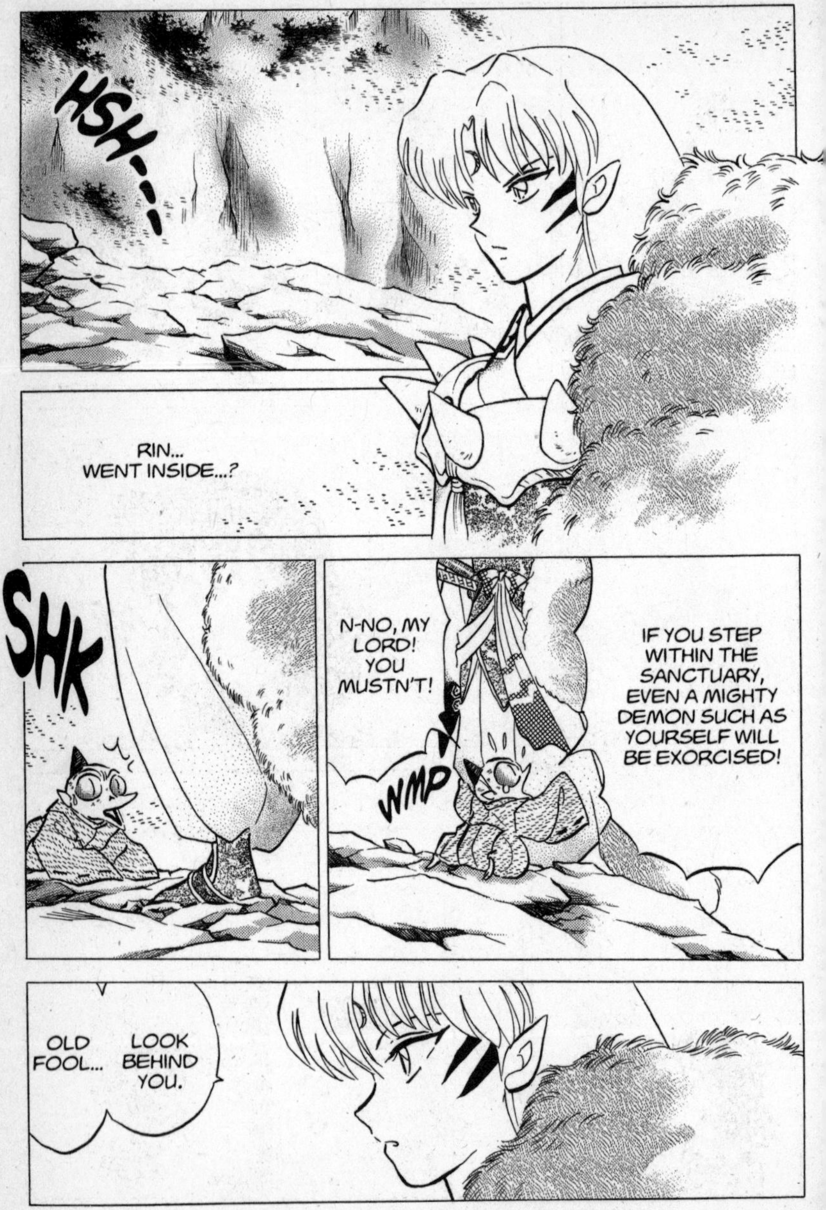
HSH---
RIN... WENT INSIDE...?
N-NO, MY LORD! YOU MUSTN'T!
IF YOU STEP WITHIN THE SANCTUARY, EVEN A MIGHTY DEMON SUCH AS YOURSELF WILL BE EXORCISED!
WMP
SHK
OLD FOOL...
LOOK BEHIND YOU.

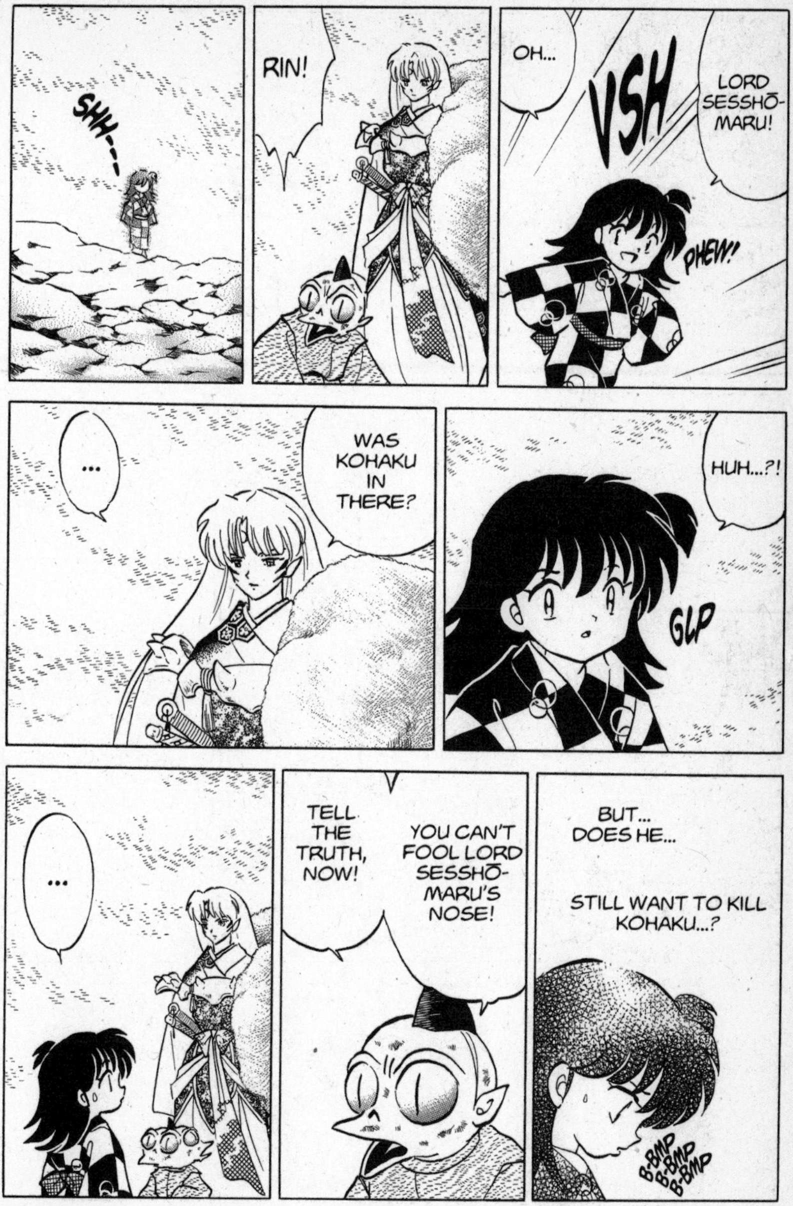
SHH...
RIN!
OH...
VSH
LORD SESSHŌ-MARU!
PHEW!
...
WAS KOHAKU IN THERE?
HUH...?!
GLP
...
TELL THE TRUTH, NOW!
YOU CAN'T FOOL LORD SESSHŌ-MARU'S NOSE!
BUT... DOES HE...
STILL WANT TO KILL KOHAKU...?
B-BMP B-BMP B-BMP

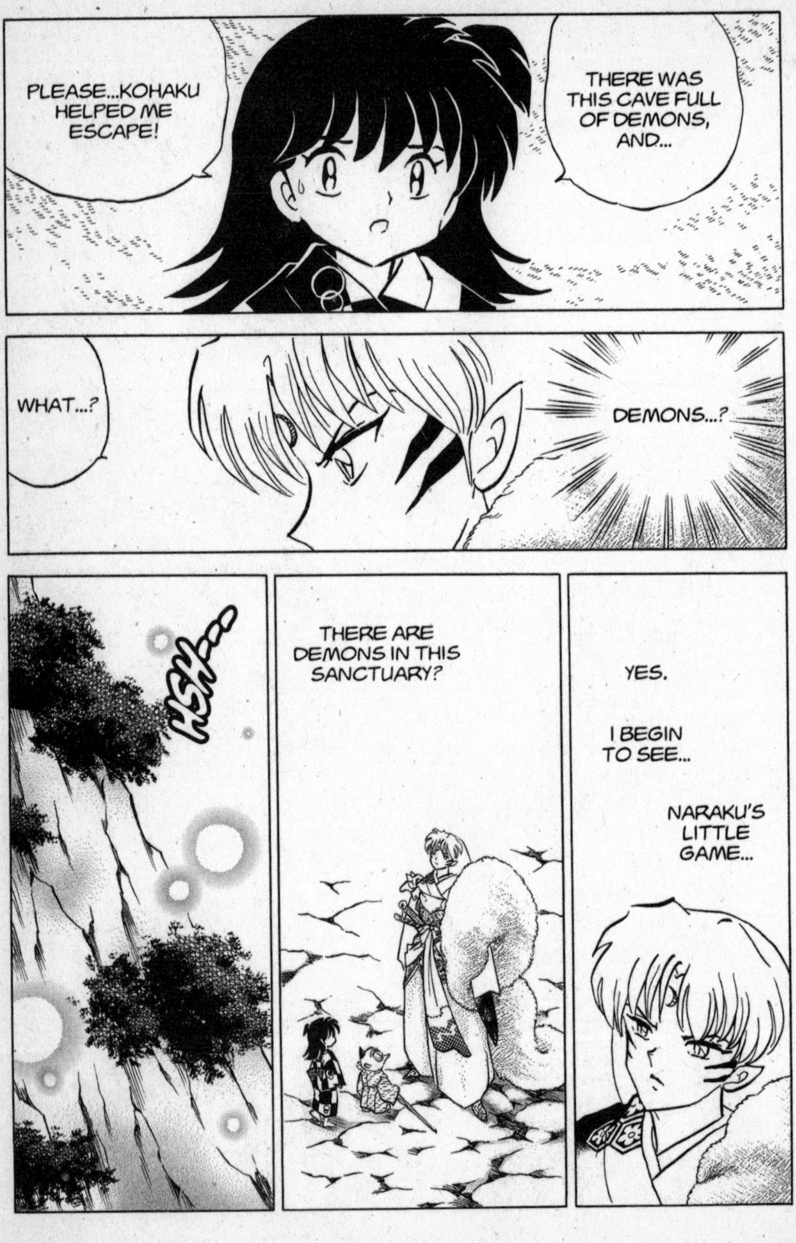
PLEASE...KOHAKU HELPED ME ESCAPE!
THERE WAS THIS CAVE FULL OF DEMONS, AND...
WHAT...?
DEMONS...?
HSH...
THERE ARE DEMONS IN THIS SANCTUARY?
YES.
I BEGIN TO SEE...
NARAKU'S LITTLE GAME...

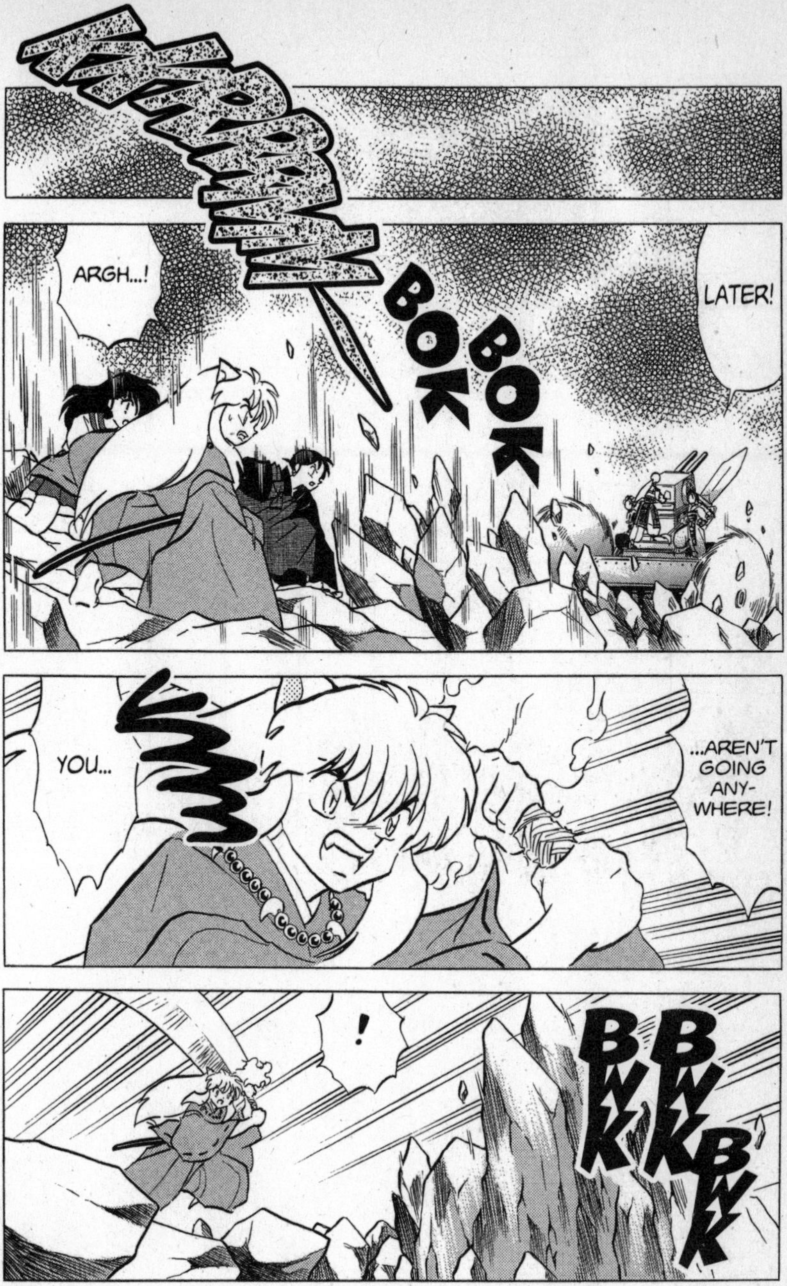
ARGH...!
BOK BOK
LATER!
YOU...
...AREN'T GOING ANY-WHERE!
!

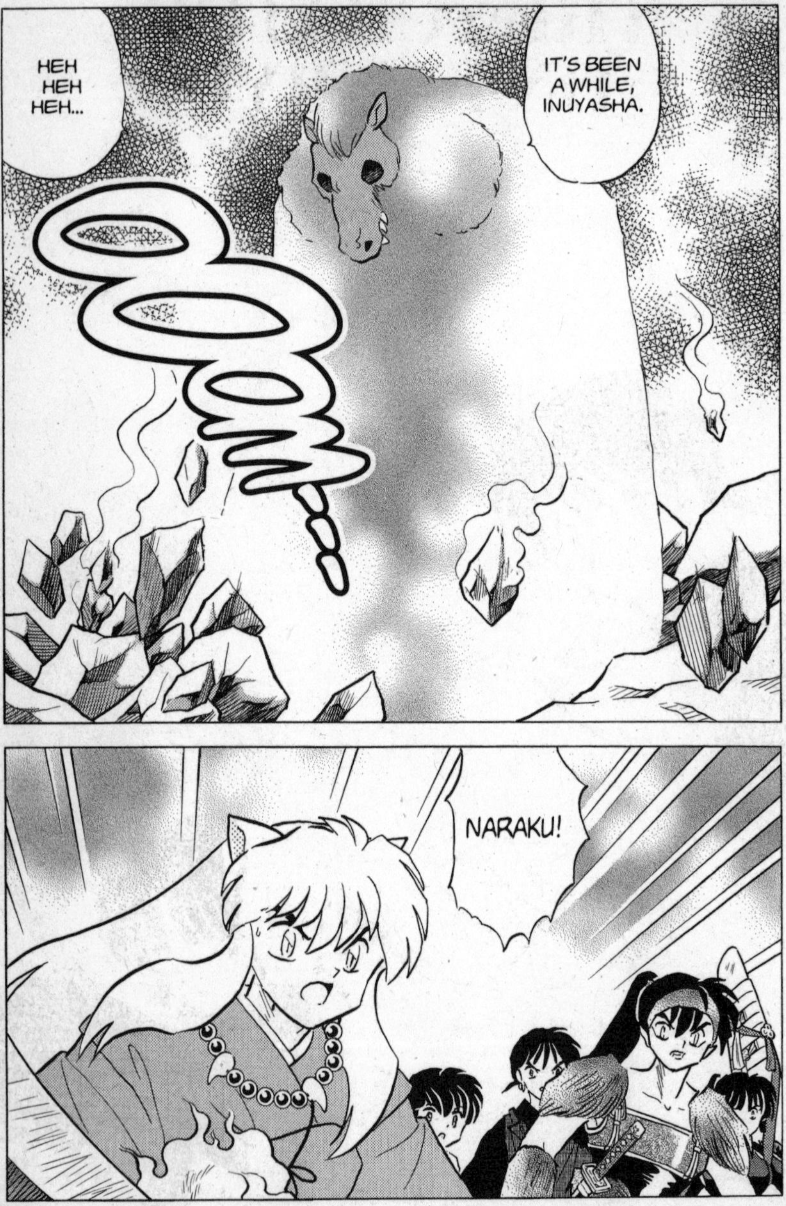
HEH HEH HEH...
IT'S BEEN A WHILE, INUYASHA.
NARAKU!

SCROLL SIX

THE SCRATCH ON BANRYU

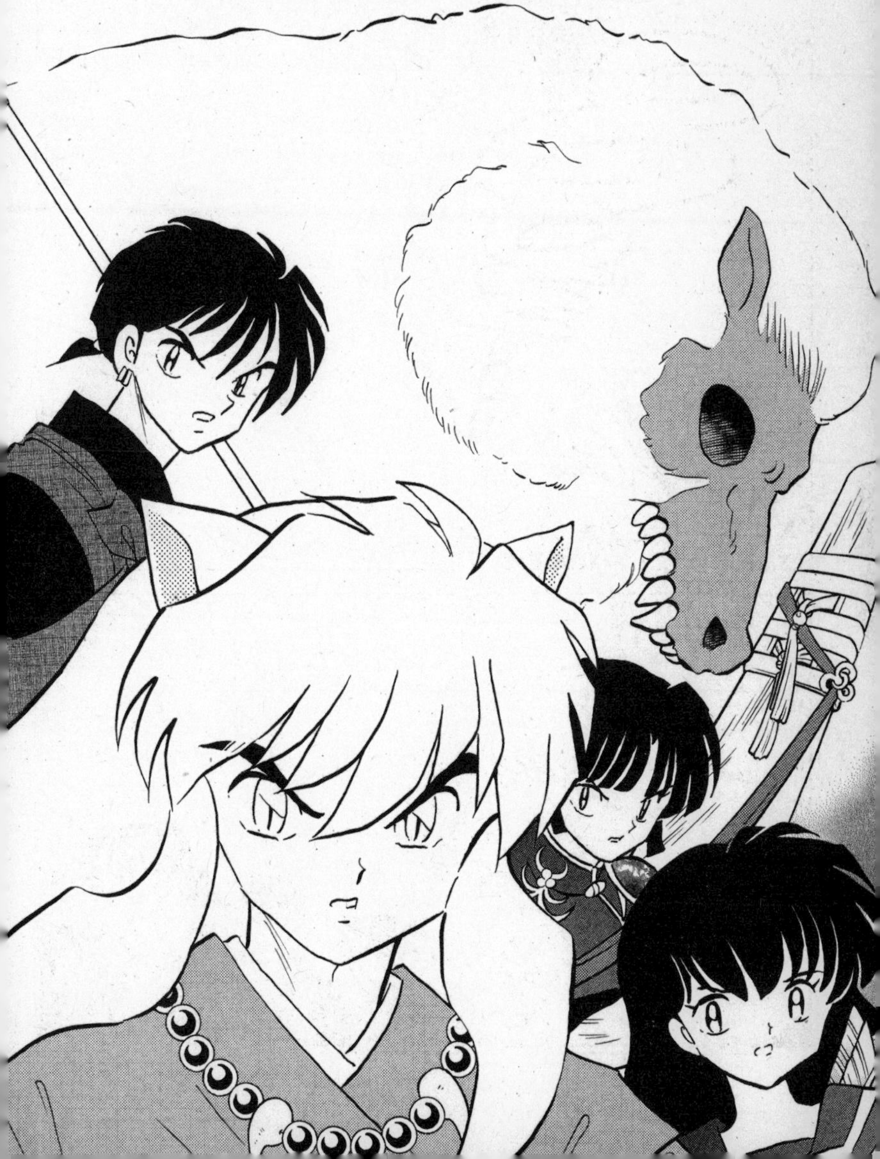

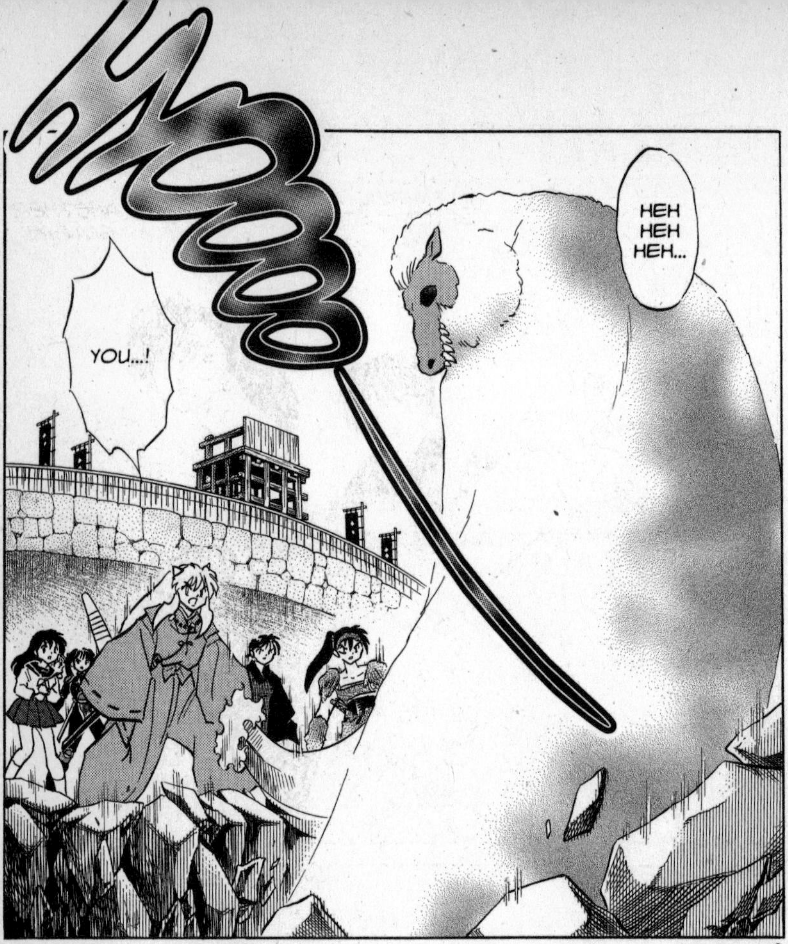
HYOOOO
YOU...!
HEH HEH HEH...
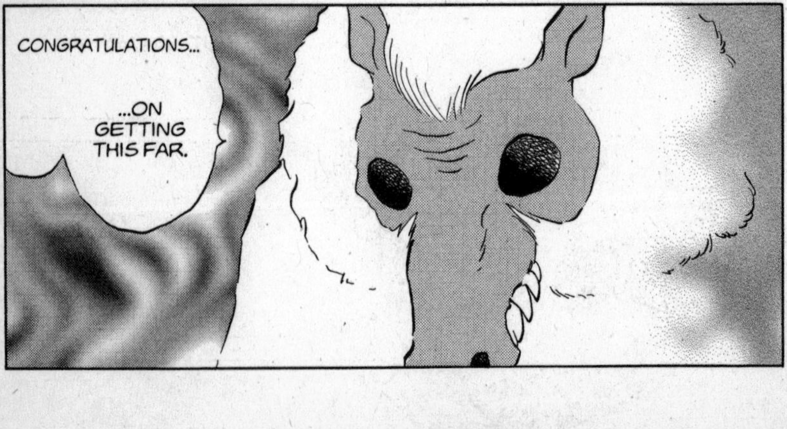
CONGRATULATIONS...
...ON GETTING THIS FAR.

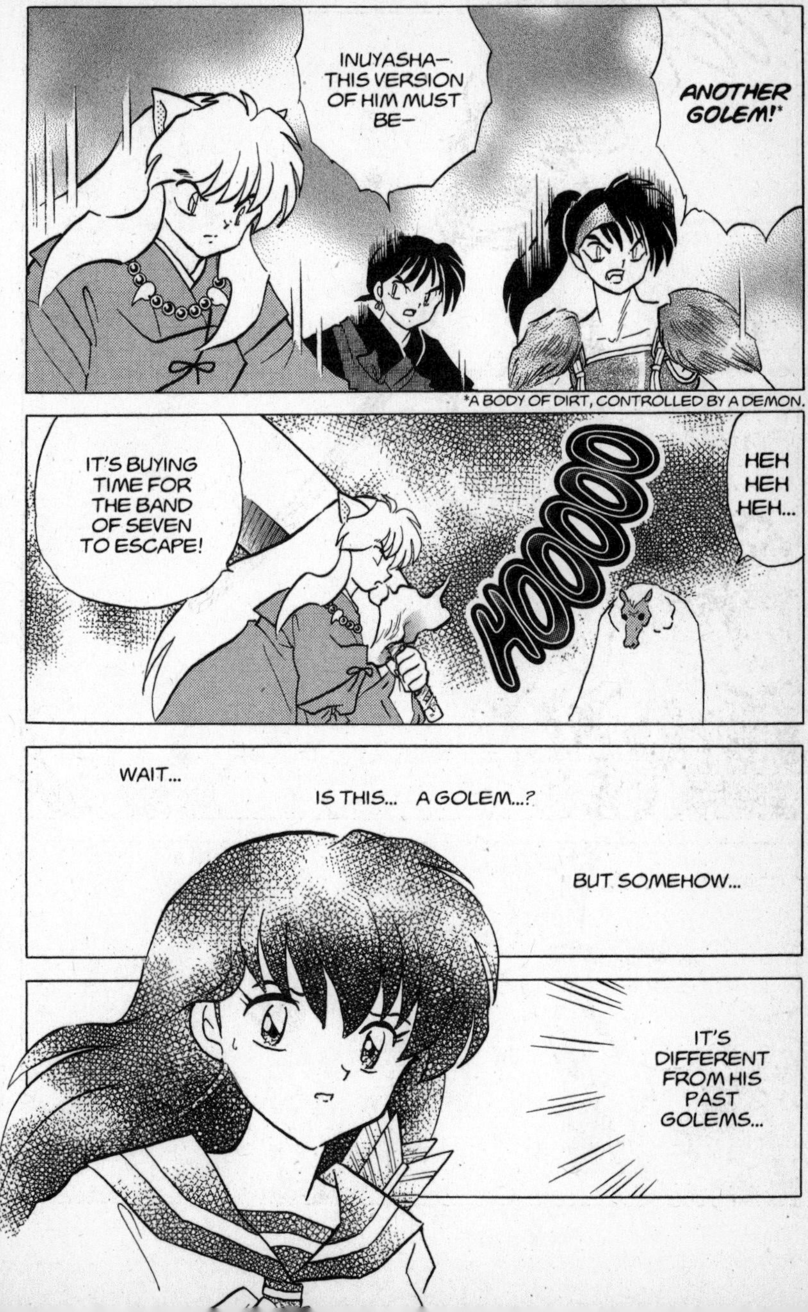
INUYASHA— THIS VERSION OF HIM MUST BE—
ANOTHER GOLEM!*
*A BODY OF DIRT, CONTROLLED BY A DEMON.
IT'S BUYING TIME FOR THE BAND OF SEVEN TO ESCAPE!
HOOOOO
HEH HEH HEH...
WAIT...
IS THIS... A GOLEM...?
BUT SOMEHOW...
IT'S DIFFERENT FROM HIS PAST GOLEMS...

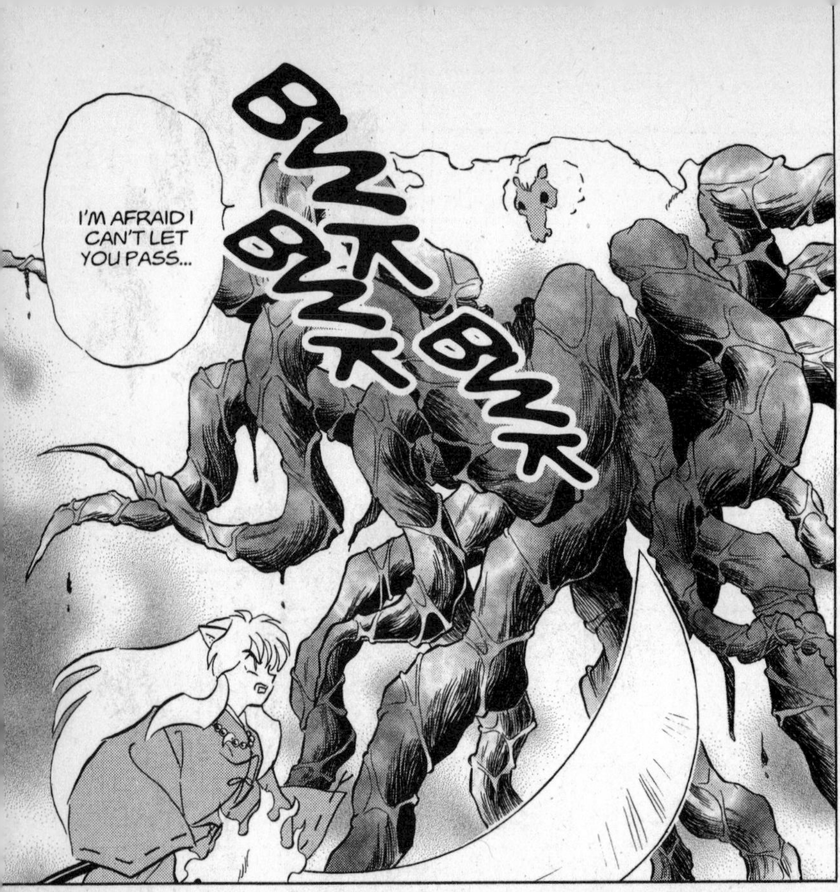
I'M AFRAID I CAN'T LET YOU PASS...
BWK BWK BWK BWK

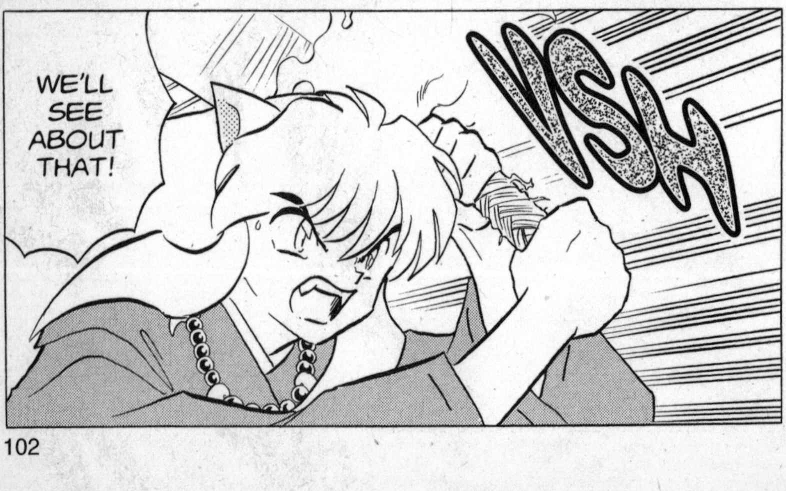
WE'LL SEE ABOUT THAT!
VSH

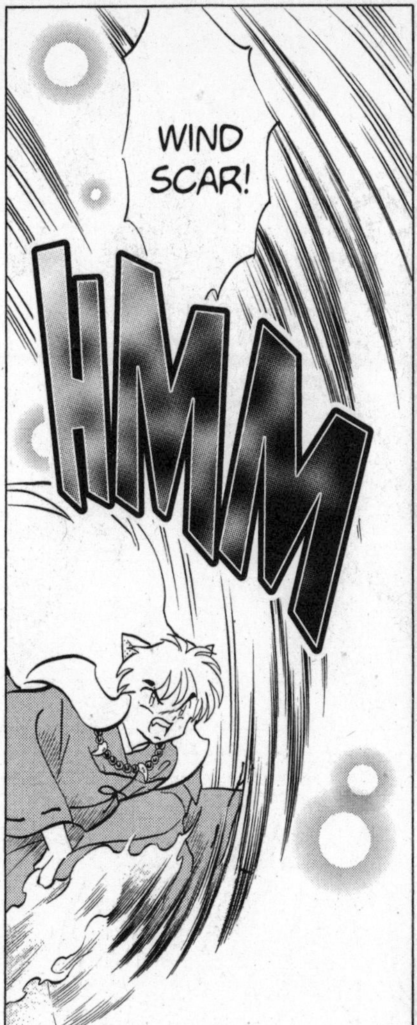
WIND SCAR!
HMM
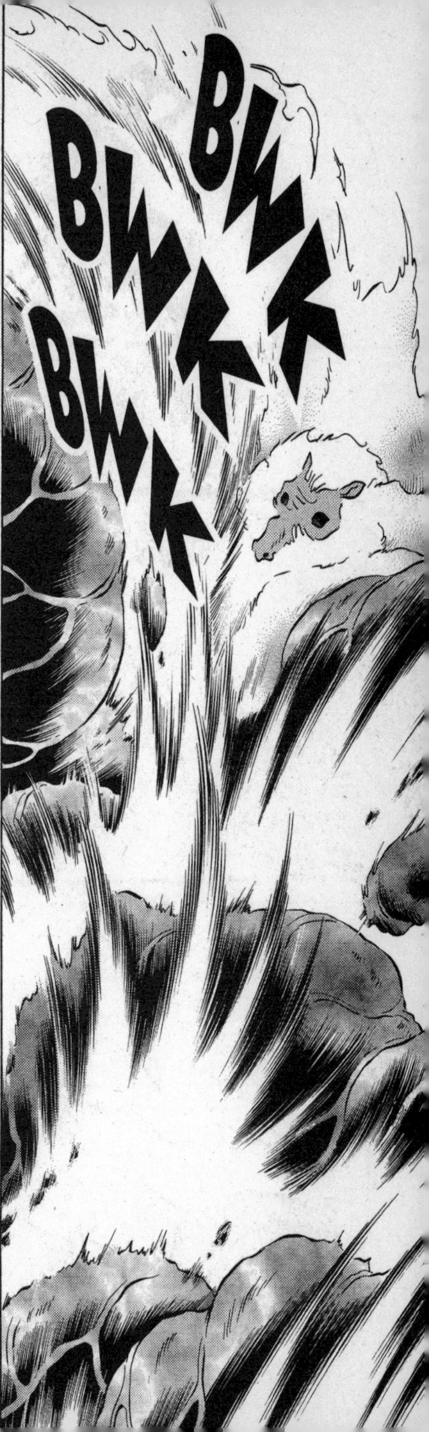
BWK
BWK
BWK

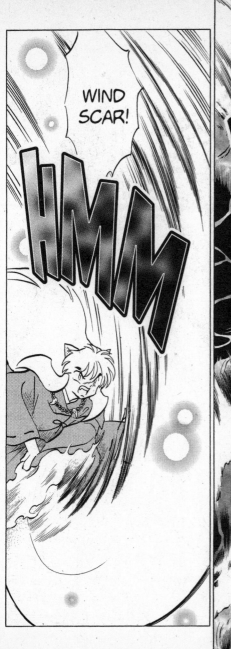

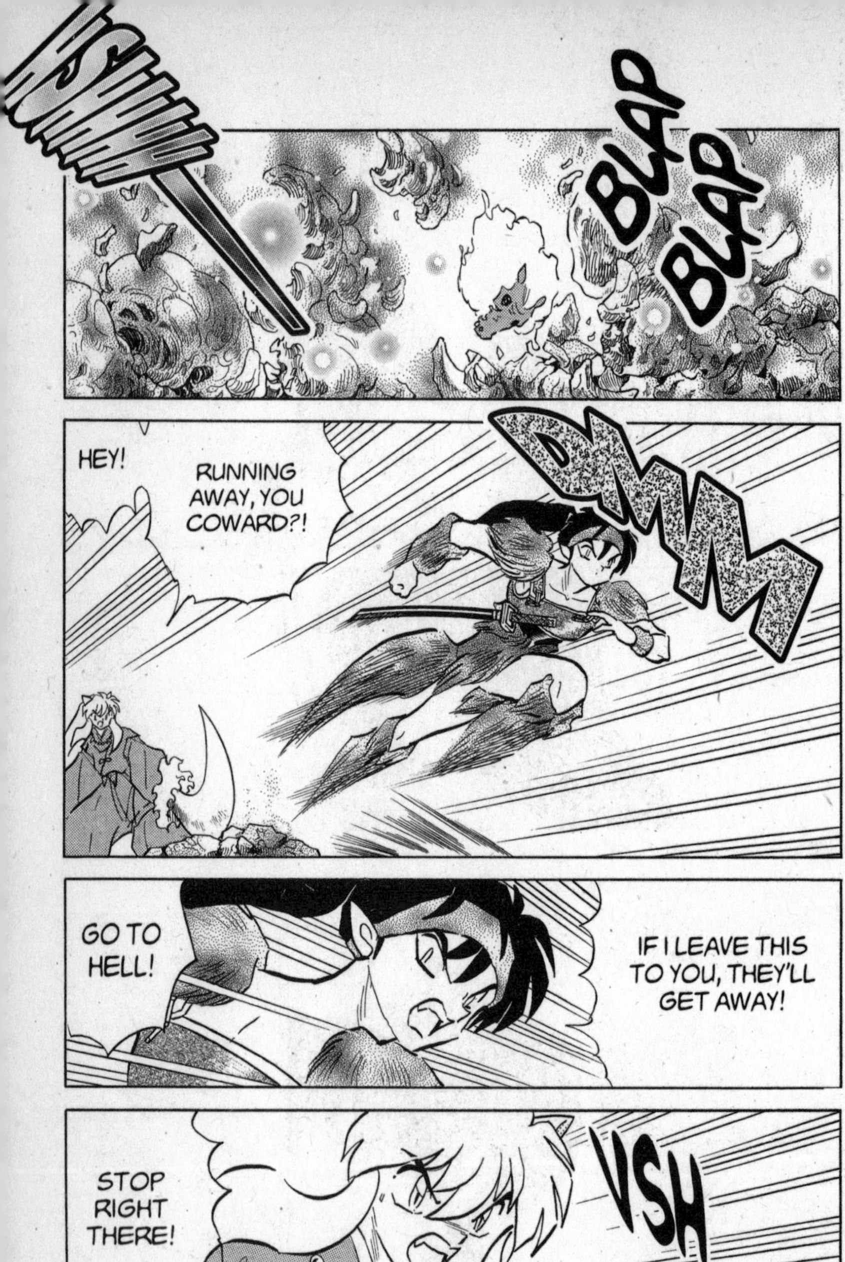
VSHHHH
BLAP
BLAP
HEY!
RUNNING AWAY, YOU COWARD?!
DWM
GO TO HELL!
IF I LEAVE THIS TO YOU, THEY'LL GET AWAY!
STOP RIGHT THERE!
VSH

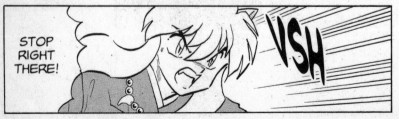

INUYASHA, WAIT!

YOU NOTICED TOO, LADY KAGOME?

NOTICED WHAT...?

THIS GOLEM'S WEIRD.

SORT OF... CLEAN, SOME-HOW.

"CLEAN?"

WHAT ARE YOU BABBLING ABOUT?

IT FEELS...

...LIKE MT. HAKUREI.

HAKUREI?!

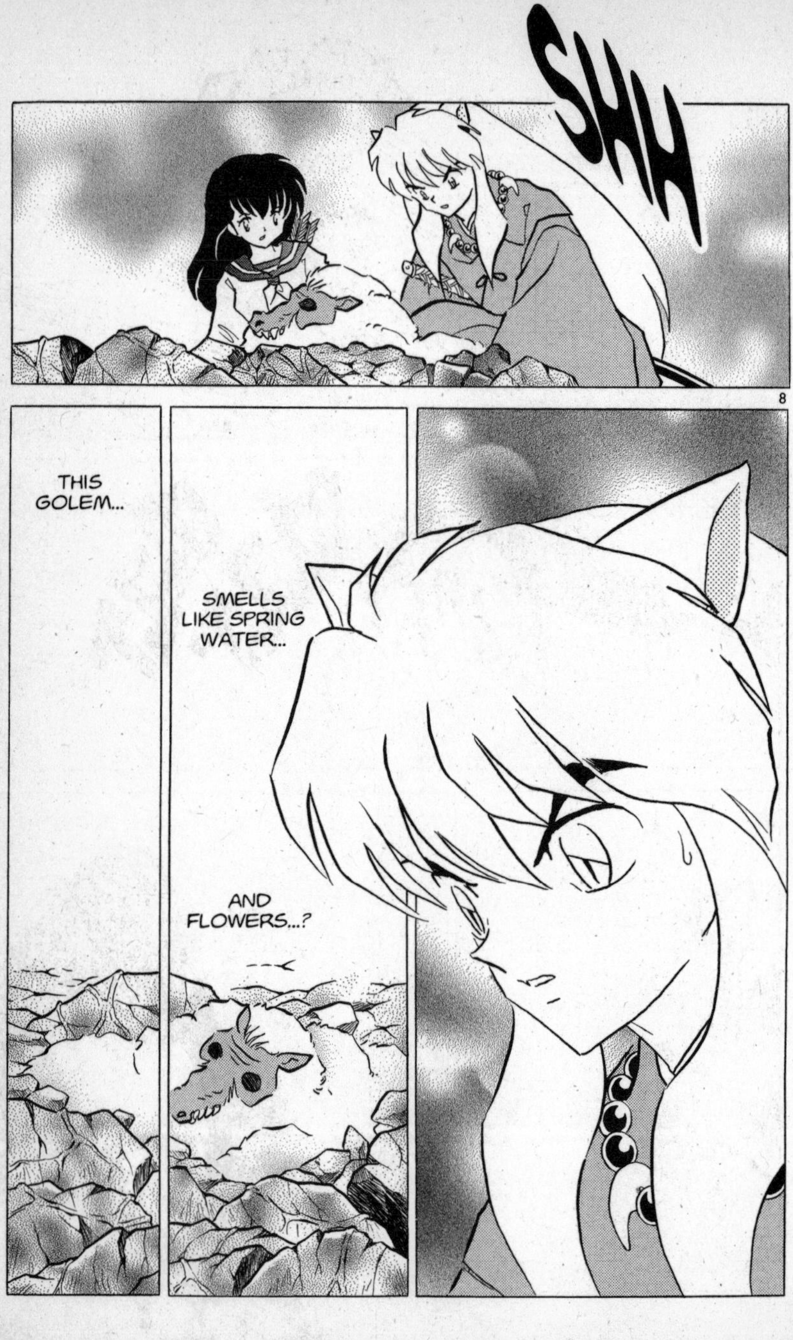
SHH
THIS GOLEM...
SMELLS LIKE SPRING WATER...
AND FLOWERS...?

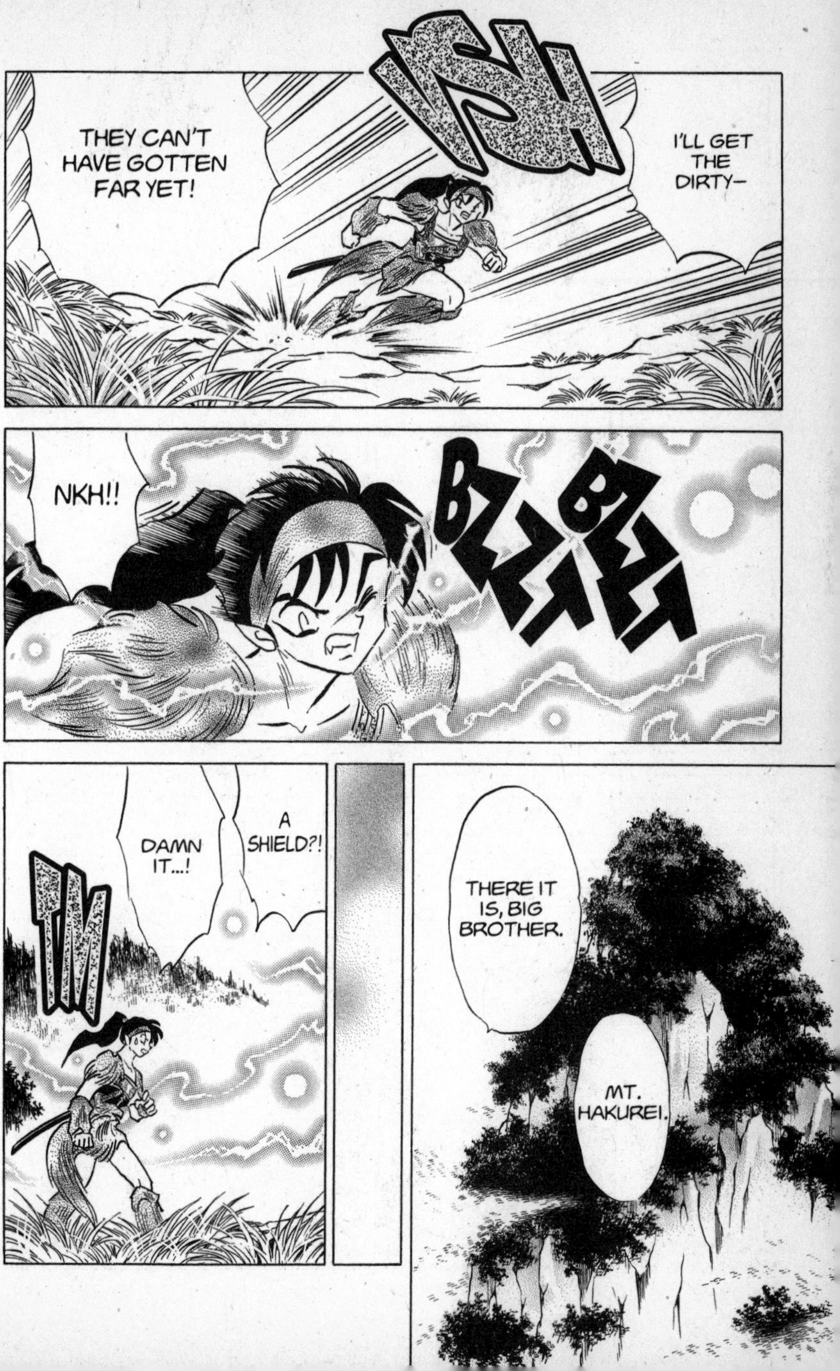
THEY CAN'T HAVE GOTTEN FAR YET!
I'LL GET THE DIRTY—
NKH!!
DAMN IT...!
A SHIELD?!
THERE IT IS, BIG BROTHER.
MT. HAKUREI.

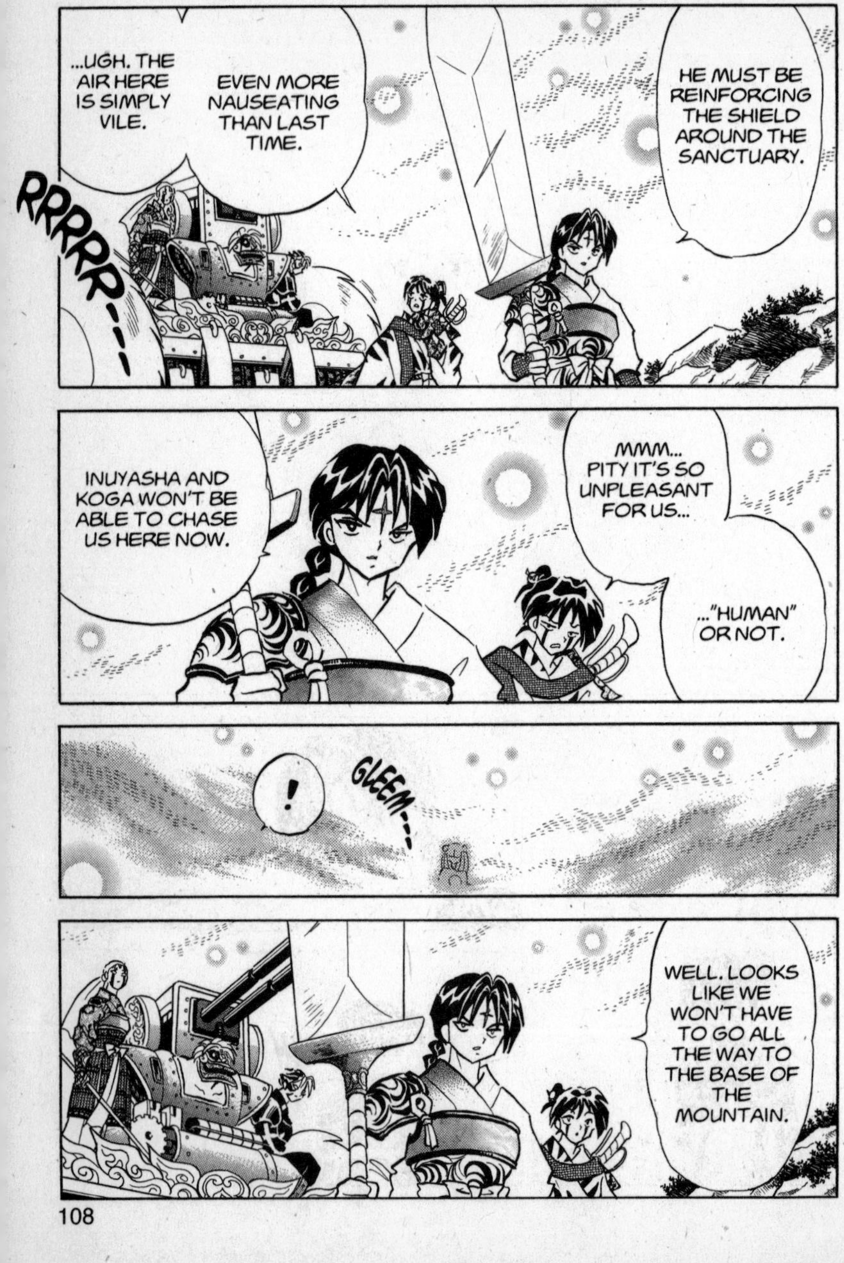
...UGH. THE AIR HERE IS SIMPLY VILE.
EVEN MORE NAUSEATING THAN LAST TIME.
HE MUST BE REINFORCING THE SHIELD AROUND THE SANCTUARY.
RRRRR---
INUYASHA AND KOGA WON'T BE ABLE TO CHASE US HERE NOW.
MMM... PITY IT'S SO UNPLEASANT FOR US...
..."HUMAN" OR NOT.
!
GLEEM---
WELL. LOOKS LIKE WE WON'T HAVE TO GO ALL THE WAY TO THE BASE OF THE MOUNTAIN.

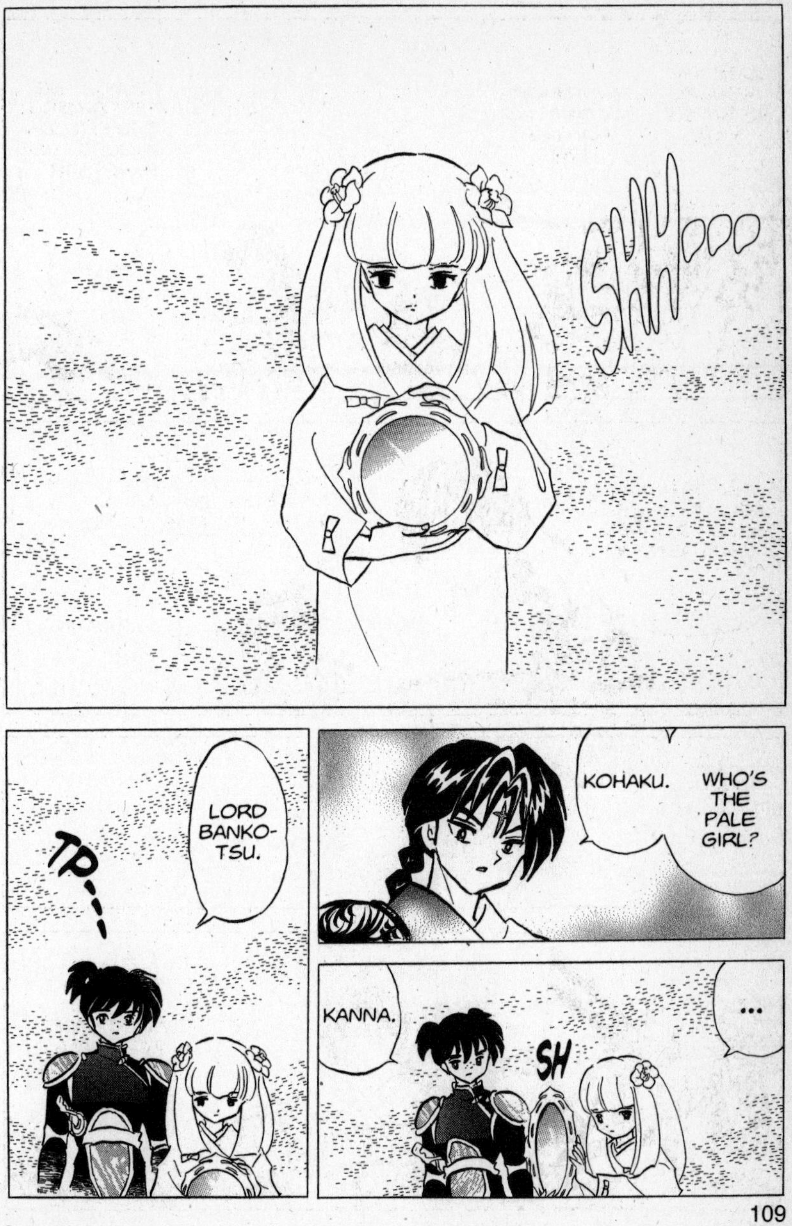
SHHOOO
LORD BANKO-TSU.
TP...
KOHAKU.
WHO'S THE PALE GIRL?
KANNA.
SH
...

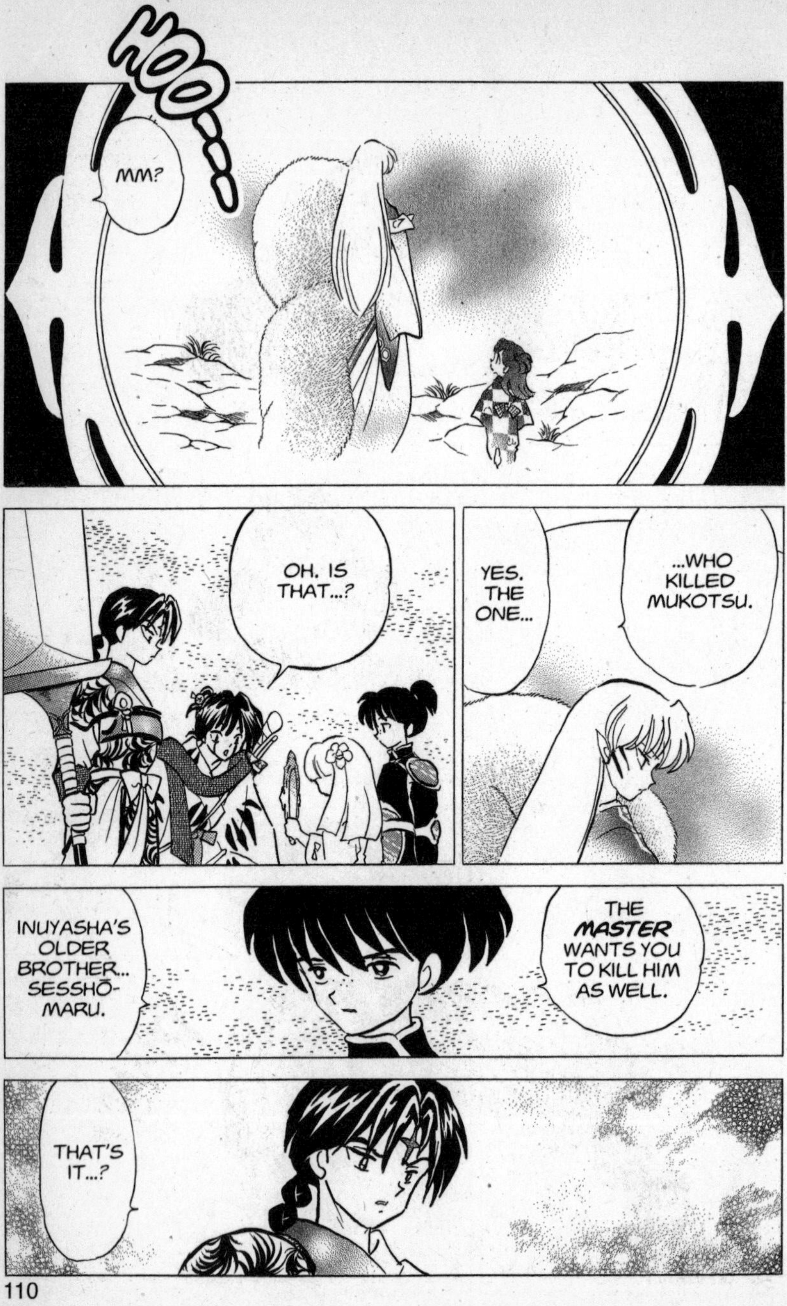
HOO-OOO
MM?
OH. IS THAT...?
YES. THE ONE...
...WHO KILLED MUKOTSU.
INUYASHA'S OLDER BROTHER... SESSHŌ-MARU.
THE MASTER WANTS YOU TO KILL HIM AS WELL.
THAT'S IT...?

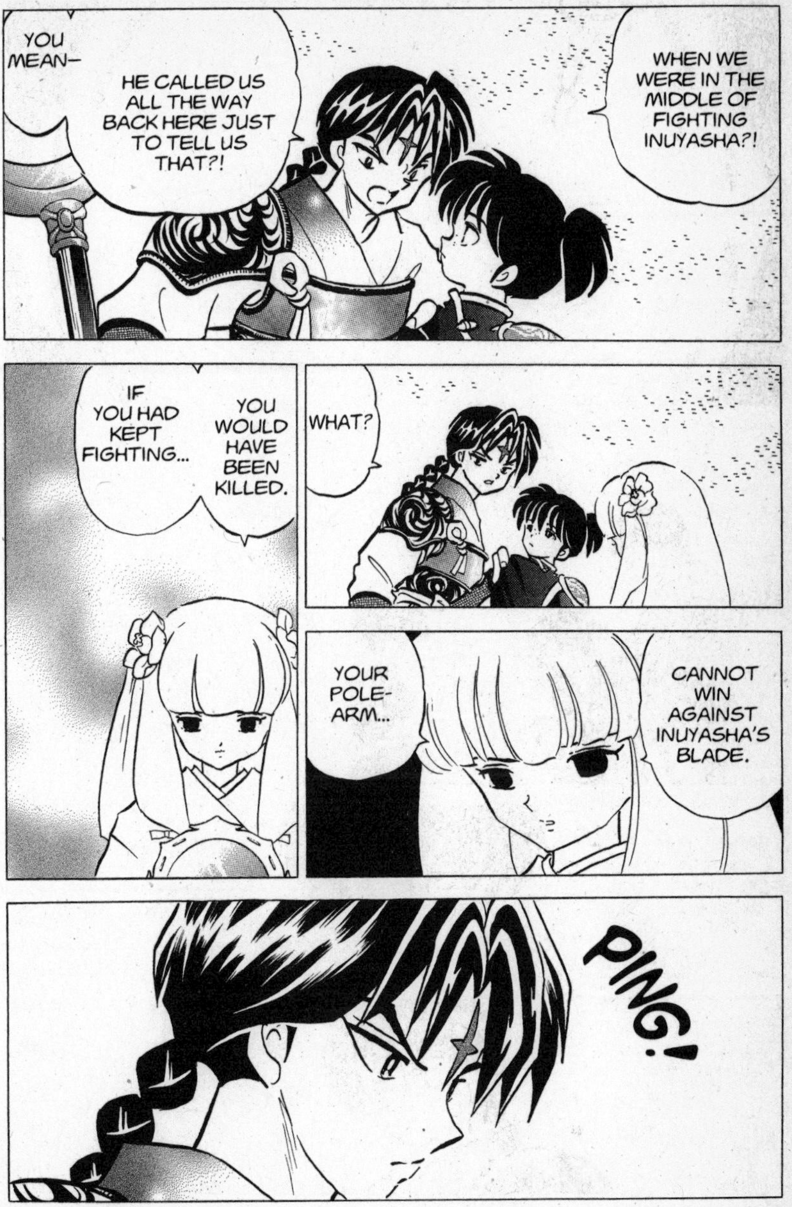
YOU MEAN—
HE CALLED US ALL THE WAY BACK HERE JUST TO TELL US THAT?!
WHEN WE WERE IN THE MIDDLE OF FIGHTING INUYASHA?!
IF YOU HAD KEPT FIGHTING...
YOU WOULD HAVE BEEN KILLED.
WHAT?
YOUR POLE-ARM...
CANNOT WIN AGAINST INUYASHA'S BLADE.
PING!

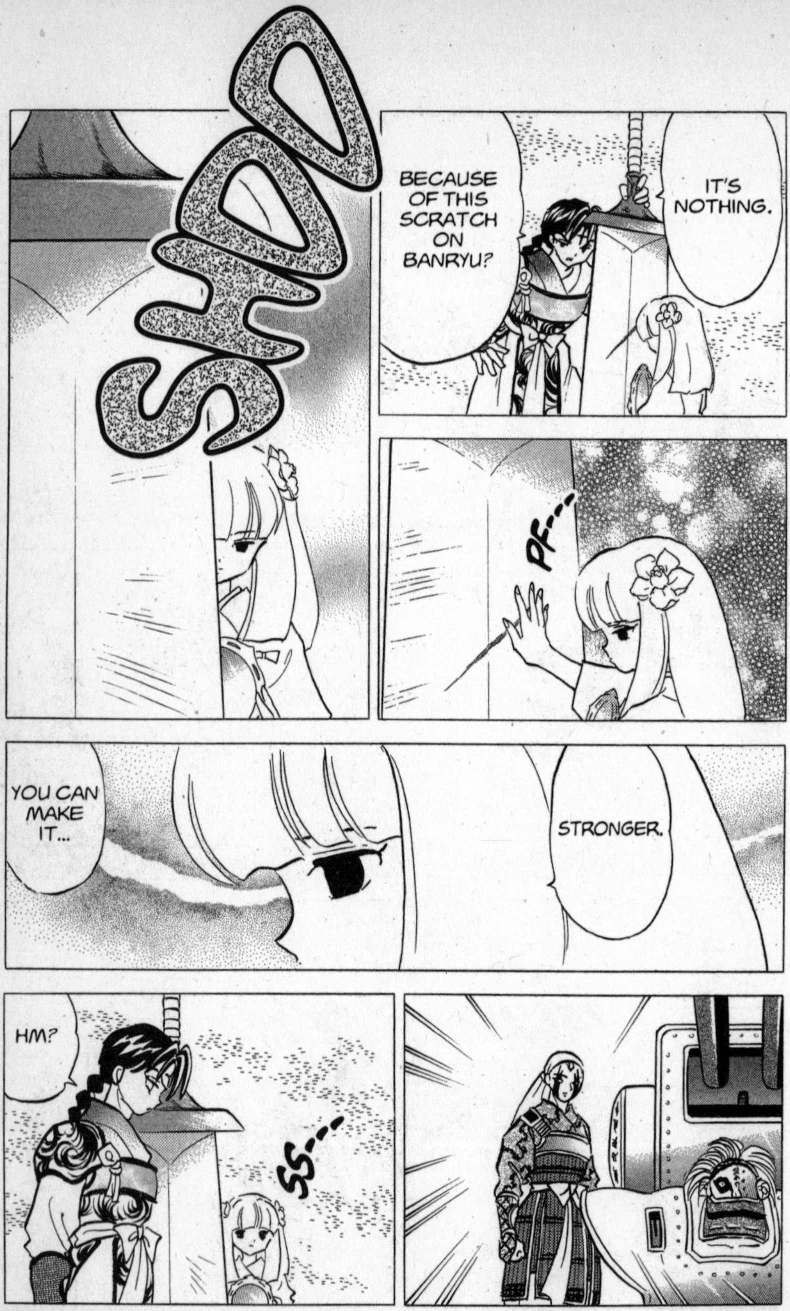
SHDD
BECAUSE OF THIS SCRATCH ON BANRYU?
IT'S NOTHING.
PF--
YOU CAN MAKE IT...
STRONGER.
HM?
SS--

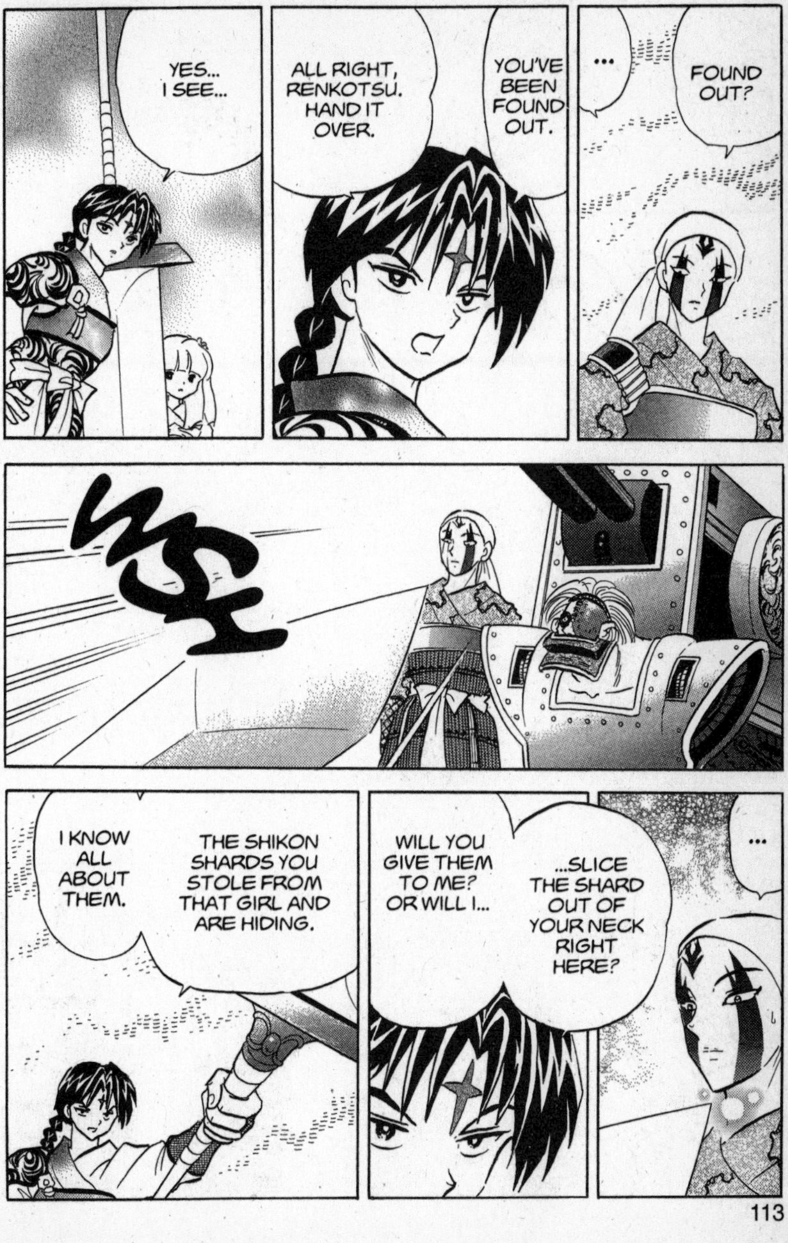
YES... I SEE...
ALL RIGHT, RENKOTSU. HAND IT OVER.
YOU'VE BEEN FOUND OUT.
...
FOUND OUT?
WSH
I KNOW ALL ABOUT THEM.
THE SHIKON SHARDS YOU STOLE FROM THAT GIRL AND ARE HIDING.
WILL YOU GIVE THEM TO ME? OR WILL I...
...SLICE THE SHARD OUT OF YOUR NECK RIGHT HERE?
...

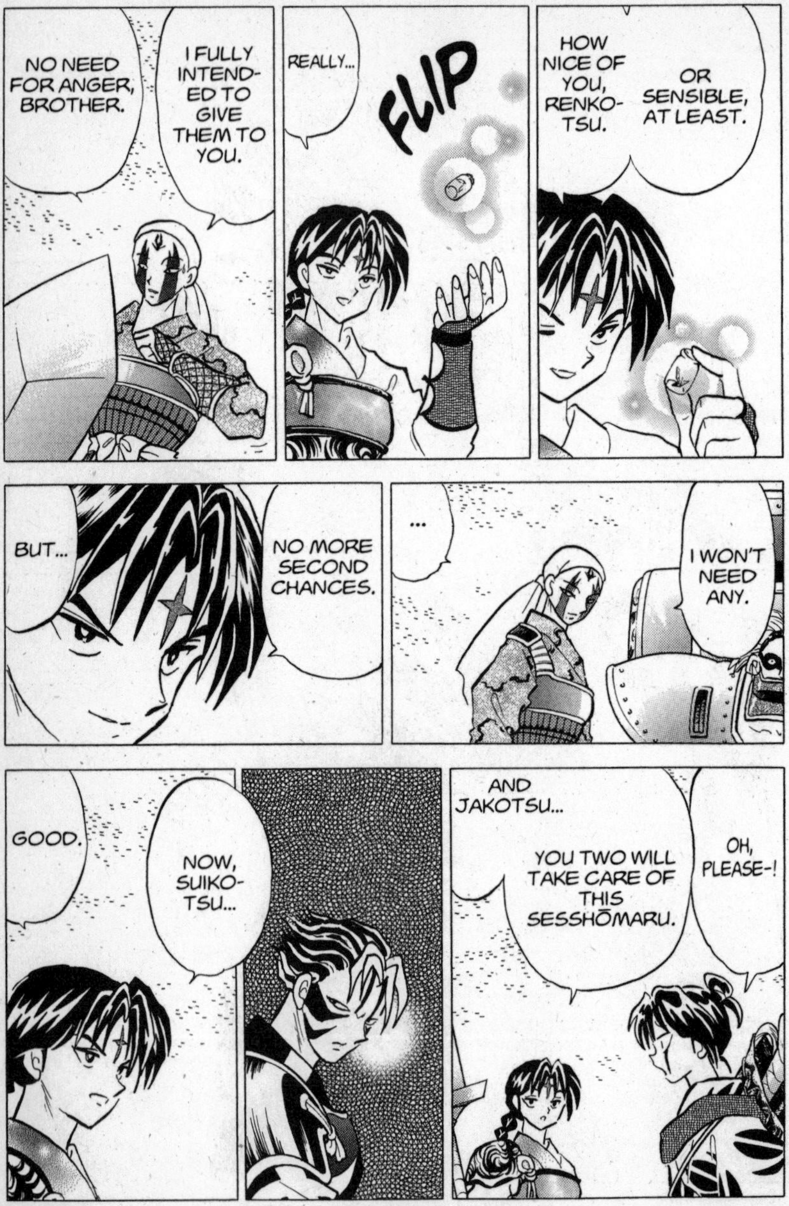
NO NEED FOR ANGER, BROTHER.
I FULLY INTEND-ED TO GIVE THEM TO YOU.
REALLY...
FLIP
HOW NICE OF YOU, RENKO-TSU.
OR SENSIBLE, AT LEAST.
BUT...
NO MORE SECOND CHANCES.
...
I WON'T NEED ANY.
GOOD.
NOW, SUIKO-TSU...
AND JAKOTSU...
YOU TWO WILL TAKE CARE OF THIS SESSHŌMARU.
OH, PLEASE-!

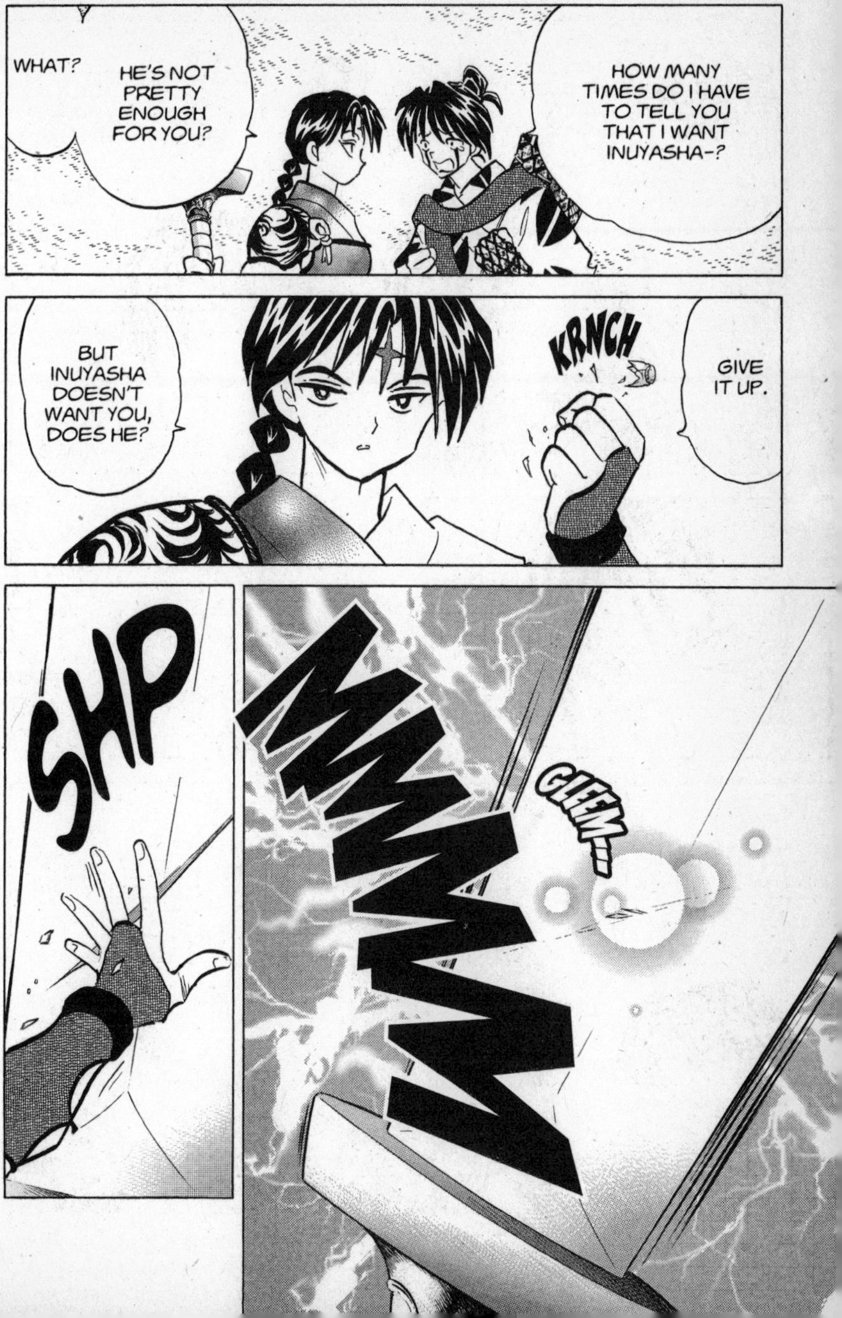
WHAT?
HE'S NOT PRETTY ENOUGH FOR YOU?
HOW MANY TIMES DO I HAVE TO TELL YOU THAT I WANT INUYASHA-?
BUT INUYASHA DOESN'T WANT YOU, DOES HE?
KRNCH
GIVE IT UP.
SHP
GLEEM-

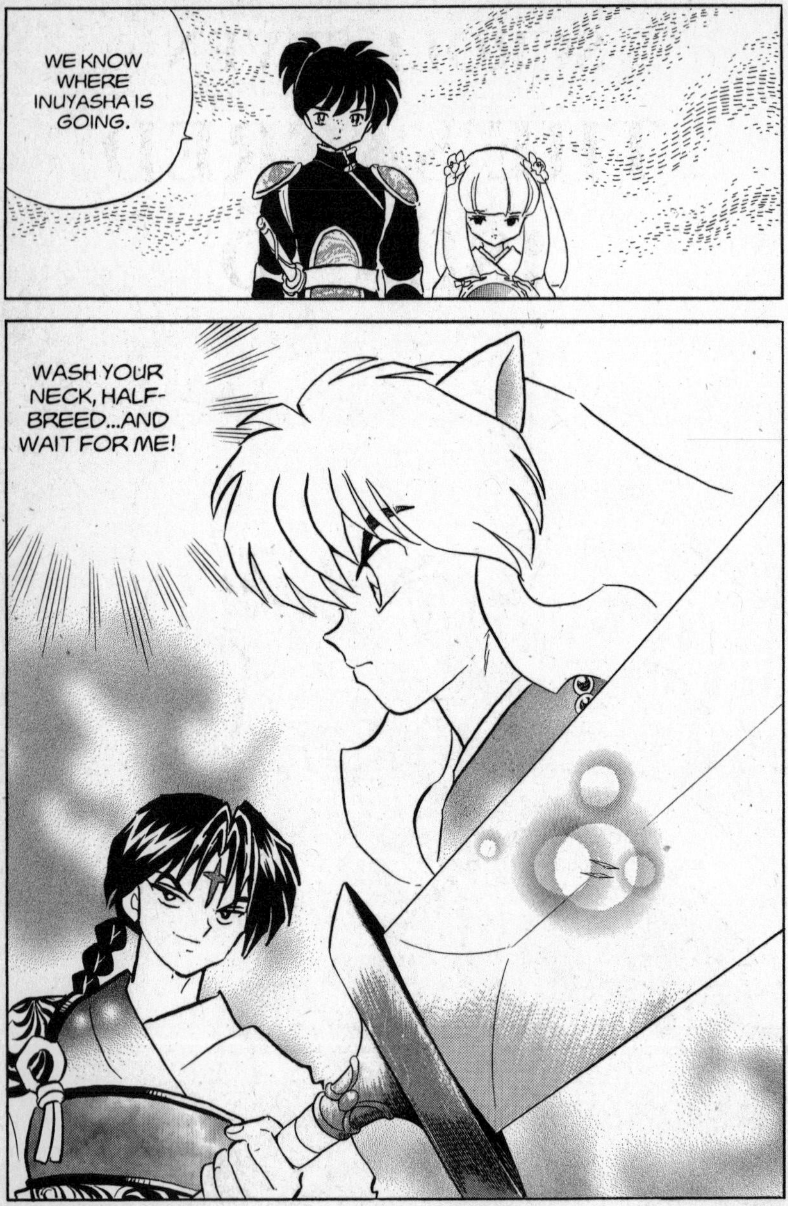
WE KNOW WHERE INUYASHA IS GOING.
WASH YOUR NECK, HALF-BREED...AND WAIT FOR ME!

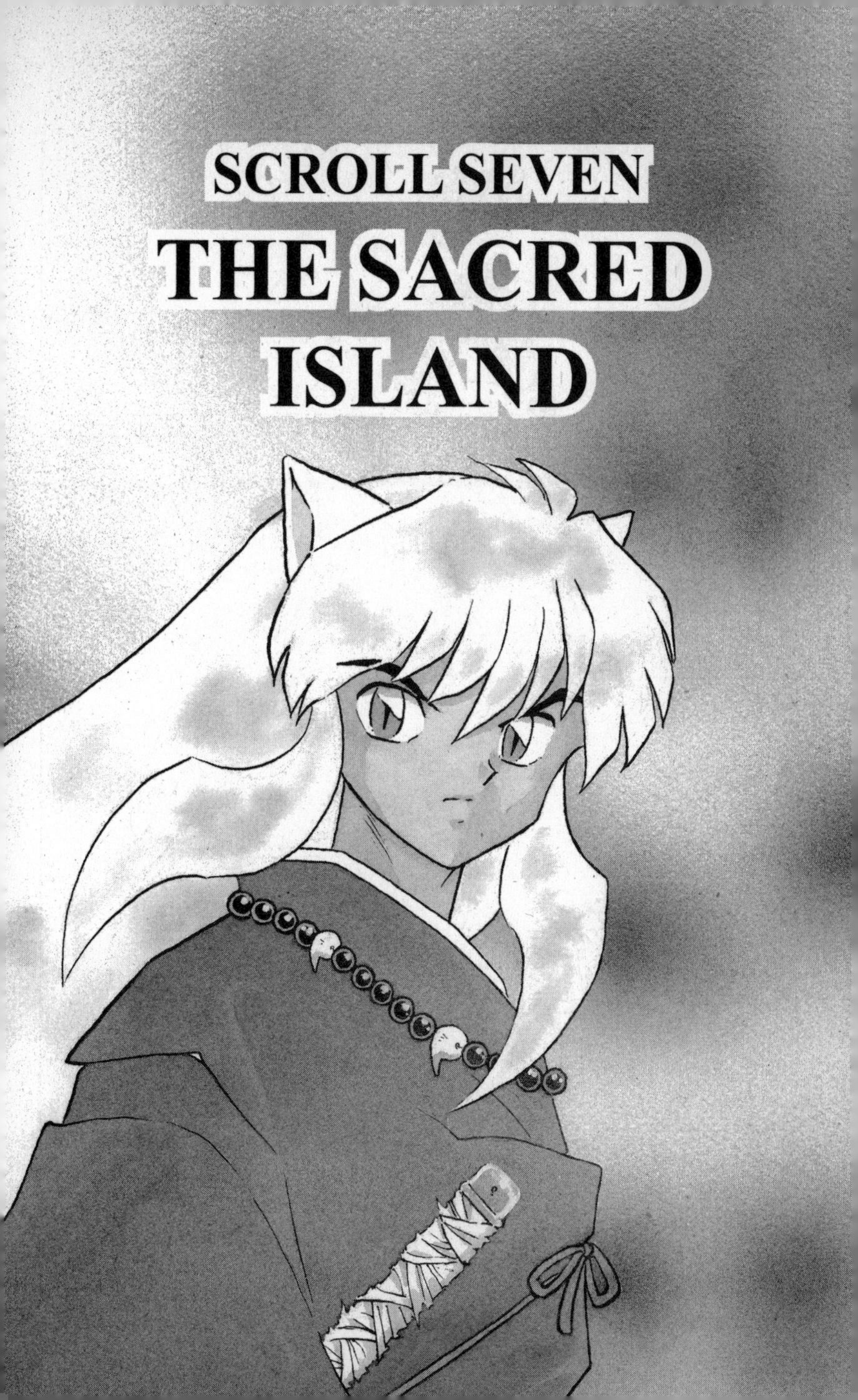
SCROLL SEVEN
THE SACRED ISLAND

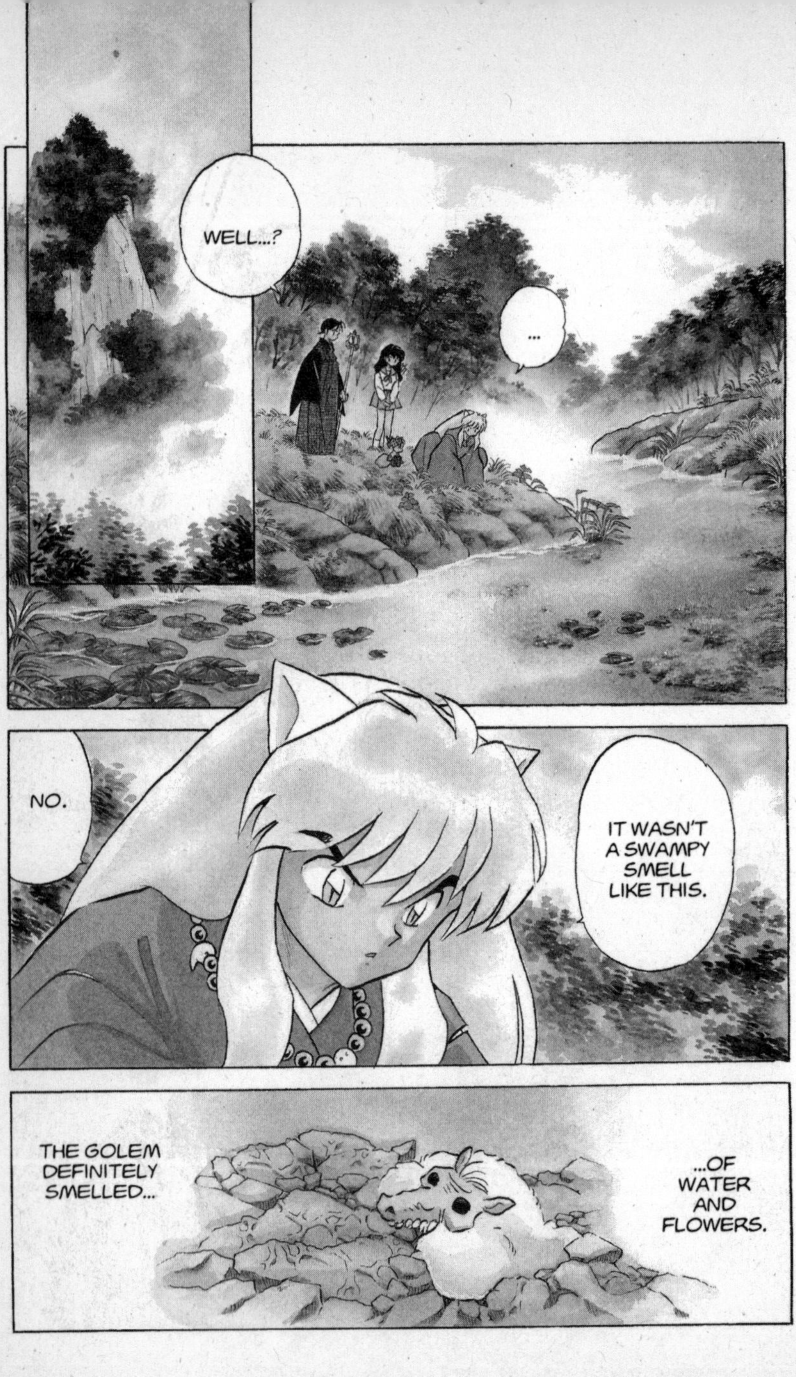
WELL...?
...
NO.
IT WASN'T A SWAMPY SMELL LIKE THIS.
THE GOLEM DEFINITELY SMELLED...
...OF WATER AND FLOWERS.

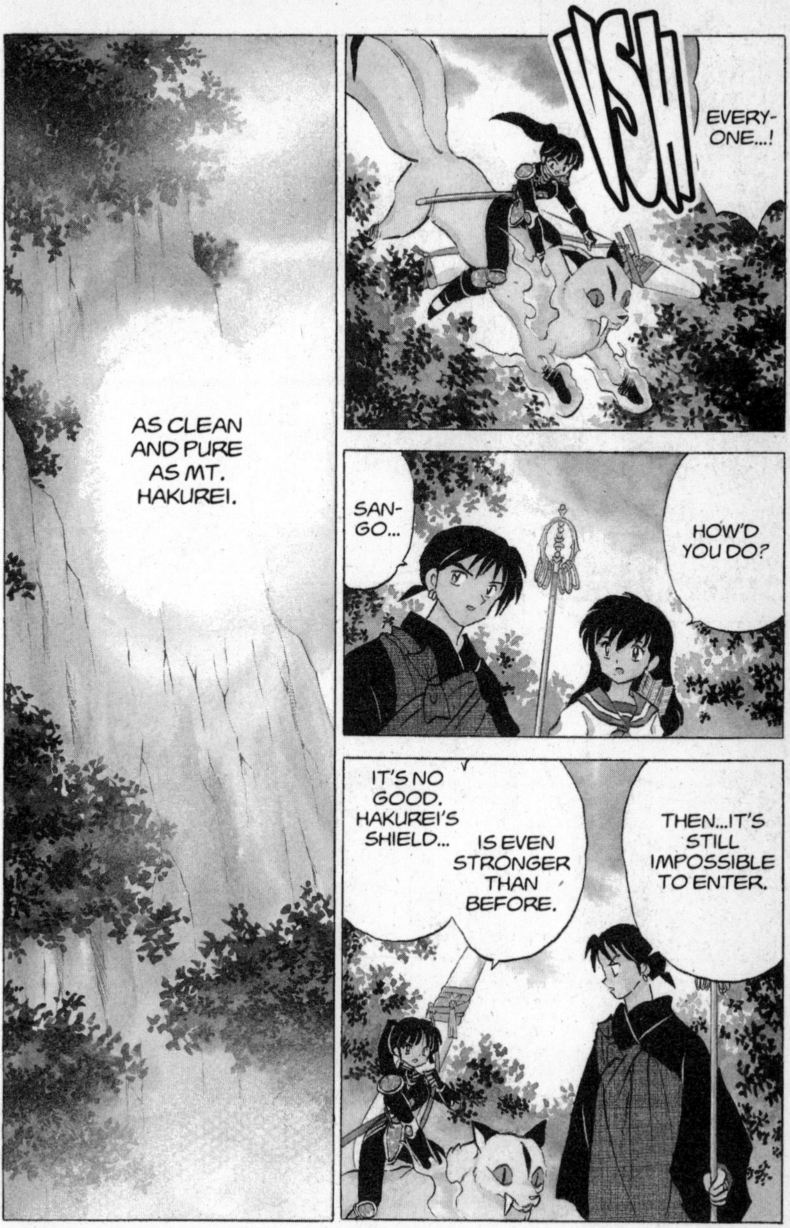
AS CLEAN AND PURE AS MT. HAKUREI.
VSH
EVERY-ONE...!
SAN-GO...
HOW'D YOU DO?
IT'S NO GOOD. HAKUREI'S SHIELD...
IS EVEN STRONGER THAN BEFORE.
THEN...IT'S STILL IMPOSSIBLE TO ENTER.

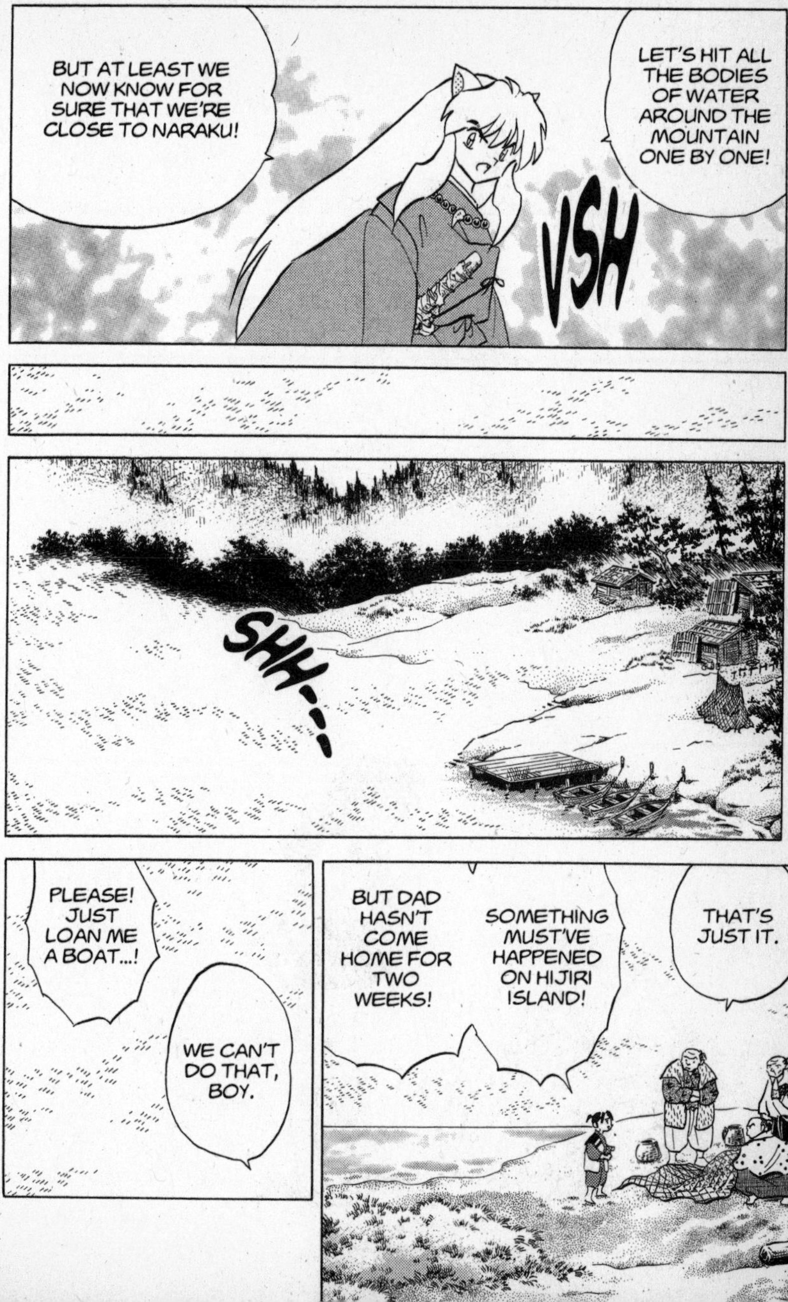
BUT AT LEAST WE NOW KNOW FOR SURE THAT WE'RE CLOSE TO NARAKU!
LET'S HIT ALL THE BODIES OF WATER AROUND THE MOUNTAIN ONE BY ONE!
VSH
SHH...
PLEASE! JUST LOAN ME A BOAT...!
WE CAN'T DO THAT, BOY.
BUT DAD HASN'T COME HOME FOR TWO WEEKS!
SOMETHING MUST'VE HAPPENED ON HIJIRI ISLAND!
THAT'S JUST IT.

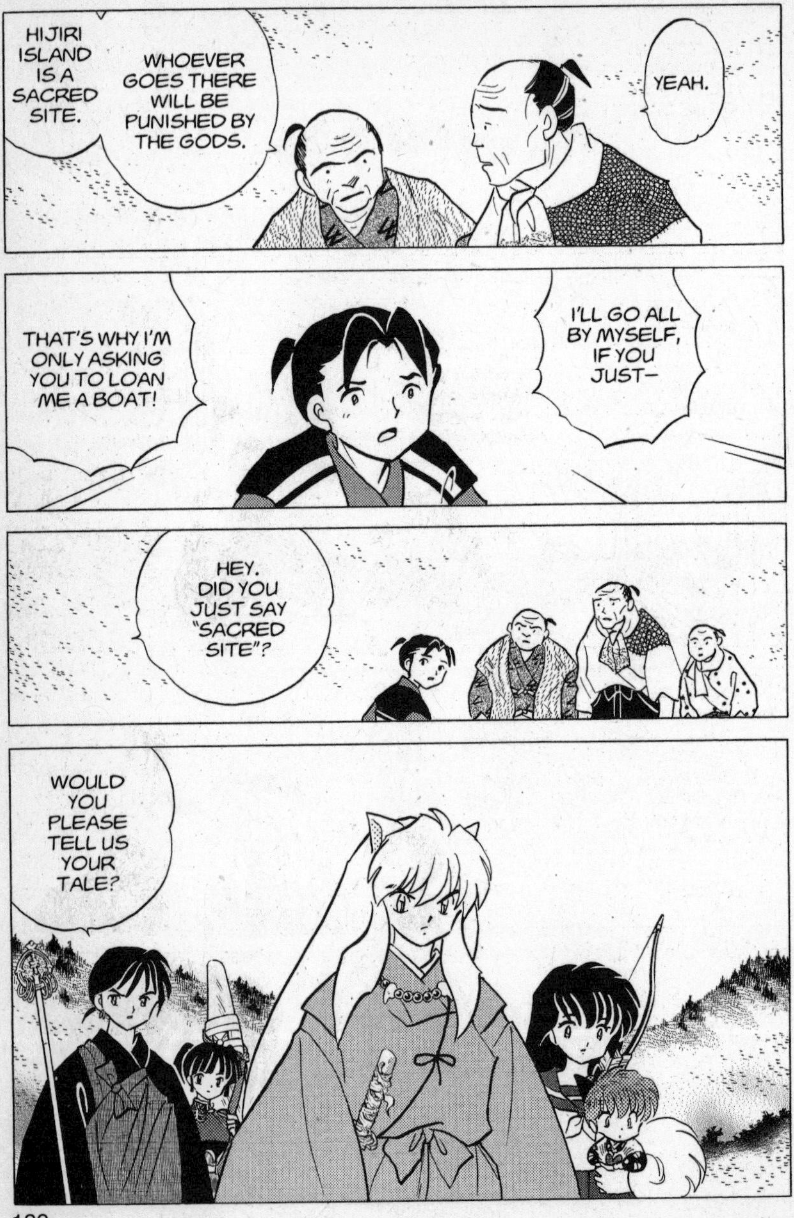
HIJIRI ISLAND IS A SACRED SITE.
WHOEVER GOES THERE WILL BE PUNISHED BY THE GODS.
YEAH.
THAT'S WHY I'M ONLY ASKING YOU TO LOAN ME A BOAT!
I'LL GO ALL BY MYSELF, IF YOU JUST—
HEY. DID YOU JUST SAY "SACRED SITE"?
WOULD YOU PLEASE TELL US YOUR TALE?

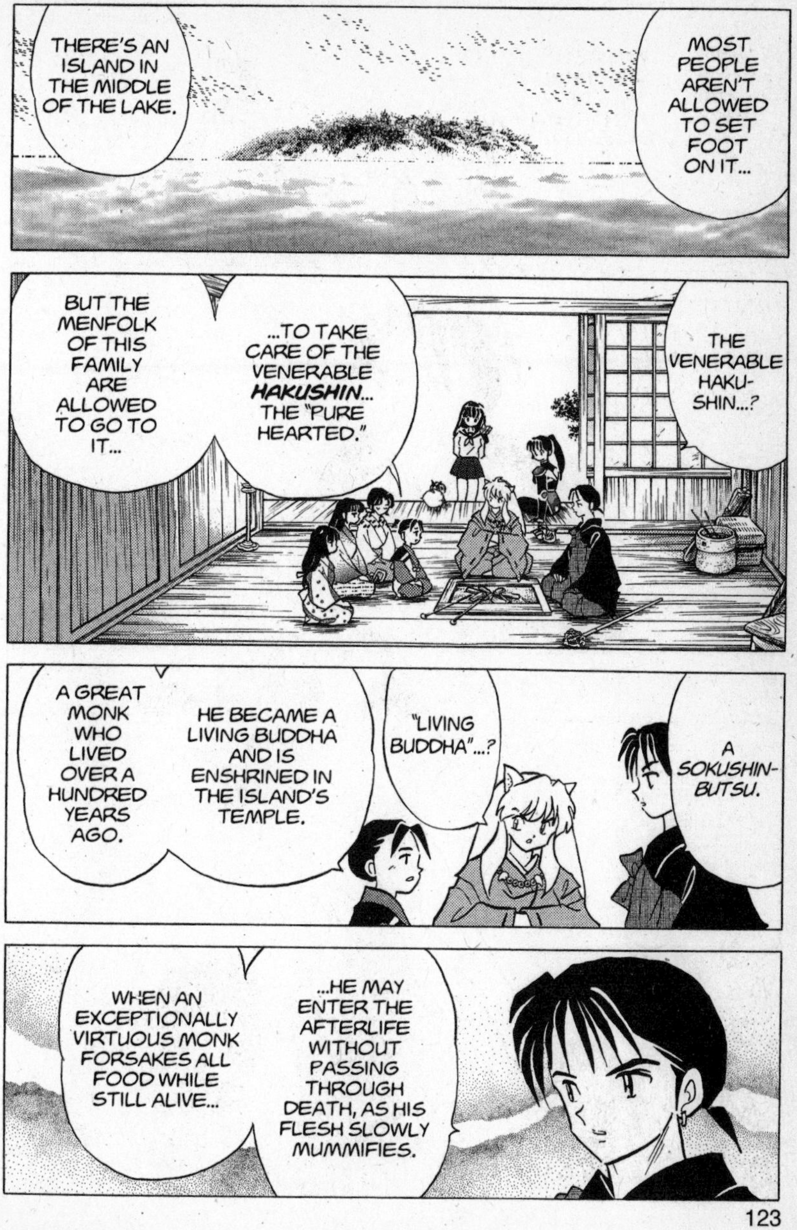
THERE'S AN ISLAND IN THE MIDDLE OF THE LAKE.
MOST PEOPLE AREN'T ALLOWED TO SET FOOT ON IT...
BUT THE MENFOLK OF THIS FAMILY ARE ALLOWED TO GO TO IT...
...TO TAKE CARE OF THE VENERABLE ***HAKUSHIN***... THE "PURE HEARTED."
THE VENERABLE HAKU-SHIN...?
A GREAT MONK WHO LIVED OVER A HUNDRED YEARS AGO.
HE BECAME A LIVING BUDDHA AND IS ENSHRINED IN THE ISLAND'S TEMPLE.
"LIVING BUDDHA"...?
A SOKUSHIN-BUTSU.
WHEN AN EXCEPTIONALLY VIRTUOUS MONK FORSAKES ALL FOOD WHILE STILL ALIVE...
...HE MAY ENTER THE AFTERLIFE WITHOUT PASSING THROUGH DEATH, AS HIS FLESH SLOWLY MUMMIFIES.

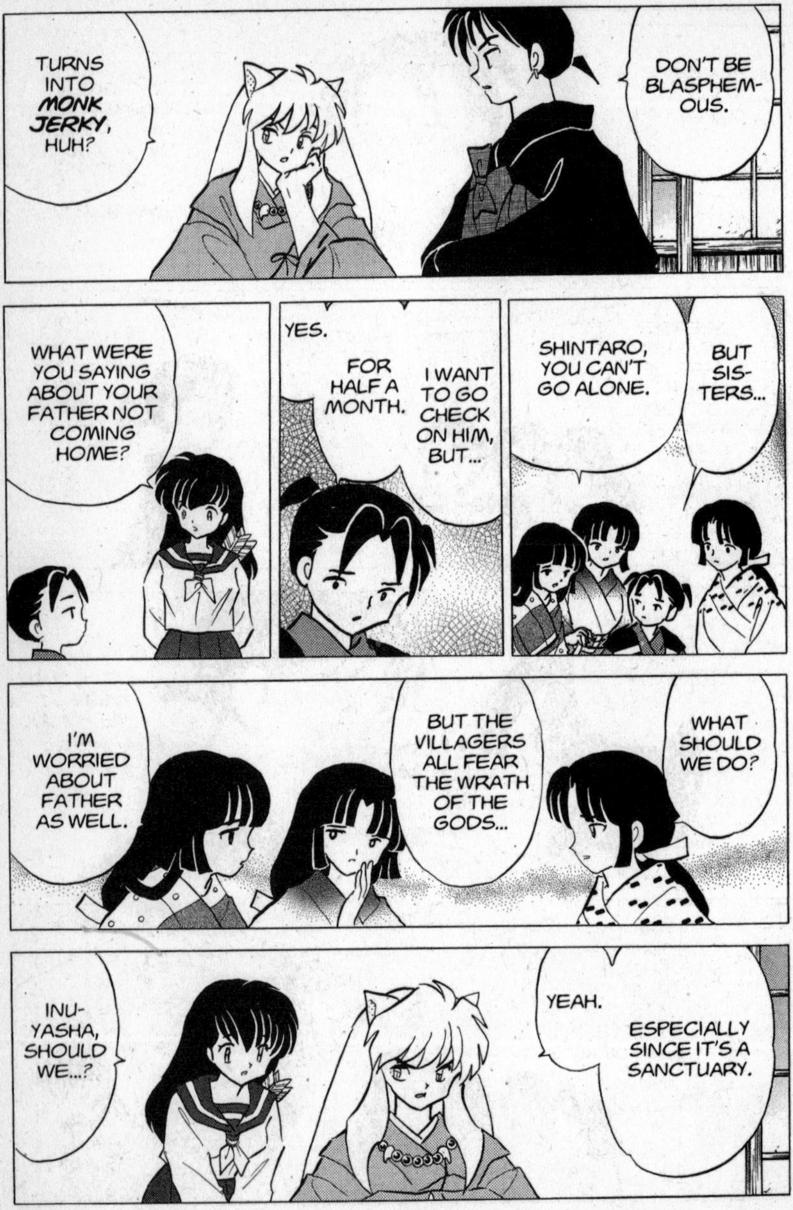
TURNS INTO **MONK JERKY**, HUH?
DON'T BE BLASPHEM-OUS.
WHAT WERE YOU SAYING ABOUT YOUR FATHER NOT COMING HOME?
YES.
FOR HALF A MONTH.
I WANT TO GO CHECK ON HIM, BUT...
SHINTARO, YOU CAN'T GO ALONE.
BUT SIS-TERS...
I'M WORRIED ABOUT FATHER AS WELL.
BUT THE VILLAGERS ALL FEAR THE WRATH OF THE GODS...
WHAT SHOULD WE DO?
INU-YASHA, SHOULD WE...?
YEAH.
ESPECIALLY SINCE IT'S A SANCTUARY.

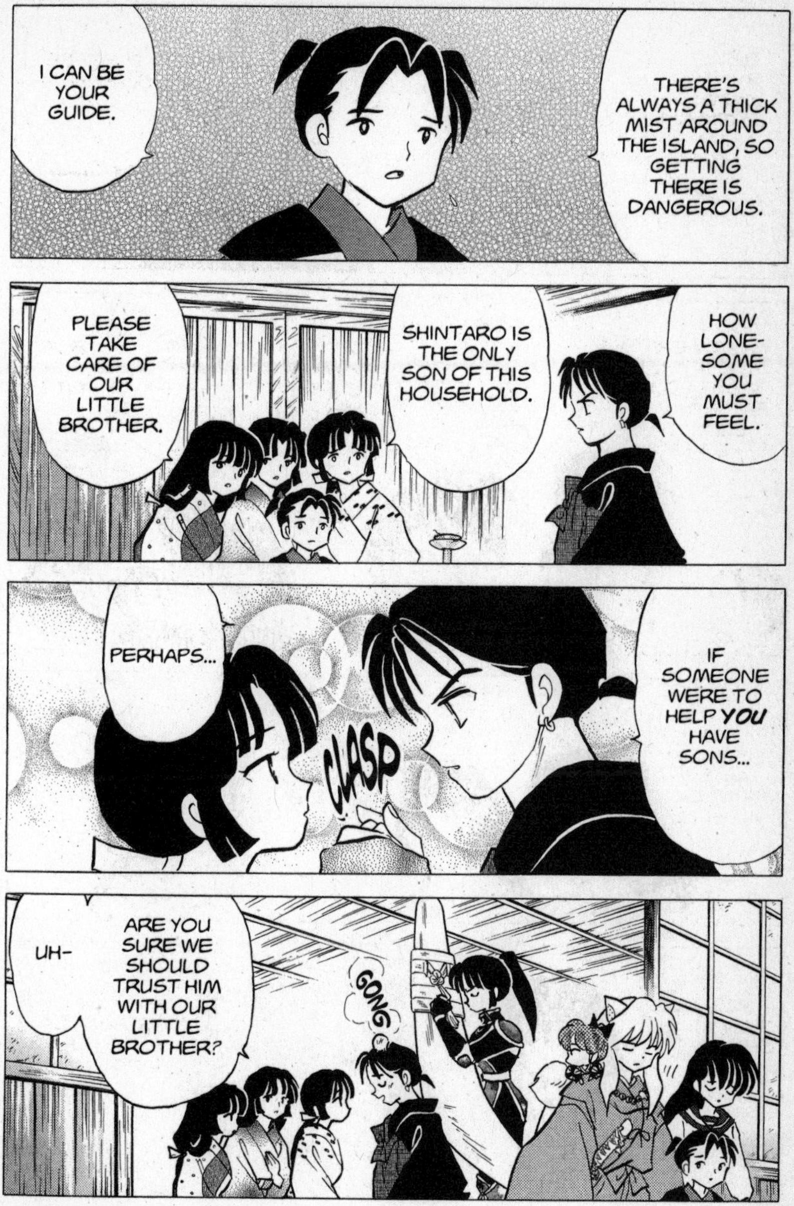
I CAN BE YOUR GUIDE.
THERE'S ALWAYS A THICK MIST AROUND THE ISLAND, SO GETTING THERE IS DANGEROUS.
PLEASE TAKE CARE OF OUR LITTLE BROTHER.
SHINTARO IS THE ONLY SON OF THIS HOUSEHOLD.
HOW LONE-SOME YOU MUST FEEL.
PERHAPS...
CLASP
IF SOMEONE WERE TO HELP *YOU* HAVE SONS...
UH-
ARE YOU SURE WE SHOULD TRUST HIM WITH OUR LITTLE BROTHER?
GONG

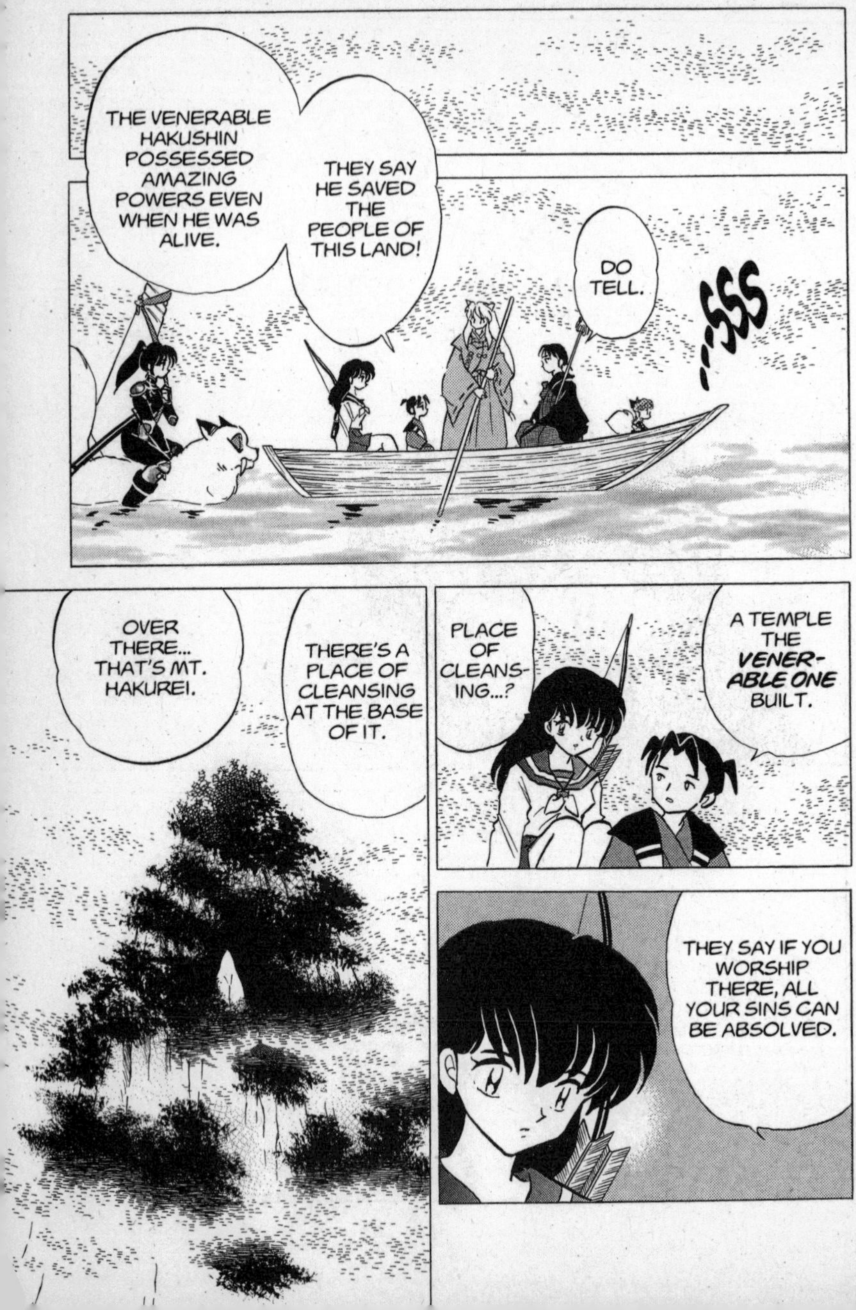
THE VENERABLE HAKUSHIN POSSESSED AMAZING POWERS EVEN WHEN HE WAS ALIVE.
THEY SAY HE SAVED THE PEOPLE OF THIS LAND!
DO TELL.
SSS...
OVER THERE... THAT'S MT. HAKUREI.
THERE'S A PLACE OF CLEANSING AT THE BASE OF IT.
PLACE OF CLEANSING...?
A TEMPLE THE VENERABLE ONE BUILT.
THEY SAY IF YOU WORSHIP THERE, ALL YOUR SINS CAN BE ABSOLVED.

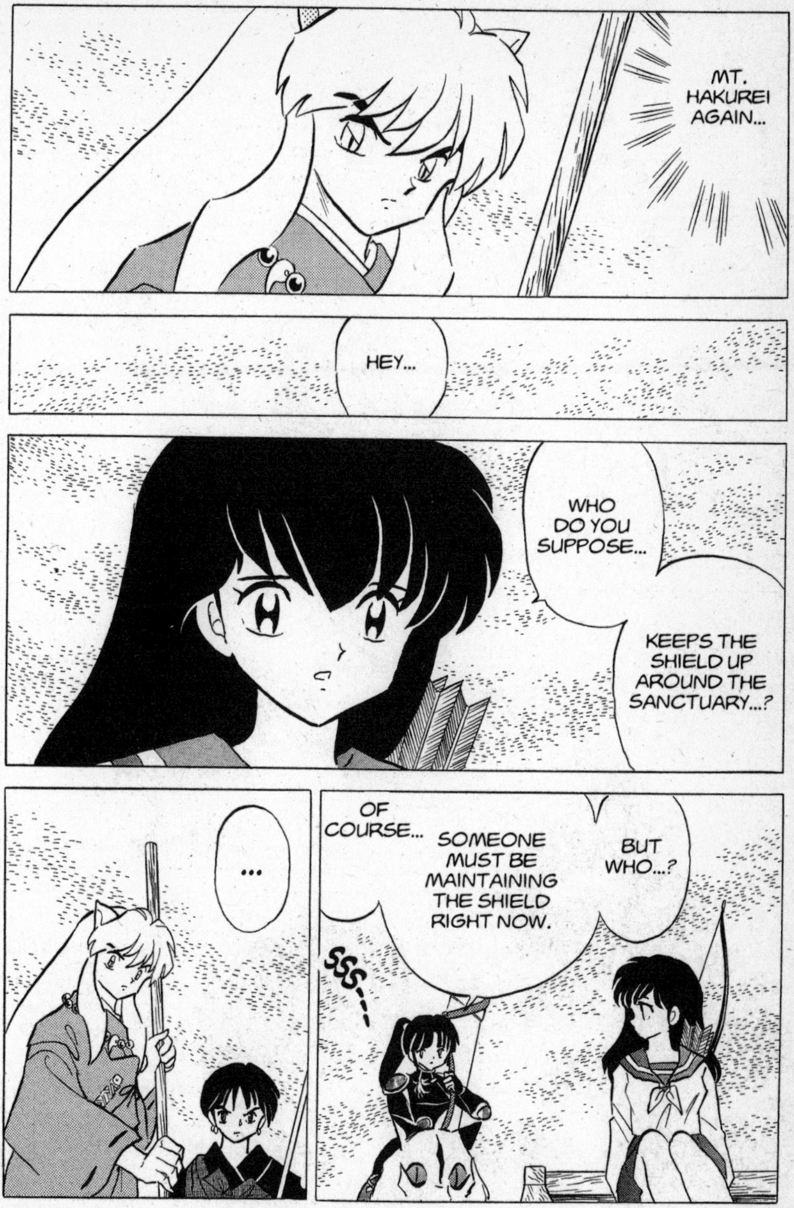
MT. HAKUREI AGAIN...
HEY...
WHO DO YOU SUPPOSE...
KEEPS THE SHIELD UP AROUND THE SANCTUARY...?
OF COURSE...
SOMEONE MUST BE MAINTAINING THE SHIELD RIGHT NOW.
BUT WHO...?
SSS...
...

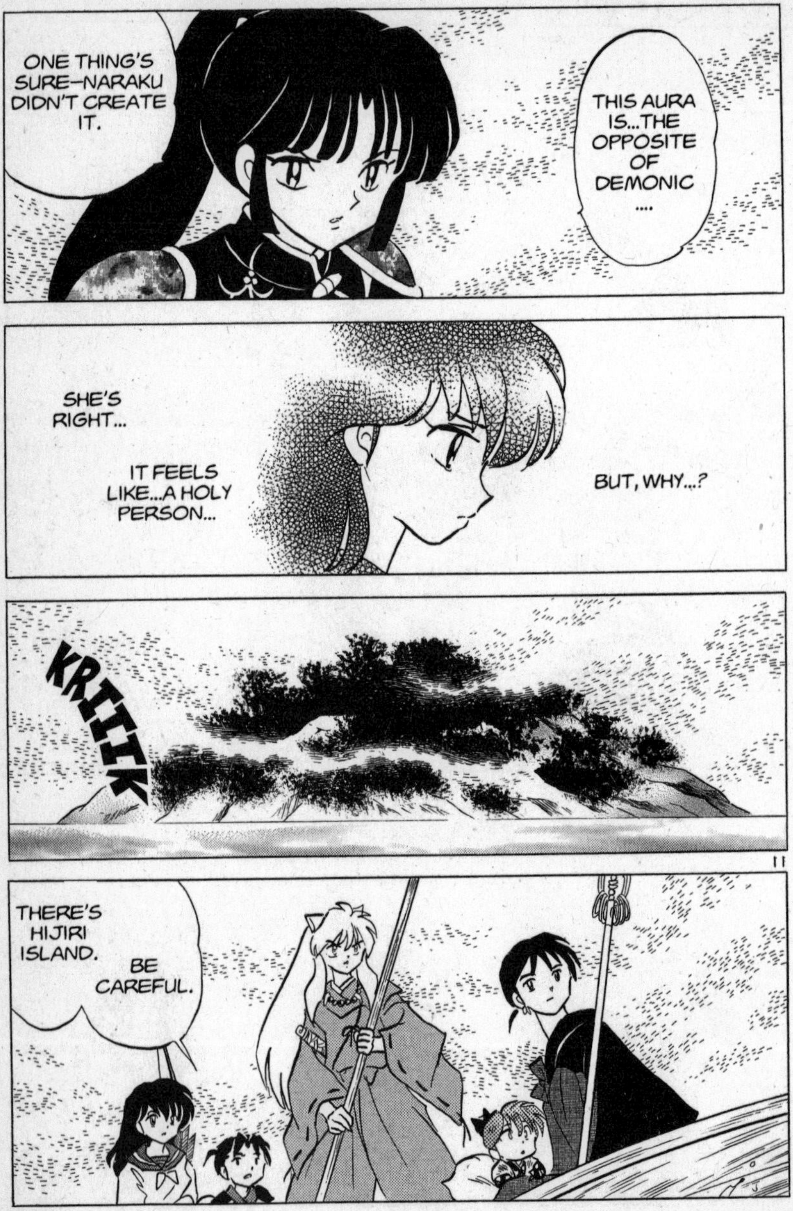
ONE THING'S SURE—NARAKU DIDN'T CREATE IT.
THIS AURA IS...THE OPPOSITE OF DEMONIC ....
SHE'S RIGHT...
IT FEELS LIKE...A HOLY PERSON...
BUT, WHY...?
KRIIIK
THERE'S HIJIRI ISLAND.
BE CAREFUL.

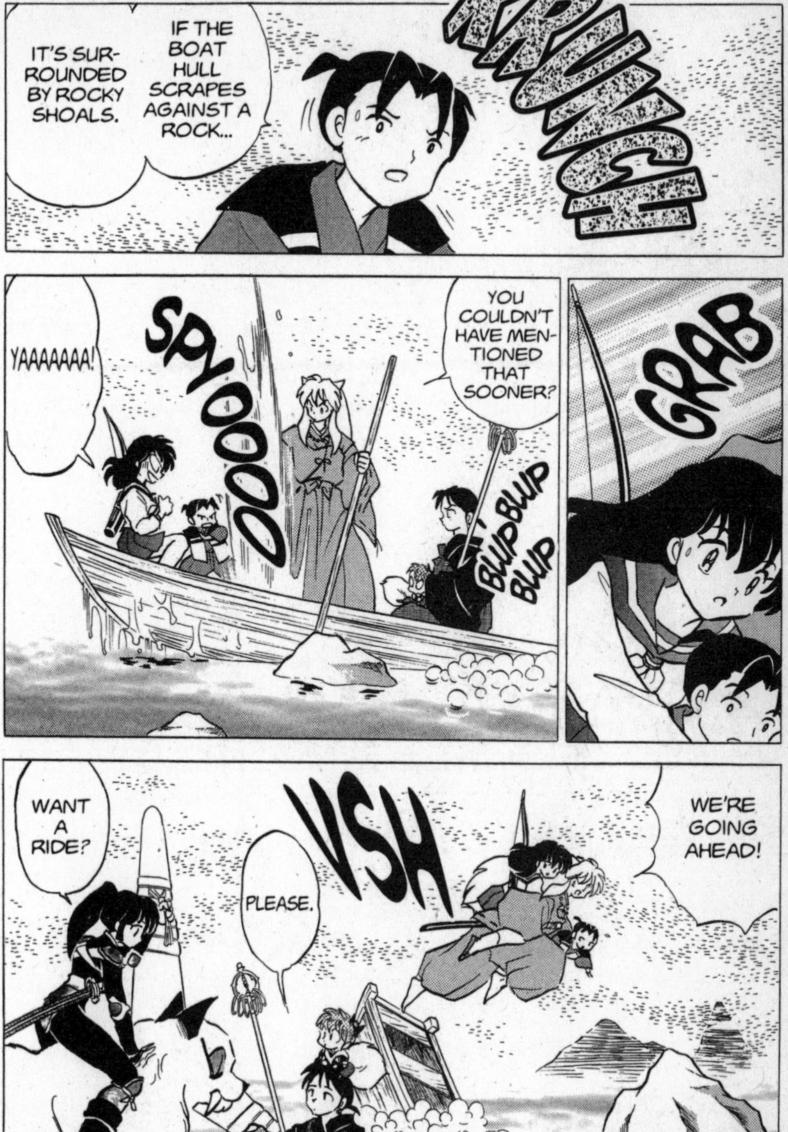
IT'S SUR-ROUNDED BY ROCKY SHOALS.
IF THE BOAT HULL SCRAPES AGAINST A ROCK...
KRUNCH!
YAAAAAAA!
SPYOOOO
YOU COULDN'T HAVE MEN-TIONED THAT SOONER?
BLUP BLUP BLUP
GRAB
WANT A RIDE?
PLEASE.
VSH
WE'RE GOING AHEAD!

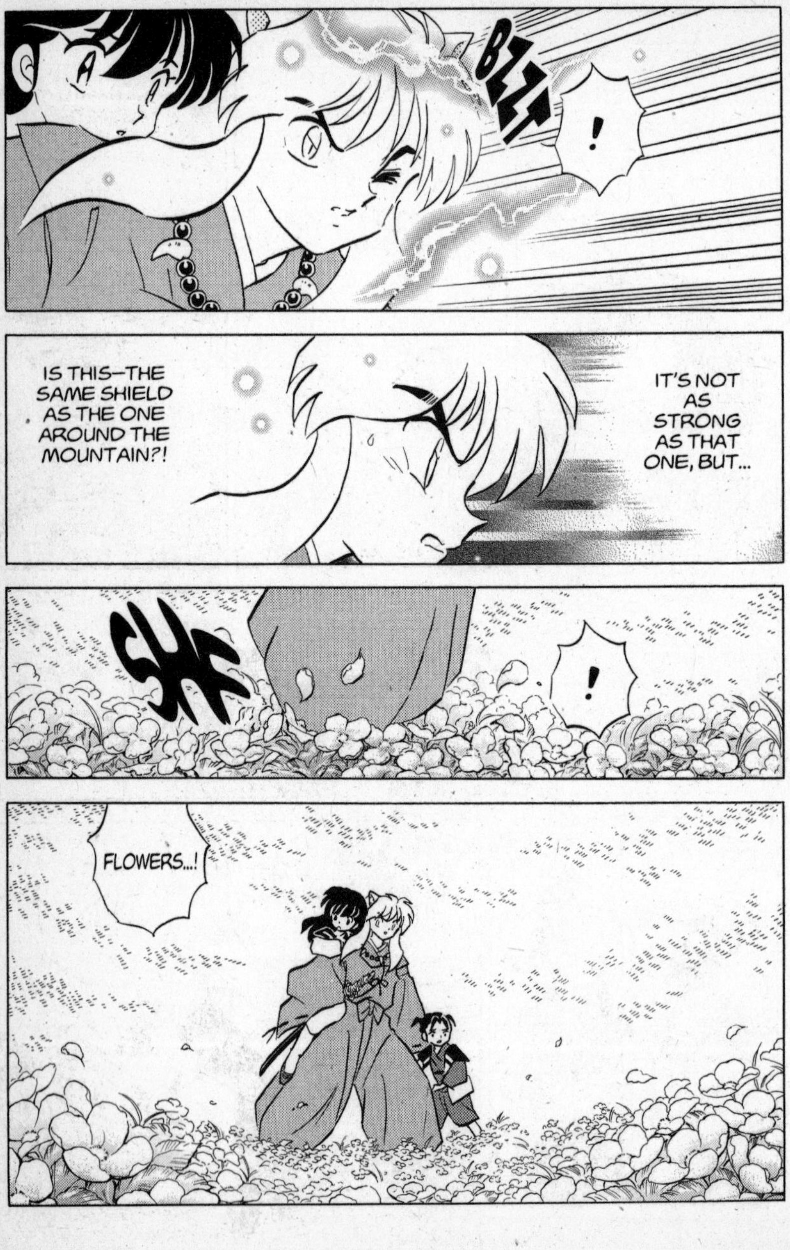
BZZT
!
IS THIS—THE SAME SHIELD AS THE ONE AROUND THE MOUNTAIN?!
IT'S NOT AS STRONG AS THAT ONE, BUT...
SHF
!
FLOWERS...!

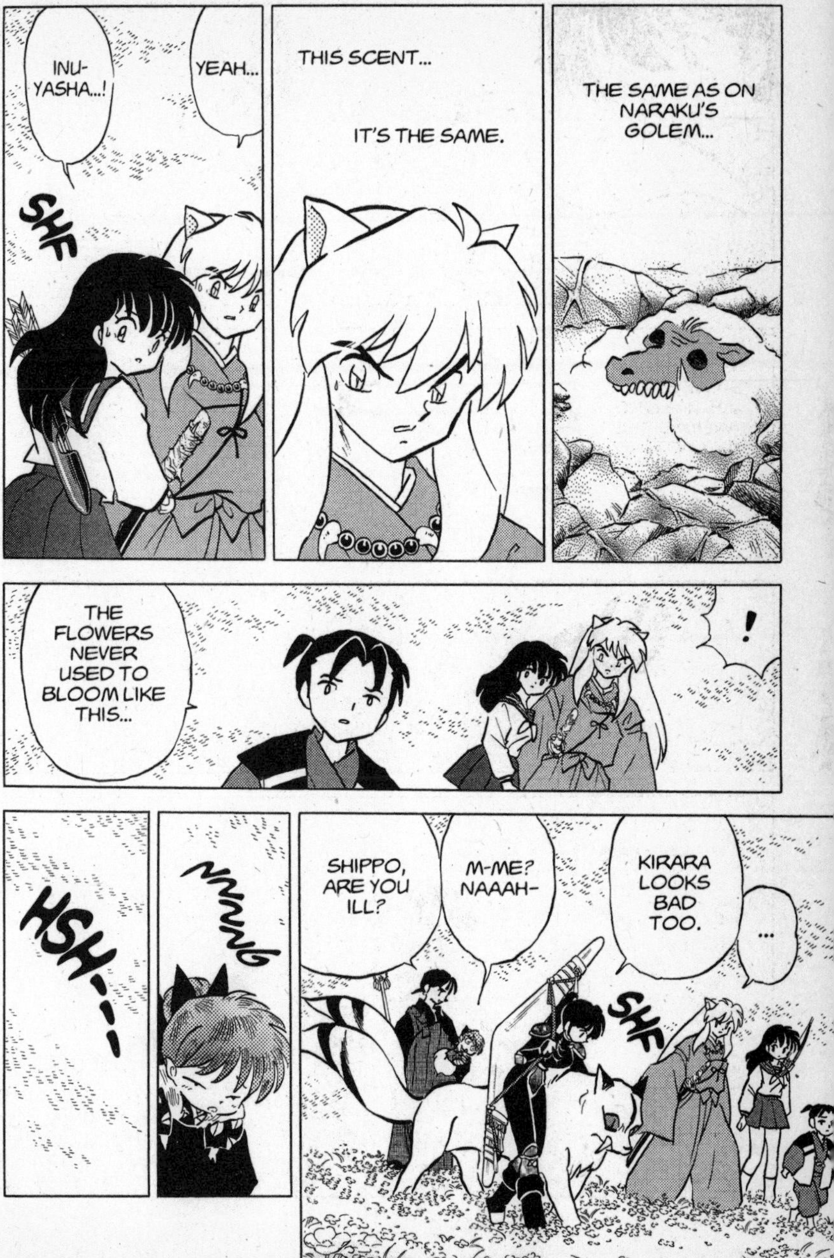
INU-YASHA...!
YEAH...
SHF
THIS SCENT...
IT'S THE SAME.
THE SAME AS ON NARAKU'S GOLEM...
THE FLOWERS NEVER USED TO BLOOM LIKE THIS...
!
HSH-...
NNNNG
SHIPPO, ARE YOU ILL?
M-ME? NAAAH-
KIRARA LOOKS BAD TOO.
...
SHF

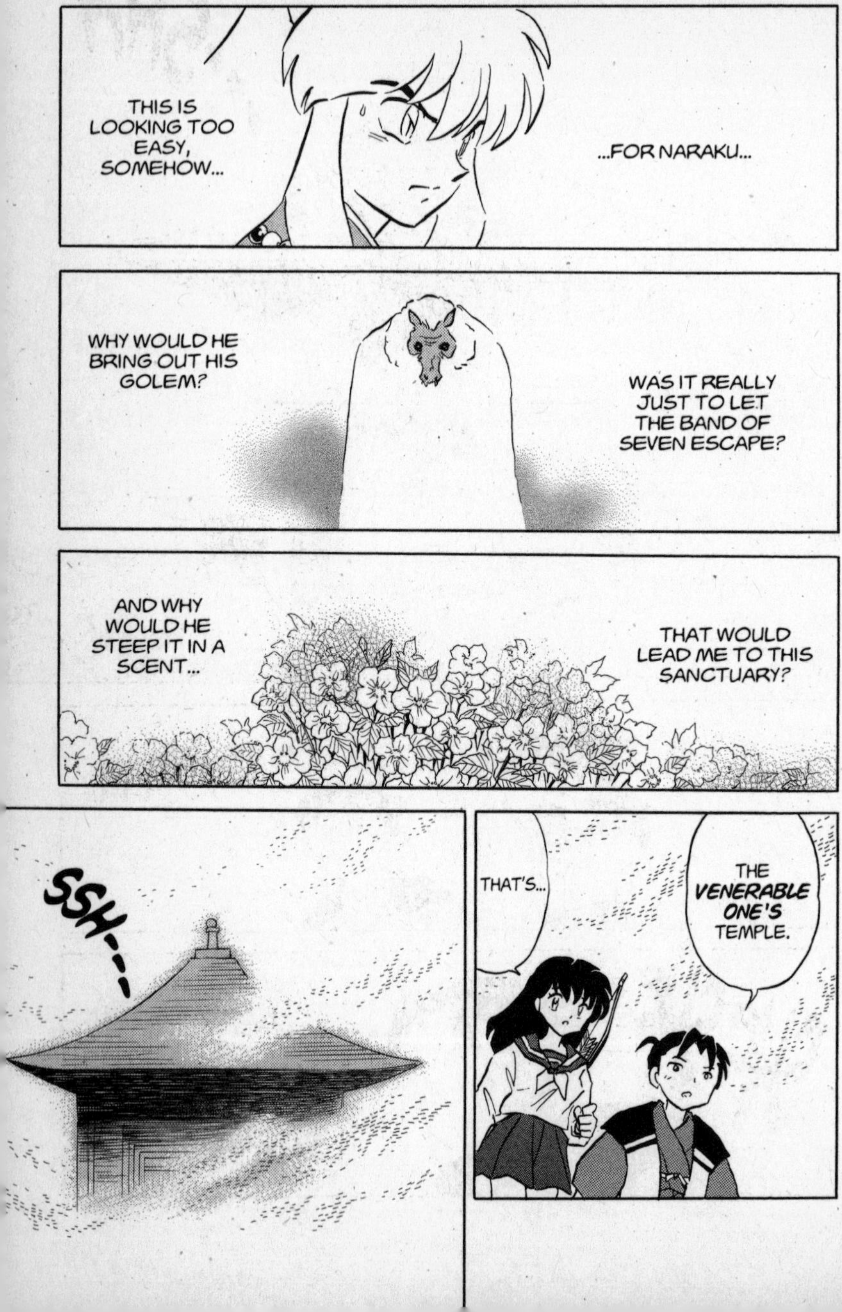
THIS IS LOOKING TOO EASY, SOMEHOW...
...FOR NARAKU...
WHY WOULD HE BRING OUT HIS GOLEM?
WAS IT REALLY JUST TO LET THE BAND OF SEVEN ESCAPE?
AND WHY WOULD HE STEEP IT IN A SCENT...
THAT WOULD LEAD ME TO THIS SANCTUARY?
SSH---
THAT'S...
THE *VENERABLE ONE'S* TEMPLE.

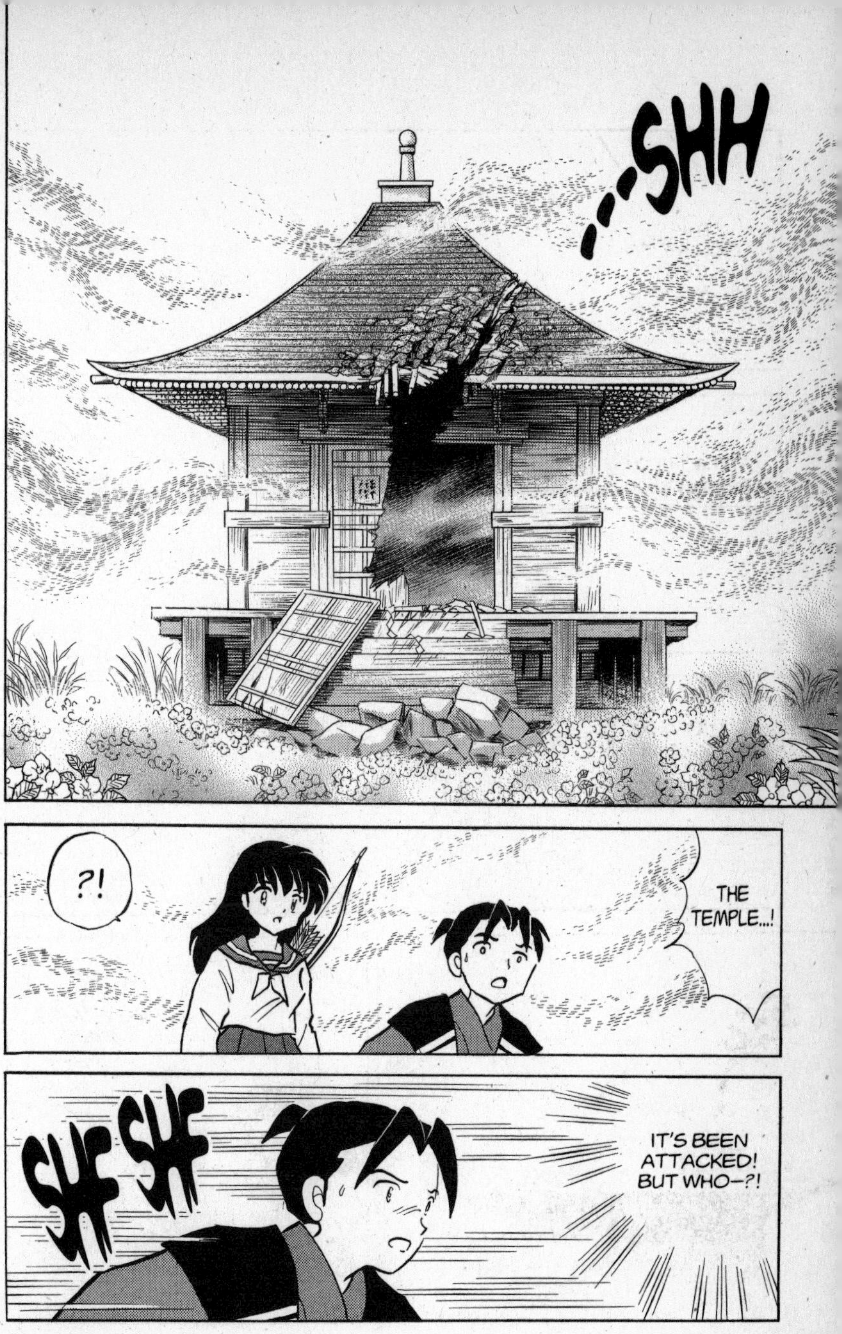
...SHH
?!
THE TEMPLE...!
SHF SHF
IT'S BEEN ATTACKED! BUT WHO—?!

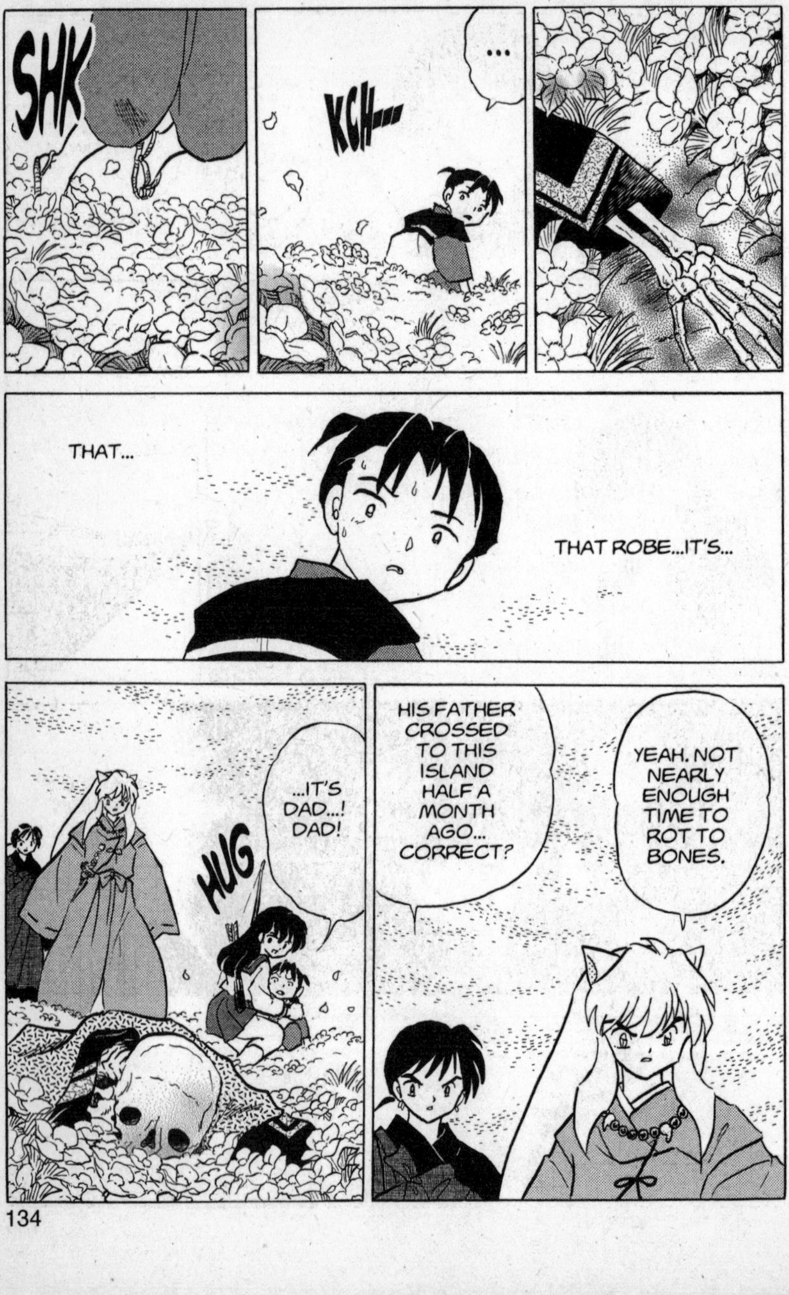
SHK
KCH...
...
THAT...
THAT ROBE...IT'S...
...IT'S DAD...! DAD!
HUG
HIS FATHER CROSSED TO THIS ISLAND HALF A MONTH AGO... CORRECT?
YEAH. NOT NEARLY ENOUGH TIME TO ROT TO BONES.

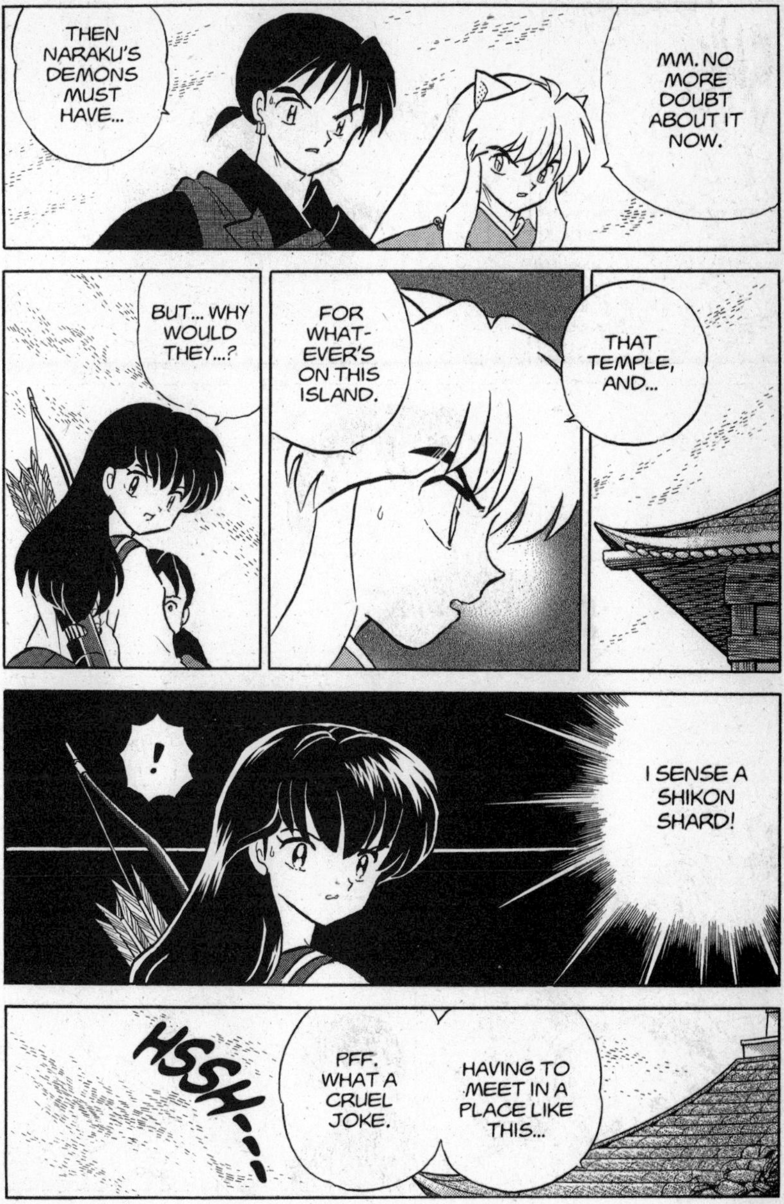
THEN NARAKU'S DEMONS MUST HAVE...
MM. NO MORE DOUBT ABOUT IT NOW.
BUT... WHY WOULD THEY...?
FOR WHAT-EVER'S ON THIS ISLAND.
THAT TEMPLE, AND...
!
I SENSE A SHIKON SHARD!
HSSH...
PFF. WHAT A CRUEL JOKE.
HAVING TO MEET IN A PLACE LIKE THIS...

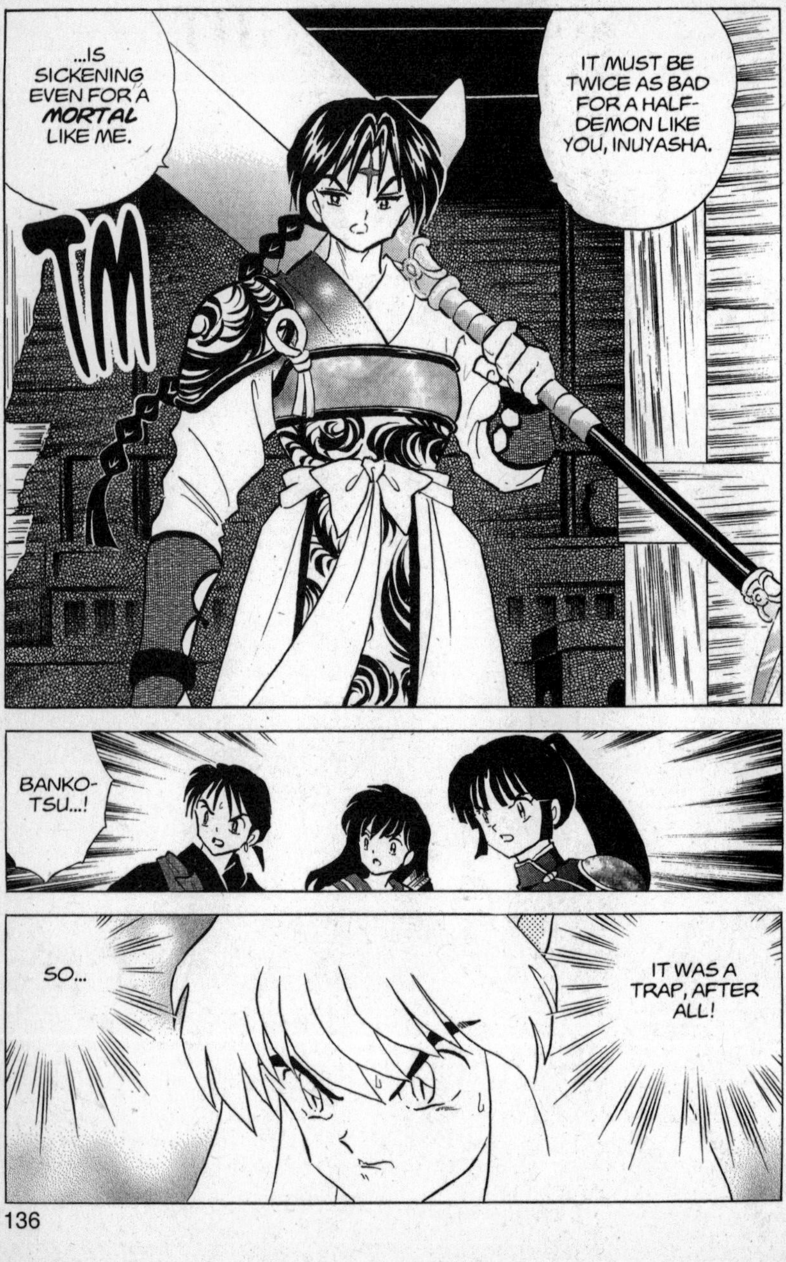
...IS SICKENING EVEN FOR A ***MORTAL*** LIKE ME.
IT MUST BE TWICE AS BAD FOR A HALF-DEMON LIKE YOU, INUYASHA.
TM
BANKO-TSU...!
SO...
IT WAS A TRAP, AFTER ALL!

SCROLL EIGHT

THE CENTER OF THE SHIELD

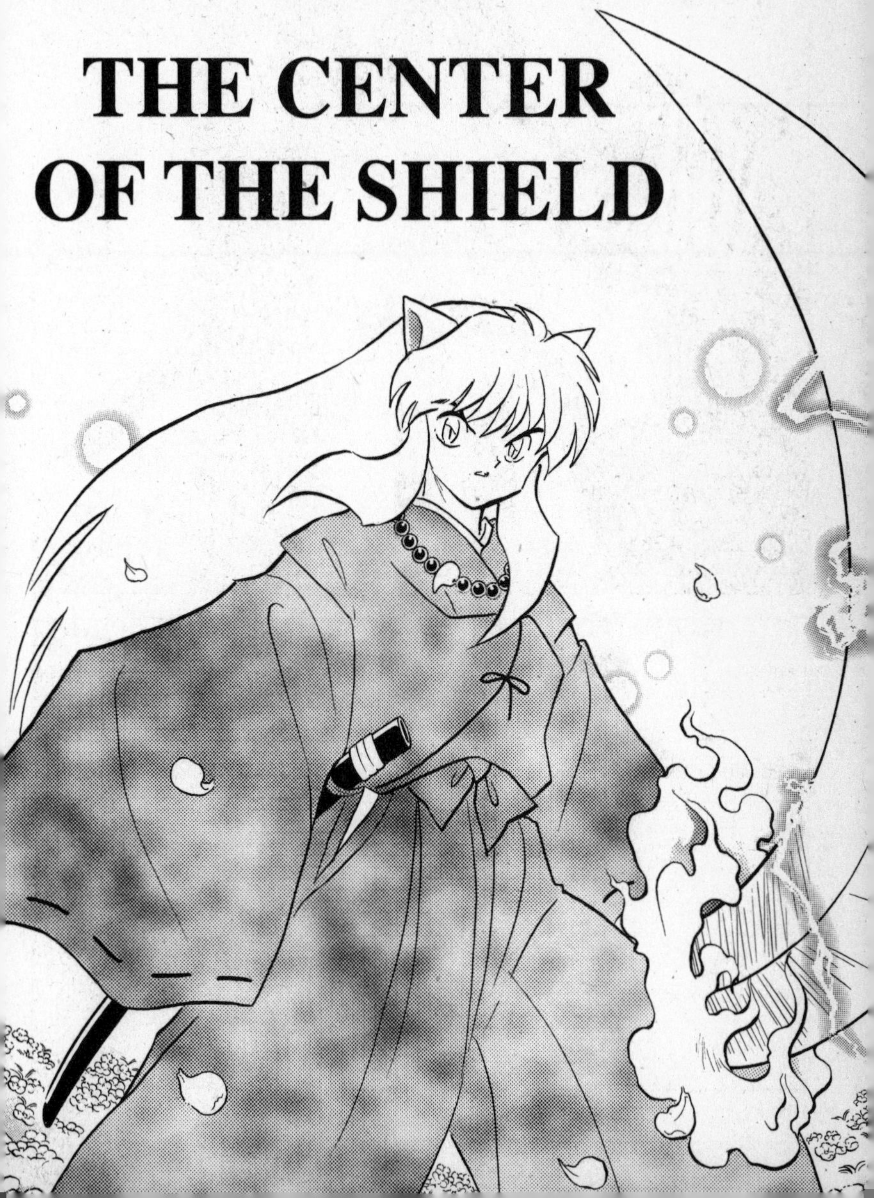

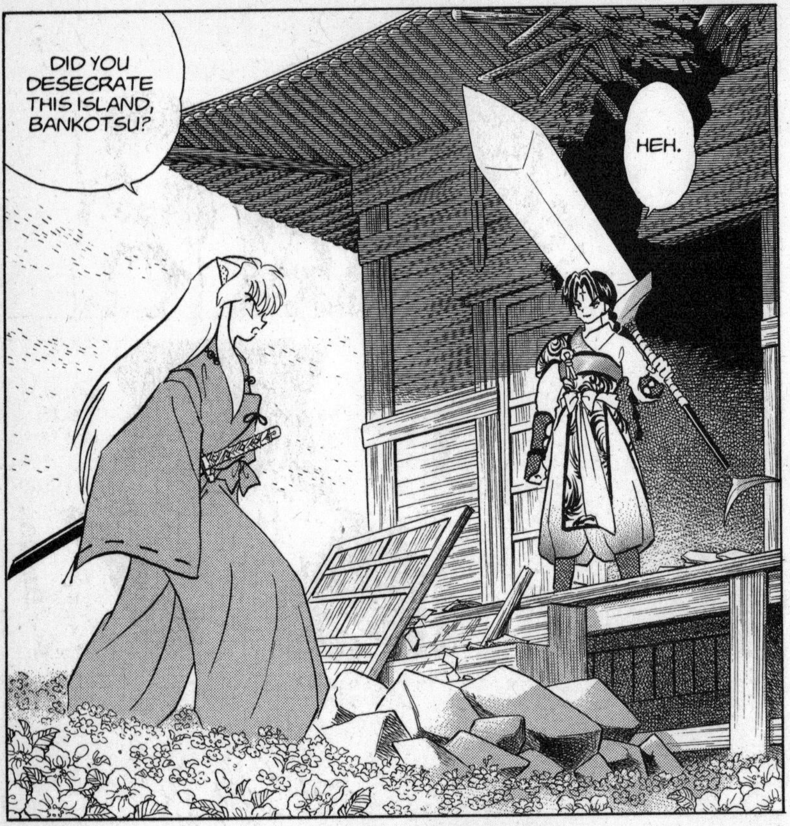
DID YOU DESECRATE THIS ISLAND, BANKOTSU?
HEH.

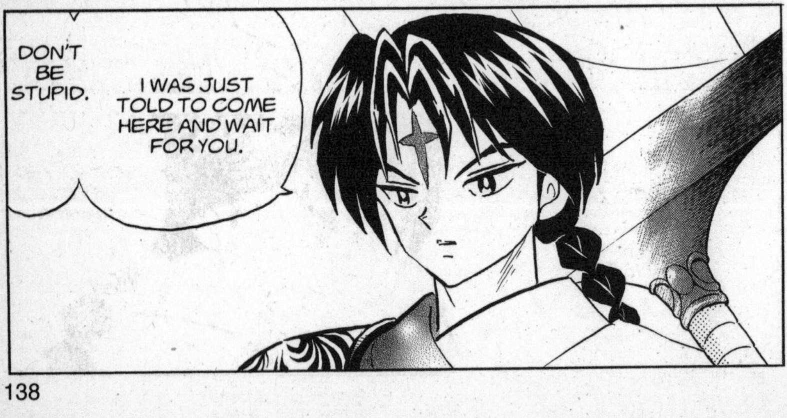
DON'T BE STUPID.
I WAS JUST TOLD TO COME HERE AND WAIT FOR YOU.

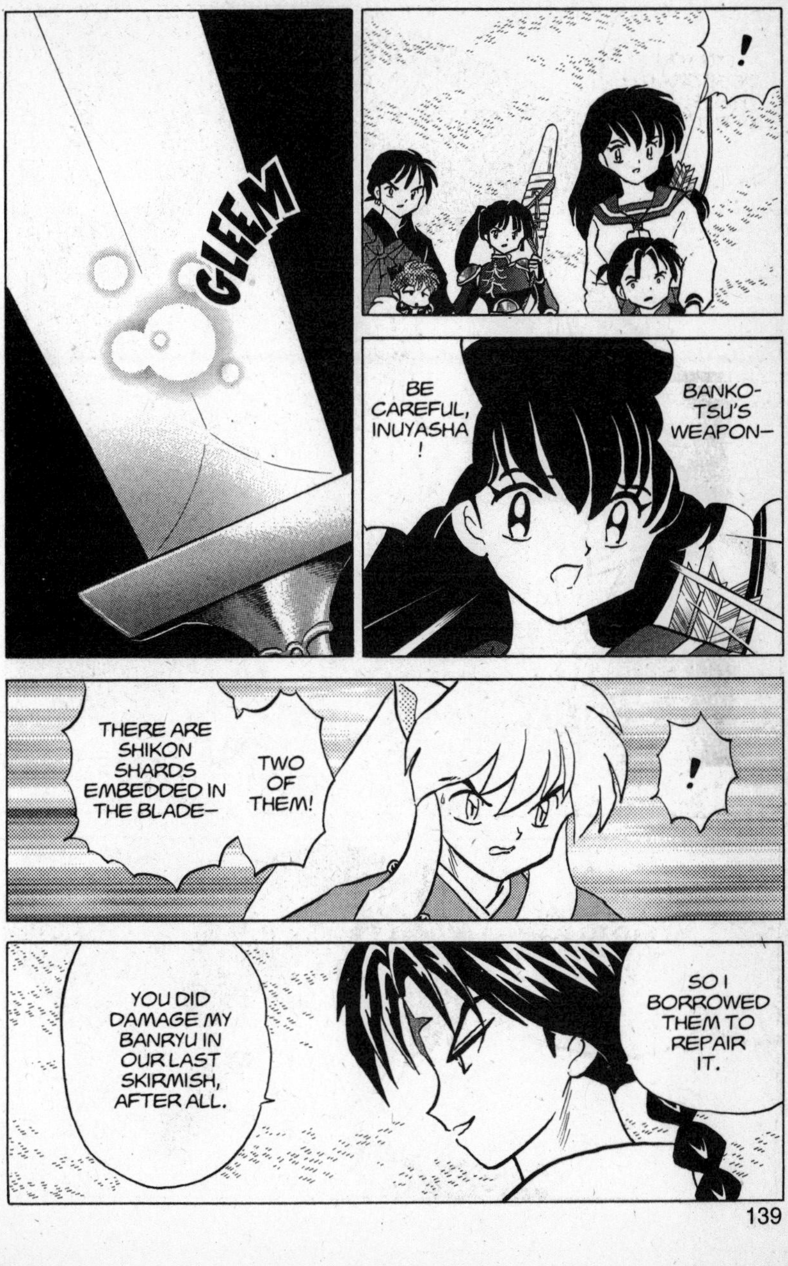
GLEEM
!
BE CAREFUL, INUYASHA!
BANKO-TSU'S WEAPON–
THERE ARE SHIKON SHARDS EMBEDDED IN THE BLADE–
TWO OF THEM!
!
YOU DID DAMAGE MY BANRYU IN OUR LAST SKIRMISH, AFTER ALL.
SO I BORROWED THEM TO REPAIR IT.

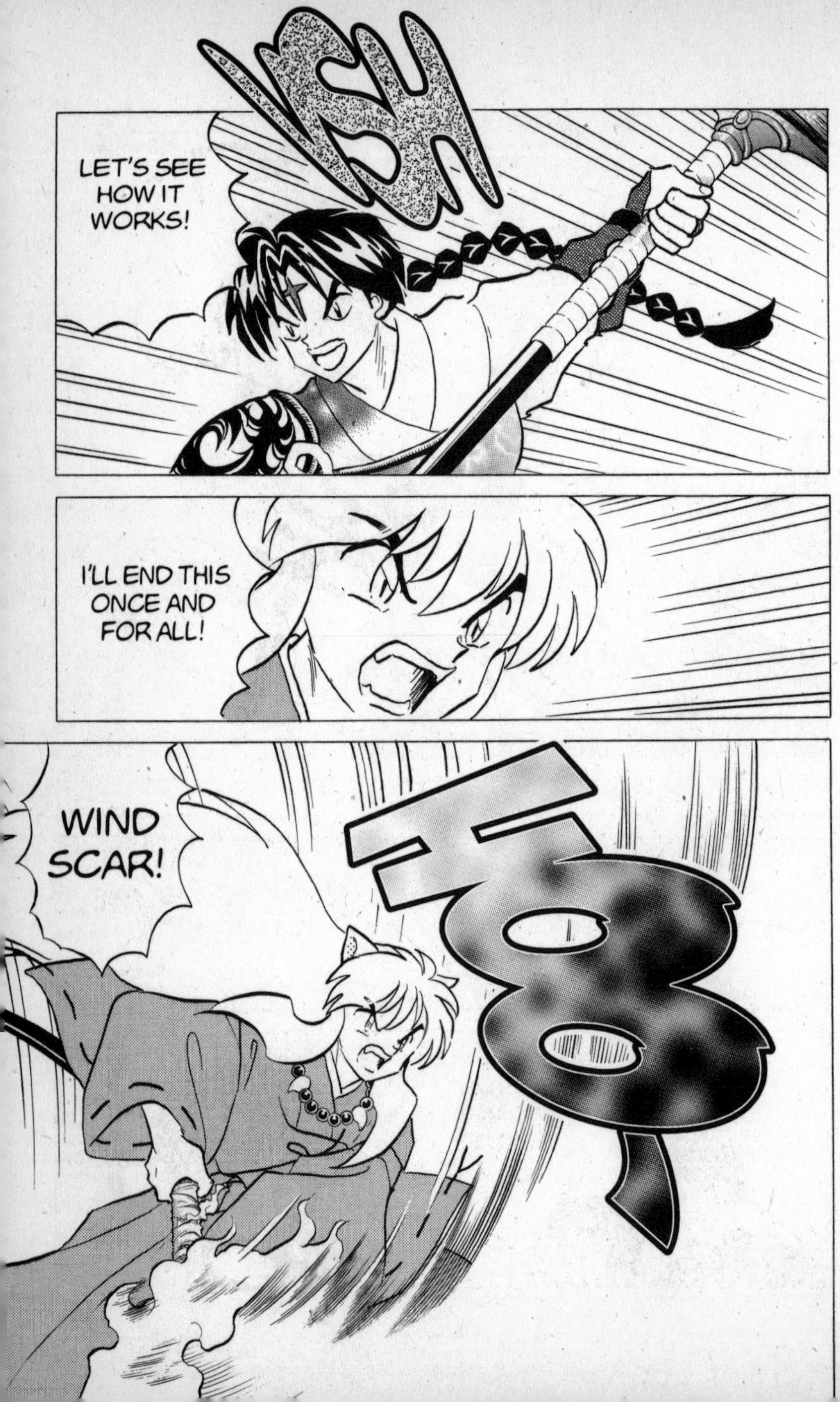
VSH
LET'S SEE HOW IT WORKS!
I'LL END THIS ONCE AND FOR ALL!
WIND SCAR!
FOO

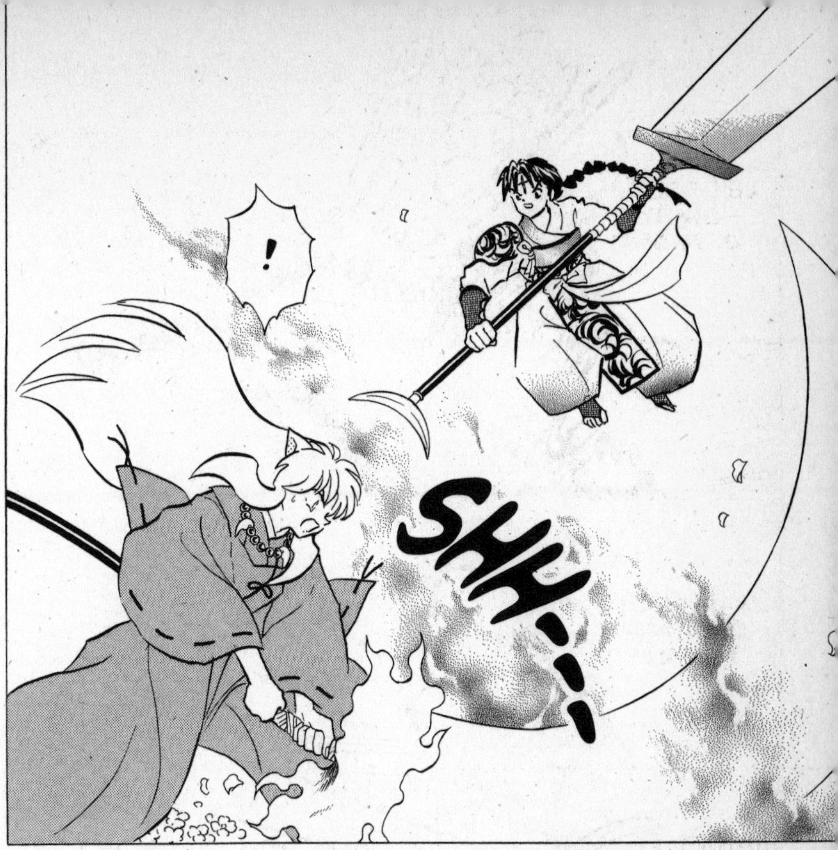
!
SHH---

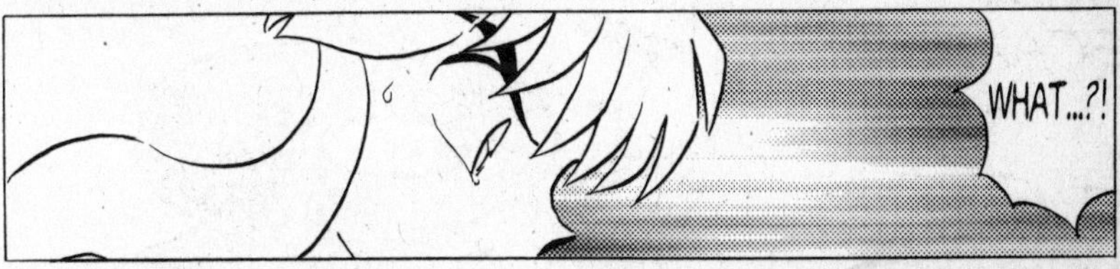
WHAT...?!

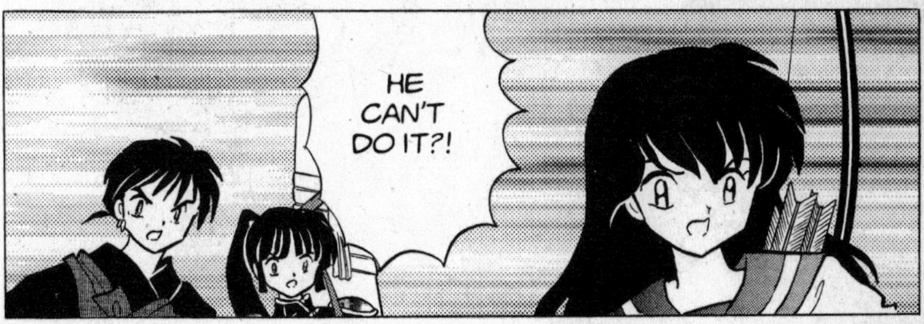
HE CAN'T DO IT?!

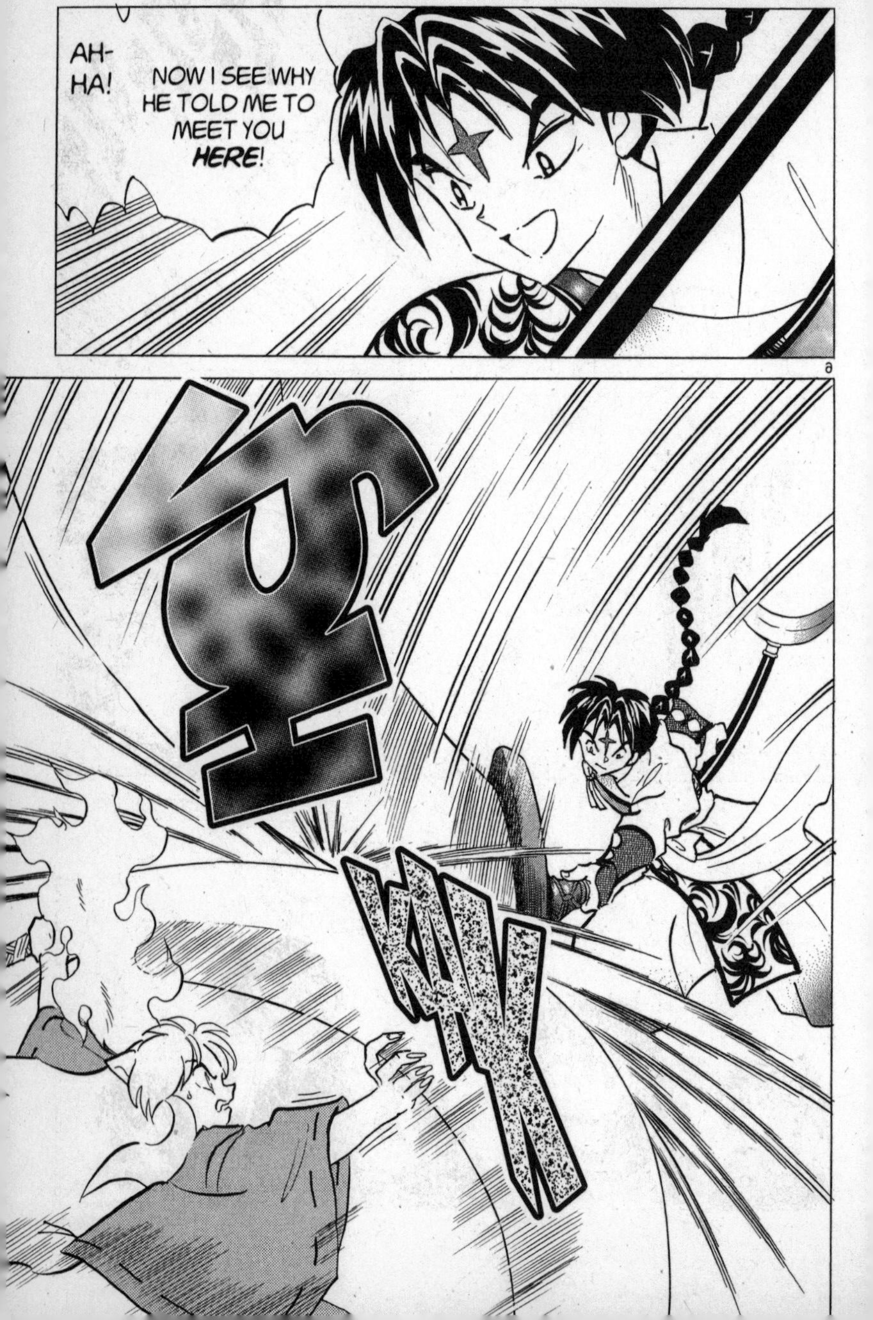
AH-HA!
NOW I SEE WHY HE TOLD ME TO MEET YOU **HERE**!

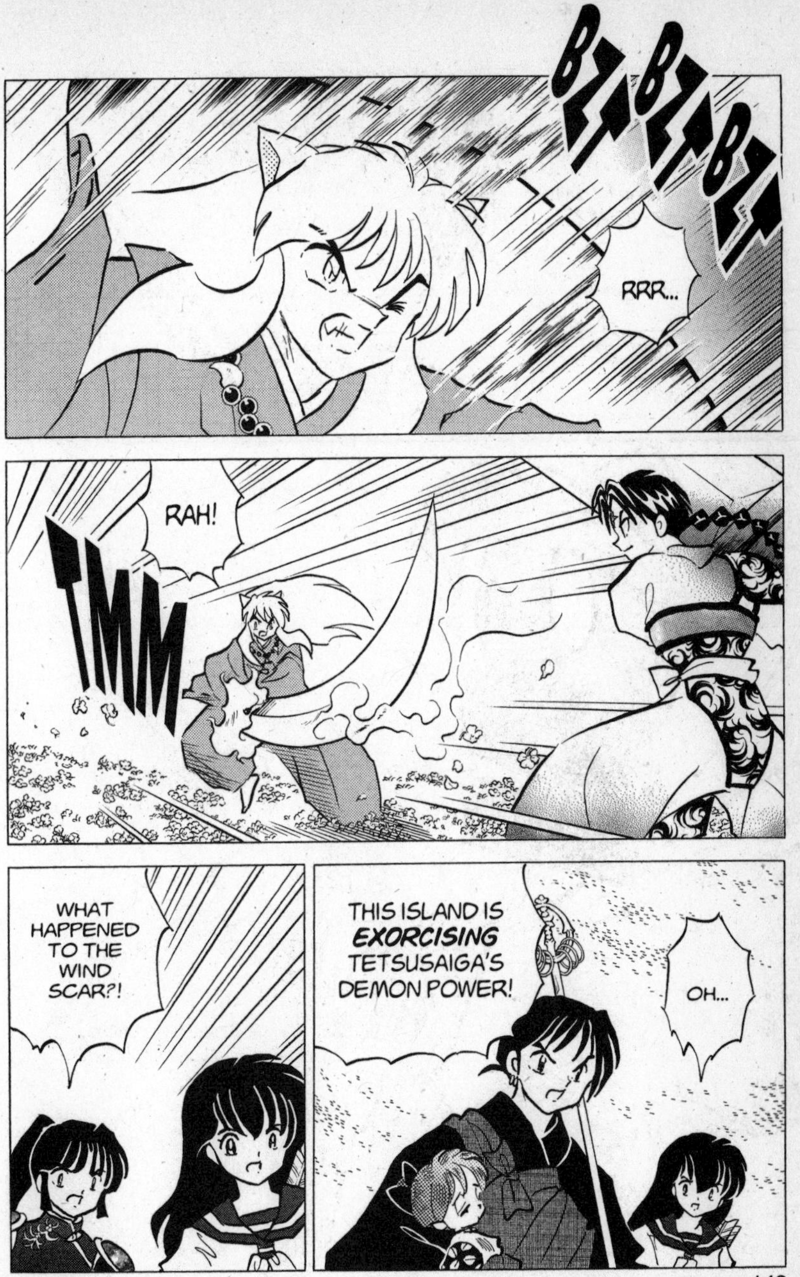
BZT BZT BZT
RRR...
RAH!
TMM
WHAT HAPPENED TO THE WIND SCAR?!
THIS ISLAND IS *EXORCISING* TETSUSAIGA'S DEMON POWER!
OH...

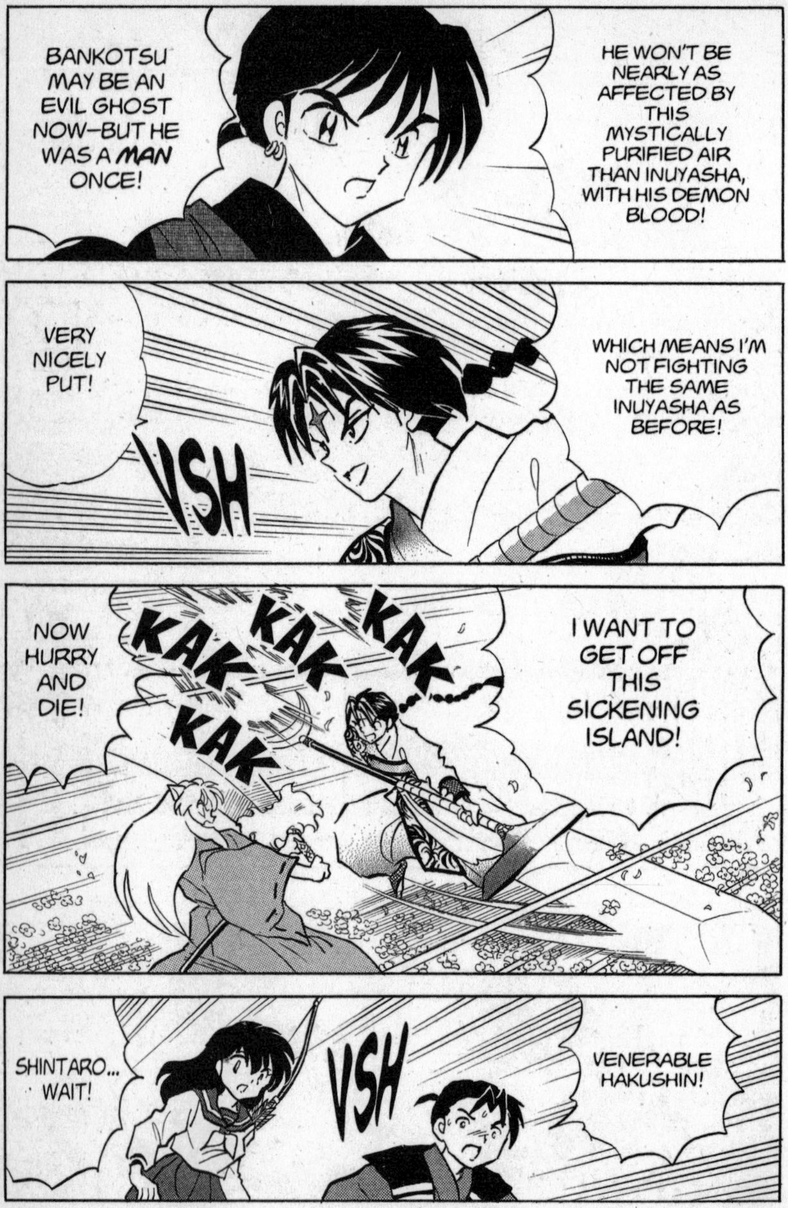
BANKOTSU MAY BE AN EVIL GHOST NOW—BUT HE WAS A *MAN* ONCE!
HE WON'T BE NEARLY AS AFFECTED BY THIS MYSTICALLY PURIFIED AIR THAN INUYASHA, WITH HIS DEMON BLOOD!
VERY NICELY PUT!
VSH
WHICH MEANS I'M NOT FIGHTING THE SAME INUYASHA AS BEFORE!
NOW HURRY AND DIE!
KAK KAK KAK KAK KAK
I WANT TO GET OFF THIS SICKENING ISLAND!
SHINTARO... WAIT!
VSH
VENERABLE HAKUSHIN!

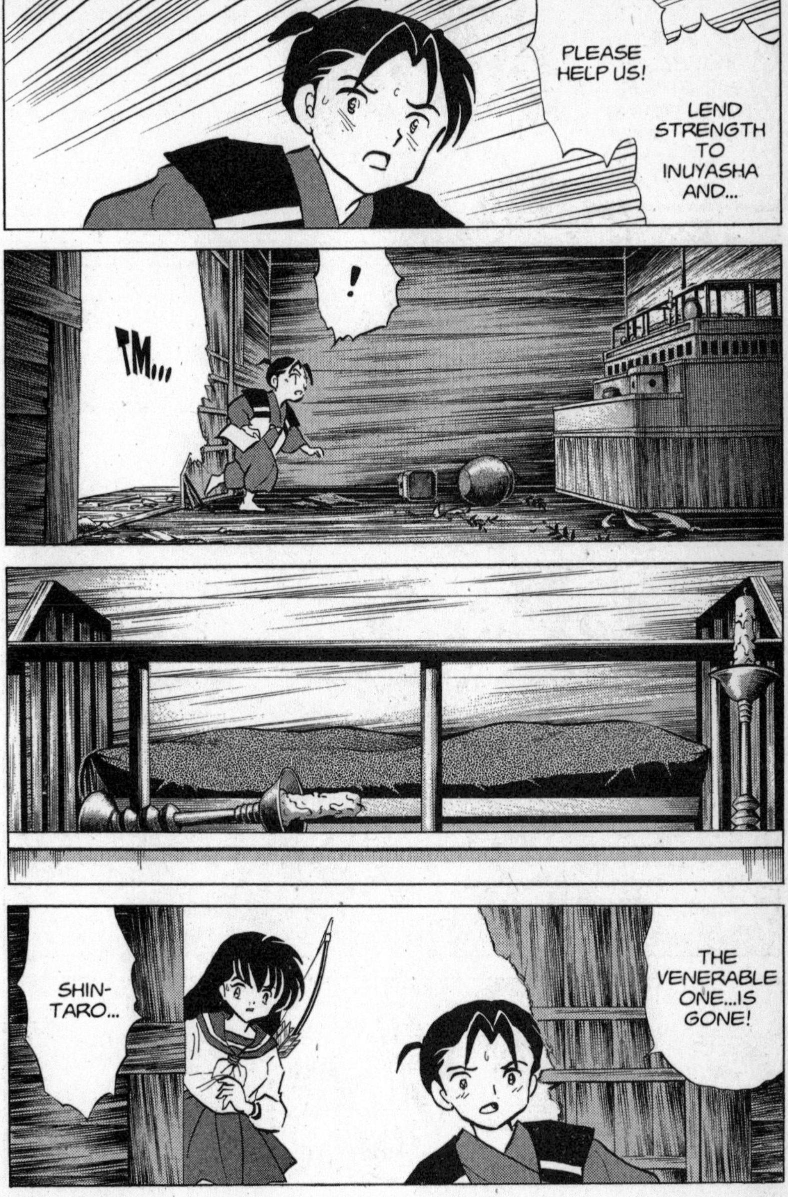
PLEASE HELP US!
LEND STRENGTH TO INUYASHA AND...
TM...
!
SHIN-TARO...
THE VENERABLE ONE...IS GONE!

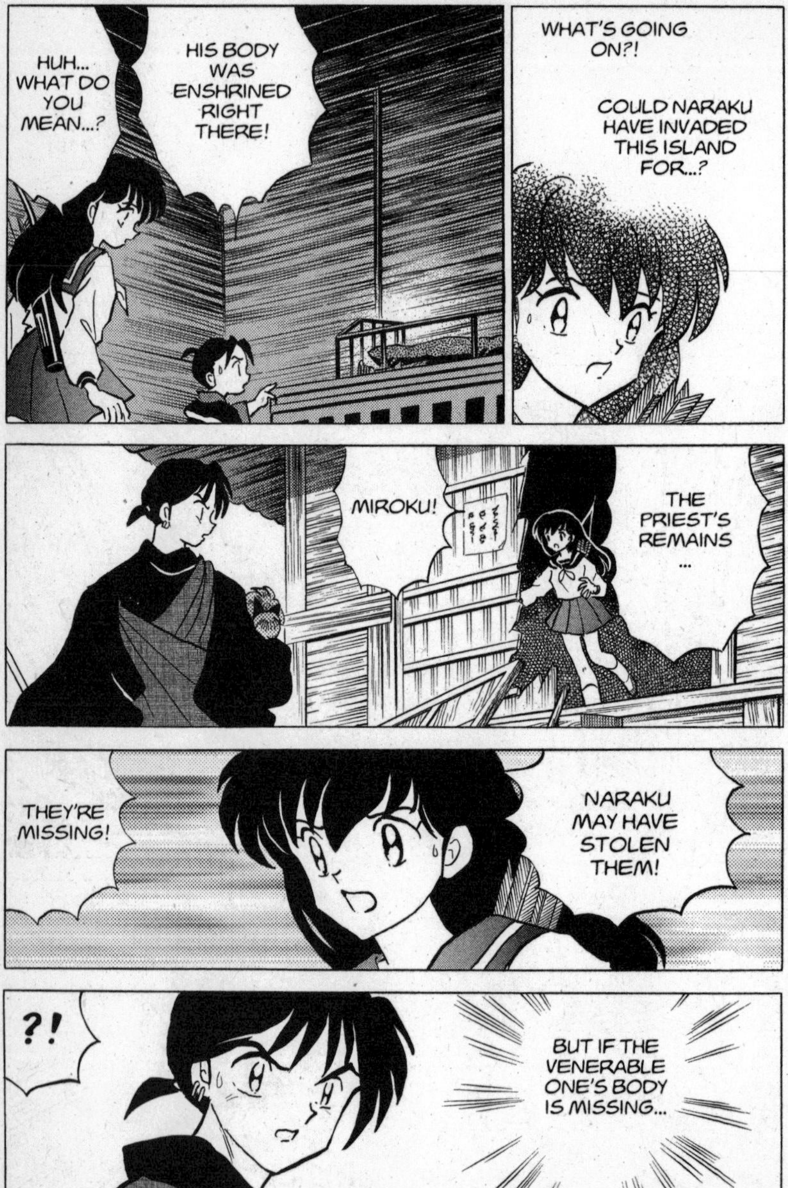
HUH... WHAT DO YOU MEAN...?
HIS BODY WAS ENSHRINED RIGHT THERE!
WHAT'S GOING ON?!
COULD NARAKU HAVE INVADED THIS ISLAND FOR...?
MIROKU!
THE PRIEST'S REMAINS ...
THEY'RE MISSING!
NARAKU MAY HAVE STOLEN THEM!
?!
BUT IF THE VENERABLE ONE'S BODY IS MISSING...

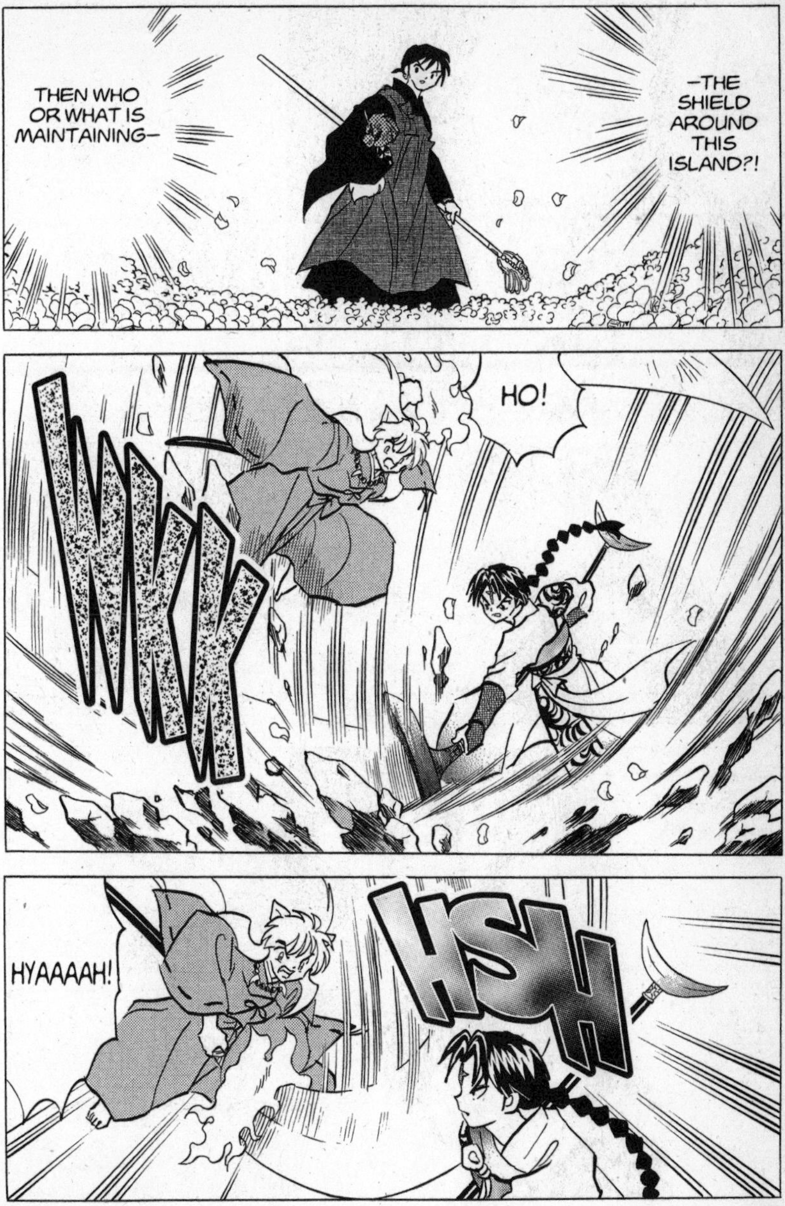
THEN WHO OR WHAT IS MAINTAINING—
—THE SHIELD AROUND THIS ISLAND?!
WKK
HO!
HYAAAAH!
HSH

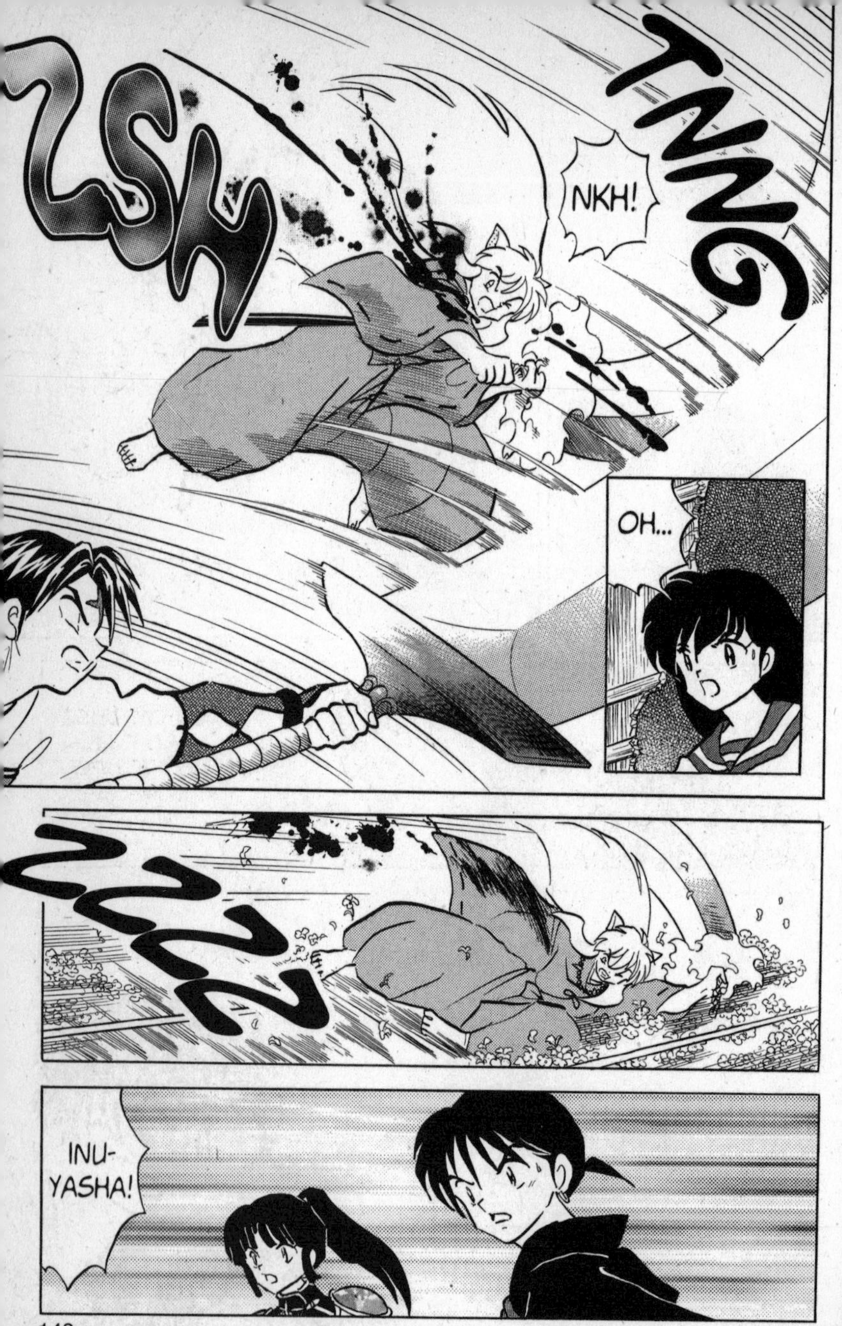
ZSH
NKH!
TWNG
OH...
INU-
YASHA!

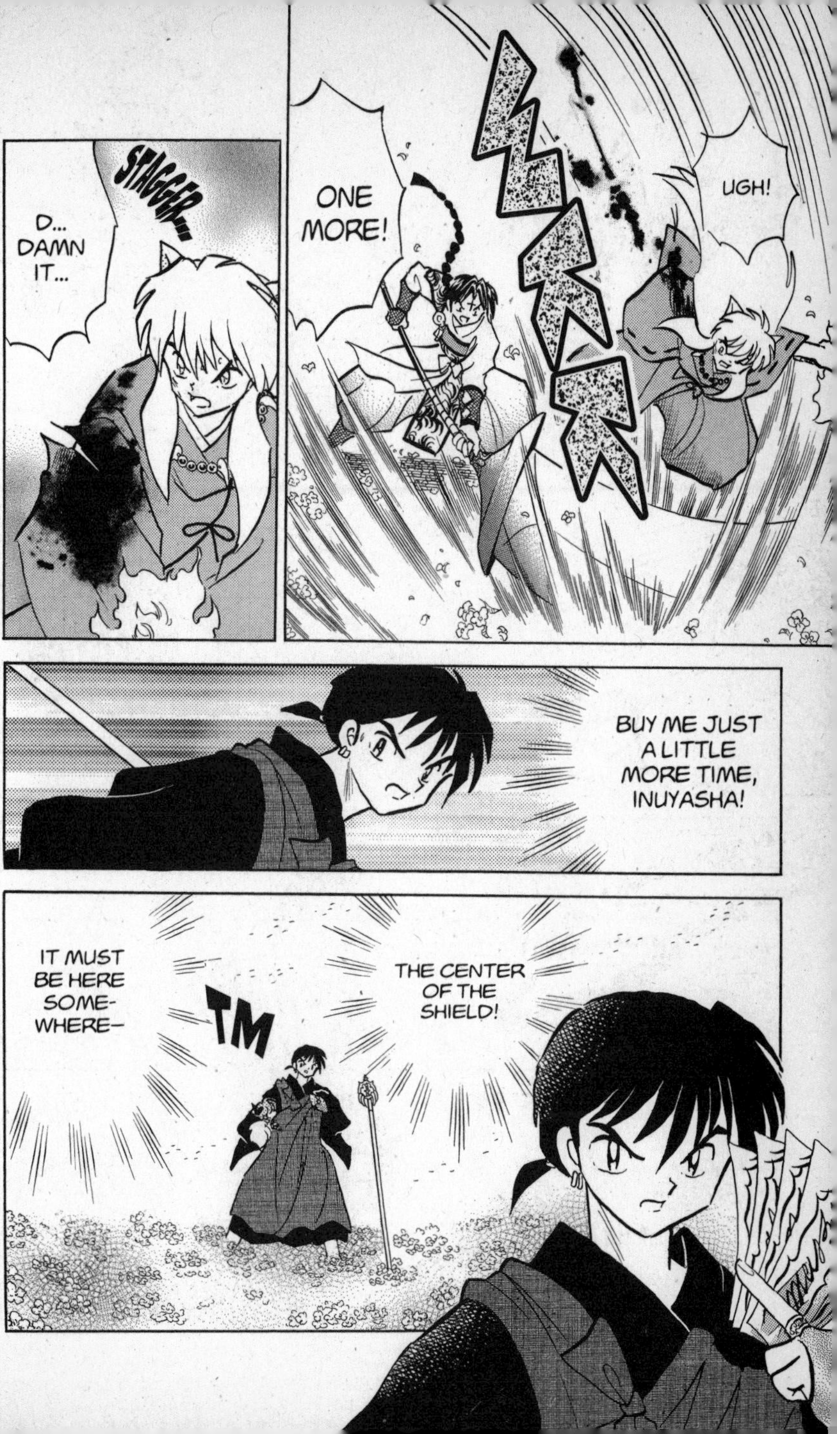
D... DAMN IT...
STAGGER...
ONE MORE!
UGH!
WAKKK
BUY ME JUST A LITTLE MORE TIME, INUYASHA!
IT MUST BE HERE SOME-WHERE-
TM
THE CENTER OF THE SHIELD!

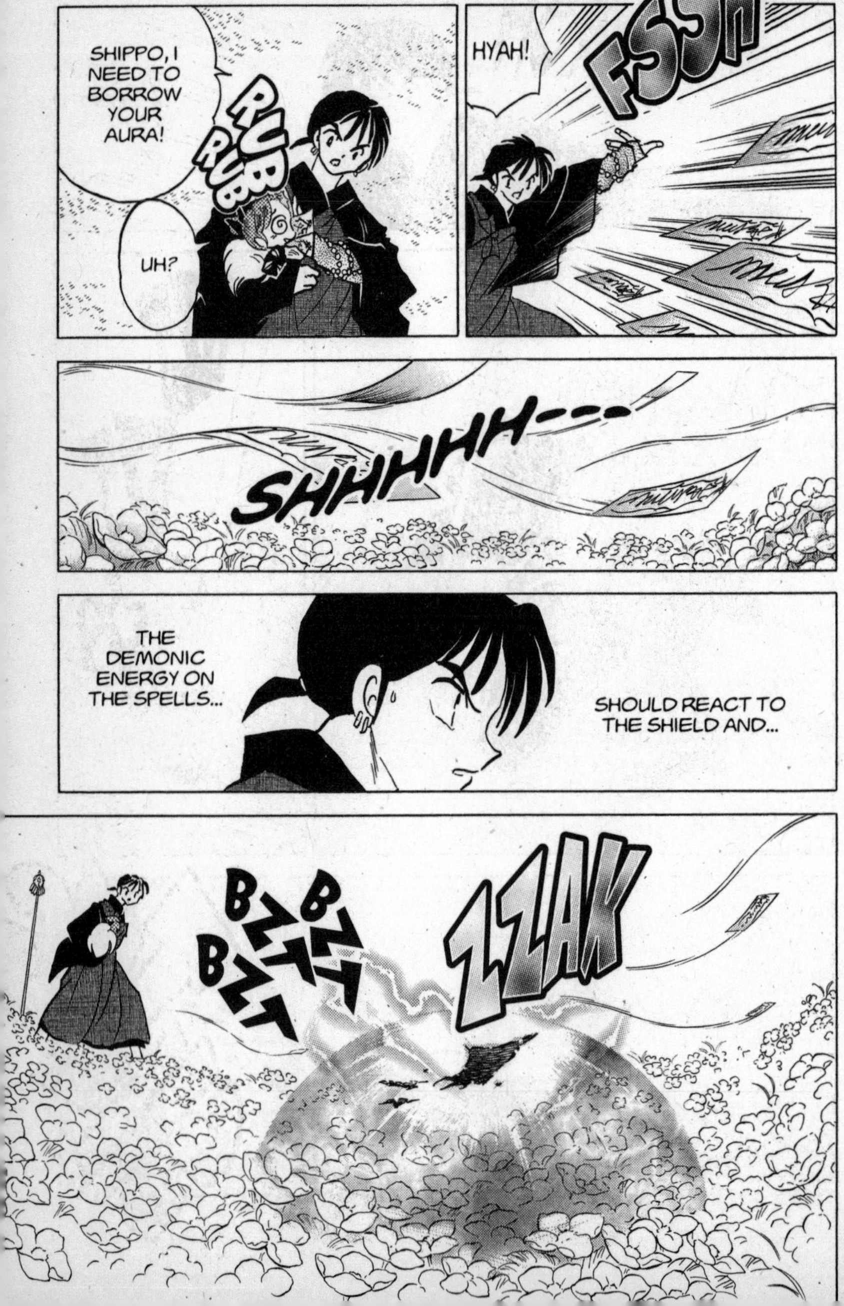
SHIPPO, I NEED TO BORROW YOUR AURA!
RUB RUB
UH?
HYAH!
FSSH
SHHHHH---
THE DEMONIC ENERGY ON THE SPELLS...
SHOULD REACT TO THE SHIELD AND...
BZZT BZZT
ZZAK

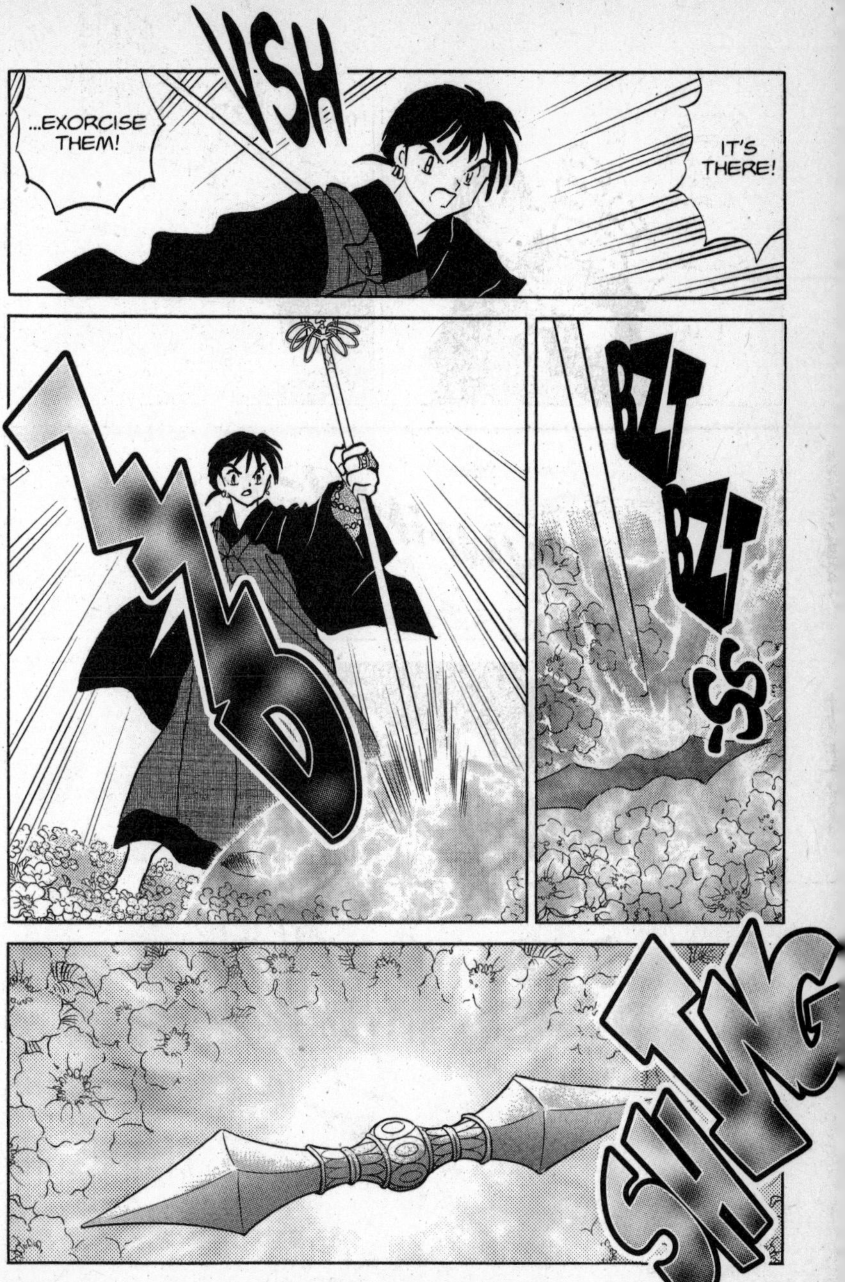
VSH
...EXORCISE THEM!
IT'S THERE!
BZT BZT
SS
SHING

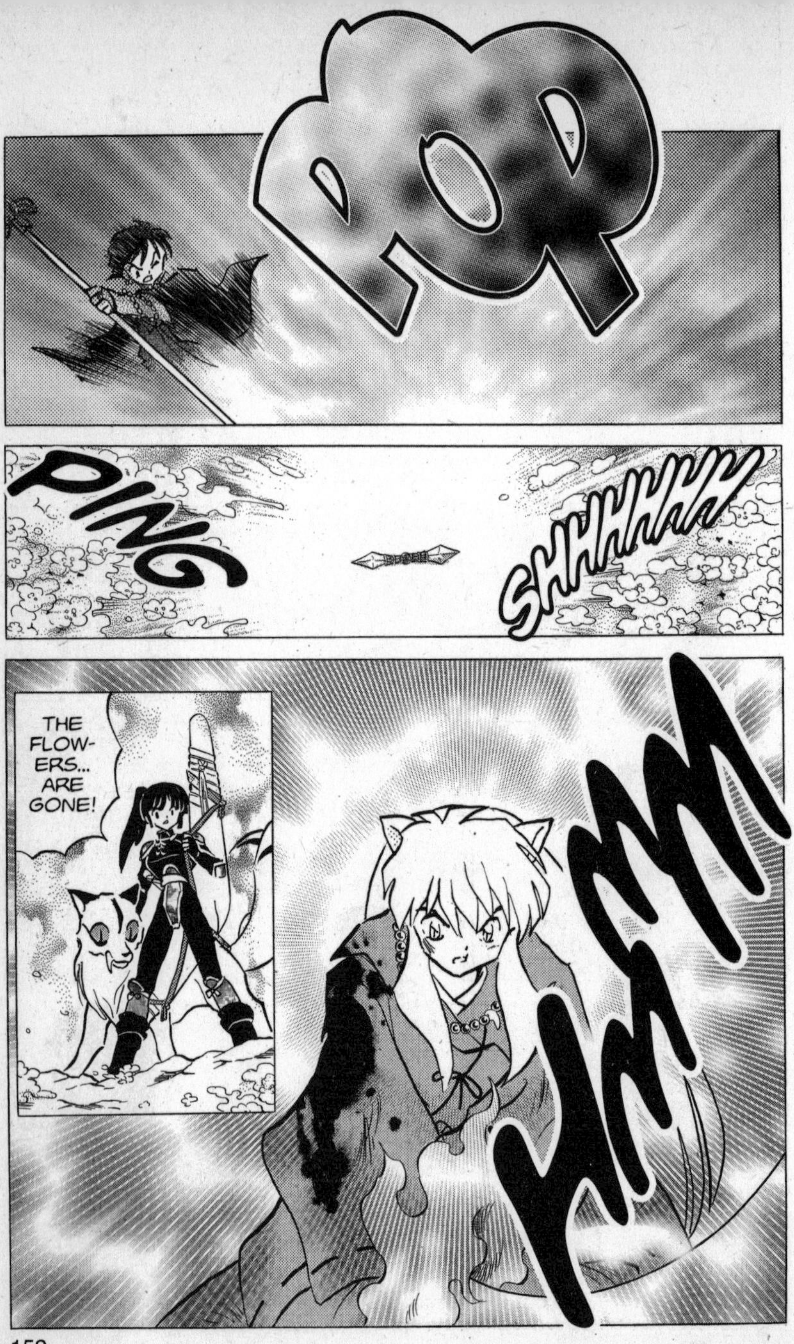
POP
PING
SHHHHH
THE FLOWERS... ARE GONE!
HMM

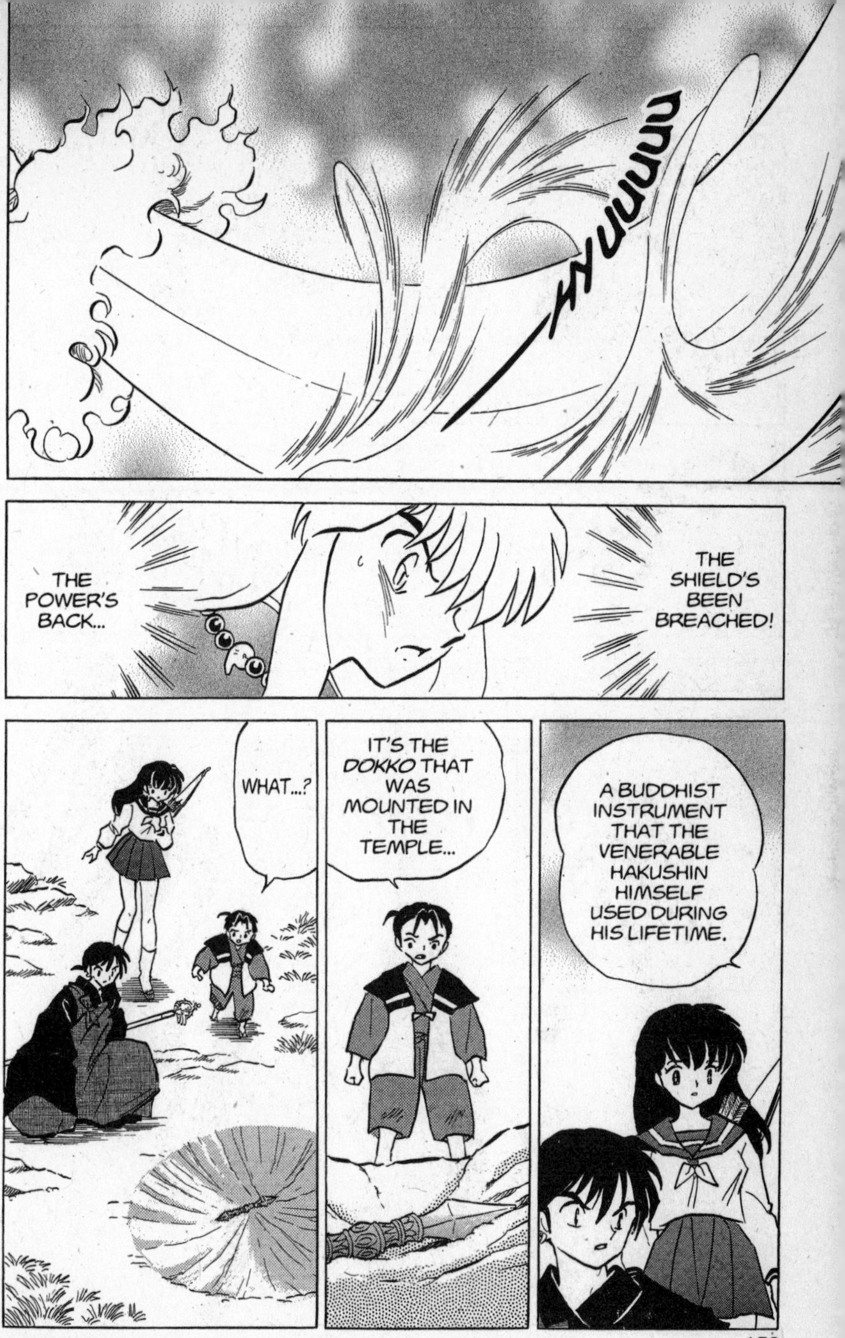
KYUUUUUN
THE POWER'S BACK...
THE SHIELD'S BEEN BREACHED!
WHAT...?
IT'S THE *DOKKO* THAT WAS MOUNTED IN THE TEMPLE...
A BUDDHIST INSTRUMENT THAT THE VENERABLE HAKUSHIN HIMSELF USED DURING HIS LIFETIME.

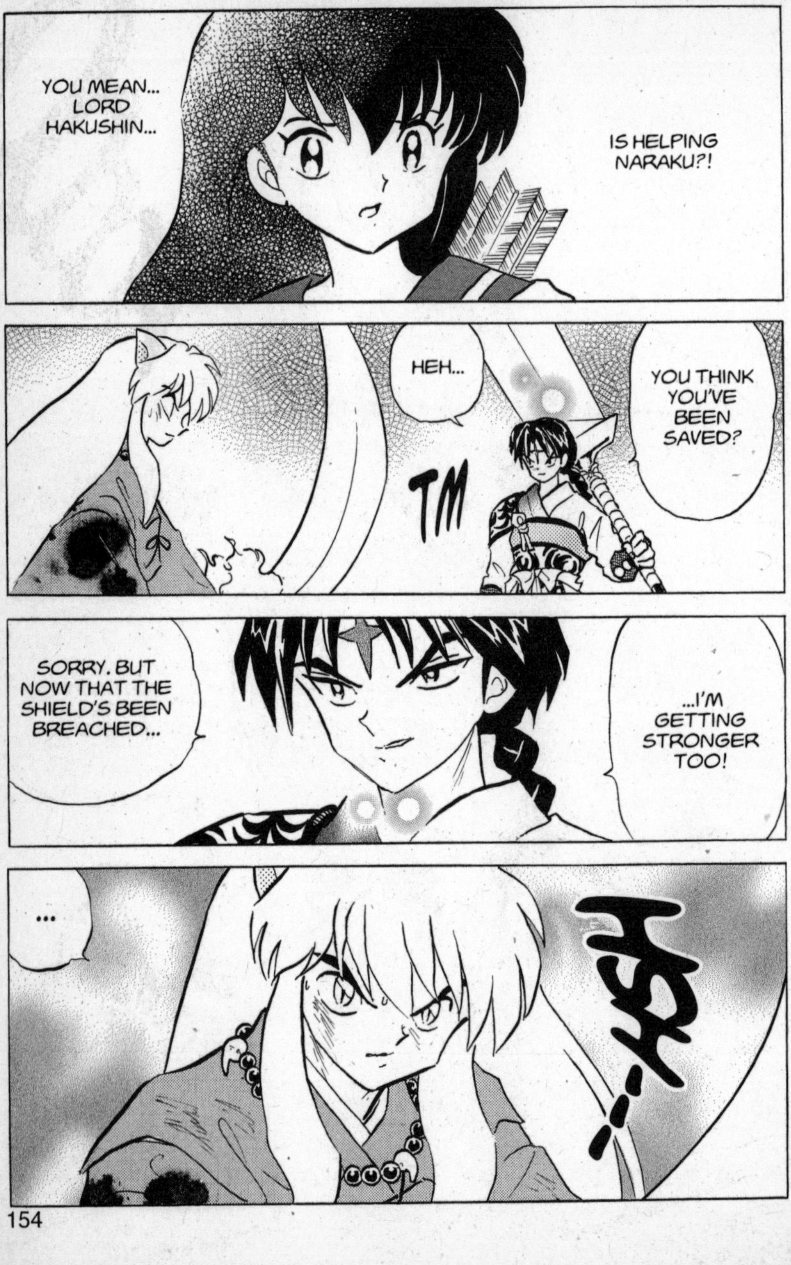
YOU MEAN... LORD HAKUSHIN...
IS HELPING NARAKU?!
HEH...
TM
YOU THINK YOU'VE BEEN SAVED?
SORRY. BUT NOW THAT THE SHIELD'S BEEN BREACHED...
...I'M GETTING STRONGER TOO!
...

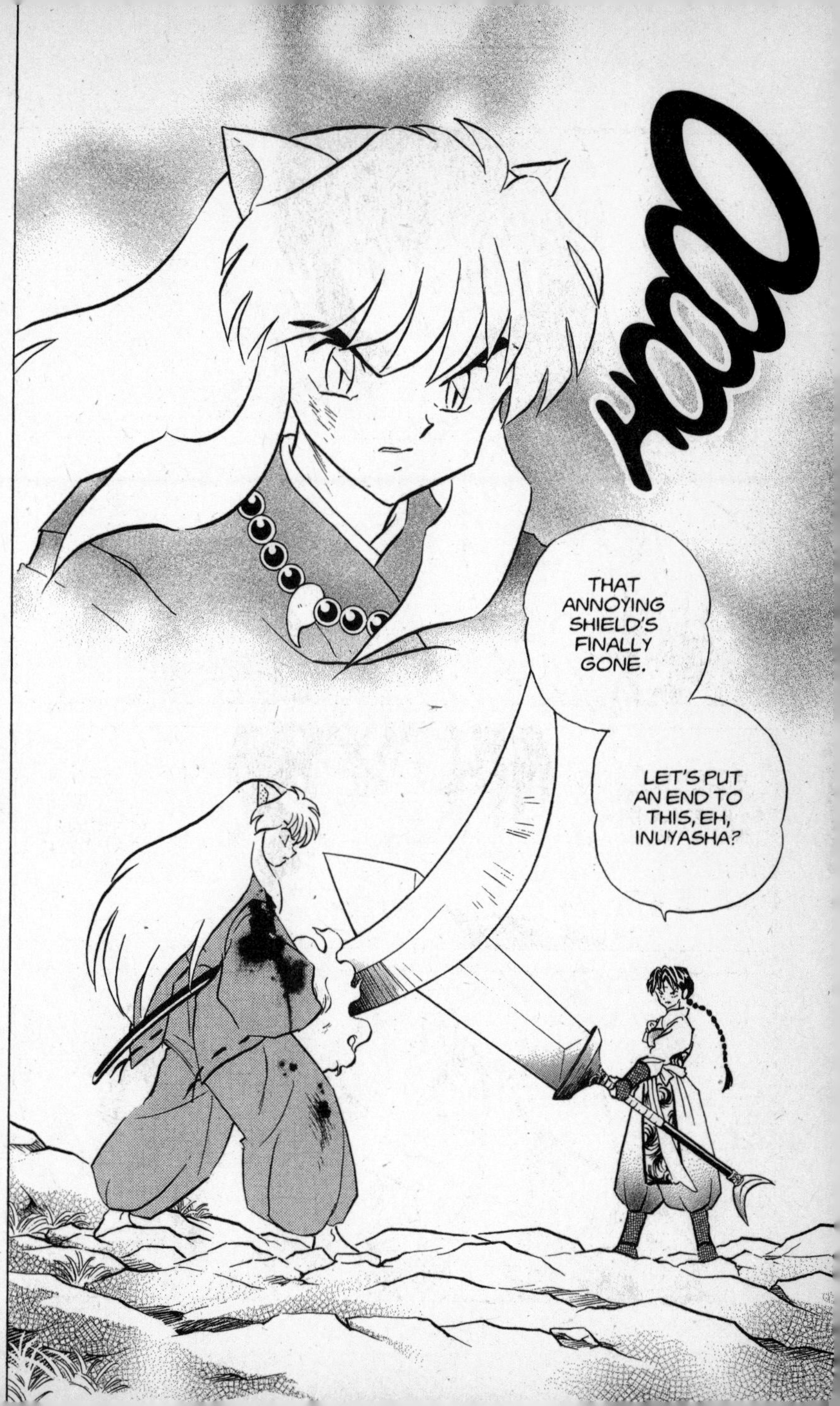

HOOOO
THAT ANNOYING SHIELD'S FINALLY GONE.
LET'S PUT AN END TO THIS, EH, INUYASHA?

SCROLL NINE

THE DOKKO

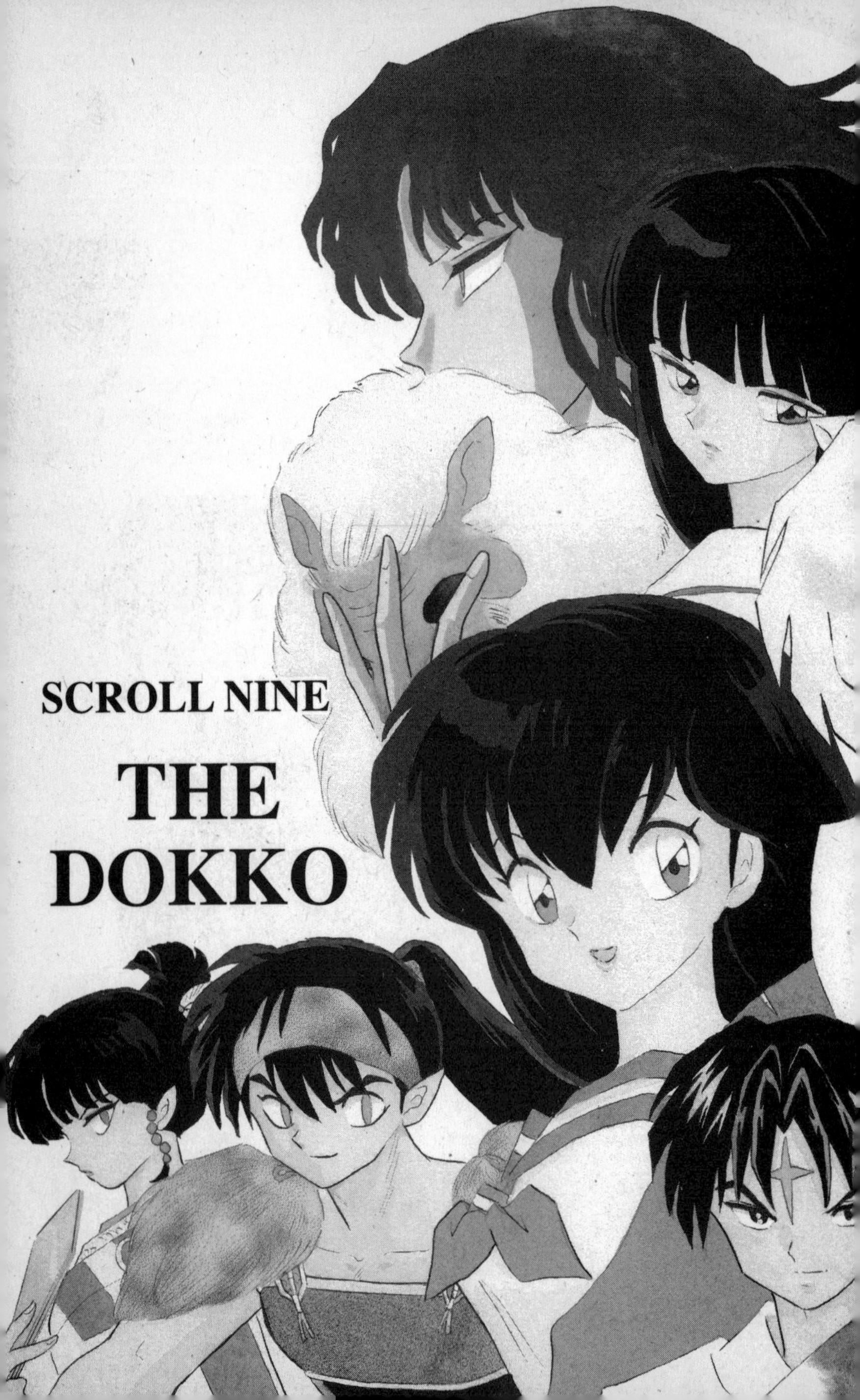

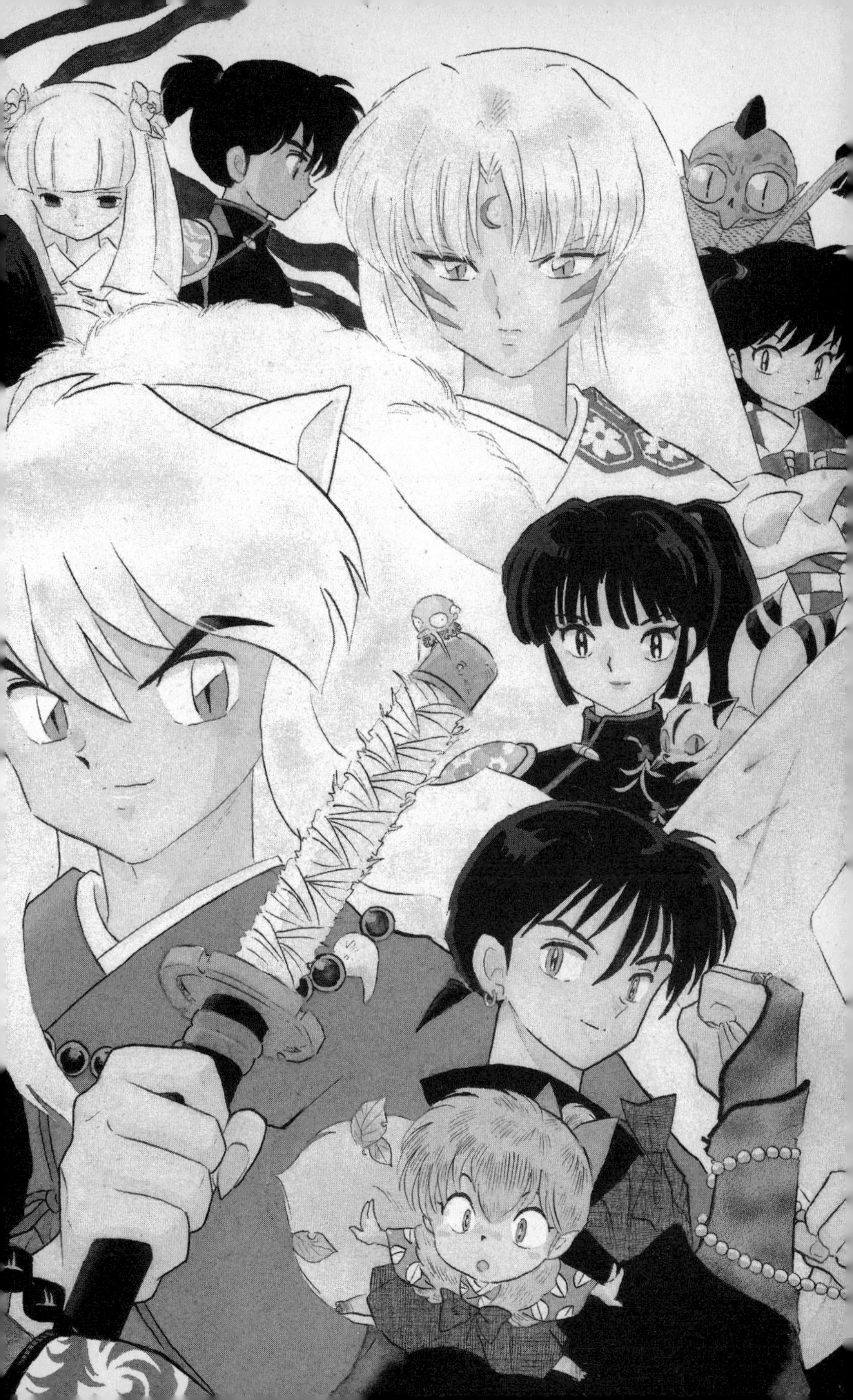

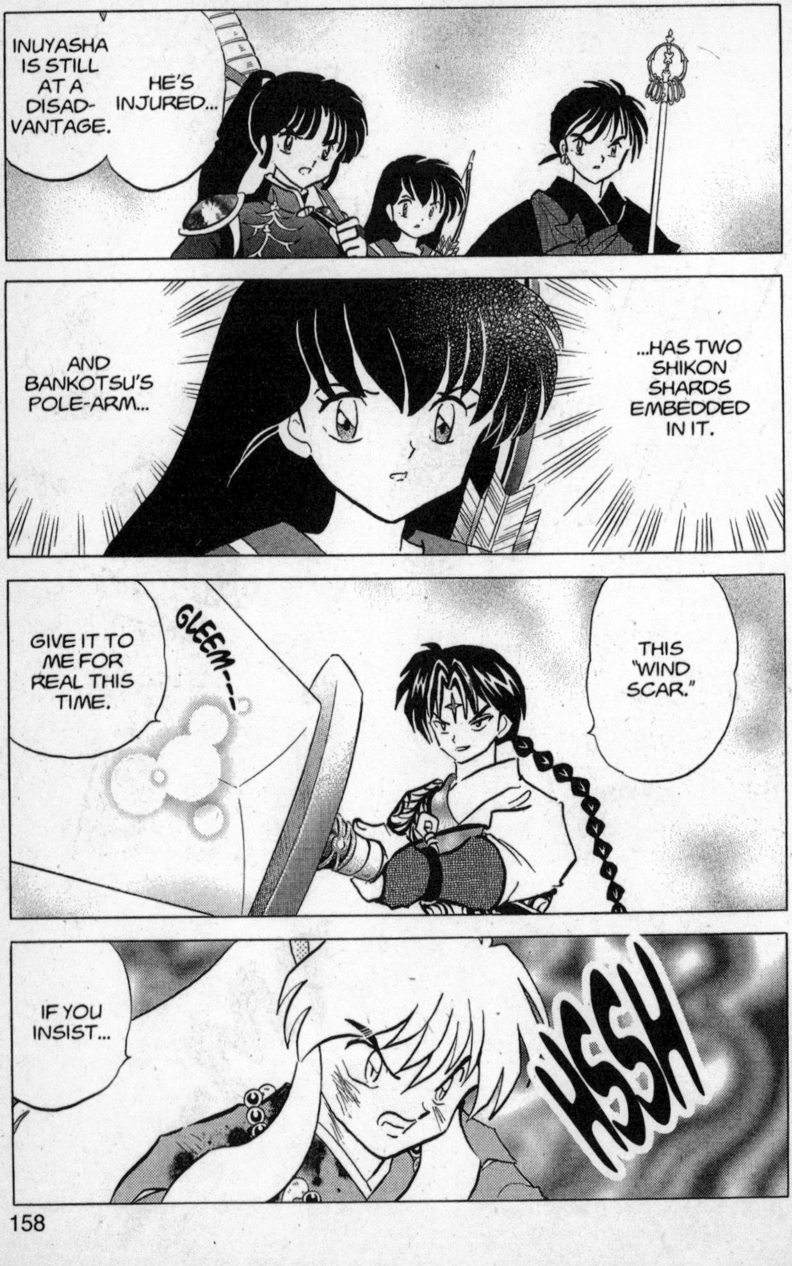
INUYASHA IS STILL AT A DISAD-VANTAGE.
HE'S INJURED...
AND BANKOTSU'S POLE-ARM...
...HAS TWO SHIKON SHARDS EMBEDDED IN IT.
GIVE IT TO ME FOR REAL THIS TIME.
GLEEM---
THIS "WIND SCAR."
IF YOU INSIST...
HSSH

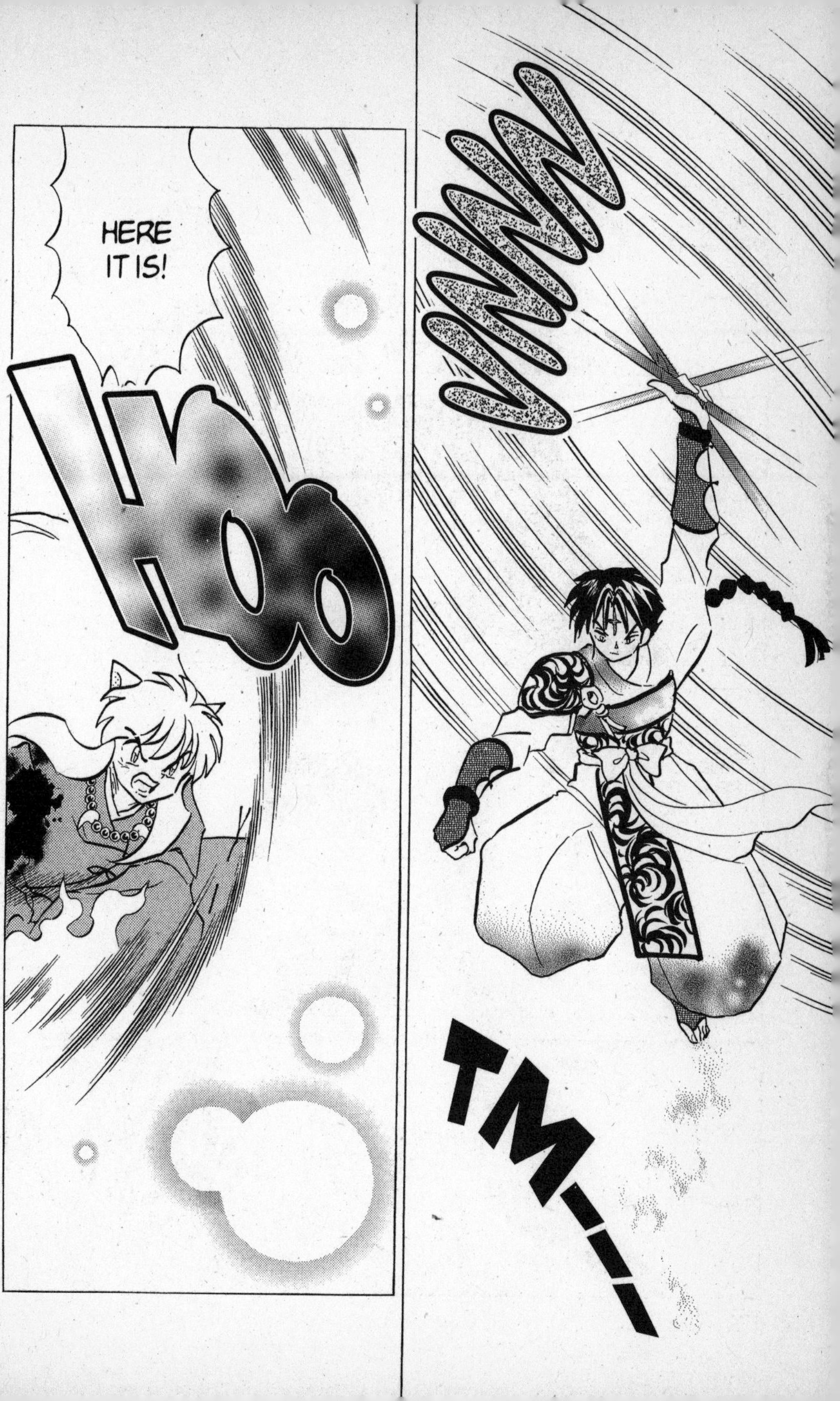
HERE IT IS!
HOO
TM---

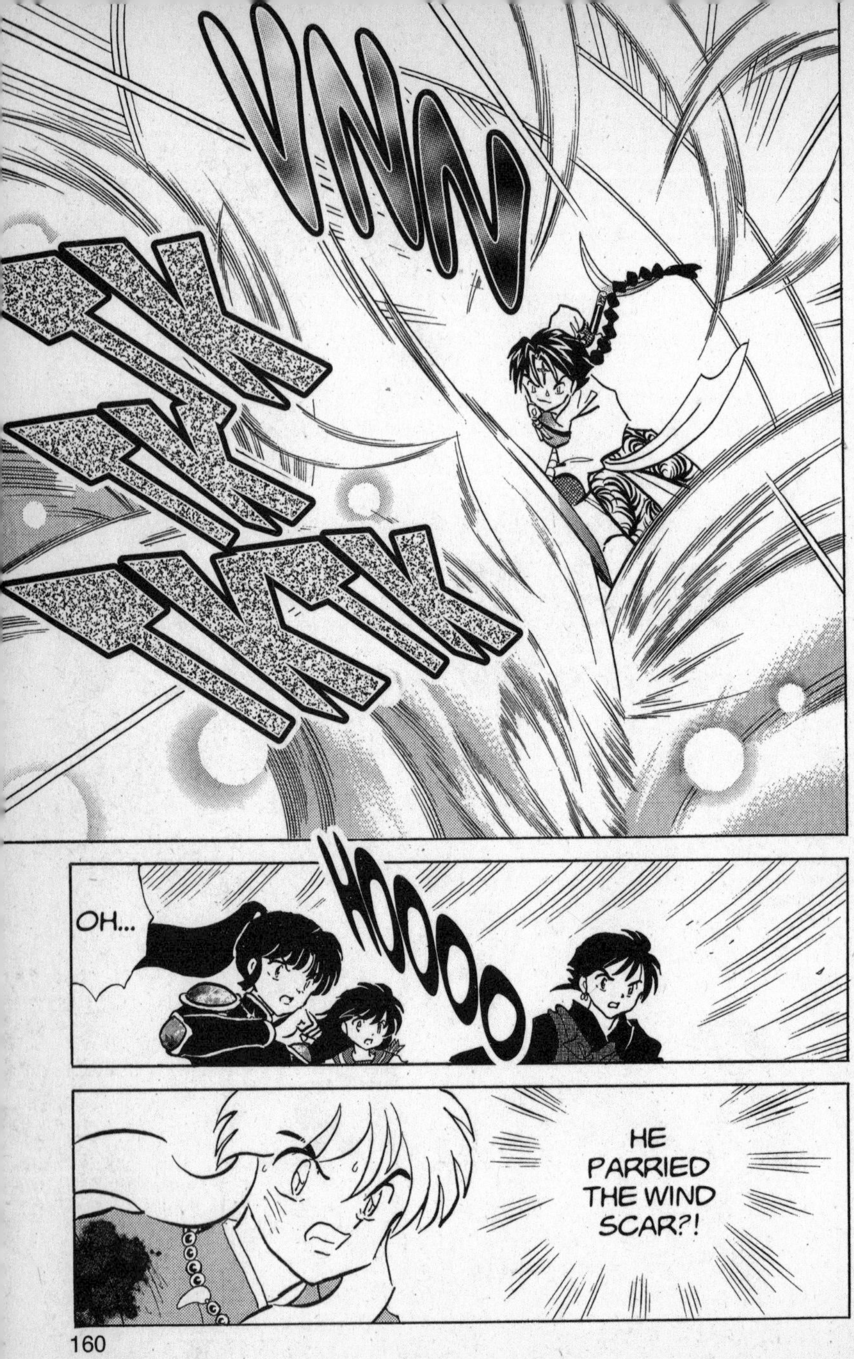
OH...
HOOOO
HE PARRIED THE WIND SCAR?!

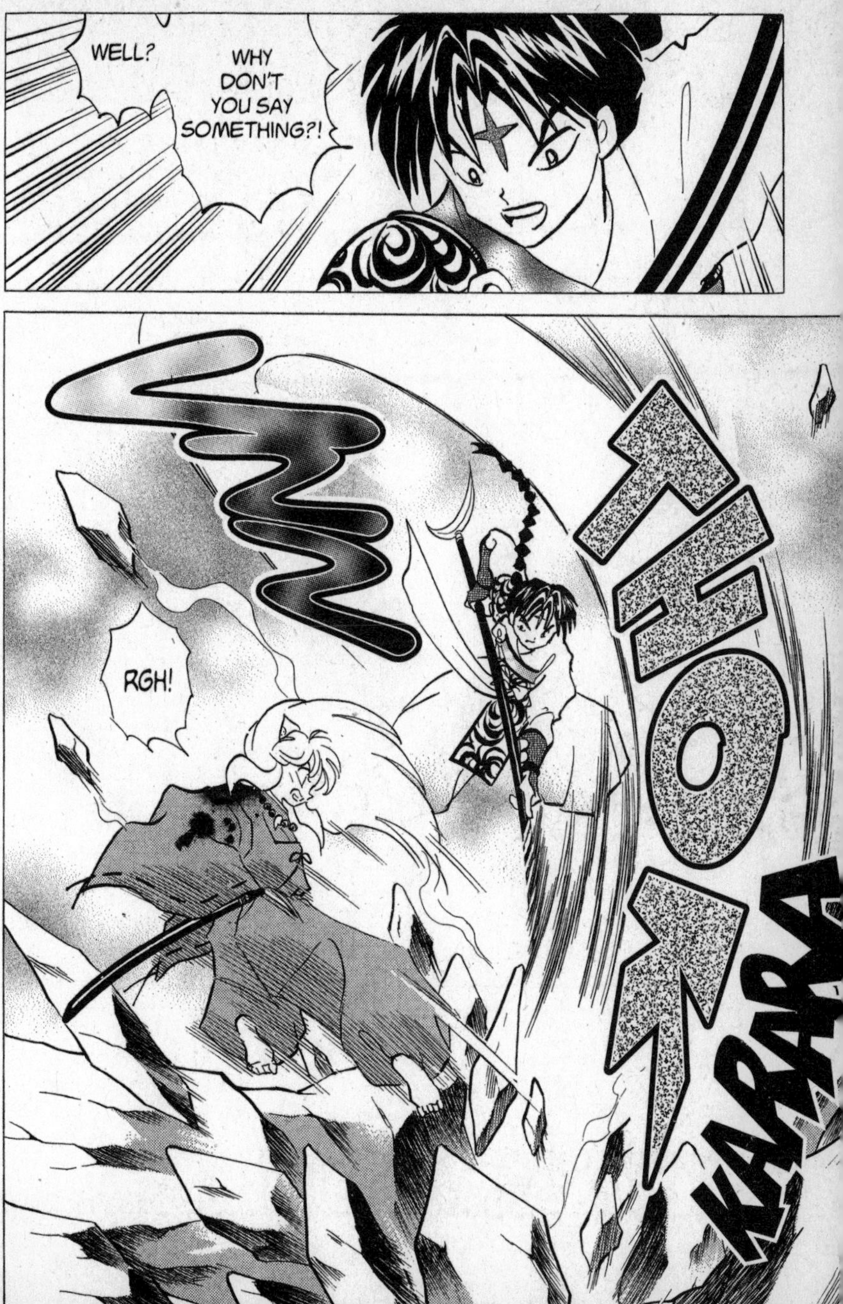
WELL?
WHY DON'T YOU SAY SOMETHING?!
RGH!
WHOOSH
KARARA

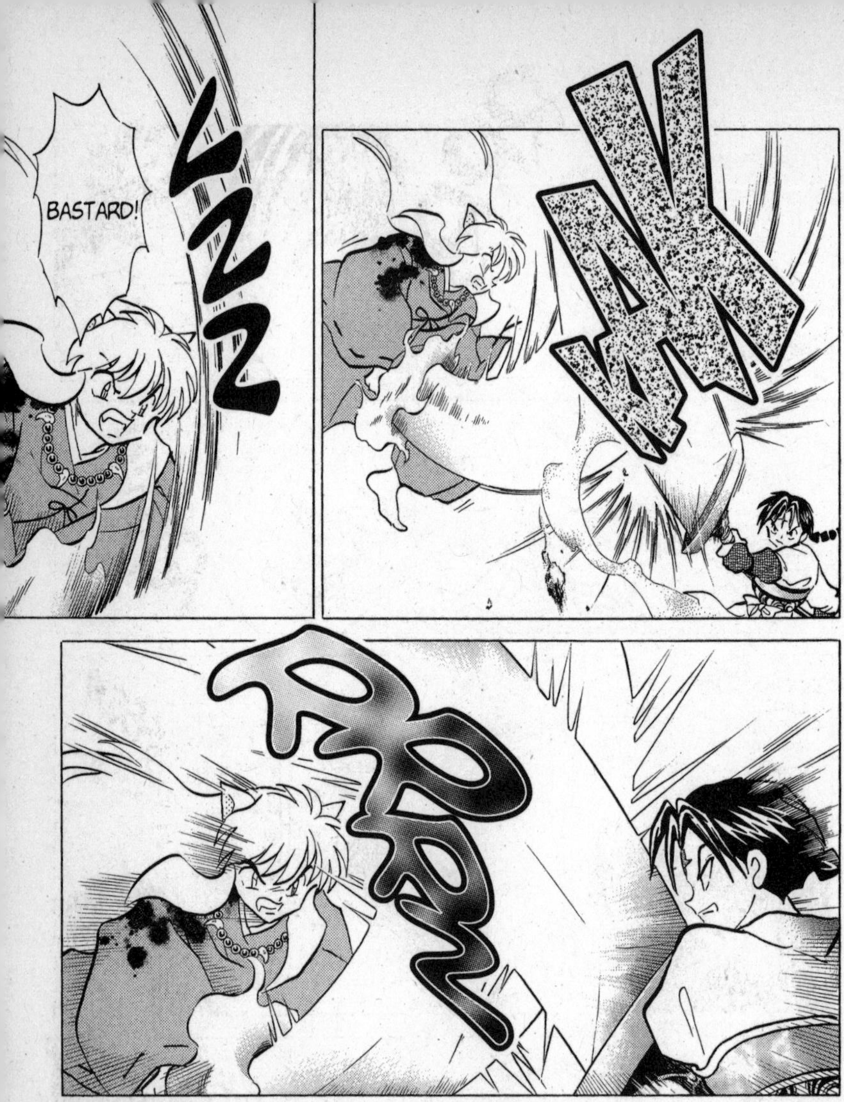
BASTARD!
CLOSE IN...
AND DEAD EVEN...

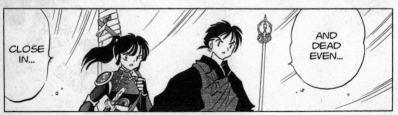

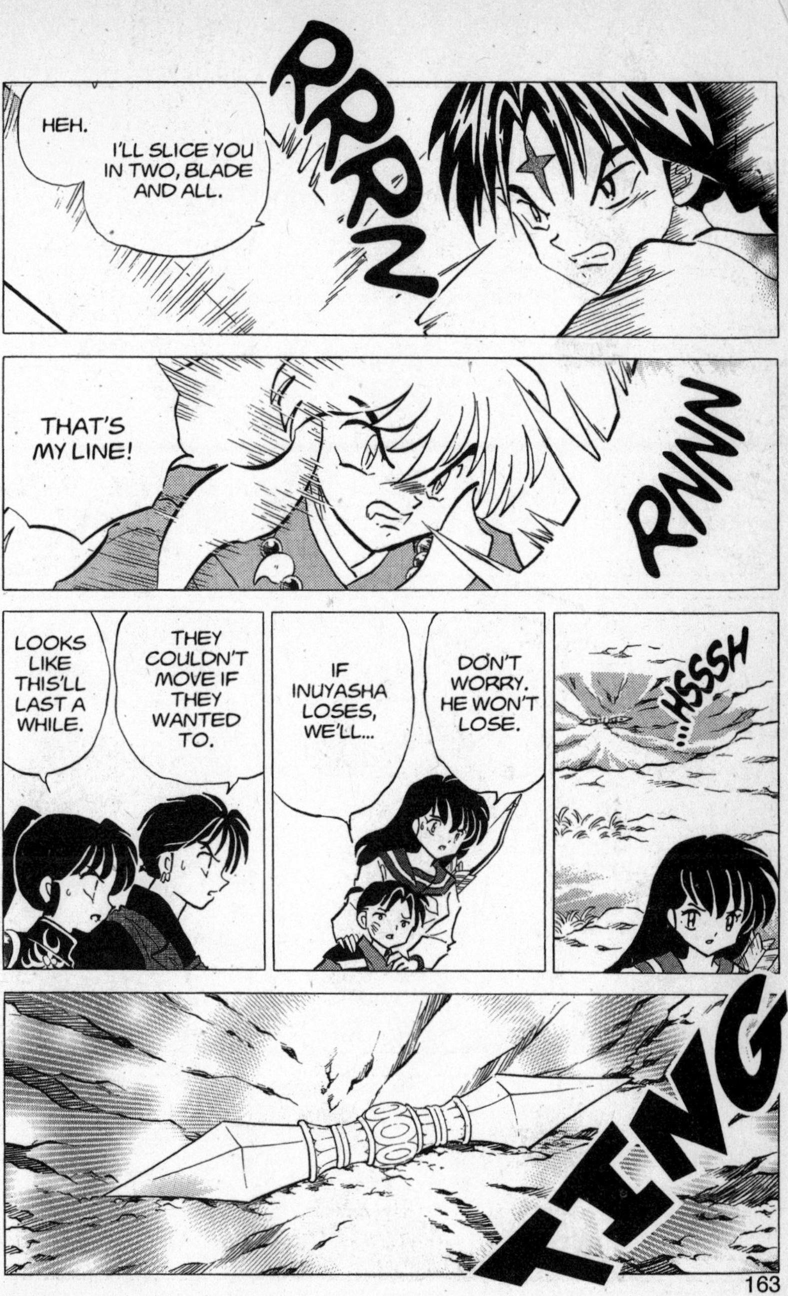
RRRN
HEH.
I'LL SLICE YOU IN TWO, BLADE AND ALL.
THAT'S MY LINE!
RNNN
LOOKS LIKE THIS'LL LAST A WHILE.
THEY COULDN'T MOVE IF THEY WANTED TO.
IF INUYASHA LOSES, WE'LL...
DON'T WORRY. HE WON'T LOSE.
...HSSSH
TING

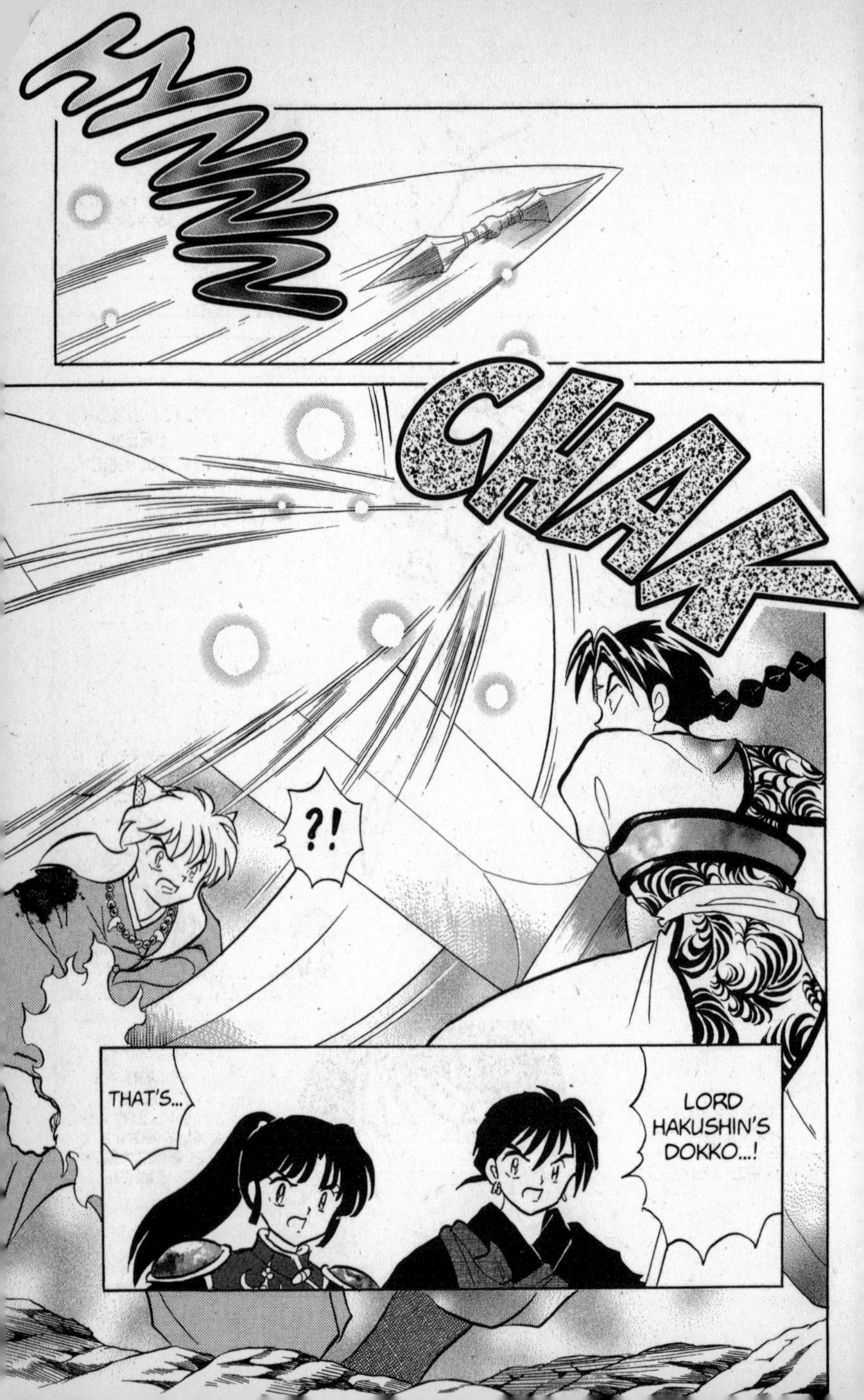

SHWWWW
CHAK
?!
THAT'S...
LORD HAKUSHIN'S DOKKO...!

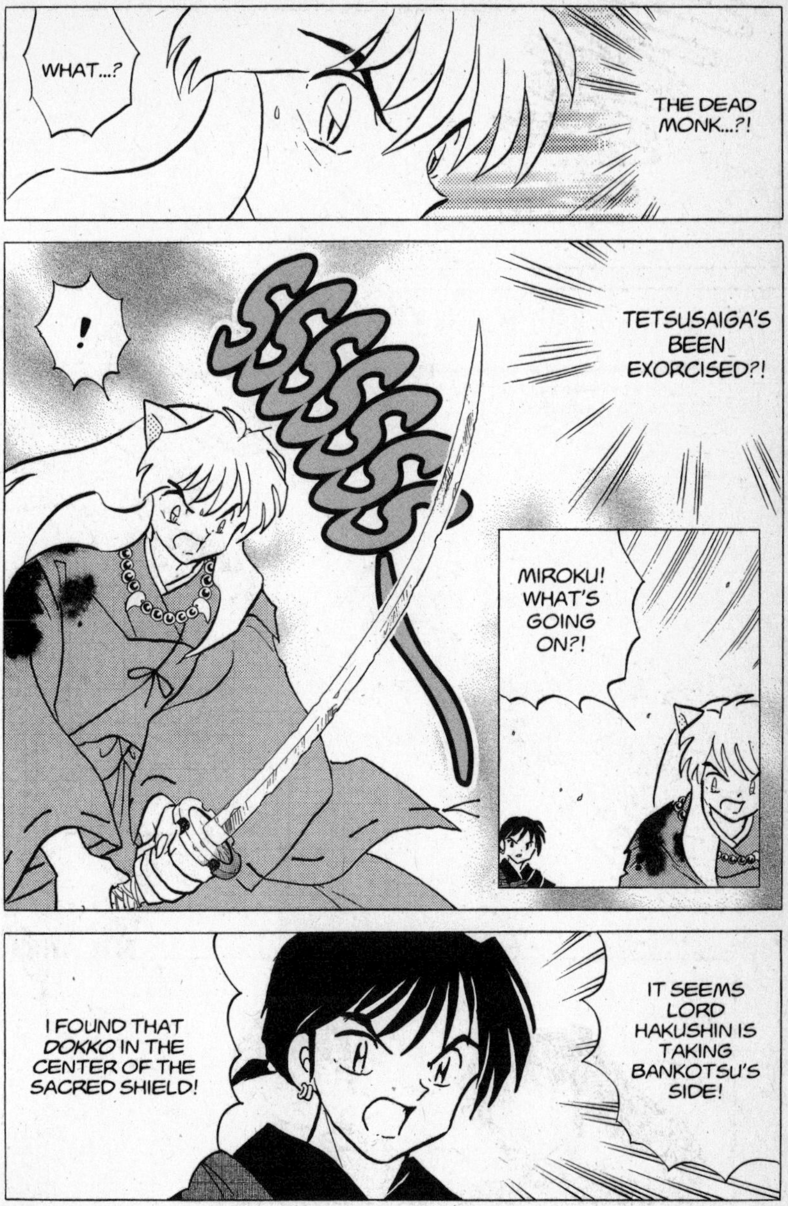
WHAT...?
THE DEAD MONK...?!
!
SSSSSS
TETSUSAIGA'S BEEN EXORCISED?!
MIROKU! WHAT'S GOING ON?!
I FOUND THAT *DOKKO* IN THE CENTER OF THE SACRED SHIELD!
IT SEEMS LORD HAKUSHIN IS TAKING BANKOTSU'S SIDE!

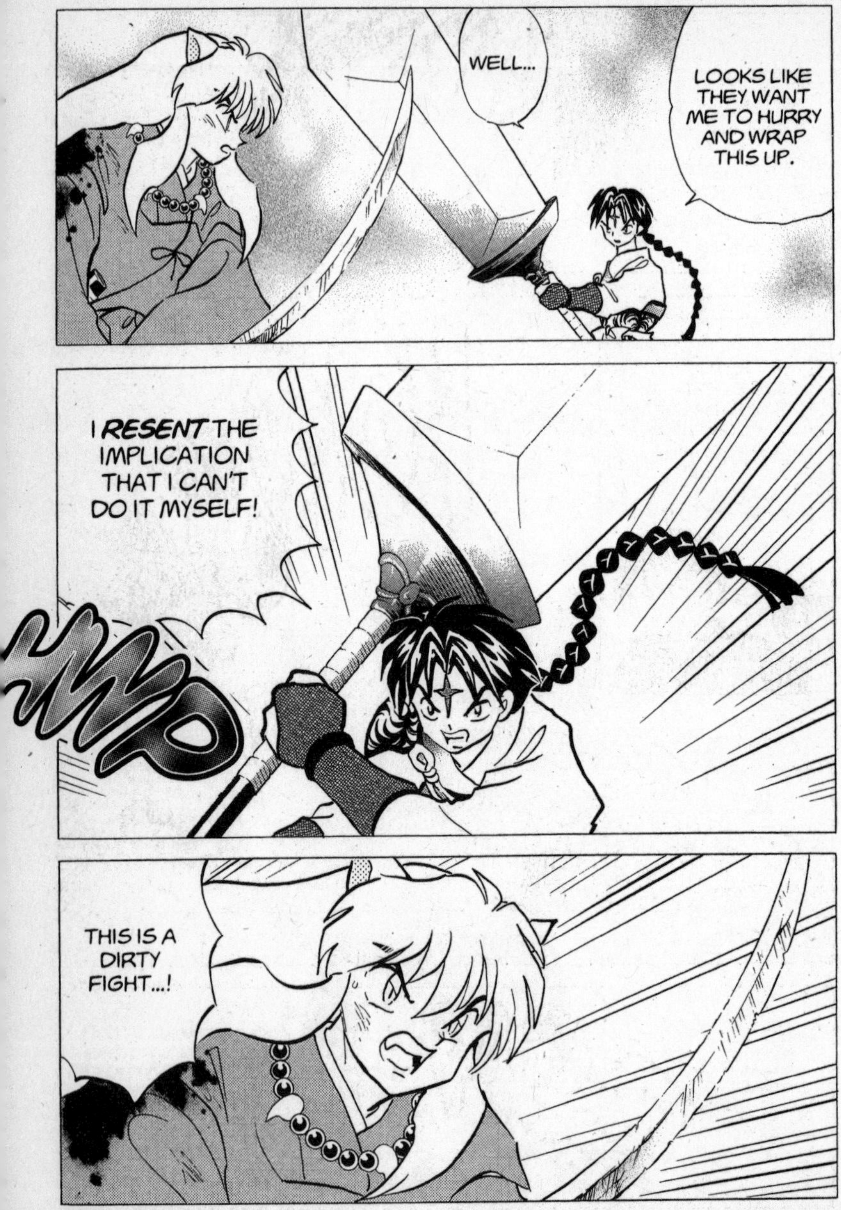
WELL...
LOOKS LIKE THEY WANT ME TO HURRY AND WRAP THIS UP.
I *RESENT* THE IMPLICATION THAT I CAN'T DO IT MYSELF!
HMP
THIS IS A DIRTY FIGHT...!

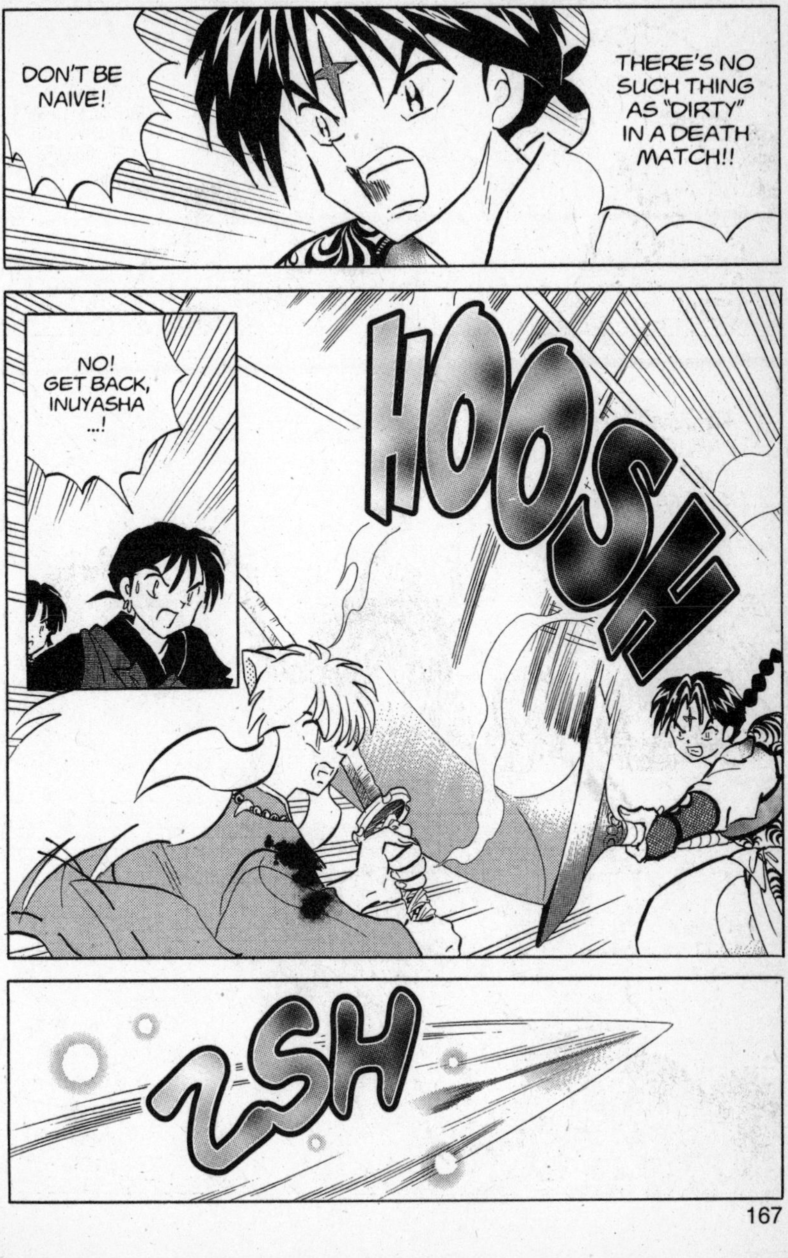
DON'T BE NAIVE!
THERE'S NO SUCH THING AS "DIRTY" IN A DEATH MATCH!!
NO! GET BACK, INUYASHA ...!
HOOSH
ZSH

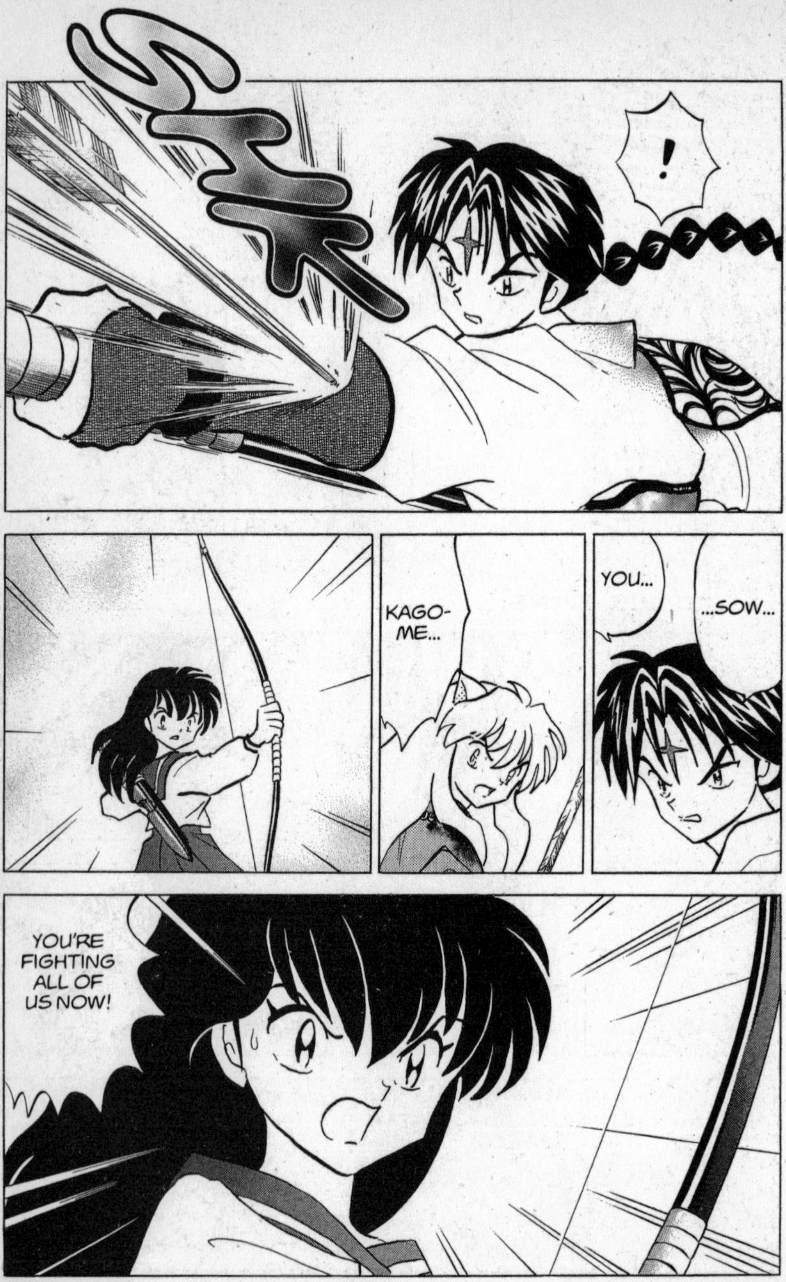
SHK
!
KAGO-
ME...
YOU...
...SOW...
YOU'RE FIGHTING ALL OF US NOW!

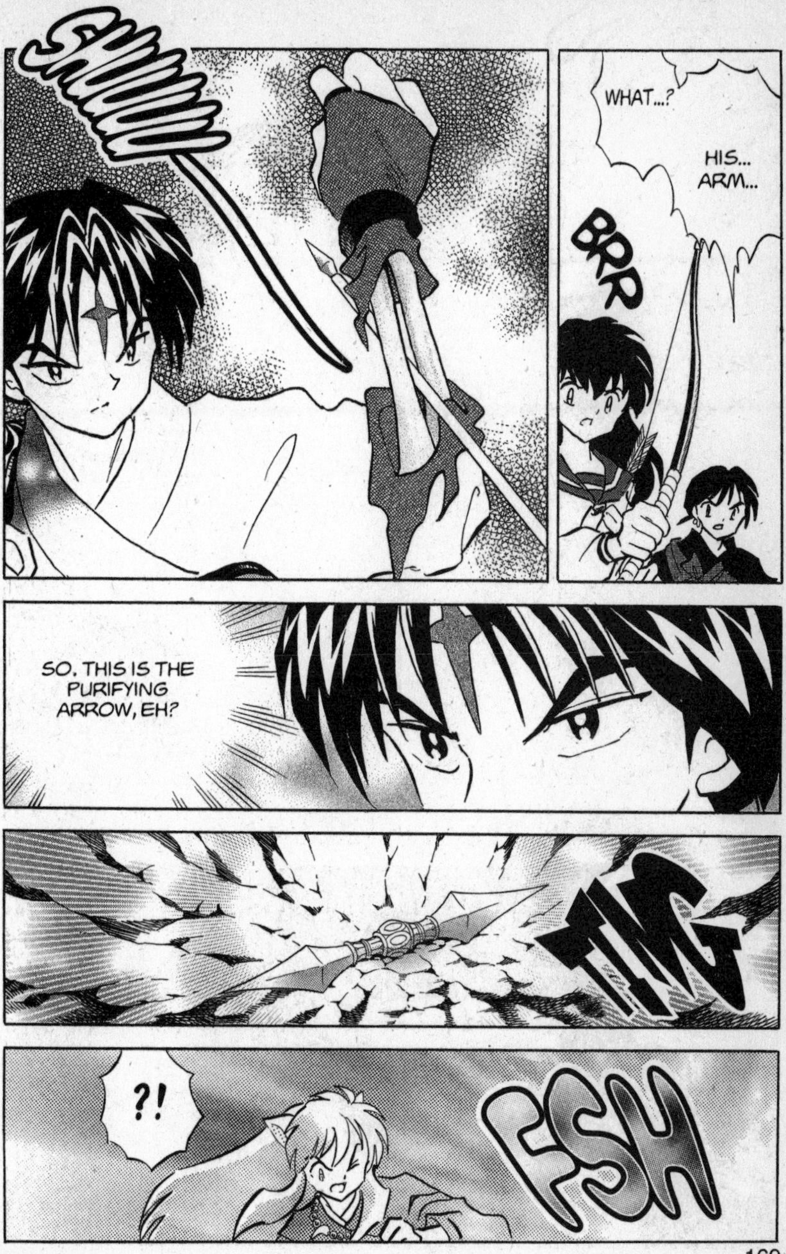
WHAT...?
HIS... ARM...
BRR
SO. THIS IS THE PURIFYING ARROW, EH?
TING
?!
FSH

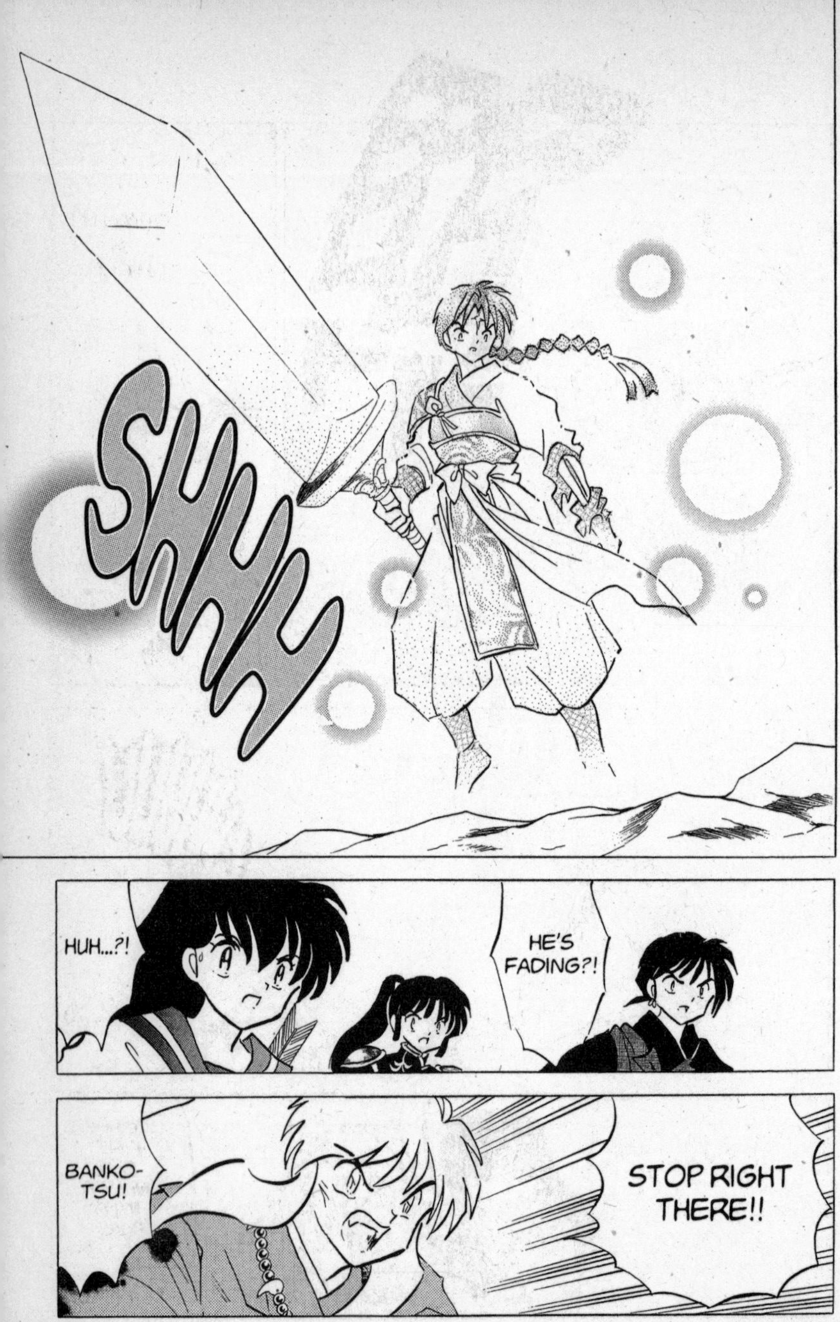
SHHH
HUH...?!
HE'S FADING?!
BANKO-TSU!
STOP RIGHT THERE!!

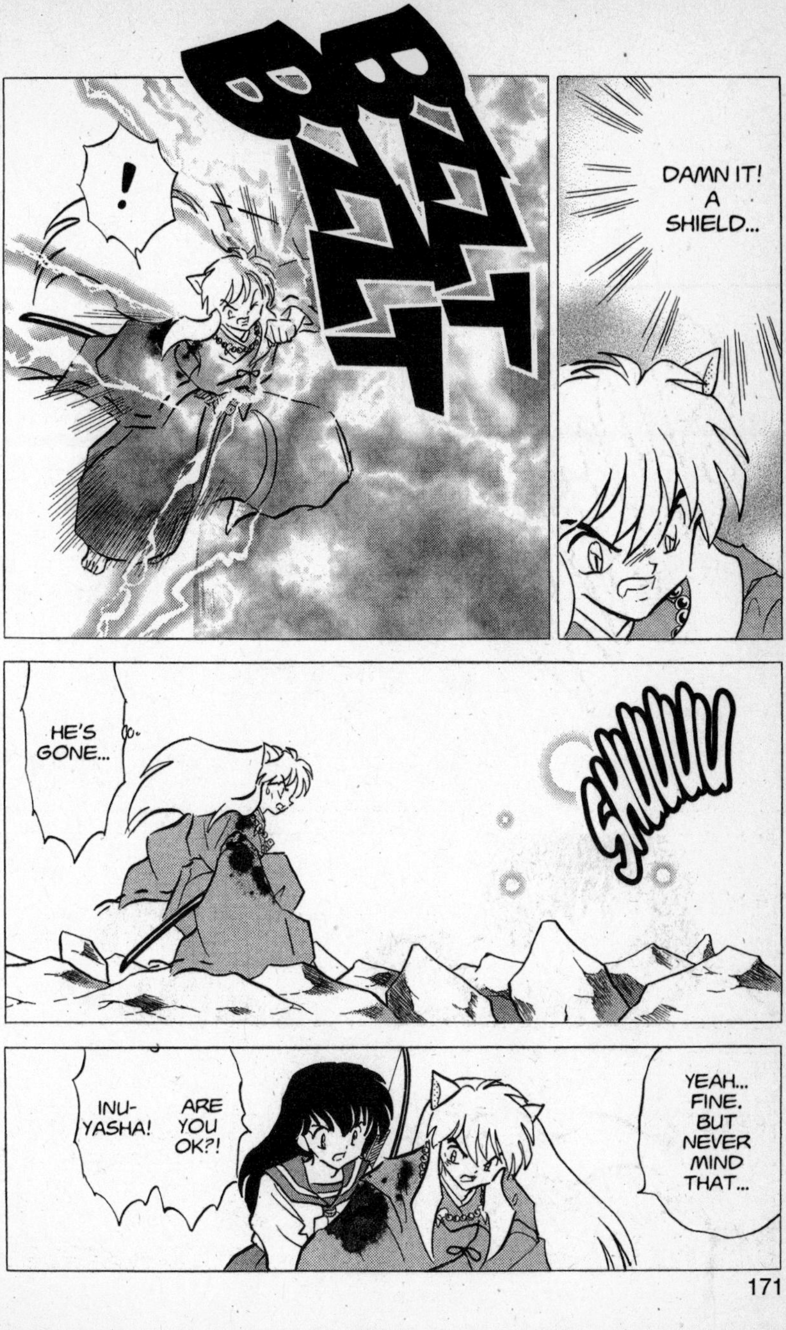
!
BZZT
DAMN IT! A SHIELD...
HE'S GONE...
SHUUUU
INU-YASHA!
ARE YOU OK?!
YEAH... FINE. BUT NEVER MIND THAT...

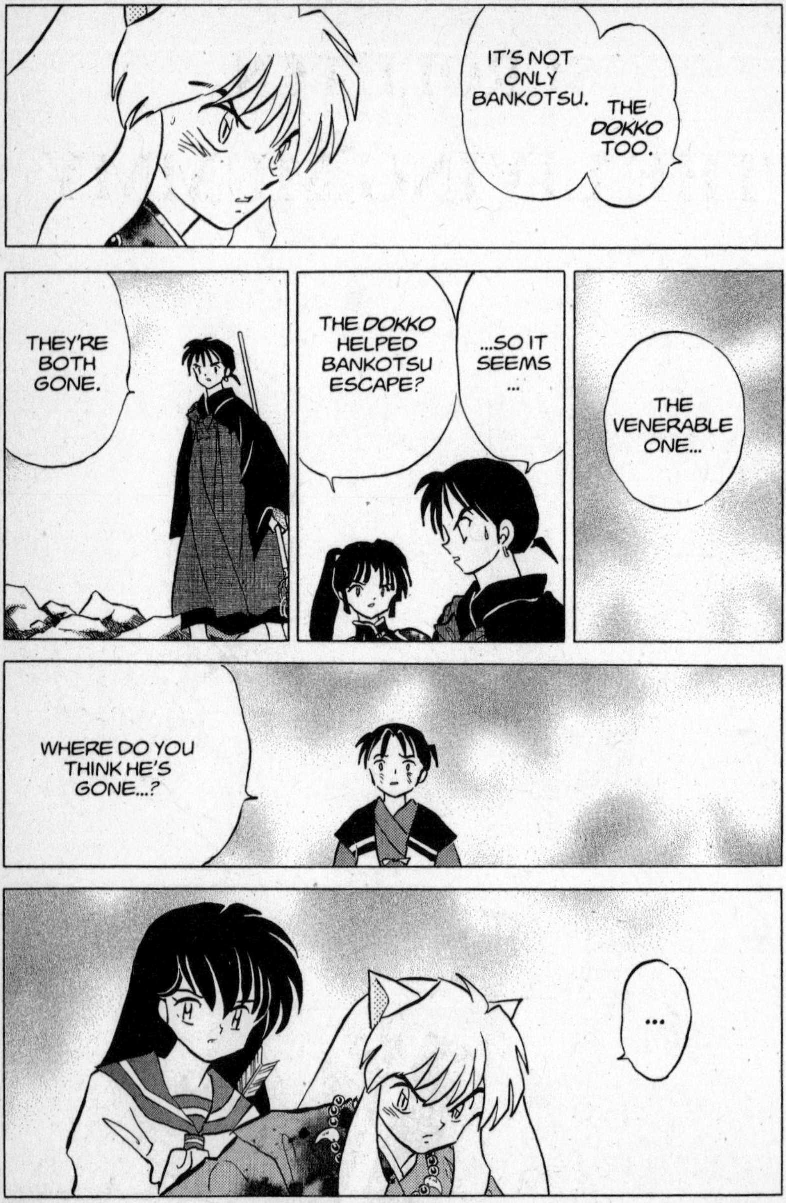

IT'S NOT ONLY BANKOTSU.
THE *DOKKO* TOO.
THEY'RE BOTH GONE.
THE *DOKKO* HELPED BANKOTSU ESCAPE?
...SO IT SEEMS ...
THE VENERABLE ONE...
WHERE DO YOU THINK HE'S GONE...?
...

SCROLL TEN
THE LIVING MUMMY

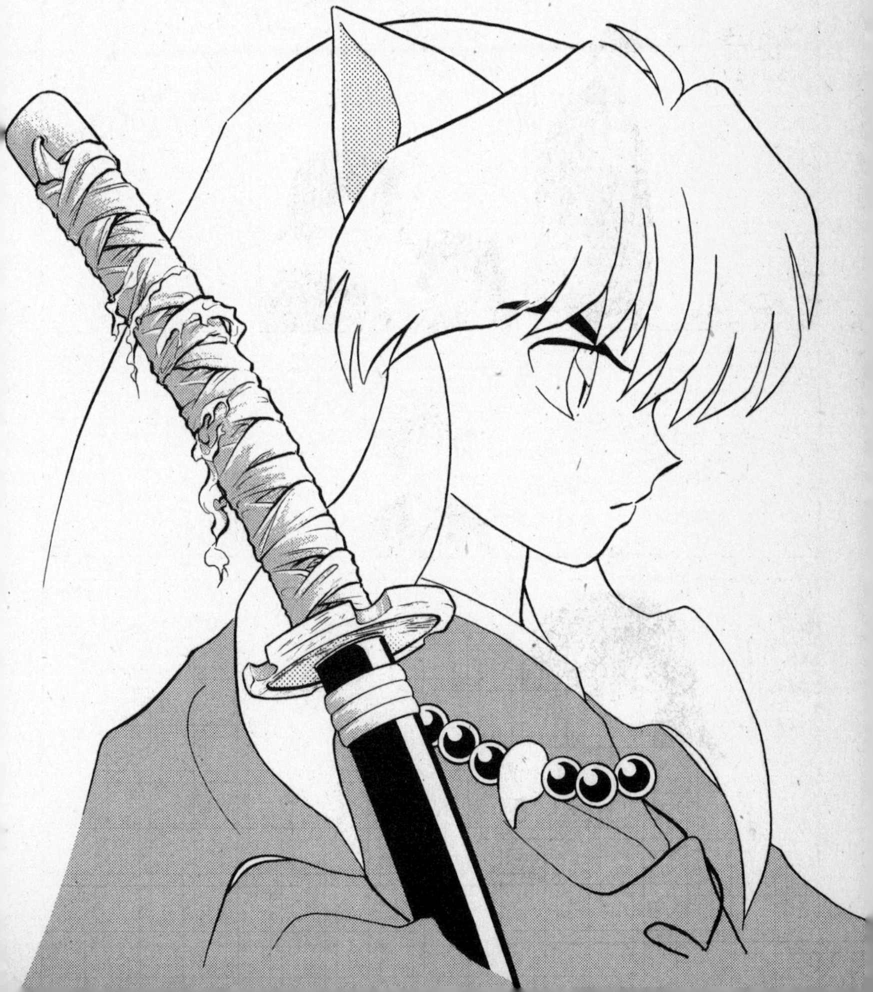

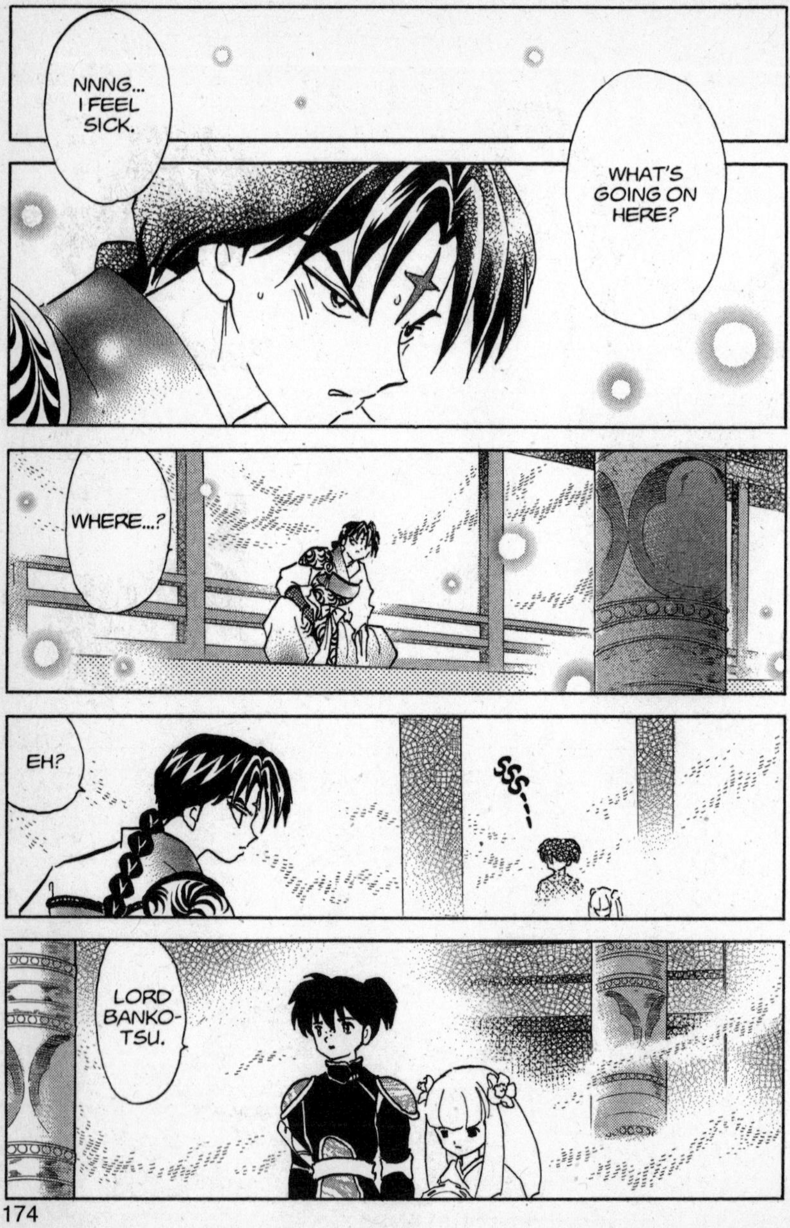
NNNG... I FEEL SICK.
WHAT'S GOING ON HERE?
WHERE...?
EH?
SSS...
LORD BANKO-TSU.

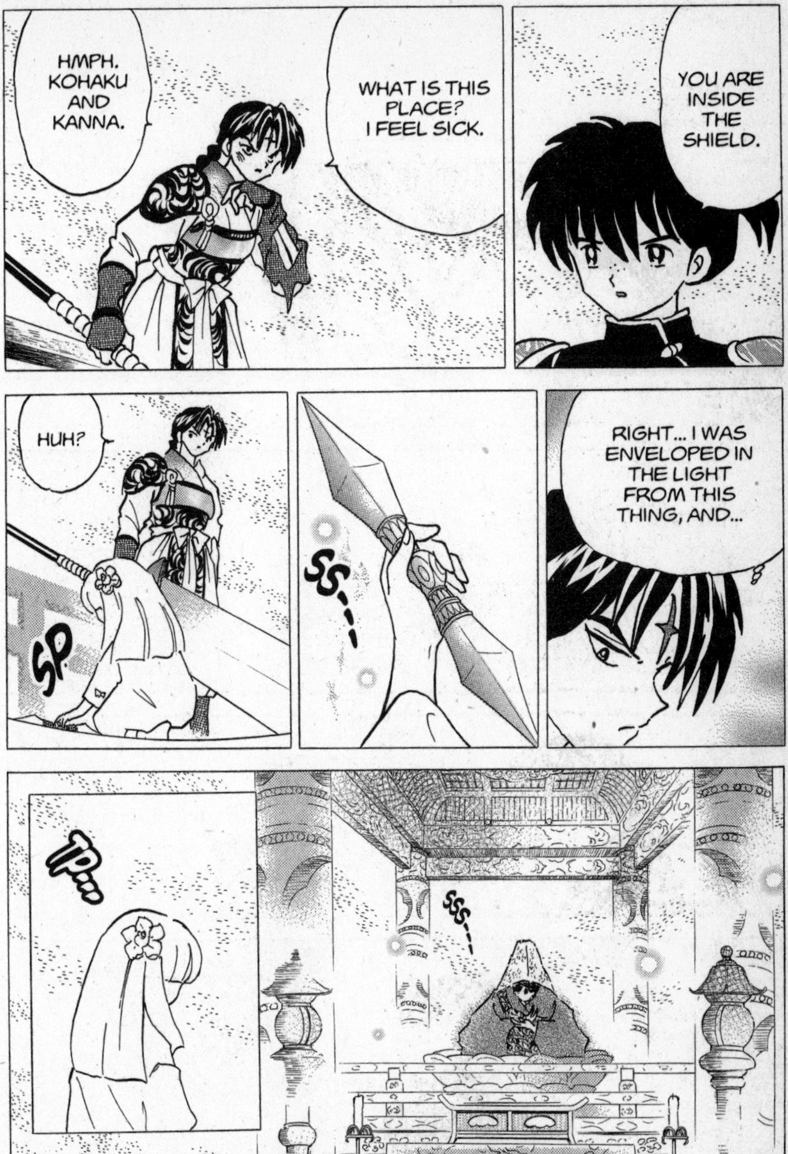
HMPH. KOHAKU AND KANNA.
WHAT IS THIS PLACE? I FEEL SICK.
YOU ARE INSIDE THE SHIELD.
HUH?
SP
SS...
RIGHT... I WAS ENVELOPED IN THE LIGHT FROM THIS THING, AND...
TP...
SSS...

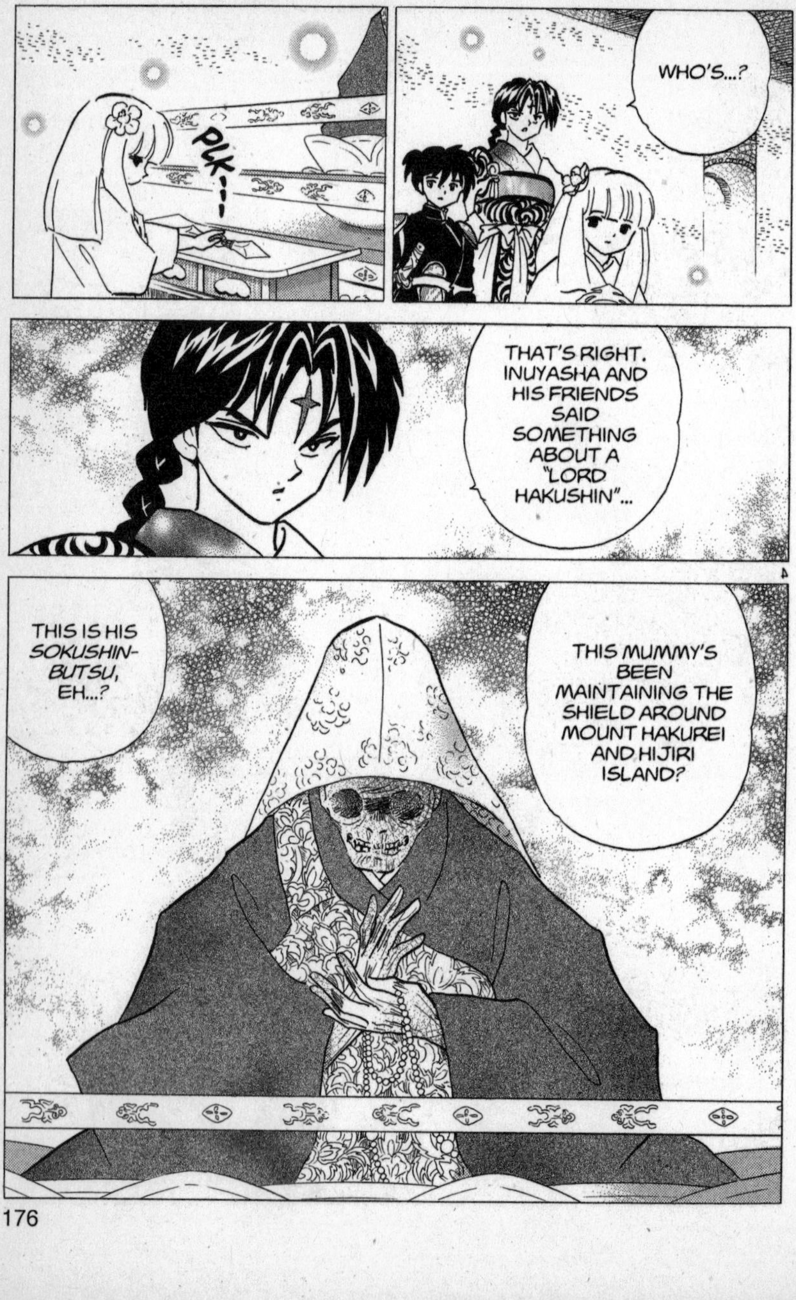
PLK...
WHO'S...?
THAT'S RIGHT. INUYASHA AND HIS FRIENDS SAID SOMETHING ABOUT A "LORD HAKUSHIN"...
THIS IS HIS SOKUSHIN-BUTSU, EH...?
THIS MUMMY'S BEEN MAINTAINING THE SHIELD AROUND MOUNT HAKUREI AND HIJIRI ISLAND?

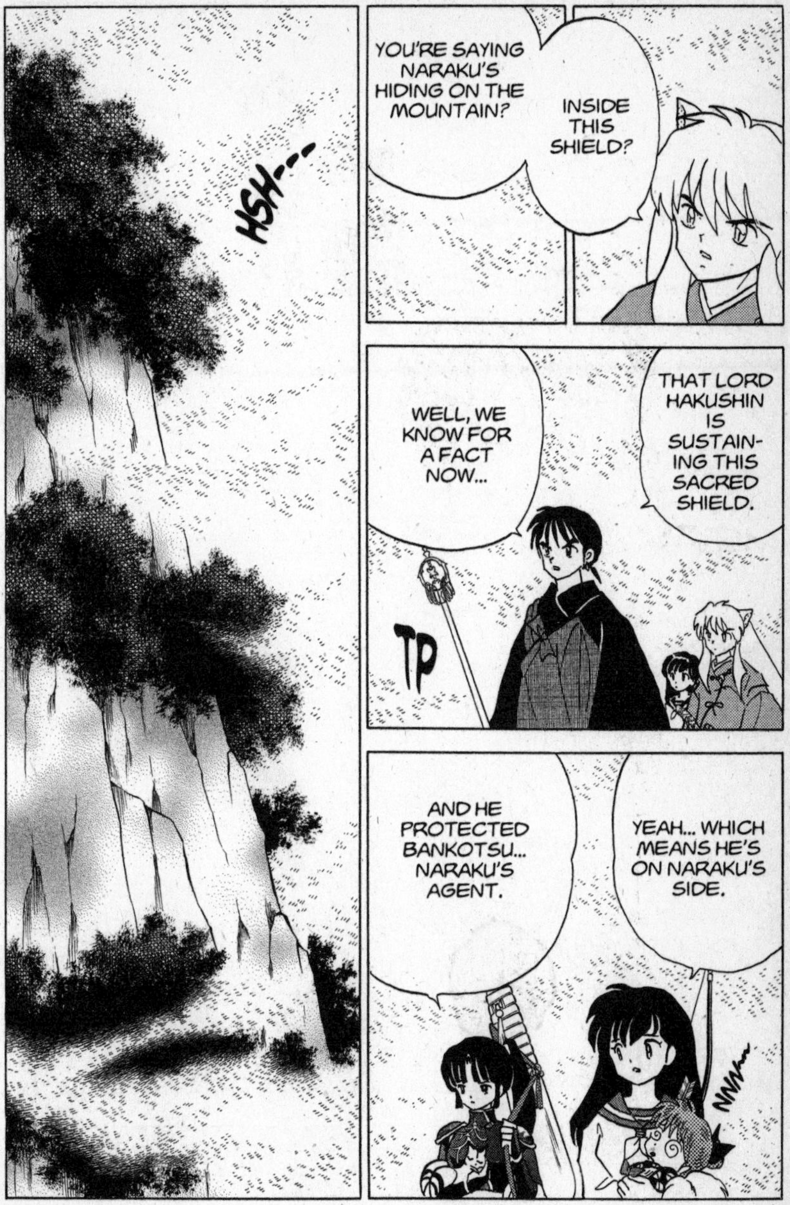
HSH...
YOU'RE SAYING NARAKU'S HIDING ON THE MOUNTAIN?
INSIDE THIS SHIELD?
WELL, WE KNOW FOR A FACT NOW...
THAT LORD HAKUSHIN IS SUSTAIN-ING THIS SACRED SHIELD.
TP
AND HE PROTECTED BANKOTSU... NARAKU'S AGENT.
YEAH... WHICH MEANS HE'S ON NARAKU'S SIDE.
NWW

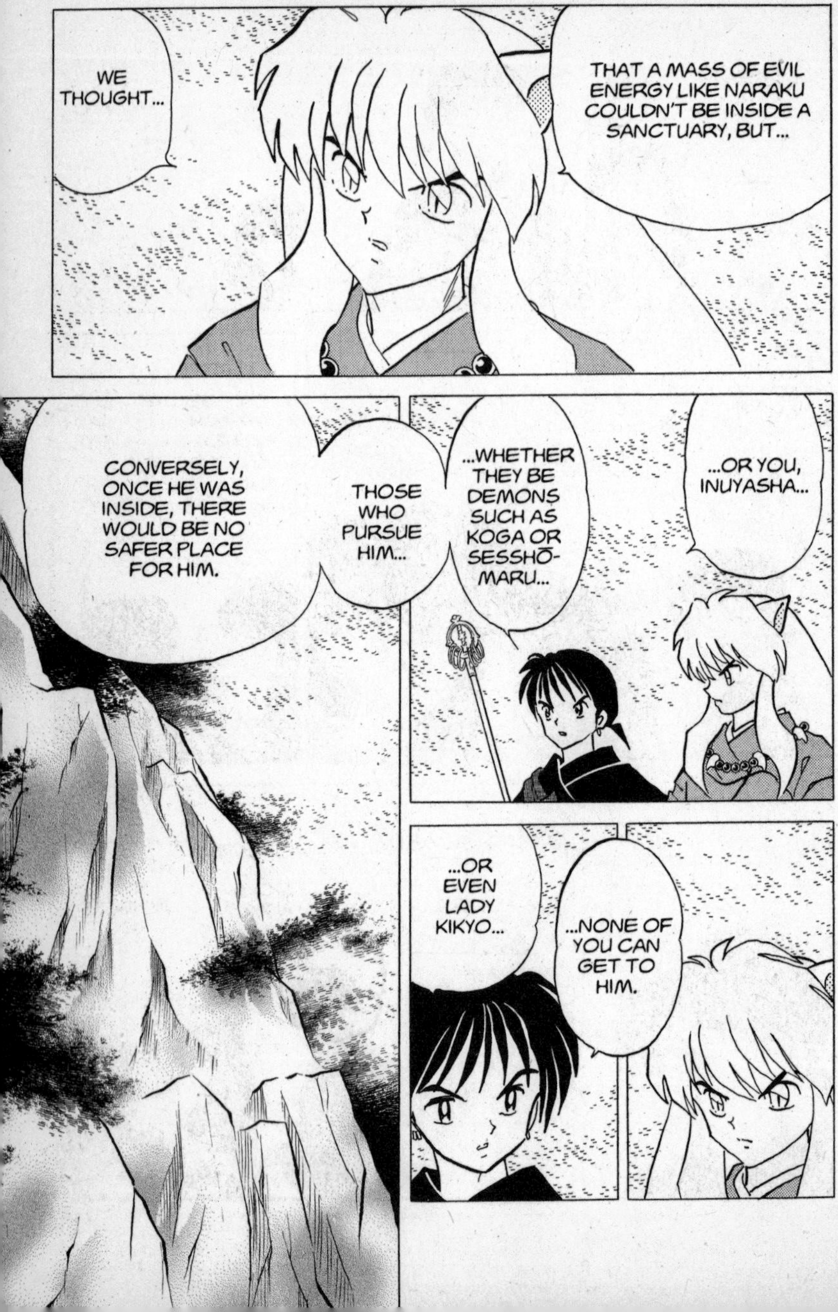
WE THOUGHT...
THAT A MASS OF EVIL ENERGY LIKE NARAKU COULDN'T BE INSIDE A SANCTUARY, BUT...
CONVERSELY, ONCE HE WAS INSIDE, THERE WOULD BE NO SAFER PLACE FOR HIM.
THOSE WHO PURSUE HIM...
...WHETHER THEY BE DEMONS SUCH AS KOGA OR SESSHŌ-MARU...
...OR YOU, INUYASHA...
...OR EVEN LADY KIKYO...
...NONE OF YOU CAN GET TO HIM.

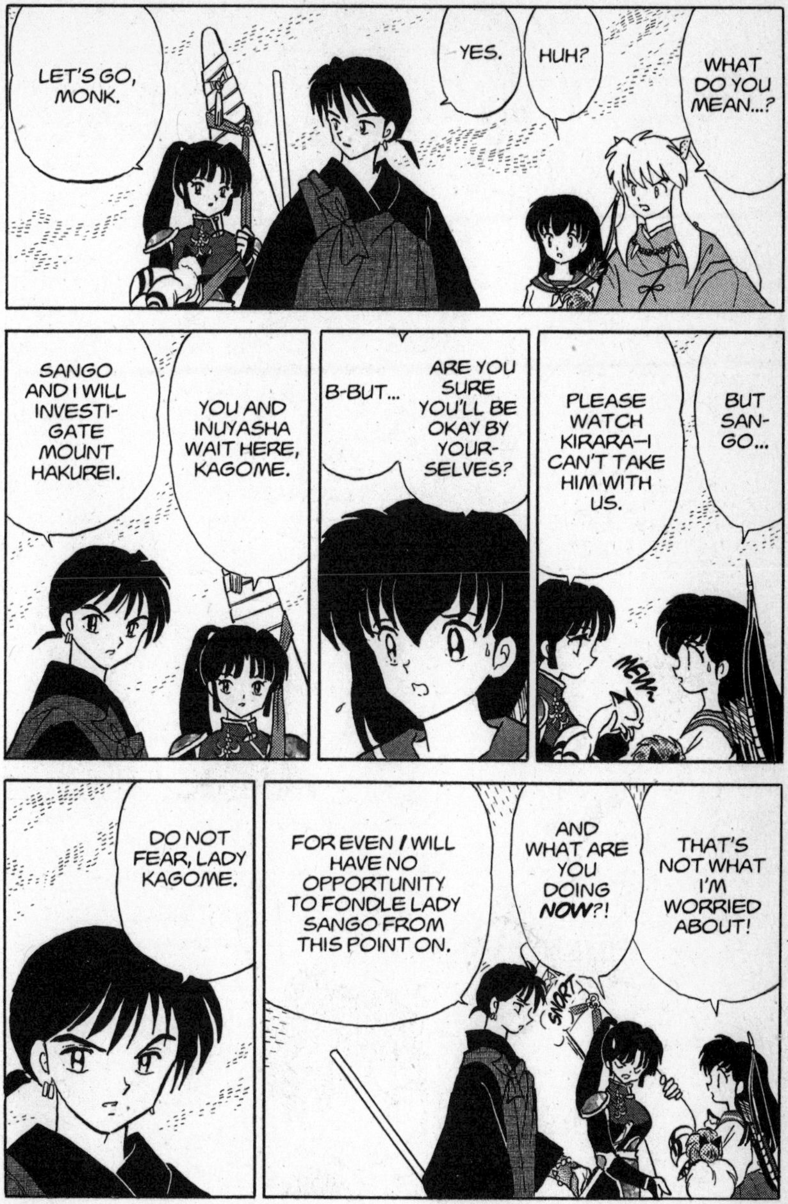

LET'S GO, MONK.
YES.
HUH?
WHAT DO YOU MEAN...?
SANGO AND I WILL INVESTIGATE MOUNT HAKUREI.
YOU AND INUYASHA WAIT HERE, KAGOME.
B-BUT...
ARE YOU SURE YOU'LL BE OKAY BY YOURSELVES?
PLEASE WATCH KIRARA—I CAN'T TAKE HIM WITH US.
BUT SANGO...
MEW
DO NOT FEAR, LADY KAGOME.
FOR EVEN *I* WILL HAVE NO OPPORTUNITY TO FONDLE LADY SANGO FROM THIS POINT ON.
AND WHAT ARE YOU DOING *NOW*?!
THAT'S NOT WHAT I'M WORRIED ABOUT!
SNORT

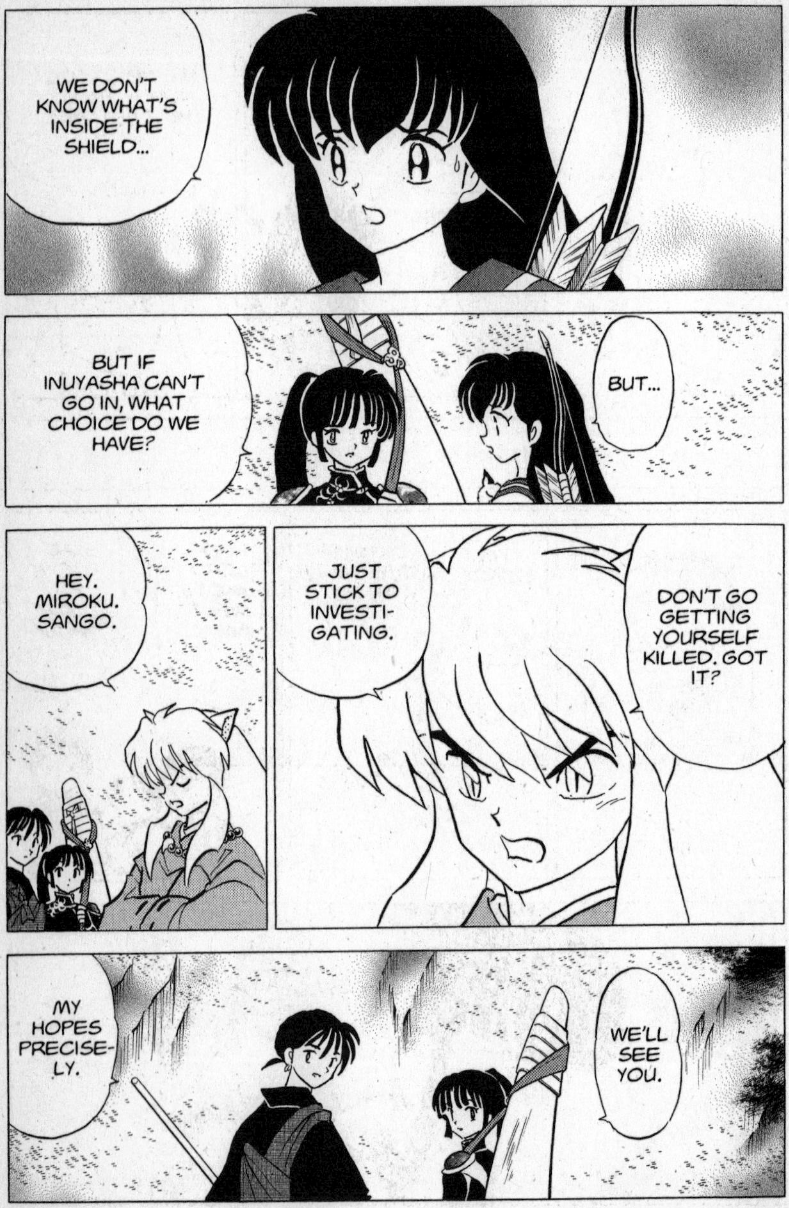
WE DON'T KNOW WHAT'S INSIDE THE SHIELD...
BUT IF INUYASHA CAN'T GO IN, WHAT CHOICE DO WE HAVE?
BUT...
HEY. MIROKU. SANGO.
JUST STICK TO INVESTI-GATING.
DON'T GO GETTING YOURSELF KILLED. GOT IT?
MY HOPES PRECISE-LY.
WE'LL SEE YOU.

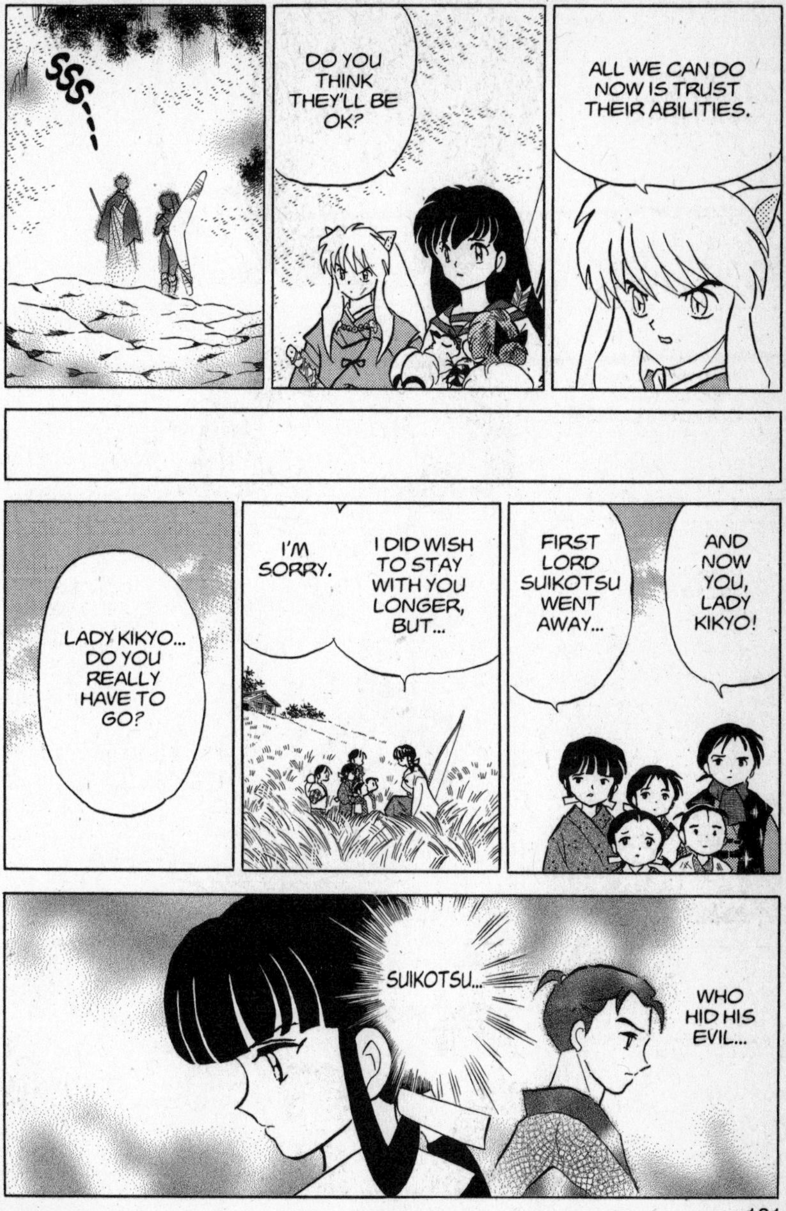
SSS...
DO YOU THINK THEY'LL BE OK?
ALL WE CAN DO NOW IS TRUST THEIR ABILITIES.
LADY KIKYO... DO YOU REALLY HAVE TO GO?
I'M SORRY.
I DID WISH TO STAY WITH YOU LONGER, BUT...
FIRST LORD SUIKOTSU WENT AWAY...
AND NOW YOU, LADY KIKYO!
SUIKOTSU...
WHO HID HIS EVIL...

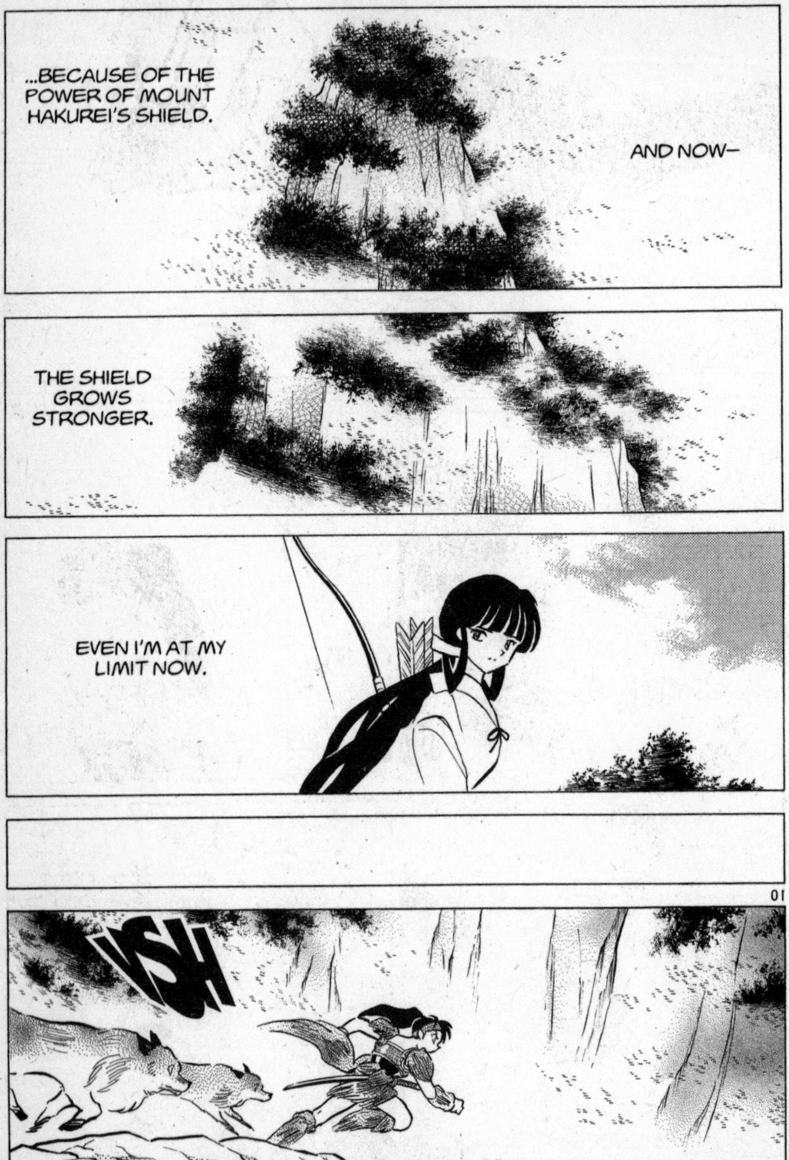
...BECAUSE OF THE POWER OF MOUNT HAKUREI'S SHIELD.
AND NOW—
THE SHIELD GROWS STRONGER.
EVEN I'M AT MY LIMIT NOW.
VSH

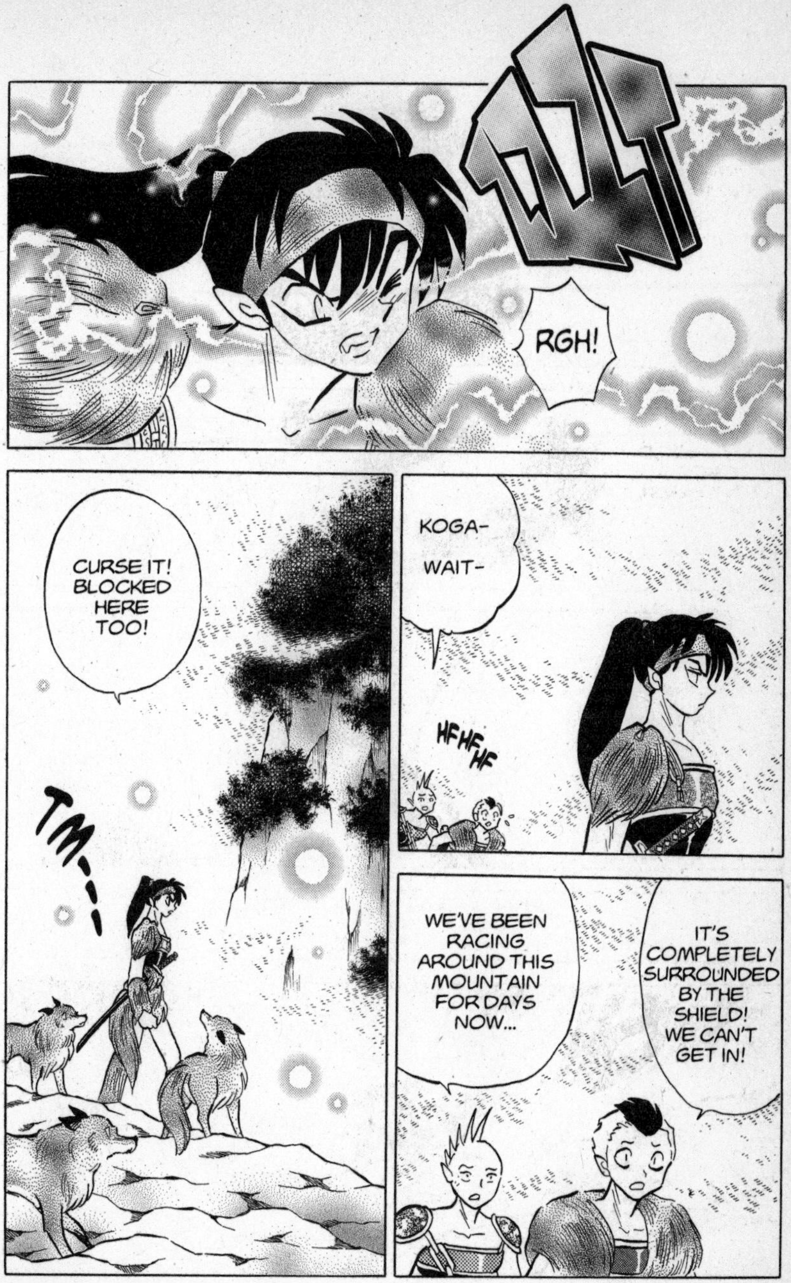
ZZZT
RGH!
CURSE IT! BLOCKED HERE TOO!
TMP...
KOGA- WAIT-
HF HF HF
WE'VE BEEN RACING AROUND THIS MOUNTAIN FOR DAYS NOW...
IT'S COMPLETELY SURROUNDED BY THE SHIELD! WE CAN'T GET IN!

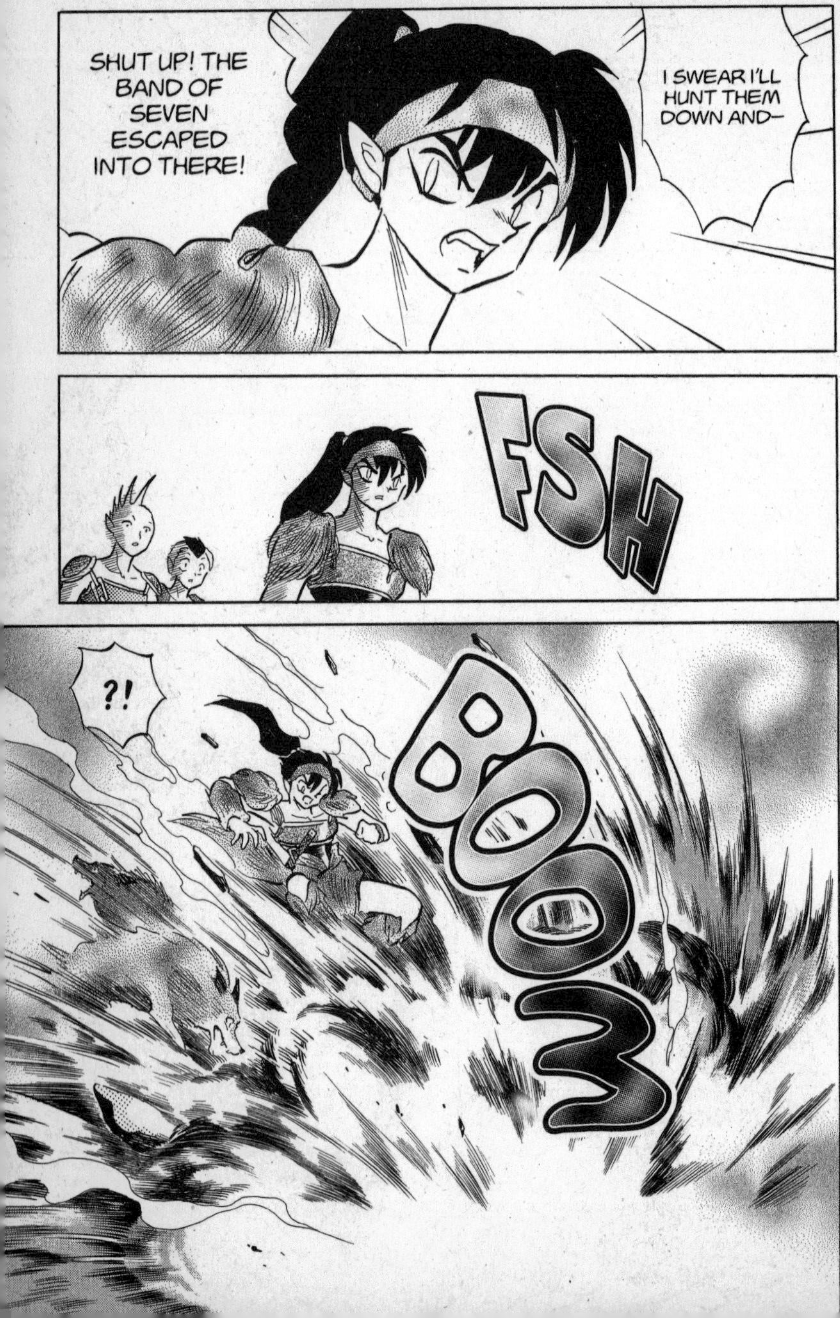
SHUT UP! THE BAND OF SEVEN ESCAPED INTO THERE!
I SWEAR I'LL HUNT THEM DOWN AND–
FSH
?!
BOOOM

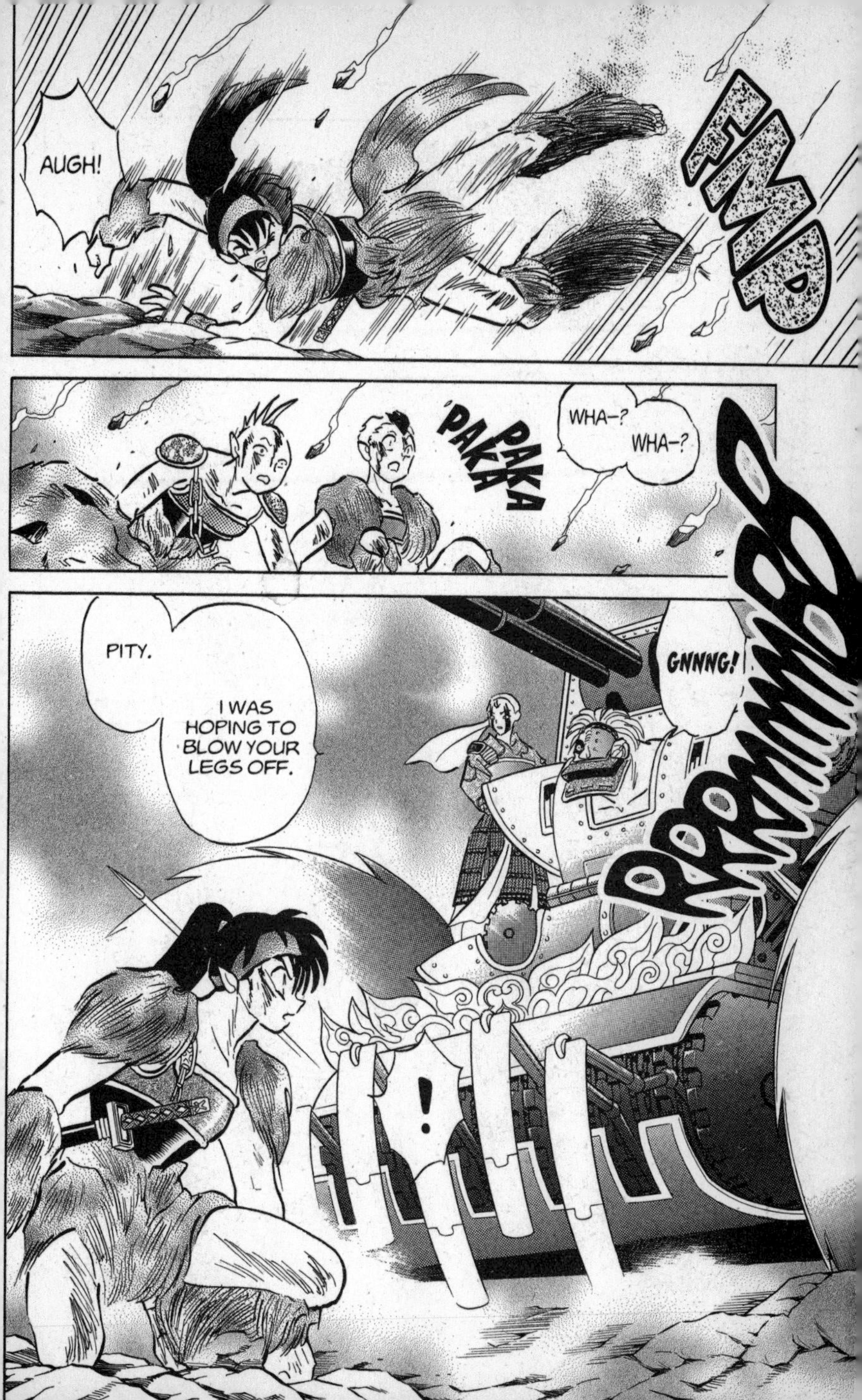
AUGH!
PAKA PAKA
WHA-? WHA-?
PITY.
I WAS HOPING TO BLOW YOUR LEGS OFF.
GNNNG!
!

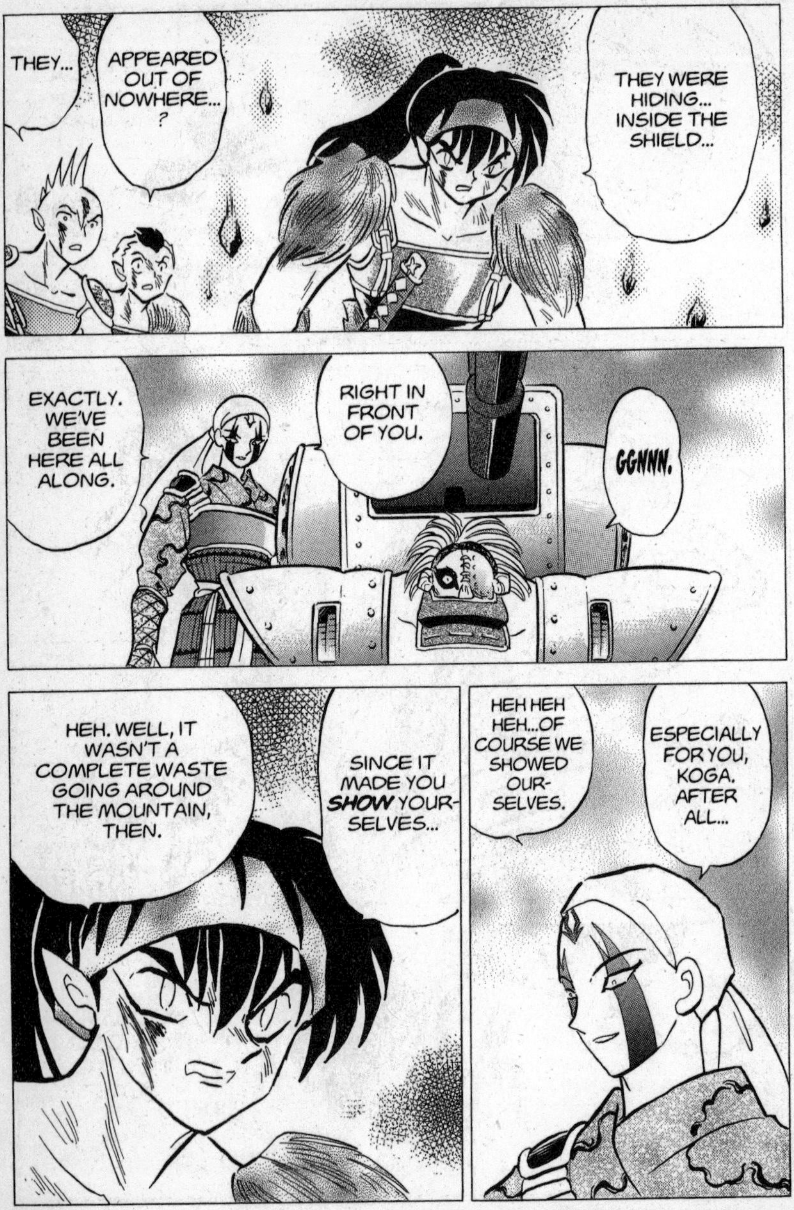
THEY...
APPEARED OUT OF NOWHERE...?
THEY WERE HIDING... INSIDE THE SHIELD...
EXACTLY. WE'VE BEEN HERE ALL ALONG.
RIGHT IN FRONT OF YOU.
GGNNN.
HEH. WELL, IT WASN'T A COMPLETE WASTE GOING AROUND THE MOUNTAIN, THEN.
SINCE IT MADE YOU SHOW YOURSELVES...
HEH HEH HEH...OF COURSE WE SHOWED OURSELVES.
ESPECIALLY FOR YOU, KOGA. AFTER ALL...

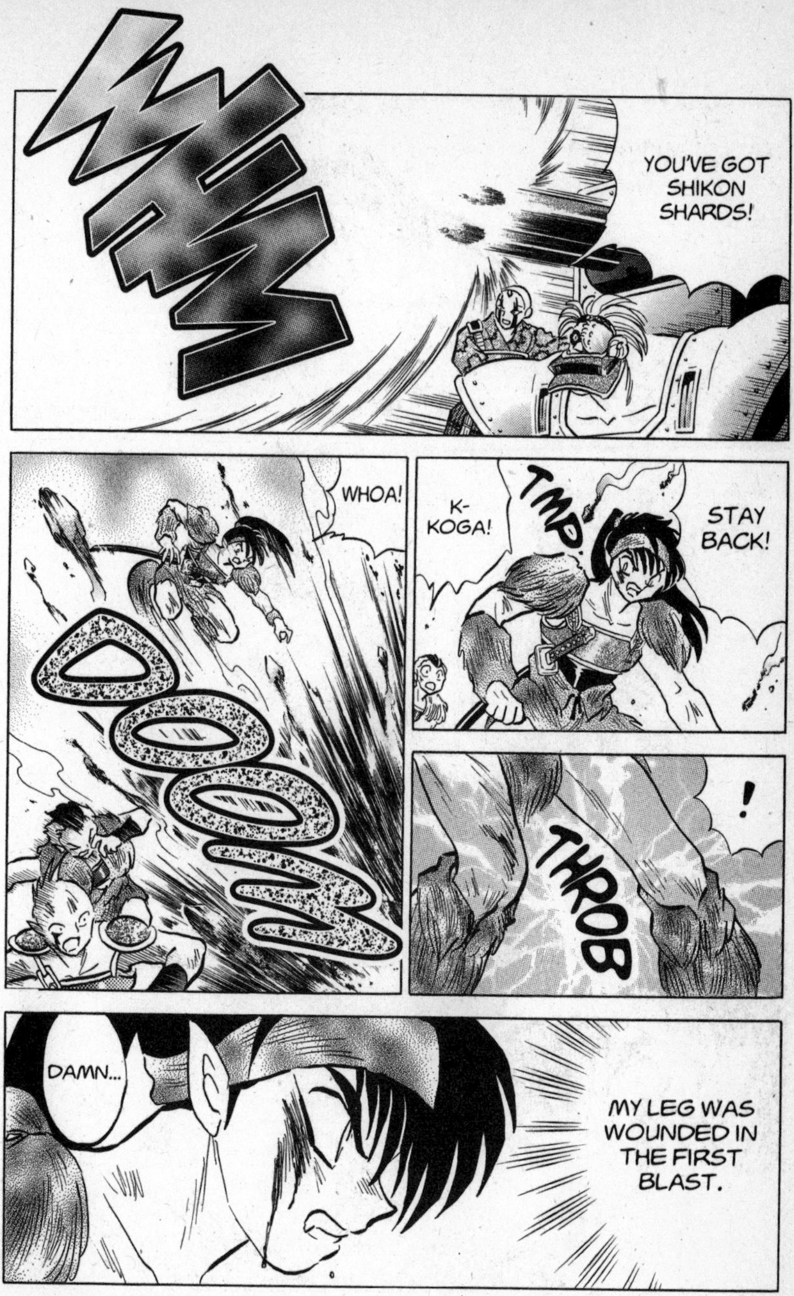
WHM
YOU'VE GOT SHIKON SHARDS!
WHOA!
DOOOM
K-KOGA!
TMP
STAY BACK!
THROB
!
DAMN...
MY LEG WAS WOUNDED IN THE FIRST BLAST.

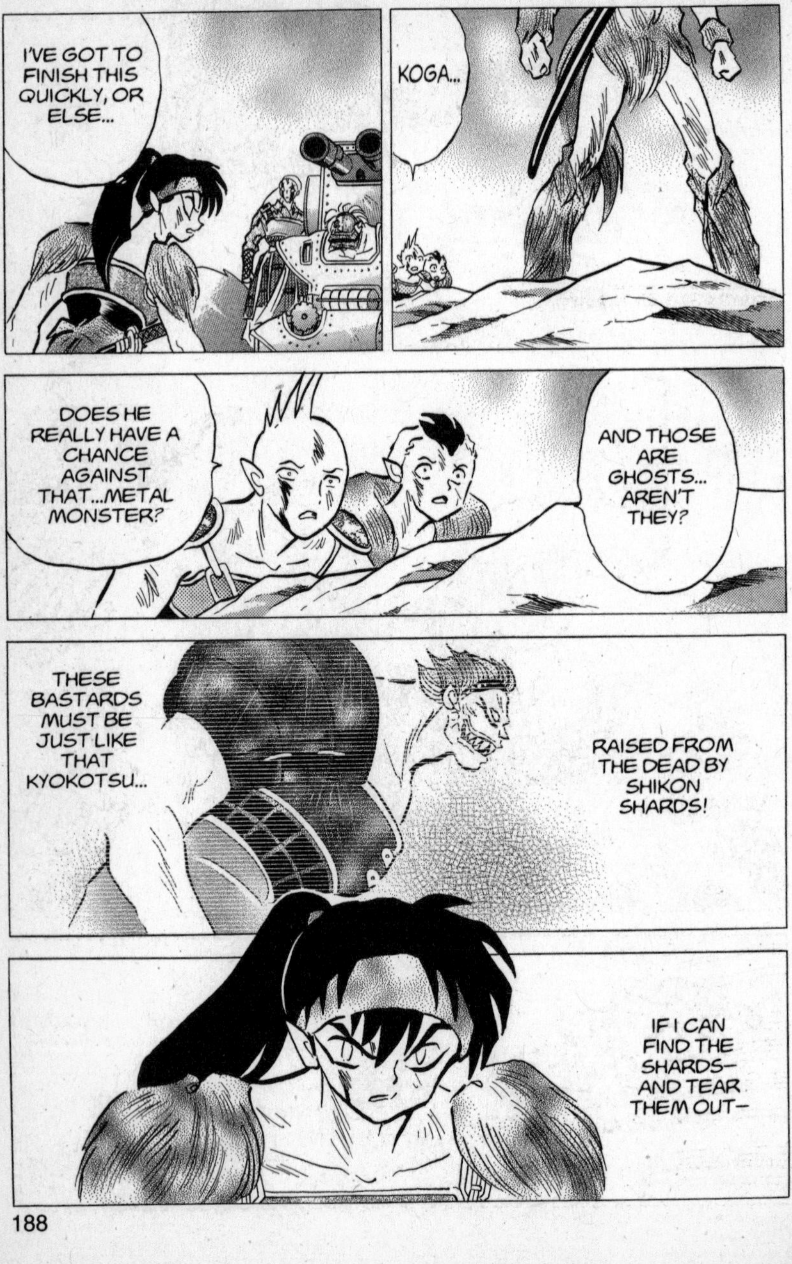
I'VE GOT TO FINISH THIS QUICKLY, OR ELSE...
KOGA...
DOES HE REALLY HAVE A CHANCE AGAINST THAT...METAL MONSTER?
AND THOSE ARE GHOSTS... AREN'T THEY?
THESE BASTARDS MUST BE JUST LIKE THAT KYOKOTSU...
RAISED FROM THE DEAD BY SHIKON SHARDS!
IF I CAN FIND THE SHARDS— AND TEAR THEM OUT—

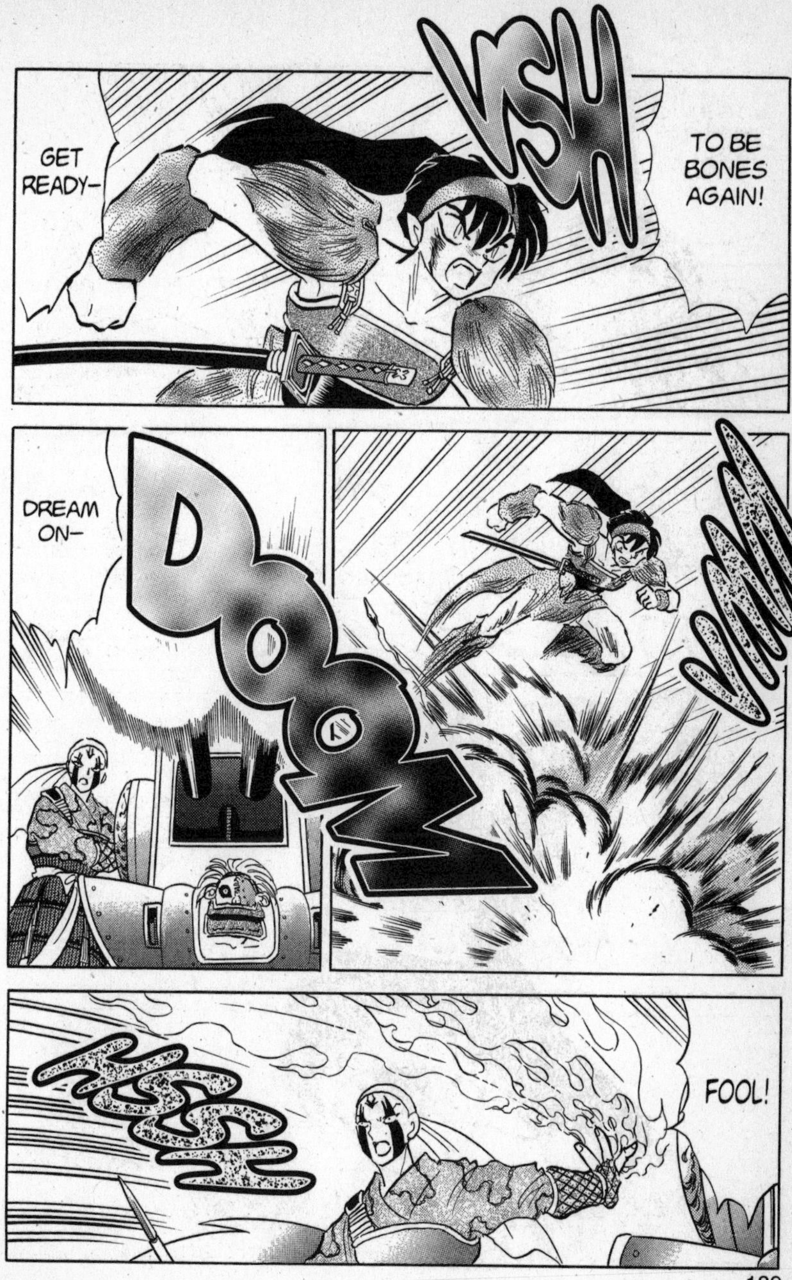
GET READY-
VSH
TO BE BONES AGAIN!
DREAM ON-
DOOM
FOOL!

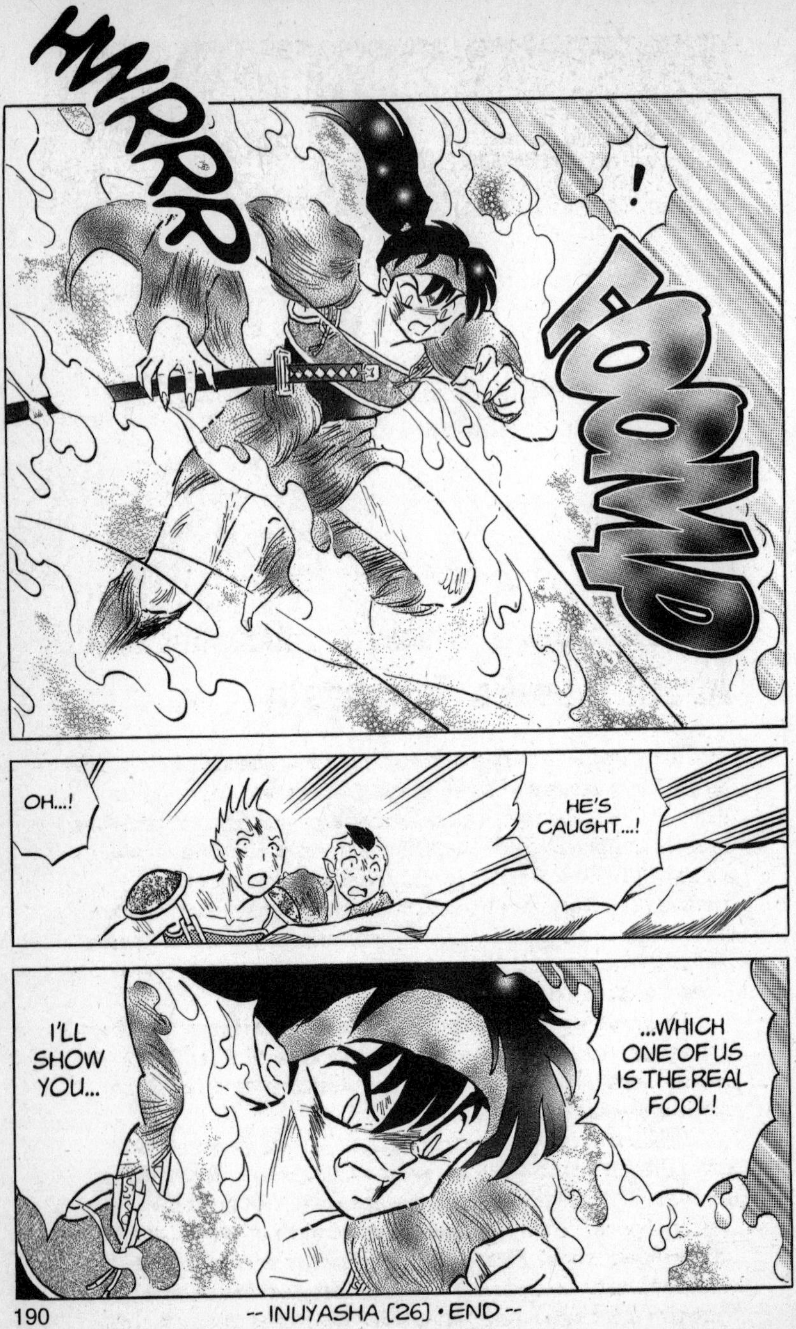
HWRRR
!
FOOMP
OH...!
HE'S CAUGHT...!
I'LL SHOW YOU...
...WHICH ONE OF US IS THE REAL FOOL!

About Rumiko Takahashi

Born in 1957 in Niigata, Japan, Rumiko Takahashi attended women's college in Tokyo, where she began studying comics with Kazuo Koike, author of *CRYING FREEMAN*. She later became an assistant to horror-manga artist Kazuo Umezu (*OROCHI*). In 1978, she won a prize in Shogakukan's annual "New Comic Artist Contest," and in that same year her boy-meets-alien comedy series *URUSEI YATSURA* began appearing in the weekly manga magazine *SHÔNEN SUNDAY*. This phenomenally successful series ran for nine years and sold over 22 million copies. Takahashi's later *RANMA 1/2* series enjoyed even greater popularity.

Takahashi is considered by many to be one of the world's most popular manga artists. With the publication of Volume 34 of her *RANMA 1/2* series in Japan, Takahashi's total sales passed *one hundred million* copies of her compiled works.

Takahashi's serial titles include *URUSEI YATSURA*, *RANMA 1/2*, *ONE-POUND GOSPEL*, *MAISON IKKOKU* and *INUYASHA*. Additionally, Takahashi has drawn many short stories which have been published in America under the title "Rumic Theater," and several installments of a saga known as her "Mermaid" series. Most of Takahashi's major stories have also been animated and are widely available in translation worldwide. *INUYASHA* is her most recent serial story, first published in *SHÔNEN SUNDAY* in 1996.

LOVE MANGA?
LET US KNOW WHAT YOU THINK!

HELP US MAKE THE MANGA
YOU LOVE BETTER!